THE JIGSAW MAN

JIGSAW MAN: THE REMARKABLE CAREER OF BRITAIN'S FOREMOST CRIMINAL PSYCHOLOGIST

LONDON · NEW YORK · TORONTO · SYDNEY · AUCKLAND

TRANSWORLD PUBLISHERS LTD
61–63 Uxbridge Road, London W5 5SA

TRANSWORLD PUBLISHERS (AUSTRALIA) PTY LTD
15–25 Helles Avenue, Moorebank, NSW 2170

TRANSWORLD PUBLISHERS (NZ) LTD
3 William Pickering Drive, Albany, Auckland

Published 1997 by Bantam Press
a division of Transworld Publishers Ltd

A catalogue record for this book is available from the British Library.

ISBN 0593 04066X

Typeset in 11/13pt Times by
Phoenix Typesetting, Ilkley, West Yorkshire.

Printed in Great Britain by
Mackays of Chatham, plc, Chatham, Kent.

I dedicate *The Jigsaw Man* to two groups of people and an individual who have irrevocably touched my life.

The victims of the crimes I have investigated, whose fear and pain can never be entirely escaped.

The operational police officers who have to try to put their own feelings aside during the working shift, and to be ordinary family men and women when they go home.

Marilyn has always been there, I hope she always will be. She can't have entirely escaped either.

ACKNOWLEDGEMENTS

Through many criminal and other difficult, sensitive cases I have worked with the most able and far-seeing investigators of their day. They have each contributed to changing the ways in which information is gathered, analysed and acted upon. I pay particular tribute to:

Detective Chief Superintendent David Baker, Commander John Grieve, Commander David Tucker, Detective Superintendent Bob Taylor, Assistant Chief Constable Tom Cook, Detective Chief Superintendent Mick Jenkins, Detective Superintendent Harry Shepherd, Detective Superintendent Ian Johnston, Superintendent Ian Gordon, Detective Chief Superintendent Duncan Bailey, Detective Chief Superintendent Brendon Gibb-Grey, Chief Constable John Stevens, Detective Inspector Keith Pedder, 'Lizzie James', Detective Superintendent Micky Banks, Detective Inspector John Pearse, Detective Superintendent Albert Kirby, Detective Superintendent John Bennet, Detective Chief Superintendent Colin Port, Detective Superintendent Tony Bayliss and Detective Inspector Gino Varriale. With the FBI, Judd Ray, Greg Cooper, 'Roy' Hazelwood and John Douglas.

When times were difficult Paul Jackson, Julian Boon and Sarah Lewis turned out to be good friends and effective colleagues.

Ursula Mackenzie, Bill Scott-Kerr, Garry Prior, Patrick Janson-Smith, Larry Finlay and Alison Barrow at Transworld, and Michael Robotham and Mark Lucas at LAW, gave the perfect balance of encouragement and pressure necessary to see the book completed.

Diane Purves, my NHS secretary, has helped to ensure that my clinical work stayed on track when I attended to criminal cases.

It is probably not possible to have been immersed in these cases without collecting some personal damage. I have found unfailing love and renewal of my emotional and intellectual life in my family, Mal, and Emma and Rufus, and Ian and Katherine.

Finally I acknowledge those other men and women who cannot be named for reasons of confidentiality and security. You know who you are – good luck. Don't ever stop, darkness will overtake us all if you do.

'. . . Let us meet, and question this most bloody piece of work,
To know it further. Fears and scruples shake us.
In the great hand of God I stand, and thence
Against the undivulg'd pretence I fight . . .'

Shakespeare, *Macbeth*, Act II scene iii.

AUTHOR'S NOTE

I have selected the particular cases reported in *The Jigsaw Man* because they show the beginnings and development of professional psychology used in the investigation of crime, and also because the fact of my involvement in each is public knowledge, with the outcome of the judicial process known. I will not discuss those cases, in the public or the private sector, where secrecy remains important.

Occasionally details of crimes or the investigative process have been obscured. This is to protect witnesses, victims, or a continuing investigation and to avoid showing would-be offenders how not to be caught.

Details which would identify individuals mentioned in the clinical cases have all been altered, except where these are a matter of public record.

1

ON TUESDAY MORNING, 22 NOVEMBER, 1983, I LOOKED OUT OF MY office window, across the terrace and the unkempt garden to the fields beyond, and saw a strange procession. Dozens of men emerged from the trees, shuffling forward in a long unbroken line. Clouds of condensed vapour billowed from their faces almost like speech bubbles that dispersed and reformed with each breath.

Occasionally, someone in the line would stop and squat near to the ground. The rest would pause, waiting and leaning a little closer to the frozen grass and mud. Although wrapped up against the cold, I saw no warmth in their faces or delight in their task.

'What are they doing?' asked Anne Chalmers, a secretary in the psychology department.

'They look like policemen,' I said.

'Mmm.'

She slipped into silence and we watched together at the window, wondering what had brought the police to our doorstep; to Carlton Hayes Psychiatric Hospital in Narborough, Leicestershire.

The large Edwardian hospital was the dominating landmark for miles around, rising out of farmland between several picturesque villages in the East Midlands. When it was built between 1905 and 1907, as the county asylum, the journey by carriage or horseback from the surrounding market towns must have seemed like a trip to the middle of nowhere. In those days, all the surrounding farmland was owned by the hospital and worked by the patients so that the institution was virtually self-sufficient. But it could never shed the image of madness that haunts all such asylums and makes them places to be feared by locals, particularly children. Perhaps this is why the name was changed in 1938 from the Leicestershire and Rutland Lunatic Asylum.

Yet Carlton Hayes wasn't an intimidating or frightening place. Once inside the main gate a visitor was immediately struck by the sense of space and tranquillity as the road swung past the gatehouse, car-park, bowling green, cricket pitch and flower-beds before reaching the main body of the hospital. The larger buildings were fashioned from red brick with steeply pitched slate rooves and two massive brick chimneys that could be seen for miles around.

I remembered my first visit, five years earlier, when I'd arrived to be interviewed for a traineeship as a clinical psychologist. Despite having been an honorary trainee for six months, I was still daunted by the sight of Carlton Hayes. The broad stone steps, oak doors, reception room and administrative corridor looked like something from an old town hall. The floors echoed and the oak doors swung on heavy hinges, with polished brass handles worn by years of turning.

The boardroom was lined with paintings of past incumbents, with their mutton-chop sideburns and stiffened collars. In the early days we could hold our departmental meetings around one end of the table but in later years the department expanded to fill the table.

I took up the post in October, 1978, and for the next three years began dealing with a broad range of patients and psychological problems. Much of my work was with out-patients at the Woodlands Day Hospital, a large country house with seven or eight bedrooms, about a quarter of a mile from the main hospital buildings. I also worked in the acute unit – a small four-ward section of the hospital where patients would be treated intensively for a few months before being discharged or moved into the longer-stay wards.

Most of the in-patients needed long term care, being psychogeriatrics who suffered from atrophy of the frontal cortex or from depression, or were younger men and women having severe psychiatric illnesses such as schizophrenia. I rarely had cause to visit the wards where the elderly patients with dementia were cared for, but am destined to never forget the wall of smell that overwhelmed everything else in those back wards. Over the decades it seemed that urine had seeped into the fabric of the building so that no matter how much it was scrubbed and polished, the smell would never go away.

Thankfully, the psychology department was set away from the

main hospital buildings in a former medical superintendent's house known as The Rosings. The two-storey red-brick house had a large bay window overlooking a small stone terrace where we'd often sit and have lunch, opening a bottle of wine and watching the hares forage in the nearby fields.

Now there were heavier feet shuffling across the feudal farming strips and icy earth. Throughout the day, the police criss-crossed the fields and gathered beneath the trees deep in discussion. Being isolated at The Rosings, it was mid-afternoon before I learned the reason for their search.

'It's a girl,' said Anne Chalmers, obviously upset. 'She's been murdered.'

'Murdered? Where?'

'One of our porters found her this morning on his way to work. She was lying beside the Black Pad.'

I'd never used the black cinder pathway, although I passed the entrance every day on my way to work. It ran along the perimeter of Carlton Hayes and acted as a shortcut between the village of Narborough immediately to the south and Enderby to the north, a walk of about fifteen minutes.

'Do you know who she is?' I asked.

'A local girl, a teenager.'

Suddenly I thought of my own daughter, Emma. She'd be on her way home from school about now and then she'd take Jess, our white retriever, for a run in the fields before it grew dark. Like many fathers I was protective, but Emma had walked home from school ever since she was a youngster.

'Who'd do such a thing?' asked Anne, getting more upset.

They'll think it's someone from here, I thought to myself. It would be a natural reaction – but the wrong one. Carlton Hayes didn't house violent or dangerous patients; most of them were so elderly and infirm that they needed assistance to go to the bathroom. The acute patients were well-known and at the Woodlands Day Hospital we were treating neurotic and anxious people who were unable to cope with the vagaries of life that sometimes overwhelmed them. They weren't seriously aggressive or violent.

That night, I watched the early evening news on television.

'Detectives are investigating the murder of a fifteen-year-old schoolgirl whose partially clad body was found this morning beside a footpath near the village of Narborough, in the grounds of Carlton Hayes Psychiatric Hospital.

'Lynda Mann, a local teenager last seen alive at about 7.30 p.m. on Monday, was discovered early today beside a local footpath known as the Black Pad. Detectives immediately sealed off the area and began tracing the girl's last movements. The cause of death has not been revealed.'

A photograph showed a slightly built, dark-haired girl with a shy smile who didn't seem big enough to fill her clothes.

In November 1983, I'd just been appointed as a senior clinical psychologist by the Leicestershire Health Authority, moving my office into the newly opened mental illness unit at Leicester General Hospital. I still visited Carlton Hayes to see out-patients at The Rosings and day-patients at The Woodlands.

As I expected, Carlton Hayes became an early focus of police interest, although I hadn't expected them to take up residence next door. An unoccupied section of The Rosings became an incident room and the murder squad brought in filing cabinets, white boards and index cards.

What were they doing for furniture? I wondered. A few years earlier, when we'd first moved into The Rosings, we had begged, borrowed and eventually had to steal basic necessities such as chairs and lamps. The hospital administration had given us virtually nothing but I'd peered through a locked window in the disused half of The Rosings and spied everything we needed covered in dust.

'Can we have some of that?' I asked the Estates Department.

'Well, no . . . ah, that's already been earmarked . . .'

'Where's it going?'

'Ah, well, I can't say.'

Enough of this, I thought. There were four psychologists in the department, three men and a woman; all of us about the same age and eager to accomplish something.

'So we're all in it together,' I said, as we agreed the plan.

'But it's stealing,' said Russel, nervously.

'No, not at all,' I reassured him, 'we're only relocating resources so as to optimize their usefulness.'

Russel said, 'So we're not breaking any locks or windows . . . I mean, I don't want to break any . . .'

'Leave it to me.'

Shouldering a ladder from the orchard, I carried it upstairs and pushed open the loft hatch. It was pitch-black inside the roof and I gingerly edged forwards careful to stay on the beams to stop crashing through the ceiling.

Finding another hatch, I prised it open and lowered the ladder down into the unoccupied half of the house – a veritable Aladdin's Cave of disused furniture and tableware. We couldn't just walk out through the front door which was padlocked, but I found a large sash window at the back overlooking the garden which I unlocked and began passing stuff through. Over the next week we made four or five trips until we had what we needed apart from carpets.

In a different part of the hospital, the old nurses' quarters, there were fine carpets lying unused, so we set about rectifying the problem. This called for a bolder approach. We agreed that three men and a woman, carrying two fifteen-foot-long carpets in daylight through a busy hospital, would probably succeed so long as we looked confident and no-one stopped us to ask questions.

It worked and I found myself with a rather comfortable office, despite the white-tiled walls which made it look like a urinal. No-one ever mentioned the missing items, although I couldn't help feeling a slight pang of guilt when the murder squad moved next door.

The Lynda Mann inquiry became a constant in my life over the following weeks as I read the local newspapers and watched the TV news, seeing the numerous public appeals and poster campaigns. The incident room handled dozens of reported sightings and also searched through decades of local records, looking for past offences or offenders who might be linked. Two more police teams moved into the cricket pavilion, overlooking the hospital's cricket pitch. One team concentrated on house-to-house inquiries in the surrounding villages; while the other dug into hospital records, trying to trace likely out-patients and day-patients who had passed through Carlton Hayes during the previous five years.

Although various theories emerged and a number of suspects were sought, by Christmas the murder squad seemed no closer to catching Lynda's killer. Officers volunteered to keep the incident room open during the holidays and the *Leicester Mercury* ran a headline, 'Please Help Trace This Maniac'.

Weeks later, I remember walking along Forest Road for a meeting at the Woodlands Day Hospital and suddenly I realized how long it had been since the murder. Looking towards the Black Pad, the remnants of black and yellow police tape twirled like forgotten Christmas decorations on the metal railings.

Why haven't they caught someone? I wondered. Do they really understand what happened?

I began to think how a psychologist would approach it – a fanciful idea perhaps, but psychology is all about understanding people's motivations and what makes us do the things we do. There were so many questions that I would ask that the police perhaps wouldn't ordinarily consider.

On that lonely footpath, in the cold and dark, two people had come together and one of them had died. There must have been some kind of social interaction between them, however brief or violent. These two people had their own families, friends and histories. What they said to each other and how they reacted had been determined by who they were and what shaped their personalities.

People respond to the same situation in different ways. For example, you could take three young women through the same streets, into the same shops, restaurants and pubs and each could see the environment differently. One might see people laughing and enjoying themselves and think of them as potential friends. Another might look at these same people and think them hostile or likely to laugh at her or ridicule her. The third woman has a perfectly realistic view that these strangers are neither good nor bad and are just going about their lives.

These three women wear different clothes for different reasons and not just because certain styles suit them. Imagine the first woman is interested in attracting attention; she enjoys being looked at so wears clothes that catch the eye. The second woman tries to avoid this – she doesn't want to stand out and is more careful and conservative. The third woman dresses to please herself and to make herself feel comfortable.

Each of them is different and will probably react to similar situations in a different way. None of this just happens. We are each the product of our pasts. When Lynda Mann walked along the Black Pad on that Monday night, she carried within her all the things that shaped her as a person and these things determined how she reacted when confronted by her killer. Did she run? Did she get angry? Was she passive?

In just the same way, I knew that her killer was more than a caricature or comic book villain. He also had a rich life which had shaped his personality and actions. What went through his mind, I wondered, when he saw Lynda? What did he see and why did he choose her? If he could do this to a young girl, what did he think of women in general? Was he likely to be intelligent? What sort of job would he do?

The wind tugged at my trouser turn-ups and sent leaves scurrying along the gutters and against the metal railings as I turned and walked away. Somewhere, still out there, Lynda Mann's killer walked the streets, ate his lunch, showered, slept and probably had a beer at his local pub.

Within a few yards, my thoughts of Lynda had been pushed aside and I pondered my meeting. It wasn't my concern, I thought. Psychologists didn't get asked to help catch killers, that was the grim job of the police and I didn't envy them.

A fortnight later, on 2 February, 1984, the coroner released Lynda's body for burial and she was laid to rest in the cemetery of All Saints Church. Her headstone read:

LYNDA ROSE MARIE MANN
Taken 21st November 1983
Aged 15 years
We didn't have time to say goodbye,
but you're only a thought away.

2

THERE WAS NO SINGLE EVENT OR WATERSHED THAT CONVINCED ME to become a psychologist. People often try to find triggers in their lives but invariably decisions or choices are the culmination of many small incidents and influences that come together or fall haphazardly into place.

As a teenager I had no interest in how things work mechanically. I didn't dismantle old alarm clocks or marvel at the workings of the wireless in my mother's kitchen. I had no particular interest in steam engines, model aeroplanes or the mechanical engineering experiments we performed at school.

Later, when I bought my first car, an old Standard 10 van with no second gear that cost me £39, my knowledge of what made the wheels turn was pathetically slim. I remember my wife, Marilyn, and I setting off on our first big outing to Wales to see her grandmother. The van's top speed was 56 mph and we trundled along celebrating our new found freedom.

At some point on the Old Road just past Chepstow I noticed that the top speed was beginning to fall. Even with my foot flat on the floor I couldn't coax more than 35 mph out of the van. When this continued falling into the twenties, I decided that it was time to find a garage. Initially I thought it might be a fuel problem. Maybe the top speed was dependent on how much petrol was in the tank – less petrol meant less speed.

A rather bored-looking mechanic with a flop of hair covering one eye climbed out of the grease pit, wiping his hands on a rag and sauntered across the forecourt to the van. I explained the problem, trying to sound authoritative about the workings of the internal combustion engine.

'What about oil?' he said.

'Oil? Ah, well, I don't think so. It doesn't squeak. Have you heard any squeaks, Marilyn?'

She shook her head.

The mechanic looked at me strangely and asked Marilyn to pull the bonnet catch. I peered over his shoulder as he fiddled with several leads and examined the battery. Then he pulled out the dip-stick.

'Look at this,' he said, holding the gleaming stick aloft.

'It looks very clean to me,' I offered.

'Clean? Listen, mate, you've got no oil.'

'Is that a problem?'

I mention this episode not just to illustrate my ignorance of most things mechanical, but as a counterpoint to where my real interests lay. While machines held no fascination for me, I was intrigued by people and how their minds and bodies work; why we do the things we do and become the people we become.

A great many of these answers lie in our pasts and mine began in May 1946, the year after peace broke out in Europe. I was born and grew up in Royal Leamington Spa, a rather grand-sounding name for a town whose grandeur had passed a century earlier. Many of the guest-houses and hotels on the Victorian terraces that had once welcomed the great and the good who had come to sample the spa waters had since been converted into flats and boarding houses.

I can't recall having a father – he'd gone by the time I was old enough to notice such things. Down the years I heard stories about him, not all of them flattering, but I never did hear his account. My earliest firm memory was growing up in a condemned basement room in Leamington. I don't know why it had been condemned, perhaps because of rising damp or subsidence, but my mother made sure it was so spotless you could have eaten off the floor.

A devout Catholic all her life, she diligently took my younger brother, Anthony, and me to Mass each Sunday at St Peter's Church, giving thanks for the help the church gave her in raising a family on her own.

During the week she did various jobs although the one I remember best is when she worked as an assistant nurse at an old people's home. It sticks in my mind because of an ancient-looking resident called Mr Blower who I met one day during the school holidays when my mother brought him his lunch. He smelled of tobacco and old tea leaves and would sit in his slippers and dressing-gown, seeming to stare out of an imaginary window. He must have been in his eighties or nineties and I was about seven.

'What's your name?' he asked me.

'Paul, sir.'

'Do you like pirates, Paul?'

'I don't know any pirates.'

'What? None!'

'What about explorers?'

I shook my head.

He sucked air through his teeth and looked right past me as if he'd forgotten our conversation in mid-sentence. But a few days later, my mother came home with some books.

'These are from Mr Blower,' she said.

They were the first real books in our household and I read them over and over. I still have them – *Lost in the Wilds of Canada* by Eleanor Stredder, *The Swiss Family Robinson* and *Treasure Island* by Robert Louis Stevenson, and *The Wolf Hunters* by James Oliver Curwood.

I suppose you could say it was the beginning of my life-long love-affair with reading. Mr Blower continued to send me books until the day he couldn't send any more. When I was old enough I joined the Leamington Library. By then we'd moved to a house in Lillington, an expanding village on the outskirts of Leamington, soon to be swallowed up by the town.

In between lay the Campion Hills which became my childhood playground. A single oak tree stood on top of the hills and from the great fork in the main branches I could look over the whole of the town and towards Warwick, the county seat, four or five miles away. The tree was a magical childhood place that became a castle, pirate ship or cavalry fort, depending upon the chosen game.

I didn't regard our family as being poor or deprived. Some had more, some had less. Similarly, not having a father wasn't particularly unusual, the war had seen to that. For this reason, I greeted the arrival of my stepfather with a degree of ambivalence. I was twelve years old at the time and didn't see any great hole in my life that he would suddenly fill.

He was a Russian who had lost a wife and two daughters in the war. An avowed anti-Communist, he fought as a major in the Russian army and afterwards fled Stalin's regime, walking from his homeland to Switzerland. Eventually he ended up in Warwickshire working as an engineer for the Ford motor company.

His ability to read English was limited – a source of frustration – but he could speak it quite well. Even so, he seemed to be a man who was horribly out of place. Having been well-educated, from quite possibly a wealthy family, with great technical skills and a history of commanding men in battle, he found himself mixing and working with people from totally different backgrounds. Even amongst the other émigrés from Eastern Europe, he seemed isolated because of his intelligence and former status.

Gaining a good education was rather a hit and miss affair at the local Catholic schools. The primary school served a wide catchment area and drew children from every social grouping, from well-to-do families to those who seemed to specialize in breeding savages. It was a harsh place, dreadful academically, where children moved through classes each year and teaching was a matter of child-minding as much as enlightenment.

I lost every nail on my fingers before the age of thirteen. Surprisingly, this had nothing to do with the rougher of my classmates. The person responsible was Mr Adams, a teacher who took a perverse pleasure in inflicting pain. His favoured means of punishment was to make a student put his fingers on the desk and then he'd use a piece of wooden dowelling, about two feet long, to whip down across the fingernails.

I wasn't particularly singled out for this treatment. It reached the stage where any boy in the class who didn't bear the tell-tale stigmata of blackened nails was reckoned to be the teacher's pet.

Another of my junior school teachers would enliven spelling by making us stand with our hands held out and for every letter we got wrong in spelling a word he would swipe us with the sharp edge of a ruler. To this day, I do not spell as well as I might because of the fear he created.

If the standard of education was deplorable, the iniquities of the English education system made things worse. At the age of eleven, students had to take an exam known as the eleven-plus which would decide whether or not they went on to a grammar school or to a secondary modern school. One path opened up the possibility of going to university, the other prepared students for life outside.

I don't know how other schools organized these exams, but my class was virtually segregated into children from wealthier families and others less well provided for. Because the grammar school required uniforms and there was an expectation that children would have cultural pursuits, it was felt that only those from the more wealthy families would have the wherewithal to support such an education.

These children were then kept in after school to be groomed and coached for the eleven-plus exam. Others, like myself, were left to fend for themselves. As expected, all of one group passed the examination while the rest of us looked at the paper and said, 'What's this?'

Thus, my future was decided and I was sent to a secondary modern school. There would be no O levels, or A levels. I was being prepared for life. The reality hit home one day when I stood at the front of a classroom and noticed that nearby a cupboard door had been left ajar. Peering inside I saw chemistry flasks, test tubes, Bunsen burners and stands – all of them a mystery to me.

I held up a test tube and asked the teacher, 'What are these?'

'Oh, put that back,' he said. 'You'll never have need of those.'

Although I wouldn't seek to rewrite my past, I think any system that decides the educational pathway of a child at the age of eleven is one of the greatest offences against the youngsters of the day.

Even as I left school, I realized that I wanted to go to university. It wasn't clear quite how, but I planned to save enough money and eventually do my O levels and A levels. This notion of further study wasn't entirely understood at home. My mother had grown up in a small village in Ireland and had very basic, straightforward priorities. A university education wasn't among them and she was fearful and overly respectful towards scholars.

I can't remember why I decided to become a police cadet – perhaps we had a couple of local bobbies who impressed me. In spite of once being carpeted by the local inspector for breaking a gas mantle in an old street lamp, I don't actually recall there being any crime in Leamington when I was growing up. That's the benefit of childhood memory. People didn't bolt their doors or lock their cars; mothers left their babies in prams outside shops and children walked to school. Crime was something that happened in mystery stories or to other people.

Like most of us, I assumed real villains were easily recognizable. Conan Doyle and Charles Dickens drew them in my imagination – extraordinary figures like Moriarty and Bill Sykes. Of course, it's not that simple in the real world.

I can pinpoint exactly when I realized that badness wasn't worn like a badge, tattoo or scar. Having become a police cadet in Warwickshire, I was stationed at Leamington Police Station when, in the early hours of Thursday 8 August, 1963, fifteen masked men stopped the night train from Glasgow to London at Bridego Bridge near Leighton Buzzard and stole £2,631,684. It became known as The Great Train Robbery and caught the world's imagination.

In policing terms it was like having a bucket of icy water thrown over you. A momentary numbness went through the whole system and people thought, Jesse James robs trains, it doesn't happen here. There was a sense of affront and outrage, particularly when the newspapers portrayed it as a Robin Hood-style robbery – the money didn't belong to anyone, it was going to be destroyed anyway and the thieves simply helped themselves, good luck to them. Unfortunately, the train driver Jack Mills had been severely beaten during the robbery and however romantic the heist may have seemed to the public, the police responded intensely to the violence done.

As a cadet I had almost no role in these events but I remember the telex machine clattering non-stop and sergeants who hadn't been out from behind a desk in ten years suddenly on the move. When they released the first photographs of the wanted men a few days later, I stared at the faces of Bruce Reynolds, Charlie Wilson and Jimmy White and I thought, they look so ordinary. They could have been someone I grew up beside or the father of a friend, or local businessmen, shopkeepers, taxi drivers, school teachers . . . anyone except train robbers.

I found myself asking, 'What happened to these ordinary-looking men which made them become who they are? How did they get here and what other choices did they have?'

The Kray twins were the same. I remember seeing early photographs of Ron and Reggie, wining and dining with sports stars and celebrities in East London. They looked like perfectly ordinary, successful men. Only later, when the photographs became more selective and people learned of their murderous careers, were they made to seem sinister.

Part of my job as a police cadet was to take meals from the café next door to people in the cells. I'd knock on the metal door and hand the tray through the slot.

'Hello, Paul,' said a familiar voice one night.

It was someone I'd been to school with, a few years ahead of me. Now he was locked up in the cells. What happened to him? I thought. What made him different from me?

I left the police force after a year but these questions stayed with me and were possibly part of the reason I became a psychologist. In the meantime, I began the first of a myriad of jobs – too many to remember, let alone name – that ranged from the shop floor to the boardroom and everything in between.

Although living at home, I enjoyed the freedom of earning money. When I bought my first pair of jeans – against my stepfather's wishes – it was more than a fashion choice. I'd earned the money and the right to choose what I wore. 'My house is full of teddy boys,' he said, sighing in disgust.

Occasionally, I went to local dances and I remember one in particular towards the end of 1963 at the Locarno Ballroom in Coventry. A young lady seemed quite keen to dance with me all night and I didn't take much notice of the band or its rather strange, gawky lead singer who kept jumping off the stage and running through the hall. It was Mick Jagger and The Rolling Stones.

A few weeks later, on 27 December, a former schoolmate convinced me to go to another dance at the Court School of Dancing in Leamington where Woody Allen and the Challengers were playing. I wasn't very interested but he lent me a coat and I tagged along.

It was noisy and crowded inside but two girls stood out from the rest. I'd been to school with one of them, who'd become a nurse, but I didn't know her friend. Tall and slender with dark brown hair, she wore a belted tartan pinafore dress and long sleeved white blouse. I couldn't take my eyes off her and she blushed when I asked her to dance.

Afterwards I walked her home to the opposite end of town. It was a crystal clear night when the footpaths and hedgerows sparkled with frost. Outside her gate, she gave me a very shy peck on the cheek and I walked six miles to get home. With every step I told myself that I'd found the girl I was going to marry.

The wedding was in early June, 1966, and we honeymooned in Tenby in Wales, staying at a guest house on the coast and travelling by train. Then we moved into the first floor Victorian flat that I was renting in Leamington. Marilyn was a personal secretary at the University of Warwick and I continued my migratory job swapping, even spending time as a croupier in a casino in Birmingham until a policeman 'advised' me that it wasn't a sensible career move for a young man.

When Emma arrived the following year – and Ian two years later – we had a mortgage and a small three-bedroom semi which we both thought was wonderful. Any dreams of going to university were put on hold as I sometimes held down two jobs to make ends meet. Meanwhile, Marilyn dealt with everything at home. I earned the unenviable distinction of having only woken up twice during the night in the combined childhoods of both my issue. When I sleep, very little can wake me.

By the autumn of 1972 I was working as an export liaison officer at Automotive Products, an international motor car components company and the largest employer in town. My job was to ensure that my designated customers had the parts available when they were needed. It certainly wasn't 'a career' and I could see the treadmill of working for someone else stretching out beneath my feet. I would never really take responsibility and could only hope that after forty years I would have enough to see me through retirement. I'd done all manner of jobs, some of them demanding but none fulfilling, and I knew that I had to find a career that would captivate and motivate me; something I would want to do for the rest of my life.

With Marilyn's support, I enrolled at night school to do my O levels with the aim of going to university. It meant coming home from work, having a meal and then peddling my bicycle to 'Thornbank', the Mid-Warwickshire College of Further Education, to be there for 7.00 p.m. I'd come home at 9.30 p.m., start the study assignments and get to bed at midnight or one o'clock.

I sat the exams in the summer of 1973 and immediately began thinking about doing my A levels. Unfortunately, I discovered there were no evening classes at Thornbank for my subjects. I'd come too far to turn back, I was going to university to change things, so why not change them now, I thought. Making an appointment to see a senior director at work, I explained that I wanted to go to college during the day and asked if I could please have a job on nights.

I became the night clerk, working 8.00 p.m. to 8.00 a.m. four nights a week. The plan was to go to class during the day and then catch a few hours sleep before work and at weekends. At worst, it would only be for a year, I thought. But having changed my job, I went to

Thornbank to enrol and discovered that the A level courses were taken over two years.

There was no point in arguing. I asked for a list of textbooks, went back home and began teaching myself during the day. My aim was to start university in October 1974, which meant sitting the A level exams within seven or eight months.

By January, I'd been provisionally offered a place to read law at Oxford and medicine at Birmingham, but both would mean moving house and getting a new mortgage without a job. The University of Warwick on the outskirts of Coventry, twelve miles away, emerged as a more attractive option; if they would take me.

'Can I help you?' asked the secretary, looking up from her typewriter. She had long straight hair and a perfectly horizontal fringe.

'I'm looking for the admissions tutor, Dr Samuals,' I said.

'I think he's probably having morning coffee but you can try his office. Turn left, along the corridor, the third door.'

She watched me go and I felt mildly self-conscious. I seemed to be the only person on the entire campus at Warwick University who was wearing a suit.

Pausing at the door, I settled myself and knocked. There was no answer.

'Are you looking for Jim?' A short, balding man had appeared from somewhere. 'He's having coffee, I'll get him for you.'

'It's OK, really. I'll wait,' I said.

'No, no, he's had long enough.' Just as quickly, he disappeared.

In spite of having worked all night at Automotive Products, I didn't feel tired. Today was too important. I'd arrived home at 8.00 a.m., just in time for breakfast and to wave Emma off to school. Then I'd bathed, shaved and polished my shoes, put on my suit and caught the 517 Midland Red bus to the outskirts of Coventry.

A man was approaching along the corridor. He looked to be about my age or perhaps a little older and wore neatly pressed slacks and a V-necked jumper. I could see him thinking, Who's this? I don't know him. He's too old to be a student and he's wearing a suit.

'Can I help you?'

'My name is Paul Britton and I'd like to join your course.'

Slightly perplexed, he said, 'Oh! I see. Well, you had better come in then.'

Although I'd never been into an academic's room before, I could have imagined this one. It had a well-used desk, several chairs, a large blackboard and hundreds of books lining the walls.

'Have you made a formal application?' he asked.

'Ah, no.'

'Well, that's normally the procedure; otherwise, I'd have dozens of people waiting outside my office door.'

'I'm sorry, I thought . . .'

He looked mildly amused. 'Well, you're here now. Why do you want to study Management Science?'

I was ready for the question, knowing it had to be asked. I told him that I wanted to be a psychologist and that Management Science at Warwick was my best hope because a third of the course focussed on behavioural science. Coupled with this, I had lots of real work experience and the university was close enough to home that we wouldn't have to move. He listened and occasionally asked questions, cocking his head to one side as if afraid to miss something.

'You're a bit older than the average student, Mr Britton,' he said uncritically.

'I'm twenty-seven. I have a wife, two children and a mortgage.'

'So much! I'm afraid I still don't quite understand why you've turned up at my door. It's not normally the way we do things.'

'It just seemed important to come and see the person who makes the decision . . . the main man.'

He laughed loudly and I felt more relaxed.

'I'm no stranger to hard work. I've had full-time jobs for the past ten years – all sorts of things. I've been going to night school to do my O levels and now I've started my A levels.'

'That's a two year course. You're talking about coming here in October.'

'I'm going to sit the exams in May.'

'Four months from now?' He couldn't hide the doubt in his voice.

'I know, but I can't wait. I'm older than the other applicants. The clock is ticking. I've got a family to support.'

He leaned forward. 'Which brings me to my next question. How are you going to cope financially with three years of full-time study, Mr Britton?'

'I'm hoping to get a student grant.'

'And what if you don't?'

'I've discussed that with my family. This is the most important opportunity we have; one way or another, we'll see it through.'

Dr Samuals leaned back in his chair, weighing up his words.

'There's quite a lot of quantitative understanding required in the sort of courses we do here at Warwick. What are your maths like?'

'I got the top grade at O level.'

'Oh! We normally look for A level maths.'

My heart sank.

'Well, let's check it, shall we?' He stood at a large roller-board and used chalk to draw the axis of a graph, labelling one 'x' and the other 'y'. Then he wrote an algebraic equation beneath. 'Can you plot the course of this equation on the graph?'

Hell's bells, I thought. I knew the form of the calculation but was far too nervous to go through the detailed arithmetic. Instead, I used my finger to draw the classic curve for the equation in the dust on the board.

He smiled. 'That's right, although it should start about half an inch lower.'

Back at his desk, he clasped his hands together and pressed them to his lips. The long silence grew uncomfortable.

Finally he spoke. 'If I were you, I would concentrate on getting A level economics. You've only got a few months. If you can get a grade D or above, we'll guarantee you a place.'

I felt like punching the air in jubilation.

'You don't know how much it means to me,' I said.

He laughed again. 'Oddly enough, I think I do.'

For those next four months, I spent every spare moment studying. However, a far more worrying concern arose. Ian was diagnosed with a debilitating hip disorder which caused him tremendous pain and meant that he couldn't walk and had to be carried or taken in a pushchair everywhere. The lubrication in the hip joints was inadequate, leading to erosion of the ball and socket.

Orthopaedic surgeons and medical experts looked at him and eventually decided to take him into hospital and put him in traction. Marilyn would get Emma off to school and then get to the hospital early in the morning and I'd come straight from work and sit with Ian during the day. It went on for weeks and was an awful time.

I managed to sit the exam while all this was going on and then had to wait for the results that would decide if all the hard work and family sacrifice had been worth it.

By mid-August I was still waiting to hear and had gone to the hospital to sit with Ian. Marilyn joined me and we spent most of the day there. Most of the nurses were known to us by now and, late in the day, one of them asked me what I did.

'I might be going to university,' I said. 'It depends on . . .'

'Oh, the results,' said Marilyn. 'They came this morning. I forgot.'

I looked at her, hardly daring to ask.

She smiled. 'You got an A.'

Even with a student grant, we lived frugally for those next three years. Fortunately, I'd married a woman who could cook amazing meals even if the cupboards looked a little empty. She gave me the space and the support to keep studying.

Within a month of starting at Warwick, a separate psychology department was established and I was able to immediately transfer across from Management Science. It didn't take me long to realize that I'd found my future career – psychology offered me the chance to not only satisfy my own curiosity but also to repair people's lives.

The human mind is still largely uncharted. Its parameters are so broad they encompass everything we do and say; all that has gone before and is still to come in our understanding of the world. How is it that three or four pounds of grey sludge in our heads can produce everything that we think we know and understand? When Mozart wrote his symphonies, when Michelangelo painted the Sistine Chapel, when Hitler ordered the Final Solution, when a teenage mother abandons her baby in a rubbish bin, when a crime victim is too afraid to walk out the front door, when a couple torture and murder young girls . . . it doesn't matter how significant the event or utterance, it all comes back to some aspect of human behaviour and interaction – to that three or four pounds of porridge that make up the brain.

Imagine a fishing net formed by a matrix of hundreds of lines with thousands of knots connecting them. Any single knot may be interesting but when you try to pick it up, all the others come with it. They are all interconnected and you can't truly understand any single knot unless you understand the principles of those around it. That's what makes psychology so fascinating. It's like having a three dimensional map that you journey upon and through.

After three years of lectures, assignments and late night essays, I graduated with a First and accepted an advanced postgraduate studentship at Leicester University. My work was connected with phobic anxiety – in particular measuring arachnophobia, the fear of spiders, and I established elaborate mazes for human subjects and spiders to explore the problem.

The move to Leicester, thirty-five miles from Leamington, hadn't been taken lightly. For Marilyn and the children it was like going to the other side of the world and they were desperately homesick. Ian, then aged seven, now walked and ran properly, although it would be years before his joint problem would be completely cured. We told him that he'd make new friends and on the day we moved into our new house he went outside and stood on the edge of the street, saying that he wouldn't come inside until he'd found a friend.

The sight of him plucked at the heart strings. Eventually, the lady who lived opposite said to her young son, 'Oh, go and talk to that little boy. He's been standing there for ages.'

Ian's wish had been granted.

Soon after starting my postgraduate work, I became an unpaid trainee clinical psychologist with the Leicestershire Health Authority, the largest in the country. My long term goal had been to work in the clinical field and I accepted a full-time salaried post when it became available nine months later.

After qualifying, my day-to-day work involved assessing and treating people who were damaged by unfortunate events in their lives. This included people who suffered recurring nightmares or acute anxiety, others had sexual problems or personality disorders; some couldn't sleep, or stop washing, or bring themselves to walk out of their front door to post a letter. There were also psychosomatic complaints from patients who thought they were paralysed or had exotic illnesses and disorders that doctors had failed to diagnose.

None of these conditions are trivial or minor, because they affect the quality of people's lives and can destroy relationships and families. I remember an eight-year-old boy coming to my office one day and giving me a pen that he'd obviously bought with his pocket money.

'This is for helping my mum,' he said nervously and dashed back to her side. For the previous six years his mum had not been able to leave her house to go to the shops or take him to the park. It had taken months of work but now she was free of her agoraphobia.

In another case a young woman in her mid-twenties was referred to me by her doctor. Martha suffered from anxiety-related problems that were putting great pressure on her marriage. She and her husband desperately wanted a baby but she hadn't been able to fall pregnant and had never actually menstruated. Coupled with this, she had quite serious hearing difficulties and these embarrassed her.

Although I tried to make Martha feel less nervous, every ounce of her being seemed to advertise her poor self-esteem and lack of confidence. Similarly, the very normal history she related was inconsistent with everything else I could hear in her voice and see in her mannerisms. Her words were telling me one story but her body couldn't maintain the deception.

I began telling her a story about how sometimes people came to me for the first time, anxious and upset, and they had notions of what might happen that were based on what they'd seen on television and at the cinema.

'They spend days beforehand preparing themselves, trying to plan exactly what they'll say, but when they step into the room they can't remember any of this and they feel stupid,' I said. 'And then, when we begin to talk about parts of their lives that are very uncomfortable, they get nervous and embarrassed. After all, I'm a perfect stranger. I know it's hard but it's like skydiving; you get to the door of the aeroplane and have to make that last step.'

I went on to explain that very often in these circumstances it turns out that their problem has taken place a long while ago when they were much younger. Perhaps an adult made them do something which upset them a great deal and they don't know how to talk about it. Sometimes they feel, quite wrongly, that they are somehow to blame.

As I continued talking, Martha began crying and eventually collapsed in tears. She described a childhood hampered by hearing problems which eventually led her to be enrolled in a school for the deaf. While at the school she was systematically sexually abused by a member of staff. The attacks started before puberty and went on for a number of years.

Unable to make herself understood and painfully shy, Martha internalized the brutality and felt it must somehow have been her own fault. I took her through the painful memories, explaining where the blame really lay. As I spoke, I could see the guilt falling away in front of me and a different person emerging.

Before Martha left the out-patients clinic she agreed to come and see me again. That evening she menstruated for the first time and became pregnant within weeks with the first of three children.

This is why I chose to become a clinical psychologist – to help people like Martha. Everything I had worked towards and dreamed about had become a reality and there was no sense of anticlimax or what happens next? I had a career that would challenge and motivate me, one that could provide for my family's future and also repair people's lives.

3

EARLY IN 1984 WHEN A TELEPHONE CALL CAME FROM DETECTIVE Superintendent David Baker, my first reaction was that one of my patients was in trouble. The head of Leicestershire CID politely introduced himself and said that my name had been mentioned to him by a colleague.

I racked my brain.

'You helped us out once before,' he prompted, mentioning the officer.

'Ah, yes,' I said, remembering the case which involved a young woman who had become dangerously infatuated with a policeman.

'To be honest it's rather out of my line, psychology,' said Baker. 'You see I'm . . . ah . . . I'm a detective . . .' he let the statement trail off.

This must be leading somewhere, I thought.

'Am I right in thinking that your work gives you an insight into what motivates people and how they become who they are?'

'Yes, in very broad terms,' I said, cautiously.

'Well, I'm involved in a rather difficult murder investigation and I wonder if you'd mind coming to see me? I'd appreciate your help.'

I was intrigued. What could I possibly bring to an investigation? My knowledge of police work came from being a police cadet at the age of sixteen and reading Sherlock Holmes stories as a child. Then I remembered Lynda Mann and stopped myself.

'Of course,' I said, 'will tomorrow do?'

'Have a good breakfast before you come,' he said, rather cryptically. 'You won't want any lunch.'

At the County Police Headquarters, on the London Road in Leicester, Baker's office was littered with the evidence of his twenty-seven years on the force. The walls carried pennants and photographs and adorning his desk was a set of the delicate scales used by drug dealers to measure their wares. In his late forties, Baker wasn't a tall man although quite heavy-set, with thinning hair and an almost cherubic face. He had a slight military bearing and favoured immaculately pressed dark blue suits with a stripe. He sat with his jacket on.

'There aren't any established rules for what I'm about to ask you,' he began, like somebody who knew that he might sound foolish. 'If I were to show you the scene of a crime, pretty much unchanged since it happened, is it possible for you to tell me things about the person who was responsible for the murder?'

I took a deep breath and again my mind went back to Lynda Mann. 'Depending on what you can show me, yes.'

He relaxed just fractionally. 'Have you heard about the death of Caroline Osborne?'

I was surprised. 'No, I'm sorry . . .'

'Her body was found last August in waist-high grass in Aylestone Meadows, beside the Grand Union Canal in Leicester. Certain aspects of the attack are very puzzling.'

I nodded.

As he continued, Baker wavered slightly, unsure of how to proceed. The previous year, 1983, had been a bad one for Leicestershire CID, with three unsolved murders. In July the body of Caroline Hogg, aged five, was found on a grass verge close to Twycross Zoo, ten days after going missing from Edinburgh's Portobello area. That same month, Caroline Osborne, a pet beautician, was murdered while walking her dogs in Leicester, and then came Lynda Mann's killing.

Caroline Osborne, aged thirty-three, had lived and worked in the corner terrace house in Danvers Road, Leicester, for seven years. She ran her business, Clippapet, in the front rooms of the house and lived in the rear and upstairs. On the day she died, she left the parlour at 6.00 p.m. to walk her dogs through Aylestone Meadows; a large green-belt area of sports fields, allotments, waste ground and walking paths. She took her black Labrador Tammy and a neighbour's brindle-coloured Labrador-cross of the same name, letting them run off their leads.

Later that night, Caroline's dog was found wandering alone by John Douglas, a local resident, who recognized Tammy and noticed she'd been in the water. He took her back to his house and then told her to go home. Three hours later, neighbours in Danvers Road heard Tammy howling and called the police.

A late-night search found no trace of Caroline. It resumed on Saturday morning and at 10.30 a.m. a police dog handler spotted Caroline's fully clothed body lying in waist-high grass.

'There are some rather disturbing aspects,' said Baker, pulling out several loose-leaf spiral-bound folders marked, 'Property of the Chief Constable'. 'Her hands and feet were bound with twine. She was stabbed in the neck five times and the chest twice, puncturing her heart. There were no signs of robbery or of a sexual assault and we haven't found the murder weapon . . .'

He paused. 'We did, however, find this . . .'

A piece of paper had been discovered lying near the body that contained a drawing of a pentagram in a circle – an image often associated with satanic or black magic rituals.

'We think the murderer left it behind,' said Baker, unable to hide his disquiet.

Opening the first spiral-bound folder, he asked, 'Have you ever seen crime scene photographs, Paul?'

I shook my head.

'I'm sorry, it's not a pleasant thing.'

The first pages consisted of area-establishing shots of the canal and towpath. The images then gradually focussed down upon the body which was pictured from every conceivable angle. It was appalling, and I had a most powerful urge to put the photographs down, close the album and walk away. I'd never seen anything like it.

Until then, I didn't know what stab wounds did to a body, or how in violent death limbs can often project at unnatural angles, or that with so much blood it was difficult to make out what had happened.

Caroline had also been photographed through each stage of the post-mortem and, as I opened a new folder, I quickly saw the difference between a person lying at a scene of crime and then washed, weighed and cleaned for the pathologist. It was like looking at a statue that is more or less perfect except for these terrible ripping holes – like a work of art despoiled by a vandal.

Forcing myself to look, I began to concentrate on what had happened to Caroline. I needed to understand the distribution of the wounds and how they were clustered. Almost unconsciously, I began asking myself questions. What sort of knife did he use? Was he right-handed (95 per cent of people are)? If so, was it possible to tell if he was standing in front of or behind Caroline when he began stabbing her? When did he tie her up? How long had she been conscious? How quickly did she die?

The answers were important because they influenced the much larger question of motivation. What did the killer seek to achieve when he murdered Caroline? A robbery that went wrong has far different implications to a sexually motivated killing.

Eventually, I closed the albums and leaned back from the desk, trying to rid myself of the images.

'What was Caroline like?' I asked Baker.

He slid a snap-shot across the table that showed her smiling at the camera, vibrant and alive. He began to give me a fairly standard description of height, weight, hair colour, complexion . . . but I stopped him. 'No, what was she like as a *person*?'

'Oh, I see . . . well . . . she was fit, hard-working, bright . . . A career-woman, I suppose. She certainly devoted a lot of time to her business. She and her husband separated about eighteen months ago and were getting a divorce. He lives down south. He checks out. As far as we can establish she had no secret life or boyfriends; nor any outside interests.'

'And no-one saw her that evening?'

Baker shook his head. 'We estimate there were probably about two hundred people in the Aylestone Meadows area at the time. About one hundred and twenty of them have come forward and no-one can remember seeing Caroline on the towpath. We've also checked with the holiday companies who rented barges and house boats on the canal . . . nothing.'

Baker couldn't hide his frustration. The inquiry had been one of the largest ever conducted in Leicestershire. Over 15,000 people had been interviewed, some as many as seventeen times, and eighty men had been arrested on suspicion for further questioning before being released.

'Can I get back to you?' I asked, as the meeting ended. 'I want to think about this.'

'Of course,' he said, shaking my hand.

'Is it possible to take some of the material with me?'

'Give me a note of what you need.'

* * *

At home Marilyn sensed something was wrong from the moment I walked in the door. I wouldn't talk about the case and at dinner-time my legendary appetite deserted me.

For the next three days I sank into the pain of Caroline Osborne's death, sifting through the details. With Lynda Mann I had only contemplated what questions to ask, now it was real. What could I tell the police about Caroline's killer? It clearly wasn't an act of the moment – the bindings and the knife were brought along for the purpose, as was the drawing of the pentagram. This suggested a degree of planning and deliberation.

Nor was it a case of a man coming across an attractive woman, becoming aroused, being rebuffed and angrily stabbing her before running away. Caroline had been disabled, tied up in a particular way and then attacked. Yet despite these elements of control, there was also a lack of sophistication. Why did he choose such a public place and such a busy time? He could have achieved so much more if he'd chosen somewhere more private. He could have exerted more control, made the bindings more elaborate and increased his pleasure. Instead, the killing was over in a matter of minutes.

This element of opportunism suggested that the killer was a stranger to Caroline, although she may have been known to him. Perhaps he'd seen her walking her dogs or been a customer at her shop.

In terms of a motive, I had no doubt that it was sexual, although not in the way that we normally think of a rape or sexual assault. It displayed evidence of a more extreme deviant sexuality. My work in the sexual dysfunction clinic at Leicester General Hospital had helped me understand that people's sexual functioning can become tied to and crossed with other things.

When men and women find themselves unable to have sexual intimacy in a way that feels good for everyone involved, the drive doesn't just go away. Sometimes they find themselves developing fetishes and vivid fantasies to such an extent that they lose the ability to sustain or enjoy sexual intercourse unless they imagine or actually have some very specific factor present, for example, certain types of pornography, underwear, footwear, or ritualistic behaviour.

Some people become so preoccupied with these things that the actual sexual act becomes less and less important or valuable so that even their masturbatory thoughts turn increasingly towards these fetishes and vivid fantasies. For a man, the woman can cease to be a mutually consenting, eager participant and instead become a depersonalized vehicle for his pleasure.

Caroline Osborne's murder was an expression of a corrupt lust. The bindings, control and choice of victim suggested a killer whose sexual desire had become mixed with anger and the need to dominate. Rather than fantasizing about some form of mutually consenting sexual contact, the killer's fantasies would feature extreme sexual aggression against women and closely mirror the events that unfolded on Aylestone Meadows. He would have rehearsed the scene in his mind beforehand – fantasizing about a woman being taken, restrained, bound, dominated, mutilated and killed with a knife.

But how did he become like this?

A sense of bitterness and anger towards women often begins early when, for example, a lonely and sexually immature young man may discover that he hasn't the necessary social skills to get girls to take an interest in him. He sees other boys and young men having success with women but it doesn't happen for him.

Feeling hurt and rejected, he may begin to blame women for his loneliness and sexual frustration. Over time, this can lead to a growing sense of bitterness and anger which can distort sexuality. Instead of fantasizing about consenting and mutually pleasurable sexual events, he may begin to link pleasure through masturbation with gross sexual violence. In his fantasies he can make women do what he wants and, more importantly, he can punish them for what he believes they have done to him.

The pentagram found near the body was the crux. Caroline's murder wasn't a ritual sacrifice. The diagram had been drawn earlier and left behind so that the scene would resemble the re-enactment of a ritual sexual sacrifice to a satanic or other black magic figurehead. This is how the killer rationalized his grossly deviant urges to control, torture and murder a woman. It gave his actions a purpose, even if totally spurious. If devil worship or human sacrifice had truly been the motive I would have expected to see far more of the elaborate preparation, degradation and theatre that is associated with the black arts.

Finding a foolscap page, I began writing down a list of psychological features that I could draw from the material. 'The lack of ultimate sophistication or practice in the killing suggests a very young man in his mid-teens to early twenties,' I wrote. 'He's likely to be very lonely and sexually immature, with few previous girlfriends, if any. He will have wanted relationships but won't have the necessary social skills to begin or maintain them.'

Point two: 'He will probably live at home with his parents or a parent.' This is quite a common feature that emerges among young men with poor social skills and no sexual confidence.

Another common feature concerned his likely employment. The inability to verbally express himself would make it difficult for him to hold down a managerial or higher clerical job. For this reason I wrote, 'He is more likely to be a manual worker in the sort of job that demands dexterity and may involve being comfortable with sharp knives.' The reference to knives had been flagged by his handiwork on Caroline's body.

'He's physically strong and athletic,' I wrote, something evident from the way his victim had been subdued and bound, as well as the force used to inflict the knife wounds.

'He may have known Caroline, or at least been aware of her, and she may have played a part in his various masturbatory fantasies.

'This is his territory. He knows the area and lives very close by – if not now then at some point in the recent past.' This explained how he managed to murder Caroline and then disappear so quickly from Aylestone Meadows that none of the people who were in the general area noticed anyone acting suspiciously or anything untoward. For this to happen, he had to be confident in his surroundings.

At the same time, to have struck in the open air, on a warm summer's evening when it was still light, involved taking considerable risks, but he was so aroused he was willing to take the chance.

'His violent sexual fantasies will be fed by pornographic magazines, books, posters and videos, some of it violent and featuring satanic themes,' I wrote. 'When you find him and look inside his house, I expect you'll find ample evidence of this, as well as his strong interest in knives.'

The fact that the murder weapon had not been found at the scene indicated that the killer may have a forensic awareness. Equally, it suggested that he might regard the knife as a treasured artefact and, therefore, he wouldn't have casually discarded it; he would have kept it close.

Going through each point with David Baker in his office, I sensed that he didn't quite know how to respond. Although grateful, he was unsure of how I could read so much into photographic and case history information that he and his colleagues had studied for months. How much weight could he give to my conclusions? Nobody, as far as we knew, had ever asked a psychologist to become involved in a murder investigation in quite this way before – it was virgin territory, without maps, and I was a guide who followed signs that David couldn't see.

Weeks were to pass, then months, and when I didn't hear from Baker again I assumed my role had ended. There was no way of gauging whether I'd been a help or not, I simply went back to my clinical work.

Fourteen months later, on Monday 29 April, 1985, I saw a newspaper poster on my way home from work – NURSE, 21, SLAIN ON FOOTPATH. Amanda Weedon had been one of our own, working at Groby Road Hospital in northwest Leicester as a state enrolled nurse not long finished her training and soon to be married.

David Baker called me that evening and next morning I found myself back in his office, listening to another briefing.

Amanda's body had been found by a teenage girl at 4.15 p.m. on Saturday, lying under a hedge alongside a tree-shaded footpath which ran between Groby Road Hospital and Gilroes Cemetery. A few yards away further along the path stood a red-brick building called The Chantry, a psychiatric halfway house where patients lived for a time before they returned to the community. A member of staff had seen 'a shadowy figure' lurking on the footpath at about the time of the attack.

Like Caroline Osborne, Amanda had been stabbed repeatedly and there were none of the normal signs that flag a sexual killing. Initially the police thought they might be dealing with a small-time mugger who had bungled his attack. Amanda's purse containing £20 and her cash-card was missing from her brown handbag.

She had withdrawn the money during the morning and gone shopping with her fiancé, Clifford Eversfield. The couple had said goodbye at lunchtime and Clifford, the manager of a local football team, Epworth, was on the touchline watching a game when Amanda was attacked. The news was broken to him when he came to the nurses' home on Saturday evening to pick up Amanda for a party.

After lunch, Amanda had walked to a friend's house in Amadis Road, Beaumont Leys. She left there at about 3.15 p.m. and went to buy a greeting card from Martins newsagent's in Fletcher Mall at Beaumont Leys. The shop assistant remembered her.

At 3.45 p.m. she started back towards the hospital through the snow flurries and bitter wind. The walk would have taken seventeen to twenty-two minutes and she would have reached the footpath at about 4.00 p.m. Her body was found fifteen minutes later. The greeting card lay nearby.

'There's only half an hour we have to account for,' said Baker, with a palpable sense of urgency.

'I need to know about Amanda.'

'It's early days,' he said, finding a folder. 'Her family comes from Burton-on-the-Wolds, ten miles north of here. Father's retired . . . used to work for Rolls Royce . . . Amanda's the youngest of three children . . . the only daughter . . . always wanted to be a nurse . . . not much else.' Baker continued reading out loud. 'She spoke to her mother three times on Friday about wedding invitations. She was getting married on July twenty-seven.'

Baker slid an album of crime scene photographs across the table, looking almost apologetic. I took a deep breath. Immediately it was clear that the pattern of knife wounds was similar to the first murder, aimed mainly at the neck and shoulders. Again there was an absence of an overt sexual assault but I had no doubt that it was sexually motivated. It was like laying one template on top of another. There were differences, but these were far outnumbered by the similarities.

'You're dealing with the same man who killed Caroline Osborne,' I said.

Baker nodded in agreement.

'The attack was sudden and not as thought out. He took a greater risk . . .'

'Which means?'

'Well, it suggests that there was some disinhibition which argues either for him being in a state of greater excitement or illness. He hasn't had the protracted interpersonal exchange with his victim – not like with Caroline – which suggests he's immature, otherwise there would have been more refinement. Sexual murderers tend to refine their techniques and increase their control over victims with each new murder. But this killer took a greater risk and even less time. There was also no attempt to bind the victim and no symbolism around the edges.'

Baker asked, 'And that means . . . ?'

'Well, it makes it far less likely that he knew Amanda.'

'So he struck at random?'

'Well, no . . . not quite. I don't think she was a random victim.'

Baker raised an eyebrow.

'There could have been a dozen women walk along the path and he ignored them. Something singled Amanda out; she attracted his attention just at the moment when he was most aroused. Maybe she looked like someone he knew, or her hair was tied in a certain way, or it was something she wore.'

Gilroes Cemetery sprawled across dozens of acres, dominating the aerial map that Baker gave me of the scene. He explained that police were searching the area, a known haunt for glue-sniffers, in the hope of finding Amanda's purse.

Almost in passing, he said that Caroline Osborne had been buried in the cemetery. Our eyes met momentarily and I could see we were asking ourselves the same question: could he have visited the grave?

The cemetery is vast and I reasoned there was a fair chance that any local person who died would finish up there. If there was a connection it was probably of mixed salience, I thought, although visiting Caroline's grave was just the sort of thing that might have heightened his arousal. In such a state, carrying a knife, it's possible he walked out of the cemetery and came upon Amanda Weedon.

The public had reported three sightings of a man or men in the area between 3.15 p.m. and 4.30 p.m. One description concerned a man seen leaving the footpath at 4.05 p.m. He was white, tall and wearing drab clothing, either khaki or olive green.

Baker explained that the murder squad was working through the massive list of suspects interviewed after Caroline's murder and also checking local records for known flashers and sex offenders in the area. My psychological description would, initially at least, help them channel their resources and focus on a much smaller pool of suspects who had the relevant characteristics.

We agreed to talk in a few days' time and I left police headquarters, driving to Leicester General where my NHS work was waiting.

Paul Kenneth Bostock, aged nineteen, of Beaumont Leys in Leicester, being six foot five inches tall and weighing fifteen stone, certainly matched the description issued of the stranger seen on the footpath.

Bostock's grandmother encouraged him to go to the police to eliminate himself and on Wednesday afternoon, four days after the second murder, he walked into Blackbird Road Police Station. He was nervous and contradicted himself several times when explaining his movements on the previous Saturday.

He had been interviewed three times after the first murder but had given an apparently satisfactory alibi. He lived with his parents in Blakesley Walk, Beaumont Leys, near to the scene of both murders. Eight months earlier the family had lived in Walton Street, around the corner from Caroline Osborne's pet parlour where they took their two dogs to be groomed.

Bostock came across as a mild-mannered giant and was a popular figure in his job as a meat processor, which obviously involved working with knives. A fitness fanatic, he jogged and cycled before or after work and had turned his grandmother's garage into a fitness studio.

He had played junior rugby with West Leicester – a natural forward because of his height – and later developed an interest in martial arts, training on Tuesday and Friday nights at a Leicester working men's club. He would arrive at the training lessons with his kit washed and neatly pressed, but rarely say anything to anyone.

'He was always calm and quiet,' another trainee Colin Underwood told the local newspaper. 'Sometimes people lose their temper if someone else accidentally hurts them, but Paul wouldn't. He was always in control of himself and accepted it as part of the game.'

Baker telephoned me later that evening and told me about the suspect.

'He's an exact fit for the description you gave us. We're getting a warrant to search his house.'

'Remember what I said to you after Caroline's murder,' I said. 'If he's your man, then I think you're going to find knives, pornography and a lot of black magic paraphernalia . . . that sort of thing.'

Baker hadn't forgotten. 'Listen, I've got another favour to ask. In the light of what you told me about the killer's motivation, I want you to talk to some of the other lads, particularly the interviewing officers. I want you to help them understand what they're dealing with.'

'When did you have in mind?'

'Now. That's police work for you.'

On the drive to Blackbird Lane Police Station, I kept asking myself why one of the most senior detectives in the county would come to a rather modestly placed psychologist and ask for help with interrogating a suspect? Interviewing is at the heart of what they do and my knowledge of their methods was slight.

As I crawled through the roundabouts on the outskirts of Leicester,

I began to think in terms of my clinical work. If I had Paul Bostock in my consulting room for assessment, the first task would be to take his history, and to do that I'd have to build a rapport with him. Not everyone wants to revisit their past and have their deepest secrets unlocked. Some fight against it or have totally blocked out the events at the heart of their problem. To overcome this requires a particular interview strategy that slowly draws back the veil.

This is all I could offer the police, I thought, along with an understanding of the psycho-sexual functioning of the killer and the nature of his deviation and sexual fantasies.

At the police station I was ushered into a large room in which half a dozen detectives sat casually, some with shirt sleeves rolled up, jackets slung on chairs and elbows resting on the table. I'd met some of them already but still felt self-conscious as Baker made the introductions and told me the boys were 'eerily impressed' by how accurate my description had been. There was no sense of me bruising any egos despite being an outsider. It said a lot for the admiration and respect they held for David Baker; if I was OK with him, I was OK with them.

Everybody in the room was convinced that Bostock was their man, particularly following the search of his parents' house. A collection of knives were found in his bedroom, displayed alongside other weapons such as swords, guns and kung fu stars. The walls were plastered with posters and drawings, some of which he'd done himself, which included black magic symbols and bondage scenes with topless women trussed up and being tortured. One of the symbols matched that found near to Caroline Osborne's body. Detectives had also found a large number of violent comics and magazines.

Baker explained to me the importance of tying up every loose end. After so much work, they couldn't afford to see a guilty man walk free at some later date because something had been overlooked or correct procedure hadn't been followed. Equally, he said it was important that an innocent man was not tricked or pressurized into making a false admission.

When it was my turn to talk, I began by describing the nature of sexual dysfunction and sexual deviation, much as I'd first explained it to Baker. I spoke about the patterns of how people develop, how they become who they are and the psychological defences they build to protect them from seeing themselves as they truly are.

'Tell me about the early interviews,' I asked.

'Well, he's not rolling over,' said Detective Chief Inspector Ian

Leacy in a gruff voice. 'To begin with I couldn't decide if he was a fucking moron or a genius. Now? Well, I don't think he's being deliberately unco-operative but whenever we get close to the big questions he clams up or says "No" or "I can't remember."'

'What's he like? How does he hold himself?'

'He's not cocky or aggressive, if that's what you mean. He says he wants to help. He keeps asking about his mum and dad. To be honest, I think he's frightened.'

I thought about this. 'OK, it's possible that he's blacked it out and literally can't remember, but I doubt it. He knows what he's done. This isn't a person who on a single occasion was overwhelmed and committed a murder – he's been out there twice. At the same time, he's been interviewed before and managed to avoid detection. It means that he's built up a certain amount of face and image which makes it harder for him to now tell a different story.'

Now I had to construct a strategy and simultaneously not tread on any toes. 'I've got absolutely no idea of how you conduct interviews. You're the experts. I operate entirely on my knowledge of how the human mind works. From what you've told me, this man isn't going to be a triumphant advocate of sadistic deviancy. He's managed to get away with this for a long while without alerting those around him, which suggests that in ordinary company he'll tend to repudiate that sort of behaviour and show horror.

'He's not going to sit there and think, "I know who I am and I know what I've done and I'm going to hold these people out." He possibly can't acknowledge what he did to these women or why he did it; he can't face the feelings of shame and judgement he thinks he's going to get, particularly from his family, so he's recoiling from talking about what happened.'

Baker said, 'So how do we go forward?'

'Most importantly, you prepare, prepare and prepare. The interviewers have to know everything there is to know about the offence, the victims and the suspect. You have to make it easy for him to talk to you and treat him as though he genuinely wants to tell you what happened, but is finding it emotionally difficult. Don't be judgemental, confrontational or show any repugnance.'

I began to lay out a strategy similar to one that I used in my consulting room when dealing with patients who recoiled from revealing incidents in their past.

'Imagine the truth is at the centre of a series of concentric circles.

You can't go straight to the heart – the suspect won't let you – so you begin way off and talk about family, his early life, school holidays and friends. Get him used to talking about these things in fine detail so that later, when you get close to the murders, you don't suddenly have to change gear from talking in general terms to fine detail. The discontinuity will throw him.

'As you do this, a rapport is building and he comes to feel good about you. He comes to know he's safe. He still knows there's a consequence, but he doesn't think you'll turn on him and call him an animal or a monster. Instead you want to understand what happened and how it came about.

'When he's comfortable talking about the minutiae of relationships and how things felt, you take him a step further, moving him closer and closer to the week and the day and the hour that Caroline Osborne was killed.

'When you get too close he'll tell you, "I don't know", or "I wasn't there", or "I can't remember". You can batter on that door but he'll push back even more strongly. Give it a rest, have a break and return later. This time backtrack a little, letting him go over old territory before bringing him back again. You must take him through the day in the most minute detail – what time did you leave? Did you turn left or right? Were your hands in your pockets, do you think?

'Then let him pick up the story and you'll find that he goes a little further and admits, "Yes, I might have seen her on the towpath."

'Don't look surprised. Don't say, "Hey, hold on, you denied that before." Instead, you say, "OK, that's fine. Where exactly was she standing? What was she wearing?"

'And so you move on until you reach another point where he can't remember or doesn't know. Don't batter on the door, pull back again and employ exactly the same approach. Don't say, "Well, this is getting us nowhere." Tell him, "Oh well, we've done very well today, let's have a break, shall we?"'

It was also very important that the interviewers explain the nature of deviant sexuality to Bostock. They had to help him know that he wasn't alone, that other people understood. I said, 'Tell him you know it's hard for him but you've heard such things before and he's not the first to have such feelings, even if he finds it hard to understand them.'

As they came closer and closer to the truth, the barriers would get bigger until eventually they reached a point where suddenly they crashed through one and the interview went straight to the heart. It happens in a rush because finally everything spills out in a sense of relief. 'Don't stop him, let him talk freely. Later, you can take him back and ask him specific evidential questions.

'After you've exhausted this, you can question the parts of his account that don't ring true. Maybe he's saying, "I was there, I spoke to her, I killed her but I didn't do the things you say, not like that."

'Now you can be more confrontational and challenging. He won't want to mention the sadistic or cruel acts – he doesn't want anyone to know – but you need the precise details.'

For the next few days I listened to the interview tapes, reviewing the questions and answers. Slowly, each of the barriers was broken down and Paul Bostock was taken back to Aylestone Meadows on that warm summer evening in 1983 when he met Caroline Osborne and later to the bitterly cold afternoon when he spied Amanda Weedon beside Gilroes Cemetery. As it turned out, he had been visiting Caroline's grave that day and as he left, he saw the young nurse. Why did he choose her?

'Because she had red shoes,' he said.

In June 1986, Bostock pleaded guilty to both murders at Leicester Crown Court and was sentenced to life imprisonment. His barrister released several letters that his client had written to a girlfriend while in prison awaiting trial. One of them said:

> *In those few moments I destroyed not only everything I have tried to be but I have ruined my victims' family's lives, my family's life and the life I planned for us together.*
>
> *The torment, the realisation of what I am guilty of, means that I can't look my parents in the eye, I can't look you in the eye, I can't face myself and I can hardly look at the detectives. If there was anything that could change what I have done, I would do it.*

By the time the trial was held, we had moved to a new house in a tiny village in Leicestershire which felt positively rural. Within a few minutes walk in any direction there were fields, woodland, hedgerows and streams. I did some of my best thinking on long afternoon walks, letting Jess run and watching the light fade.

The house was quite modern and had enough space for an office – a useful extra when I didn't know how my career would develop with the NHS.

The Bostock case had been a one-off, I thought, but it did answer my questions about the possible benefits of using a psychological approach to analyse a crime. It could clearly be used to narrow down the number of potential suspects and allow investigators to effectively focus their resources. By saying the offender was male and aged between his mid-teens and early twenties, it dramatically reduced the number of potential suspects. By saying he was unmarried, living at home with a detailed local knowledge, it narrowed the number again. Then it was possible to sharpen the focus still more by indicating the manual nature of his work, his athleticism and comfort with knives.

I couldn't tell the police Paul Bostock's name or his address, but I knew things about how he lived, what went on inside his mind and his motivation.

4

THE HEART OF MY WORK HAD ALWAYS BEEN THE ASSESSMENT AND treatment of people who were damaged by unfortunate events in their lives – victims rather than perpetrators. By 1986, I found myself seeing patients wall to wall, morning to evening, one every hour. Perhaps not surprisingly the extent of the challenge diminished over time, although the impact of their pain on me didn't.

At about this time, I found my clinical work taking on a more pronounced forensic (crime-related) strand. There was nothing to flag this change but my consulting room seemed to contain a growing number of patients who had committed crimes or were on the verge of doing so; as well as the victims of their actions.

This had started off as the occasional referral growing out of my work in the sexual dysfunction clinic at Leicester General. For example, a local GP would write, saying, 'Dear Paul, I have a patient who seems to fit most of the criteria for retarded ejaculation. Unfortunately, he also complains of feeling sexually attracted to his sister's children. He says that nothing has happened yet, but obviously I would appreciate it if you could arrange to examine him quickly.'

Other cases were court referrals of offenders who had perhaps been charged with indecent exposure, shoplifting or criminal damage. It might be the defence solicitor looking to find something in mitigation or the magistrates trying to understand what they were dealing with before passing sentence. There were also people who hurt themselves sexually and others who had worrying urges and wanted help before they acted upon them.

Working with forensic patients requires a completely different mental-set to non-forensic work because rather than having a natural affinity with a person in trouble, you first have to overcome the realization that the person sitting opposite might have urges to do terrible things. Your first instinct is to be harsh with them instead of automatically wanting to help someone in need.

That summer I became aware that the post as head of the Regional Forensic Psychology Service had fallen vacant. For the first time I thought seriously about how far I wanted to go in this direction. It certainly meant a more highly graded post, with more money, but also a move away from the broad ranging clinical work that I so enjoyed.

It meant providing a full-time in-patient service for people who were at the least attractive end of the clinical spectrum – the most dangerous, depraved and damaged minds in the system would finish up at my door. Did I want to spend all of my working life immersed in their horrible crimes and sharing the pain of their victims?

I thought about this for a long while and spent many nights at the kitchen table talking it over with Marilyn. The situation was complicated by my ambition to add occupational psychology to my clinical work. This covered areas such as occupational stress, teamwork and risk factors in business. Having come from industry and commerce into psychology in the first place, it seemed a natural progression.

Yet I couldn't deny that I was fascinated by the criminal mind. What made someone want to batter a woman or rape a young child? What were the triggers that caused one person to become violent and destructive and another to be a caring, conscientious member of the community?

I knew that I could help people. If I could treat, for example, a sex offender at an early stage of his career, then dozens of people might never become victims. Just as importantly, by treating victims I could repair the damage and free them from their pain. Surely, this *had* to be worthwhile.

I was interviewed for the post in July for an appointment that would begin in September. In the meantime, I continued my clinical work and prepared to enter Sheffield University as a part-time post-graduate student studying occupational psychology.

It had been two and a half years since Lynda Mann had been murdered near Carlton Hayes Hospital and I still occasionally drove past the Black Pad on my way to see a patient. The crime had never been solved but periodically new appeals for help were made, normally on the anniversary of her death. This is how it remained until Friday 1 August, 1986, when I noticed the front page of the *Leicester Mercury* as I bought milk from a corner shop.

> HUNT FOR MISSING SCHOOLGIRL
> *Senior detectives and uniformed police with tracker dogs have joined a huge search of the Narborough area for a 15-year-old girl who disappeared last night not far from a spot where another schoolgirl was found murdered three years ago.*
> *Dawn Amanda Ashworth of Mill Lane, Enderby, has not been seen since she visited friends in Narborough yesterday afternoon. She left their house in Carlton Avenue, Narborough at 4.30 p.m. and disappeared.*

At midday the following day, Dawn Ashworth's body was found alongside a footpath, this one running to the east of Carlton Hayes Hospital and known locally as Ten Pound Lane. Like Lynda she had been a pupil of the local Lutterworth Grammar School.

For the next week this second murder dominated the local and national headlines. Being so busy, I caught only occasional snatches of radio bulletins or sightings of newspapers but I knew there was a real fear in the community.

This time the police quickly made an arrest, picking up a seventeen-year-old youth from Narborough. He was a kitchen porter at Carlton Hayes Hospital, working in the large canteen that provided meals for patients and staff. On 11 August he was charged with Dawn Ashworth's murder and remanded in custody.

Within a few days a letter arrived on my doormat from the Local Health Authority – the formal contract confirming that I was to be the new head of the Regional Forensic Psychology Service. There was, however, a catch. The department didn't feel that I could take on the added responsibility while doing a further university course. I'd been expecting to get financial support for my studies at Sheffield University but it was made clear that this wouldn't be forthcoming. Perhaps if I deferred it for a year and concentrated on my new role the finance could be found in the future, they suggested.

I had a decision to make. Did I carry on as planned – now having to fund myself – and perhaps upsetting the powers that be? Or did I turn the university down and hope to win a place the following year? I began to doubt whether I wanted the new post, the office and forensic career after all.

Shortly before 9.00 a.m. on the first day of September, I pulled into the car-park at Arnold Lodge, Leicester, and surveyed my new domain. It was a rather squat two-storey brown-brick building surrounded by a sixteen-foot-high chain-link fence. Most of the windows were of reflective glass that couldn't fully open.

This was a regional secure-unit housing about twenty-four patients but with plans to eventually have sixty beds. The fence and control room announced immediately that the residents were meant to stay inside, at least for the short term and normally a maximum of two years. All the same, the place didn't look *that* secure. What am I getting myself into, I thought.

Inside, the overriding impression was one of darkness. The ceilings seemed oppressively low, dragged down by the dark stained wood that had been chosen to decorate the interiors. There were locks on every door and the central control room was wired up to respond to 'incidents' anywhere in the complex.

It was very different to the light airy corridors of Leicester General. People would now be watching my every movement. We often forget that the staff spend longer in closed institutions than most of the inmates.

The men and women at Arnold Lodge were mostly aged between eighteen and forty. Some of them had done dreadful things or had the potential to do so – arsonists, paedophiles, rapists, sadists, killers . . . They were young, physically fit people and I could sense an energy in the unit, but it wasn't something exciting, rather it was something that had to be watched.

Among the patients I had to treat was a woman in her mid-twenties who had set fire to a shopping centre; a twenty-one-year-old who had tried to cut his father's throat; a man who believed his young daughter was the devil's child and thought he had to mutilate her eyes and body before strangling her; and another man with sadistic fantasies who tied up his former girlfriend, tortured and then killed her.

Such people had gone through the legal process, been convicted or detained under the Mental Health Act. Some of them had been sent to prison or a secure hospital such as Rampton in Nottinghamshire.

Later they were transferred to Arnold Lodge for further specialist treatment on their way back to the community. It became our decision whether they still posed a risk to society or not, although some patients with particularly violent histories could only be released with the consent of the Home Secretary.

In general, if offenders were considered a grave and immediate risk but still treatable they were sent to a high security hospital. We took people who were grave risks or immediate risks but not both. The logic was that an escaped resident might be very dangerous but only in very particular circumstances, or vice versa, they might be an immediate risk but not a serious danger to the community.

Many of the patients were sent to Arnold Lodge directly by the courts, providing they met the risk management requirements and their psychological difficulties were treatable within the unit's timescale. Others came to us from normal prisons, having developed problems while incarcerated. At the same time there were out-patient clinics for offenders and crime victims. These tended to be referrals by local doctors, occasionally solicitors and more often from clinical psychologists working in the NHS who didn't have the inclination to take would-be axe murderers into their care.

My area of responsibility was for the whole of Leicestershire, Nottinghamshire, Derbyshire, Lincolnshire and South Yorkshire – an area of roughly 1,000 square miles. For the first few months, until I filled the posts around me, I *was* the forensic psychology service for a population of over five million. It would take me two hours to drive to Barnsley, or to Lincoln. Then I'd meet a local GP, probation officer, or psychologist (getting to know my referral sources) and then be on the road again.

Nothing could have prepared me for how relentlessly grim it proved to be. Each day brought disbelief and sadness until my growing professional carapace became strong enough to protect me from even the worst details. Many perpetrators had histories which revealed that they, too, were victims who had suffered abuse, neglect or violence in their formative years. If I was to help them, I had to understand what had happened and why.

Nearly three months into my new job, on 22 November, I had a phone call from a local journalist on the *Leicester Mercury.* He asked me if I could tell him the psychological characteristics of the person who killed Lynda Mann and Dawn Ashworth.

'There's someone in custody,' I said.

'Haven't you heard the news? He's been freed. It's this new blood test – genetic fingerprinting.'

Slightly taken aback, I told him that I couldn't comment. I'd never heard of genetic fingerprinting or DNA tests. Remarkably, the process had been discovered only a few miles from my office, at Leicester University by Dr Alec Jeffreys, a young scientist who had been investigating the possibility of examining the genetic differences between people by isolating their DNA. Every human cell contains the blueprint of the entire human body carried as coded information in the form of DNA (deoxyribonucleic acid) arranged into groups called genes. Since genes govern heredity, Jeffreys reasoned that if he could isolate DNA material from a cell and present it as an image it would be individually specific. The only people on earth with identical DNA maps would be identical twins.

The technology had enormous possibilities in medicine, science and the law, but until 1986 it had mostly been used in paternity and immigration disputes. That changed on 21 November when the kitchen porter from Carlton Hayes became the first alleged killer to be set free as a result of genetic fingerprinting.

For Leicestershire CID, the result was a public relations disaster. The killer of two schoolgirls was still at large and an innocent teenager had spent more than three months in jail. David Baker faced a grilling at the news conference afterwards. The arrest had not been 'a blunder', he said, the youth had been charged after tape-recorded questioning in the presence of a lawyer. 'He is not responsible for certain aspects of that murder.'

'Has he been totally eliminated?' a journalist asked.

'No-one has been totally eliminated.'

Lynda Mann had been killed almost within sight of my office and I remember contemplating who might have done such a thing. Three years later, with a second girl murdered, David Baker gave me the opportunity to ask the question in earnest. His telephone call was brief and short on detail. He didn't trust hospital switchboards and wanted to meet.

Leicestershire had a new police headquarters, purpose-built on a large campus outside the city and only a few miles from Narborough. The entrance foyer looked like a reception for a motorway hotel and after following the jinking corridors I found

Baker's office which was larger than his old one but rather sparse. The souvenirs from past operations either hadn't made the journey or hadn't been unpacked.

He introduced me to Detective Superintendent Tony Painter, a tall, fit man with a Romanesque face, aviator glasses and a local accent. Close to Baker's age and experience, the two of them looked as if they'd probably risen through the ranks together. Baker was the quieter of the two but no less assertive.

'We've got problems, Paul,' he said, nursing his chin in his hands. 'We were convinced that we had caught a murderer. We had a confession; we had witnesses who put him at the scene; he knew details about Dawn's death that were never made public. We charged him and then his father reads a bloody magazine story about genetic testing and starts demanding that we give the boy one.' He paused and looked up. 'I suppose you've met Dr Alec Jeffreys?'

I shook my head.

He continued, 'Well . . . anyway . . . he does a test that we've never heard of and comes back and says, "You've got the wrong guy." You can't challenge it. How do you challenge brand-new science? Nobody else in the bloody world knows anything about it.'

There was a short silence as the question seemed to bounce around the room.

Baker said, 'I want to know what we did wrong.'

'What exactly do you want *me* to do?'

'As far as I'm concerned, the investigation was faultless. But I'd like you to go over the interviews with the kitchen porter. I want to know if we in any way conveyed to him information that he then gave us. Were the interviews oppressive? Did we pressurize him into making confessions and admissions? How did he know the things he knew?'

Painter explained that there were about fourteen tapes of interviews conducted over several days at Wigston Police Station. A lawyer had been present for most of the sessions.

'But that isn't the first priority . . .' interrupted Baker. 'We have a lot of frightened people out there . . . parents who don't know whether it's safe for their kids to walk home from school . . .'

Painter said, 'One minute we got the guy and the next we've got Jack shit.'

Baker added, 'Bottom line, we have a double-murderer still out there and I want you to help us catch him.'

Better prepared this time, I knew exactly what I needed. 'It means going right back to the beginning and studying the entire investigation.'

Baker replied, 'Fine, whatever you want. We're not hiding anything.'

Tony Painter had headed the investigation into Dawn Ashworth's murder and he would take me through the inquiry from day one.

Dawn had a part-time job during the school holidays, working at a newsagent's shop in Mill Lane, Enderby. On 31 July she left the shop at 3.30 p.m. According to a friend, 'She was happy and in high spirits all afternoon being very excited about going on holiday with her parents to Hunstanton on Saturday.'

At home, Dawn told her mother she was going to have tea with schoolmates in Narborough. She'd by home by 7.00 p.m. because she was going to a birthday party for a little boy for whom she babysat. She even dropped back into the newsagent's shop to buy a box of Smarties as part of her gift.

She left the shop at 4.00 p.m., heading for Narborough. Dawn was five feet three inches tall and wore braces on her teeth. She had dark brown straight medium-length hair. She was wearing a mid-calf-length white skirt, a white sleeveless polo-neck top and multicoloured sleeveless top with a denim jacket. She was known to have only £10 on her.

The most direct route to the homes of her two girlfriends was via Ten Pound Lane, a mixture of farm track and footpath that ran from the sports fields of Brockington School, Enderby, between fields to the east of Carlton Hayes Hospital until it emerged onto the Leicester–Coventry road at Narborough.

To the east, running almost parallel to Ten Pound Lane, was the M1 motorway which cut across the eastern tip of Narborough and turned directly north through Enderby near the sports fields.

Dawn had a choice as she walked towards Ten Pound Lane. She could turn left over the motorway footbridge and then follow a path to King Edward Avenue, or turn right and take the shorter route down Ten Pound Lane.

In Narborough, Dawn visited several friends and the last person to see her was Mrs Valerie Allsop, the mother of one schoolfriend from Carlton Avenue. She'd seen Dawn walk past the front window as she was leaving.

Dawn appears to have then retraced her steps, walking towards home. A passing motorist sighted her at 4.40 p.m. crossing King Edward Avenue, as she headed towards the farm gate across the entrance to Ten Pound Lane.

Her half-naked body was found by police at noon on Saturday in a corner of a field next to the footpath. It was almost totally concealed by grass, nettles, twigs, branches and leaf litter which had been heaped on top.

Painter opened the first album of crime scene photographs. With the foliage cleared away, Dawn was visible lying on her left side with her knees pulled up toward her chest. She was naked from the waist down although her underpants were hooked around her right ankle and white shoes were on her feet. Her bra was pushed up over her breasts and a trail of dried blood was smeared across her left thigh. She'd been in the field a considerable time in the middle of summer and the insects had found her first. Although her eyes were closed, the lids and orbits were marked out in a creamy white mucus left by their passage.

I wanted to look away. I wanted to give the young girl some semblance of decency and turn the camera aside. Taking a deep breath, I turned the pages, mentally noting the numerous scratches, insect bites and nettle stings on the body.

Painter turned to the pathology report, explaining the important details. Dawn had two abrasions on her upper left forehead, a swelling over her left cheek and bruising from the left eye down to her jaw-line. There was a cut inside her mouth caused by her braces and other abrasions on her face, chest and the back of her neck. Some of these injuries occurred when her body was being moved and concealed, according to the pathologist.

She died of manual strangulation and possibly received a knife-hand blow before a stranglehold was imparted, possibly a forearm pressed against her larynx by an assailant behind her.

Dawn, a virgin, had been viciously raped and sodomized. The pathologist reported, 'When one considers the amount of bruising in relation to the larynx I have to suggest that the sexual attack occurred after strangulation and, therefore, at or after death.'

This was important, although I didn't want to say anything to Tony Painter until later. The timing of the penetration can often reveal clues about the murderer's motivation. There is a major difference between the psychological functioning of a rapist who panics and kills his victim to protect his identity and someone who takes perverse pleasure from abusing his victim at the moment of her death or after death.

Initially the murder squad focussed their attention on a young man who'd been seen fleeing from the area. A woman motorist had to brake sharply to avoid hitting the man as he ran across the Leicester–Coventry road under the M1 bridge on King Edward Avenue at about 5.30 p.m. on the Thursday. Thirty minutes earlier, a worker at Marston Radiators on the far side of the six-lane motorway heard two screams coming from the area where Dawn had been found. A courting couple who were seen cuddling in a nearby field at about 4.35 p.m. were sought and two independent witnesses, including a local farmer, reported seeing a man crouching in the grass and in the hedgerows on an embankment on King Edward Avenue at 5.30 p.m.

'And then there was the kitchen porter,' said Painter. 'Four different witnesses reported seeing his motorbike parked near the M1 bridge between 4.30 p.m. and 5.30 p.m., and a man was seen carrying a very distinctive red crash-helmet, like the porter's.'

'How did you pick him up?' I asked.

'On the Sunday evening, a lad pushing a motorbike approached one of our boys at the checkpoint on Mill Lane in Enderby and said he'd seen Dawn walking towards Ten Pound Lane on Thursday afternoon. The officer took a note of his name and we followed it up and spoke to him two days later. That was the kitchen porter.'

Painter drew my attention to several statements. Another employee at Carlton Hayes had returned from holiday on the day Dawn went missing. The next day, Friday, he was visited by the kitchen porter who told him that Dawn's body had been found 'in a hedge near a gate by the M1 bridge.'

'We didn't find her for another fourteen hours,' said Painter incredulously. 'How did he know about the gate leading from Ten Pound Lane and it was only ten minutes' walk from the footbridge over the M1?'

Similarly, at 1.45 p.m. on Saturday the kitchen porter had told a local man that Dawn's body had been found. Yes it had – less than two hours earlier – but the news hadn't been made public. How did he know?

'We pulled him in for questioning a week after the murder.'

'And?'

'He made certain admissions but was rather inconsistent. He'd say one thing, then deny it in the next breath; or talk in riddles and blame someone else. He admitted being on the path with Dawn, described how he attacked her and gave details of how the body was hidden. I don't care how fertile this kid's imagination is, there's no way he could have made it up and been so accurate.'

Painter produced several more statements which related to the sexual preferences of the seventeen-year-old, who apparently had come to the police's attention previously for having anal intercourse with a fourteen-year-old girlfriend on a local railway embankment. In another incident he admitted fondling a nine-year-old girl during a sexual assault that was verified by witnesses.

The police had obviously gone looking for corroboration and appeared to have established a circumstantial link between the kitchen porter and the anal assault on Dawn Ashworth.

Painter said, 'When you listen to the tapes you'll see what I mean. He admitted it, denied it, admitted it, denied it and then said, "I want a blood test. It's not me."'

I asked – 'Did the genetic fingerprinting link both murders?'

'That's the only good bit of news – we're looking for the same man.'

Silently, I considered the implications of this statement. If it was the same man, then he had already killed twice. What's to stop him striking again, I thought.

Painter drove me to the scene and we parked at the foot of Ten Pound Lane on King Edward Avenue. After checking in at the mobile incident room, a caravan, we walked up a concrete ramp leading to a gate that marked the entrance to Ten Pound Lane. Weak sunlight filtered through the hawthorn bushes on either side of the footpath. Autumn had arrived late and there was still a lot of greenery among the brambles and tangled bushes.

After a quarter of a mile the path started to narrow and the hedge closed around it creating a narrow green-sided gorge, broken occasionally by farm gates leading to adjacent fields.

'You can see where a lot of it was cleared during the search,' said Painter, breathing more heavily. 'In some sections the nettles and brambles were shoulder-high.'

'And she was here at what time?' I asked.

'A motorist saw her in King Edward Avenue walking towards the farm gate at 4.40 p.m. It would have taken her another ten minutes to reach here.'

So much undergrowth had been cleared, it was hard to picture the scene as it looked on the afternoon Dawn was attacked, yet I clearly recognized it as a pocket of isolation. First contact had to have been on the footpath and it began with an exchange – a conversation, or a threat, or simply a look. Depending on how Dawn reacted, she may have been able to influence what happened next but I didn't know enough about her to predict her behaviour.

She probably died on the path and then her body was taken through or lifted over a nearby gate into the corner of a field. The grass and nettles were quite high because the farmer's tractor would swing and miss the elbow formed by the hedges.

A withered bunch of flowers lay propped against the gatepost. Painter said that the Ashworth family had been devastated by the murder and continued to bring flowers back to mark the spot.

'Once you start, how do you stop?' he asked. 'Do you say, "Well today I won't do it any more." Then how do you get over the guilt of not doing it any more?'

Unlocking the padlock with a key, we pushed against the gate which groaned on rusty hinges. It would have taken two hands to open, I reasoned, which meant that Dawn had probably been lifted over. I felt the unevenness of the ground beneath my feet and noticed the clumps of stinging nettles and brambles. It all helped to recreate a picture of what had happened.

We walked further along Ten Pound Lane towards Enderby and I noticed where the footpath forked and one path led towards the footbridge that crossed the M1 and the other to the playing fields. How exposed is the crime scene? I asked myself. Is it possible to park a car on the M1, walk down the footpath, commit a murder and take off?

Five fields away, on the western edge of the hospital grounds, was the scene of Lynda Mann's death. We parked at the Woodlands Day Hospital and walked along Forest Road towards the entrance to the Black Pad.

A few yards along the black cinder pathway, I looked through the iron fence into the small woodland glade where Lynda's body had been found. The footpath was now flanked by street lights but in 1983, on a cold November evening, it was very dark and quiet.

Again we had a teenager who had been acquired on the footpath. She was then taken through a gateway and killed amid the silver birch and holly trees only yards away. Like Dawn, she was found lying with her legs slightly open and a branch underneath. I couldn't understand the significance of this, if any.

The post-mortem had revealed abrasions on Lynda's cheek and chin as well as heavy bruising around her collarbone and upper chest. Painter suggested that the killer had knelt on her as he tightened her scarf around her neck. There was no sign of entry into her vagina or anus but dried semen had been found matted in her pubic hair. 'Sexual intercourse was attempted and premature ejaculation occurred,' the Home Office pathologist had concluded.

At supper that night, I tried to push the memories of the day aside and talk about normal domestic things. After the dishes had been washed and cleared away, I helped Ian with his homework and then wandered into my study, locking the door. Tony Painter had given me copies of statements, pathology reports, maps and aerial photographs.

Now I had to properly reconstruct what happened – not just through the eyes of the victims but also the predator. The Osborne/Weedon case had given me confidence and allowed me to develop a framework. Four questions had to be answered – what happened, how, to whom and why.

These same questions apply to my clinical work, particularly when dealing with victims, but in a slightly different way. In my consulting room I see someone who is damaged or in pain and I have to find out who they are, psychologically, and how they got there. In this case, I didn't have a victim across the table from me and had to rely on others to tell me about Lynda and Dawn.

All the pain is focussed on that third question and the more I learned about them – about their strengths, weaknesses, loves, hates and fears – the greater the pain because they became closer to me. This must happen to the police, I thought, and the obvious tendency is to push it away and just focus on whoever committed the crime. I couldn't afford to do that. The rigour with which I answer each of the first three questions dramatically affects the answer to the fourth. In a sense I have to imagine that this man is in my consulting room chair and I'm conducting a one-sided interview. If I know exactly what motivated him to kill a woman, I can put a precise shape to his personality functioning. Then I can move back through his life from the offence and begin drawing up a picture of his family, friends, relationships and schooling.

As a child what relationship did he have with his mother and father? What would it be like now? How did he get on at primary school and secondary school? Is he likely to be of average intelligence or less so, or more? Given that he did this to a particular woman, what does it say about his feelings, perceptions and assumptions about women in general? Is he likely to have had many girlfriends? Would he have one now? What sort of work is he likely to be doing? Would it be skilled or unskilled? Does he have the social functioning to hold down a long-term job?

Sexual deviants like this man and Paul Bostock aren't unknown. They can be found in prisons, special hospitals, regional secure-units and sometimes in out-patient clinics up and down the country and throughout the world. Although I had only been a forensic clinician for barely three months, I had already taken the histories of half a dozen men who fantasized about raping and killing young women. My clinical exposure was increasing all the time and I had access to journals, case presentations, books and research papers from psychologists and specialists who had conducted similar interviews in Britain and overseas.

This is what I drew upon when I sat down and looked into the mind of the Narborough killer.

Two days later, I was back in Baker's office. I had several pages of handwritten foolscap notes in front of me.

'He's a local man or has good local knowledge,' I said. This was indicated by his ability to disappear quickly after the offences and not attract undue attention from possible witnesses. No-one had been able to provide a description that was accurate enough to identify the killer or prompt suggestions from the public.

'Everything indicates a single offender. Sexual psychopaths rarely hunt together and one person could have moved the bodies.' At the same time, I felt that he wasn't a classic loner or stand-out suspect. If he had been then someone in the local villages would have named him as being an odd sort who made women feel uncomfortable or acted strangely.

This strongly suggested someone older and more secure, who was less likely to attract attention; someone perhaps in a marriage or a relationship. This man was more controlled and had been able to keep his cool when confronted by door-to-door enquiries about the crimes.

Painter asked, 'So he could have a wife or girlfriend?'

'I'm saying that just because a man is in a relationship you shouldn't discount him. Each time he's been able to control himself long enough to maximize his chances of success of not being caught. He's careful and makes plans. People like this are more able to get into a relationship.

'You also have to ask yourself how he's managed to maintain his position and keep his secret without attracting suspicion even though he lives in a tight community. He knows his neighbours, they know him, but he doesn't stand out. You have to ask, "Why is that?" Again, it suggests that he's older and perhaps in a relationship.'

Baker asked, 'So his family might be shielding him?'

'No, I doubt it. Some aspects of his behaviour will possibly make those close to him feel uncomfortable, but I doubt if they know he's a sexual murderer.'

Baker said, 'How old?'

'At least his late twenties.'

'And clever?'

'I'd say average intelligence when you look at the degree of care and planning.' This was indicated by the ease with which he acquired the teenagers in locations that suited his purposes and then escaped afterwards.

'You're dealing with a sexual psychopath and the nature of his deviant sexuality is probably driven by fantasies, just as Paul Bostock was driven. He periodically experiences a growing urge for sexual control and domination. He needs to express this through aggression, to overpower, dominate, rape and kill a woman. If you look at your records, this man will have come to your attention, perhaps for only minor indecency offences.'

I could see David Baker previously struggling with this. The conceptual leap between a man flashing his erect penis at a woman and someone raping and killing was too great, yet I knew that the same irresistible urge could drive both and one could build towards the other.

I'd interviewed flashers in a clinical setting and while their reasons sounded rational, when you unpacked their pasts other elements tumbled out. For men visual stimulus is very important, which is why there are pornographic magazines full of pictures of naked women. Some flashers mistakenly assume that if a woman sees an erect naked penis it has a similar effect on her and she'll become so filled with lust, she'll have sex with them. Other offenders expose themselves because seeing a woman for real is far better than looking at one in a magazine – it has possibilities. There is also sometimes an aggressive or revenge element – something has happened in their own earlier life, they've been rejected or ridiculed by a woman and they want to shock and frighten and dominate.

All of these reasons can become mixed up and you can't take one strand and say, 'There's the explanation,' because it's misleading.

There are many levels of deviant behaviour and if one plotted them on the axis of a graph, invariably you see a steady rise. Someone begins with minor offences and progresses up the scale. The murders of Lynda and Dawn didn't come out of the blue. Their killer started with lesser offences and escalated through these stages.

Painter asked, 'So he might have raped before, but not necessarily killed?'

'Yes. But not all rapes are reported or detected,' I said.

'And he's likely to kill again.'

'Yes, when the urge becomes strong enough. He isn't celibate. He needs and wants sex. Yet there were three years between the killings and during this time he's likely to have found sex in some other relationship. He may have intercourse with his wife or girlfriend several times a week but this won't be enough. He has another aspect of his sexuality that has to be satisfied.'

Although the physical assaults were very similar, Painter picked up on the differences and asked why there had been no anal assault on Lynda or attempt to hide her body.

'A murderer isn't always uniform in his actions. Sometimes circumstances are different and don't allow replication, or a victim can alter events by something she says or does. At the same time, the killer will have become more confident in the time between the murders and this will affect his actions. I want to ponder that for a little longer. From a psychological point of view the vaginal and anal attacks have to be separated, because given there was no confusion over the genitalia in either case, they were intended as separate acts, and I'm not clear what sequence they happened in.'

Baker asked, 'Is there a chance that he knew the girls?'

'Yes – or knew of them,' I said.

'Is there any particular reason why he chose them?'

This is a question that I'd asked myself the previous evening, propping two snapshots of the girls on my bookshelf. Both were pretty in a young way, yet they were clearly capable of being viewed sexually by a person who was interested in women rather than children.

This predator had gone out looking for a victim who fitted certain criteria. She had to be old enough to be sexually stimulating for him but also non-threatening so that she wouldn't attack him or ridicule him in a way that spoiled it for him. Lynda and Dawn were perfect – old enough to be sexually attractive but young enough to be insecure and unworldly. That's why he'd chosen them.

When I finished, we sat and had another coffee while Painter told me about developments. Since the kitchen porter's release more than a thousand messages had been logged by the incident room at Wigston Police Station. Fifty officers were working on the double-murder hunt, concentrating on Dawn Ashworth because her death was still fresh in the public's mind.

Two Detective Inspectors, Derek Pearce and Mick Thomas, were in charge of the suspect and house-to-house teams. They were retracing their steps, interviewing suspects and asking every witness if they could remember just a little bit more. Meanwhile, the *Leicester Mercury* prepared a special four-page edition containing every known fact about the murders. Special constables delivered it by hand to every house in Narborough, Enderby and Littlethorpe.

On 18 December *Crimewatch UK* screened a reconstruction on BBC1 focussing on the youth seen running out of Ten Pound Lane at 5.30 p.m. Thirteen million people watched the programme and afterwards sixty viewers rang in from as far afield as London and Northern Ireland. The hunt went on.

In the meantime, I began listening to the police interviews with the kitchen porter. Slipping the first tape into the cassette player, I heard the seventeen-year-old begin answering questions confidently but in a quiet voice. He said that he'd known Dawn about three weeks and had seen her walking about the village. That Thursday, 31 July, had been his day off and he'd slept until ten or eleven. In the afternoon he rode his motorbike along King Edward Avenue towards Narborough. Near the motorway bridge he saw Dawn walking towards the gateway into Ten Pound Lane.

'How did you know it was Dawn?'

'By her hairstyle and the way she walked. So I knew it were Dawn.'

'Do you know her very well?'

'Just by looks. That's all.'

'What was she wearing?'

'A sort of white skirt and a yellow or white jacket. I thought I'd stop and talk to her and ask her where she was going, and that. Then I thought, I've got to get home and do this oil because it might be running out quick. It got to leaking drip, drip, drip fairly fast, so I just drove straight home.'

When told about the motorbike seen parked under the bridge and the youth seen carrying a motorcycle helmet, the porter denied it was him.

'If you stopped and had a chat with her, for goodness sake, tell us. Because if you tell lies, even though you may not have had anything to do with it, it makes you look worse. I think you stopped and parked under the bridge. You may well have spoken to her . . .'

'Yeah, I can remember now,' said the porter.

'You stopped under the bridge, didn't you?'

'Got under me bike and had a look to see if the oil were coming out.'

'And what did you say to her?'

'I just seen her approaching the gate.'

Questions went back and forth making little headway. At one stage the teenager said he went up Ten Pound Lane, then he claimed it was the day before.

Finally the police interviewer went straight to the point, 'The thing is, did you intend to kill her?'

'No.'

'So what happened?'

'Right, I seen her walked up the lane. Pulled down the side, got off me bike. Started talking to her. I asked her where Queenie was and Michael. She said, "I don't know." I said, "Where are you going?" She says, "I'm going home." I walked her halfway up the lane and I goes, "Will you be all right?" She says, "Yeah." So I turns around to come back. Got straight on me bike and goes straight home.'

Again the line of questioning petered out. Growing more upset, the suspect pleaded that he couldn't remember and said he'd be blamed.

In the next interview he was taken through his sexual history and admitted having regular sex with a fourteen-year-old girl on a local railway embankment. Once or twice 'I could have slipped and gone up her bum but I don't know,' he said. Then he recanted and denied having any prior sexual experience or even having masturbated.

As yet, he hadn't provided any detail that only the killer could have known, although his rambling answers and constant changes of direction suggested he was of below average intelligence.

When asked how he knew that the body had been found, he said Dawn's elder brother had told him. Dawn didn't have an older brother. He also denied ever having met the police constable on Sunday evening, claiming the policeman had made it up 'trying to get me in trouble'.

He sometimes seemed to be answering entirely different questions to those asked.

Changing the tape, I recognized Tony Painter's voice. He showed the teenager a photograph of Dawn Ashworth. 'I think you were responsible.'

Detective Sergeant Dawe said, 'I don't think you intended to kill her.'

'I can't remember. I probably really went mad, and I don't know it.'

Dawe asked, 'Did you fancy her?'

'Yeah, a little bit, but I can't remember any more.'

Painter said, 'Describe to me exactly what happened.'

'She'd gone down and I started putting me hands on her top. She weren't struggling at the time until I put me hands up her skirt. See, I walked her up lane and started to touch her bum. And she moved toward me and tripped over a bit. I continued to feel her and she struggled but I held her down. Then me head started spinning as if I was drunk. I couldn't remember no more until I were running away . . . I just went mad. I couldn't help it. Dawn said she wouldn't tell nobody about it. It was like someone else took over. I just went mad. Like it was someone else in me that told me to do it. I didn't want to do it. Someone were forcing me to do it. Making me arms and legs go all over. At first she let me but then she went down. She struggled and me mind went blank. I don't think it were me that did it. But when I finished and were getting up I ran off.'

Almost immediately, he denied everything and became upset. 'I never touched her. Why should I get the blame? I never even talked to Dawn . . .'

On Friday morning the interviews began again. Dawn was alive when he left her, he said. He panicked.

Painter asked, 'What did you do to make her not move?'

'I think it was when I laid down on top of her.'

'Where were your hands?'

'On her arms.'

'And what were you doing to her when you were laying on top of her?'

'Just had a laugh and a joke with her. I said to her, "I ain't going to let you go." She just started laughing. She was crawling all over me.'

'So what did you do?'

'Moved up toward her face and sat on her chest and that's what done it. Sat on her chest.'

'Was that before you hurt her or afterwards?'

'That were before.'

'How did you feel when she stopped moving?'

'Dunno.'

'Come on, tell us more.'

'When I realized she weren't, I thought, Oh shit, oh Christ! I just got up and went back down the lane. I thought she'd had a heart attack or something like that.'

'Where did all this take place?'

'Near the hedge by the ditch. I can't remember because I know I didn't do it. That's why I can't remember for certain.'

In a later interview he tried to remember more.

'Well, I got as far as putting me hands up her top. Then I put me hand up her skirt. She said, "No". I forced. She started shouting. I put me hand over her mouth to shut her up . . . Then she were lying there still. I just pressed really hard on her mouth with me hand over her nose and her mouth. She suffocated. That's all in my memory. I couldn't leave her where she was so I hid her.'

'How did you hide her?'

'With a load of brambles underneath a hedge.'

'How did you leave her? In what sort of position?'

'On her front.'

'What? Lying on her stomach, on her side, on her back?'

'Side.'

When questioned further, he explained how he pressed his fingers around Dawn's throat to make it appear as though she had been strangled. Then he took her drawers off and had sex with her. Afterwards, he lifted her over the fence and hid her body.

During the following interview sessions, the porter was quizzed repeatedly about the details of how Dawn had been acquired and attacked.

'How did you knock her down?'

'I put me feet behind her and pushed her.'

'A few minutes ago you said that you'd already gone through the gate into the field.'

'It was a mistake, that was.'

'Where did you do all this? In the lane or in the field?'

'In the gateway.'

'When you say you took her pants off, did you take them right off?'

'Yeah.'

'What did you do with them?'

'I don't know. Just chucked them away.'

'But you've just described how you put them back.'

'I put everything else back. I put her skirt back on. Bra back on. Shirt. Tucked that in and that's it . . .'

'How were you rough with her?'

'I don't know.'

'Just tell me.'

'I hit her.'

'What did you hit her with?'

'That.' He raised his fist.

'Where?'

'In the face. It was here, round the chin.'

'Around the chin?'

'I think so, yeah. I hit her in the mouth.'

'Did you do anything else?'

'I just hit her three times.'

'Was that before you indecently assaulted her?'

'Yeah.'

'Was that because she didn't want to do it?'

'Yeah.'

Near the end of the interviews, the kitchen porter was asked to explain again why he had killed Dawn.

'. . . she started panicking so I thought, If I leave her she'll tell her mum and dad and I'll be in trouble. So I did something about it. She started screaming so I put me hand over her mouth and with me other hand I fingered her. I took her pants off and had sex with her and buried her and that's all I remember doing. I walked straight back down the lane.'

On the face of it, the teenager's admissions sounded conclusive, yet punctuating his answers were constant denials and U-turns. At the same time, I could get no sense of calculated deception or someone constructing a defence; the kitchen porter simply rambled, often aimlessly.

I could see why David Baker was troubled. Whatever the reason, the teenager had a remarkable knowledge of the location, injuries and the attempt to conceal Dawn's body – most of which had never been made public.

There were four possibilities. One that he simply made it up and by some amazing coincidence his fantasies or his lies were so correct that it led him to be charged; the second that the police had unwittingly conveyed the details to him; the third that he was a participant in a two-handed murder but didn't leave any semen or forensic evidence at the scene; and the fourth that he witnessed what had happened.

The first option was too far-fetched. If he'd given vast amounts of incorrect detail and amongst it provided a few pieces that were correct, I'd have been more likely to entertain the possibility.

It was also clear from listening to the tapes that the police hadn't fed him information and, despite their obvious frustration at his erratic answers, there was no indication that he'd been pressurized or browbeaten.

My psychological analysis of the crimes had indicated a lone killer, which ruled out the possibility of the kitchen porter being a participant. That left only the fourth option – did he witness the murder, or stumble upon the body afterwards? It was time to revisit Ten Pound Lane.

I pulled off King Edward Avenue and retraced Dawn's last walk along the rutted farm track. This time I'd remembered my wellingtons although the extra weight made the incline seem steeper. I walked all the way along the path and turned right towards the M1 footbridge. Occasionally, I stopped and turned, checking the line of sight and seeing where the farm gate and a particular section of footpath disappeared from view. You could have been on the path and seen what happened that afternoon.

Closer to the footbridge, I stepped into the corner of a field and looked across at Ten Pound Lane. Because of the elevation, I could see clearly where Dawn had been found as well as the spot where she was most likely acquired. Someone crouching or sitting near the hedge could easily have watched what happened virtually in secret.

But why would he say that he touched her? And was the vantage point close enough for him to know that Dawn's underpants had been pulled down and that she'd been left lying on her side?

These were questions that the tapes couldn't answer.

A few days before Christmas, I reported back to David Baker and Tony Painter. From their point of view I couldn't tell if I was delivering good news or bad news. Both were fairly confident before I started that the police interviewers hadn't contaminated the kitchen porter's recollections or applied undue pressure.

'Is this kid innocent or is he a co-conspirator?' asked Baker.

'It's not that cut and dried,' I said. 'He wasn't fed information during the interviews or pressured into making a false confession if that's what you mean.'

'Then he had to have been there?'

'Quite possibly. I think he might have seen what was going on.'

'Jesus!' Painter shook his head.

'It also explains the differences in his accounts about Dawn Ashworth and Lynda Mann. In one he was remarkably accurate and in the other seemed to have no idea. It suggests he wasn't involved in the first murder.'

Baker nodded and pushed back his chair. 'So we carry on looking for the killer.'

'I'm afraid so.'

He rose to his feet. 'Well, we're going to end this once and for all. If technology can find this kid innocent then technology can show us who the real killer is.'

'What do you mean?'

'We're going to find the man who shed the semen.'

Baker explained that he'd been granted permission to carry out voluntary blood tests on every male resident of Narborough, Enderby and Littlethorpe. The age span would take in anyone aged between fourteen and thirty-four at the time of Lynda's murder and also every non-alibied male who'd lived, worked or had some connection with the three villages in the previous five years, including patients of Carlton Hayes hospital.

The boldness of the plan took me by surprise. Before the Bostock case, no-one had used a psychologist to profile a murderer, yet Baker had been open to the possibility and broken new ground. Now he was launching a unique operation to DNA test thousands of people.

'Of course, it has to be voluntary,' said Baker. 'We're sending letters to each of the men, asking them to submit blood and saliva samples so we can eliminate them from the inquiry.'

It can work, I thought, considering the possibilities. The thinking was brilliant. We all agreed that a local man or someone who had lived locally in the recent past was the killer. Most of the men would willingly submit, ruling themselves out of the investigation. Those who didn't would come under closer scrutiny, drastically shrinking the pool of possible suspects.

What are the killer's options, I thought. If he gives the samples, the laboratory technicians will link him to the murders. If he doesn't take the test, the police will come calling and this time turn over every stone.

'What if someone takes the test for him?' I said, thinking out loud.

Baker replied, 'We're going to want proof of identity. It won't be fail-safe but hopefully good enough.'

'If someone took the test for him, it would have to leak out,' I said. 'They won't be able to maintain the silence, especially if the testing stays in the news.'

On 2 January, 1987, the story broke and the *Leicester Mercury* announced: BLOOD TESTS FOR 2,000 IN KILLER HUNT. The national press quickly picked it up and journalists arrived from London to report on the operation. Soon they were joined by counterparts from around the world.

Two testing sites were set up at the Danemill School at Enderby and Blaby District Council in Narborough. Letters were then posted to men born between 1 January 1953 and 1 January 1970 who lived in the three villages. There were two testing sessions, morning and evening, three days a week.

Blood and saliva samples were taken by police surgeons and then sent to the East Midlands Forensic Centre's laboratory in Huntingdon and the Home Office's central research establishment at Aldermaston.

The first sample was taken on 5 January and by the end of January 1,000 men had taken the tests. The laboratories struggled to keep up but fell well behind. Suddenly the 'two month operation' was beginning to look like a serious miscalculation. At enormous cost, it would run months longer.

On a positive note, there was a 90 per cent response to the letters. Men were genuinely volunteering when they had no legal requirement

– a sign of how strongly the communities wanted to catch the killer. All those who didn't respond to the letters earned closer scrutiny, although initially many of the murder squad spent their time criss-crossing the country, chasing men who had moved out of the area.

The media had labelled the tests as 'The Bloodings' – a term meaning to give the first taste of blood to the hounds before the hunt. My own involvement in the case had ended, but periodically I read stories or heard it mentioned on television. I knew that Baker and his team were under pressure as the cost of the operation mounted.

Among the thousands of men who'd been interviewed and logged during the inquiry was Colin Pitchfork, a twenty-five-year-old baker who had moved from Leicester to a new housing estate in Littlethorpe several weeks after Lynda Mann's body was found.

When asked about the evening she disappeared, Pitchfork said he dropped his wife Carole at an evening class in Leicester at 6.00 p.m. and then returned home to babysit their three-month-old son until he picked her up again at 9.00 p.m. when the class finished. It meant that he wasn't alibied at the crucial time, but because he hadn't lived locally at the time of the murder and the killer wasn't thought likely to have taken a baby along with him, he was given a low priority classification.

There were thousands of names on the computer, each of them given a classification and listed under various categories depending on their age, address, criminal background, alibi and association with the area, for example visiting a relative or attending the hospital.

Computers were still relatively new in criminal investigations in Britain so it was very difficult to cross-reference names and salient facts to see if they turned up more than once in the inquiry. For this reason Pitchfork didn't attract attention, even though he eventually appeared on three different indexes: the resident list, the prior sexual offences list and the out-patient list at Carlton Hayes where he'd been referred by magistrates after an indecent exposure conviction in 1980.

He'd worked at Hampshires Bakery in Leicester since he was sixteen years old and at the age of nineteen had met his future wife Carole while both were volunteers at the Dr Barnados Children's Home in Leicester. When their son was born in August 1983, Carole was keen to move out of the city and chose Littlethorpe because her father lived in Narborough.

A blooding request was sent to Pitchfork in January 1987 and a reminder two weeks later when he failed to report. Before this aroused any close scrutiny, a blood and saliva test was given on Tuesday evening, 27 January, at Danemill School. A passport was given as proof of identity along with a driving licence.

In due course, a letter arrived at the house in Haybarn Close saying that Colin Pitchfork's test was negative, eliminating him from the murder inquiry.

By April, the murder squad had blooded nearly 4,000 men and teenagers, although the results were still running way behind. The response rate was 98 per cent, well above expectations, but the list of possible donors kept growing and the costs escalating.

Throughout the summer the operation continued, with mobile blood vans visiting housing estates and factories, but by then the murder squad was cut back and the media began asking questions about whether it had been an expensive waste of police resources and taxpayers' money.

David Baker deserved a break and it came on 1 August when an 'oven hand' at Hampshires Bakery, Ian Kelly, aged twenty-four, was drinking at a Leicester pub with workmates and the conversation turned to Colin Pitchfork.

'Colin had me do that blood test for him,' said Kelly.

'What test?'

'The one for that murder inquiry.'

Kelly explained that Pitchfork had buttonholed him and spun a yarn about having already taken the test for someone else – a friend who'd been in trouble for flashing when he was younger. He explained that he hadn't lived in the village when the first girl was murdered, so he thought the police wouldn't bother testing him.

Six weeks later, a bakery manager who had listened to the conversation mentioned it to a local policeman. The information was relayed to the murder squad and a comparison was made between the signatures on the house-to-house file and the blood testing form – they didn't match.

On Saturday 19 September, Kelly was arrested at his home and immediately broke down and admitted giving a blood sample for Pitchfork. He explained how Colin had cut and replaced his passport photograph with one taken of Kelly and then driven him to the school, waiting outside while the samples were taken.

As Kelly was charged for conspiracy to pervert the course of justice, detectives arrived at the house in Haybarn Close, Littlethorpe, taking Colin Pitchfork into custody at 5.45 p.m. After reading him his rights, a detective asked, 'Why Dawn Ashworth?'

The baker shrugged. 'Opportunity. She was there and I was there.'

Because I have no official link to the investigations that I assist in, it's not uncommon for me to hear nothing about the outcome. In this case it wasn't until months later that I discovered the details of Colin Pitchfork's arrest and interviews. David Baker invited me to a Mess Dinner for the Leicestershire Constabulary, a sort of night out with the top brass that is held several times a year.

Pitchfork's confession was described as 'cold' with no sign of remorse. On 21 November, 1983, he'd dropped his wife at college and gone cruising, looking for girls to flash. His baby son was in a carrycot on the back seat as he drove from Leicester to Narborough and turned up Forest Road beside Carlton Hayes.

He passed Lynda walking towards Enderby and then parked his car in the driveway leading to the Woodlands Day Hospital. Then he waited beneath a street lamp as Lynda approached. When he exposed himself, he expected her to run towards Enderby but instead Lynda ran back towards the Black Pad and into the darkness.

Pitchfork confessed, 'This is the thing I don't understand about flashing. One per cent of the time you get someone who goes mad and screams and you have to disappear quick. But all the others walk by you. Just walk by you and ignore you. But she turned and ran into a dark footpath. She backed herself into a corner . . . her two big mistakes were running into the footpath and saying, "What about your wife?" She'd seen my wedding ring.'

Lynda, he said, had tried to talk him out of raping her. She partly undressed herself, too terrified to scream or fight. Pitchfork claimed to have fully penetrated her and became angry at suggestions that he'd ejaculated prematurely. He also said that he began strangling her while still inside – something not supported by the facts but probably a crucial part of his fantasy.

Pitchfork had seen Dawn Ashworth while out riding his motorcycle on an errand to pick up ingredients for a cake. She had just walked across King Edward Avenue and entered Ten Pound Lane. He parked his bike and followed.

'Nobody ever saw me. They saw lots of other people, I guess, but not me. There I was in broad daylight, wearing jeans and a jumper and a bottle-green nylon parka jacket.'

He followed her along the path, jogging to catch up. Turning, he forced Dawn towards the farm gate, putting his hand over her mouth and pushing her into the field. The gate was off its catch.

Pitchfork ignored her pleas not to rape her. Afterwards she had sat up and said, 'Have you finished? Can I go now? I won't tell anybody. Please. Honest. Just go and leave me alone. Please.'

Then he strangled her from behind with his forearm across her throat.

Throughout the interviews, no matter how the questions were framed, Pitchfork denied having sodomized Dawn. He explained the attacks in vivid detail but insisted that he didn't touch her after death and had made little effort to conceal her body. Both of these answers didn't tally with how Dawn had been found and the injuries she sustained. Baker remained puzzled by the inconsistencies and question marks still remain, but he happily raised a glass to celebrate having caught the man he'd referred to as 'Chummy' throughout the investigation.

If I had wanted an apprenticeship or an overview into how police investigations were carried out, Baker had given me one and done it brilliantly. I don't think anyone could have made it more transparent and explained it so lucidly. He did, however, have an apology to make.

'It was some advice you gave us that I didn't appreciate enough,' he said. 'You told me that the killer would have minor sexual offences in his past. I didn't listen to that. You were right.'

5

IN AUGUST 1988 A TYPEWRITTEN LETTER ARRIVED AT THE HEAD office of Pedigree Pet Foods Ltd in Melton Mowbray, Leicestershire, addressed to Mr John Simmens, the managing director. It was attached to a tin of dog food which outwardly looked no different to the millions of others sold every year or, indeed, to those stacked in my own pantry.

> *This is a demand to Pedigree Pet Foods to pay £100,000 per year in order to prevent their products being contaminated with toxic substances.*
>
> *The accompanying tin of Pedigree Chum has had its contents mixed with toxic chemicals. These chemicals were selected because they are colourless, odourless and highly toxic. They are virtually undetectable to a pet owner before feeding.*
>
> *If payment is not forthcoming from Pedigree Pet Foods of Mars Limited, a large number of similarly contaminated tins will appear on retailers shelves throughout Great Britain.*
>
> *Initially, only Pedigree Chum dog food will be poisoned. When sales of that product have slumped another will be sabotaged if payment has not been received. The process will be repeated until payment is finally made or your company dissolves. Its fate will then be an example to other pet food manufacturers . . .*

Although I didn't know it then, almost every major manufacturer and retailer is subject to occasional angry letters or crude attempts to extort money. Sacked employees, irate customers, vanquished suppliers, jealous rivals – the motives are numerous but rarely are the threats serious.

This time, however, the accompanying product had been cut open, spiked with poison and resealed with the label concealing the incision. It was so skilfully done and well camouflaged that no-one could have suspected.

The blackmail letter warned that five contaminations would be made daily at supermarkets throughout the country, with the media informed by coded telephone calls. In total £500,000 was to be paid in instalments of £100,000 into various building society accounts to be nominated.

'When your company agrees to pay, it will place an announcement in the personal columns of the *Daily Telegraph* which will read: "Sandra, happy birthday darling. Love John,"' the letter said.

'Sandra and John' were to be codenames for Pedigree while the blackmailer used 'Romeo and Juliet' in all letters and telephone calls. He gave a deadline of 1 December, 1988.

David Baker phoned while I was mowing the lawn. My heart sank. I liked Baker a great deal but the very mention of his name immediately conjured up images of some brutal crime. As much as I wanted to help, I couldn't claim to enjoy even the smallest part of it except the ending when I could then try to forget.

Perhaps Baker sensed my disquiet for he quickly mentioned that no-one had died or been raped. Even so, the urgency in his voice was obvious and I met him the next morning in his office.

'Three questions, Paul,' he said, shuffling paper in front of him until he found a copy of the blackmail letter. 'Firstly, is it serious? Secondly, what can you tell us about the person who did this? And thirdly, what options have we got?'

Malcolm Cairns, the Assistant Chief Constable (Crime), sat across the table alongside Baker, Ian Leacy and Detective Inspector Tim Garner. It fascinated me to watch the interaction between the officers. The police hierarchy is very authoritarian, although flexible, and you can immediately recognize the most senior officer in a room because everyone else defers to him as 'Sir', 'Boss' or 'Guv'.

In this case, Malcolm Cairns as an ACC (Assistant Chief Constable) was Baker's superior yet he was a policy-maker and administrator rather than a greatly experienced criminal investigator.

He didn't have Baker's insight or know-how but still had to be given the appearance of running the meeting. It was a delicate interaction.

Having Cairns present automatically flagged the case as being different. It struck me as odd because no-one was dead and there wasn't a killer running loose. Then I realized that with a murder there is a perception that the worst has already happened – the crime has been committed and now must be solved – whereas an extortion attempt has an immediacy because it is still being committed.

Baker slid the blackmail letter across the table. I studied the language and construction of the sentences. There are formulae with which you can estimate the reading and writing ability of a writer; and by looking at the layout and structure it's possible to see if someone comes from a particular background because they replicate a certain style. It's similar to when I write a string of psychological reports for the courts and then find my private letters begin to read like legal documents.

'Is it a crank or a nutter?' asked Cairns. 'Should we take it seriously?'

Looking at the intellectual integrity of the letter, I couldn't see anything 'mad' about the author. There was no indication of psychological looseness; no obsessional political or corporate punishment themes, no *clang* associations – where the previous word is the stimulus for the next word rather than the meaning of the sentence as a whole. When people with psychotic illnesses write things, depending upon the illness, and its severity, they often start off making a particular point and as the sentence proceeds it becomes lost and the next word or clause is determined by the clause before.

'It's a feasible amount of money given the size of the company,' I said, looking at the £500,000 demand. 'Neither ridiculously high nor so small that the investment in planning and the risk involved doesn't make sense. What can you tell me about the paper?'

Baker said, 'It's widely available. The letter was photocopied so I don't think we're going to find prints. We'll have a make on the typewriter in a few days.'

All of this suggested that the blackmailer had an awareness of the investigative process. He'd also done his research, addressing the letter directly to John Simmens rather than simply writing, 'a senior executive' or 'the managing director'.

The contaminated tin was still at the police laboratory but it seemed unlikely that the poison had been introduced during the manufacturing process. The product had been purchased and then adulterated by someone who knew how to use a soldering iron and to soak or steam off a label. It said loudly and clearly, 'This isn't a game, I'm serious, you've been warned.'

I took away a copy of the letter along with my notes and promised to come back with my thoughts. There wasn't much to go on but every chance that I'd learn more if the blackmailer kept his promises.

Secrecy, of course, was vital and I didn't mention the threat to anyone, not even Marilyn, although it became awkward when she caught me removing cans of Pedigree Chum from the shelves in the cupboard.

'What are you doing?'

'Nothing really.'

'Well what's happening?'

'We're just having a change of brands for a while, OK? There's no problem.'

Two days later, back at Leicestershire Police Headquarters, I listed the psychological characteristics of the blackmailer. Intellectually he was average or above average, educated at ordinary secondary level but probably not university level. This was clear from the structure and language used in the letter.

There was carefulness and preplanning, along with tenacity and persistence. Someone had spent time experimenting on cutting and resealing the tin until they got it right. This suggested a more mature man – someone who had the patience to plan and explore; someone who had an awareness of forensic clues.

Everything about the letter's author indicated a non-committee; the words and structure had a singularity about them, as if written by one person rather than several making suggestions. Also, the more people involved in such an operation, the greater the risk.

'The primary motivation is greed, that was clear. He may enjoy the game, but doesn't embellish or over-complicate things.'

When I finished, Baker asked me if I'd join the management team of the inquiry to advise on strategy. This was a major new step. Five years earlier, when I first gave Baker a psychological analysis of Caroline Osborne's killer, he was simply trying to understand what he was dealing with. Now there was an appreciation that a psychological analysis could do more than reveal who someone was – it could help predict what that person would do next.

Pedigree's crisis management team was ushered into the room. The very urbane John Simmens sat in the centre, flanked by a public relations director who shook everyone's hand, carefully working the room; and a corporate lawyer who potentially had more influence than all of them.

Right from the beginning I became aware that Pedigree had a different agenda to the police. For Baker and his team the first priority was to protect the public and catch the extortionist. The company also wanted to protect the public but had an additional responsibility to the board and its shareholders. The commercial implications were never far from the surface.

Pedigree was a subsidiary of the Mars Group, a major international corporation with its corporate headquarters in America. Even so, Pedigree had enough freedom of movement to make decisions and act quickly rather than getting bogged down in protracted discussions overseas. This made it easier to implement strategy and change course when necessary.

'Is the threat serious?' asked Simmens, going straight to the most important question.

'Yes, it is serious.'

'OK, what do we do now?'

'Well, we can do a number of things. The first priority is to make sure no-one gets hurt.'

'I agree,' said Simmens, 'and we also don't want to panic our customers.'

Baker concluded, 'Which is why we need a strategy.'

Simmens asked about the likelihood that the blackmailer would simply go away if his demands were ignored.

'I don't think so,' I told him.

'And from our point of view that isn't good enough,' said Baker. 'We have someone out there who has committed a serious offence. If he goes away, where is he going to come back?'

The conversation turned to security and possible means of preventing a contaminated tin being put on a shelf. Pedigree and the police had already been in touch with the major food retailing associations to discuss security measures at major supermarkets. Unfortunately, there is a conflict between security and making stores attractive places to shop. You can't put a brand below the counter and have people ask for it – they're going to wonder why.

Simmens said, 'Let's say we pull every can of Pedigree Chum off the shelves. Maybe there's nothing in them. What do we do then?'

The PR man shook his head. 'We spend millions of pounds a year establishing our brand images. We're in a highly competitive sector of the market where consumer confidence and loyalty is vital. At a stroke, something like this can set it back for years. The shelves are cleared, customers move on to another brand, they don't forget.'

'There's no point in clearing the shelves,' I said, 'because if you do, he'll just go on to the next product. You can't win that way. All you do is complete his threat.'

They looked relieved.

Pedigree's counsel mentioned the possible repercussions. 'If he carries out his threats and one of our customers loses a pet, we'll face a backlash for having maintained a silence.'

'That's why you have to weigh up the commercial risk against the actual risk of contamination and then devise a strategy that balances all of those things,' I said. 'We have to somehow stop this man from carrying out his threat and, at the same time, draw him into the open where the police can catch him. To do that, we have to make contact with him and negotiate.'

I could see they were uncomfortable with the idea.

'Right now he's calling the shots. You have to keep him in the field and very gradually turn him round. Make him believe that you're co-operating but there are limitations – not restrictions that you choose, but things you have no control over. By only meeting his demands in a particular way at a particular level, you can reduce his expectations.'

Simmens asked, 'So the police make contact?'

'No. Pedigree makes contact. The blackmailer doesn't know the police are involved.'

The lawyer expressed concern about paying money and setting a dangerous precedent for the future.

'It's a matter for you and the police whether or not you choose to pay something. If you say no, absolutely, then you have to reckon with this man carrying out his threat in some way. It's your decision.

'I suggest you pay a limited amount, just enough to keep him playing the game and stop him carrying out his threats. But you can't do things entirely his way; you're playing but not doing exactly what he wants; there are problems, you're sorry, you're trying to help . . . that sort of thing.

'Right now he has most of the control but gradually we can wrest that away from him as long as we keep him in play.'

Simmens asked, 'How do we do that?'

'You don't,' said Baker. 'We do it for you. We place the advertisement in the newspaper and see what happens. I want to put some of my men into Pedigree on a dedicated telephone line. We want our man to call.'

On 31 August, the following message appeared in the *Daily Telegraph* personal columns: 'Sandra, happy birthday darling. Want to help, must talk, phone 0674 ******. Love John.'

A second letter arrived, this time providing a list of accounts at the Halifax, Abbey National and Nationwide building societies. Each had been opened in the joint names of John and Sandra Norman over a two-month period beginning in September 1986. The savings books, cash withdrawal cards and Personal Identification Numbers (PIN) were sent to an accommodation address in Hammersmith, West London.

This put a whole new number into the calculation. There were literally thousands of automatic teller machines throughout the country with customers allowed to draw up to £300 a day from each of their accounts.

The blackmailer could withdraw the money from anywhere, removing it bit by bit from thousands of different locations. He could get someone else to collect it for him – possibly a team of people. The ramifications were enormous. Normally, the most dangerous moment for any blackmailer is at the pick-up point – the specific place and time when he breaks cover to collect the money. This time there were thousands of pick-up points – how could the police guard them all? The concept was brilliant.

When David Baker told me the details, I sensed his disquiet. Much of his prior thinking had been based on the belief that they'd catch this man when he tried to pick up the payment.

There was an up-side, however. You can't pass enormous amounts of money through automatic tellers. For someone to get £500,000 it would mean making tens of thousands of withdrawals. Each time he punched in the PIN, the computer would show us exactly where and when. We could track him, in a fashion, and look for patterns to his movements.

This man had shown an awareness of how police gather information. He knew that accounts could be traced and descriptions sought about who opened them. So he did it all by mail, never having to set foot into a branch office and risk being filmed by security cameras. He also knew about accommodation addresses and that no-one ever notices who comes and goes; or you can have someone pick things up for you. In two years of planning, he'd created a complete ring of dead ends. It was fascinating but immensely frustrating.

'We've found something like this before,' said Baker.

'Where?'

'In Norfolk. Someone took a shot at Bernard Matthews, the turkey farmer. The blackmailer wanted £50,000 and used almost the same MO – building society accounts using false names and accommodation addresses, cash-point cards, the full bit. Surveillance was a bloody nightmare.'

'What happened?'

'He didn't take enough precautions and kept going back to the same cash-point machines. That's how we got him.'

'And where is he now?'

'Banged up. He got six years.'

Baker second-guessed my next question. 'As far as we know he worked alone,' he said. He added, 'The trial judge refused to allow details of the plan to be published because he said it was so clever . . .'

'Which means that someone independently came up with the same idea or someone found out.'

'Exactly.'

The police negotiators stationed at Pedigree stalled for time, slowing things down and apologizing for the delays. They didn't make concessions but neither did they challenge the blackmailer. They used language such as, 'Yes, we understand your situation but you must understand ours. We're taking you seriously, I guarantee it, but we can't just put £100,000 in these accounts, people ask questions – the tax office, our accountants, the main board. We have to keep this quiet, you understand. We have to be careful.'

Further messages were exchanged and on 28 October the first of five controlled payments was made into the Norman accounts. During the next seven weeks £56,000 was lodged but the police had arranged to block most of the accounts so that money could only be withdrawn from two investment accounts at the Halifax Building Society. Already the balance of control was subtly shifting.

Pedigree, of course, denied any knowledge of the account difficulties, telling the blackmailer it was obviously a building society mistake. They couldn't be expected to ring up and ask why – the extortion attempt was secret.

Meanwhile, the Leicestershire CID was organizing one of the biggest undercover surveillance operations ever seen in Britain. Codenamed Roach, it involved hundreds of detectives from various regional crime squads who were staking out automatic teller machines at Halifax branches. Even with such a huge task force, it still wasn't possible to cover them all.

At the same time, the building society's main computer was programmed to slow down its response to requests for cash and to alert the police as soon as the relevant PIN codes were punched in.

A week after the first payment was lodged, a cash withdrawal of £300 was made at Reading, south of London. Afterwards, they were made almost daily from machines as far north as Glasgow, as far south as Exeter and as far west as Aberystwyth in Wales. Most were made after 11.00 o'clock each evening.

'He's not going to use the same machine twice,' said Baker, disappointed but not surprised. The chances of a quick arrest were diminishing but there were still some positive signs. No contaminations had been discovered and with each new withdrawal the blackmailer risked being picked up by one of the surveillance teams.

The geographical spread of the withdrawals prompted questions about whether it might be the work of a gang rather than an individual. Could one person be covering so much territory?

At home in my office I'd set up a map of Britain and was marking off the locations of each new collection. An interesting pattern began to emerge. The blackmailer would withdraw money on consecutive days in locations such as Dalston, Aberystwyth and Bristol. It was almost like a circuit which could bring him back to London where a significant number of the withdrawals were being made. Studying the motorway system, I reasoned that a single person could be making the collections and, if so, he was probably living near London, although there weren't enough details to make it immediately obvious exactly where.

What else did I know about him? It wasn't a young man's offence, not a twenty-three-year-old. No, he's fully mature and able to reflect and be patient; he spent two years waiting to launch his plan and for a twenty-three-year-old two years can seem like for ever.

He has the freedom to travel overnight so he won't work nine to five in an office, otherwise he'd have to take sick leave or holidays and that attracts attention. More likely, he's unemployed, retired or doing shift work. He's probably not married or living with someone; he'd have to answer too many questions about where he goes at night and how he gets his money.

Looking for the signs he left behind was different from my previous police cases. There was no crime scene to analyse and the events weren't the grisly product of a perverted mind or sexual deviant. Instead of seeking emotional or sexual gratification, this offender was motivated by greed.

Every burglar, bank robber, kidnapper, embezzler, rapist, terrorist or vandal is a unique person. Good or bad, no two people are the same and each time I interview someone, or get called in by the police, there's a different person that I have to try to meet in my consulting room or find within a crime.

In some ways it's easier to deal with people who are motivated by greed or revenge because they're more easily understood; they're closer to the rest of us. We can understand the motivation, whereas we struggle to comprehend how some sadomasochistic psychopath could rape and mutilate another human being.

We all know about people fiddling their tax returns and overstating their lost luggage claim, but we don't use nasty words like fraud or extortion. Instead, it's considered almost fair game to put something over on the government or an insurance company. Consider this, if someone found a foolproof way to rig the National Lottery so that no-one suspected and a particular set of numbers came up, how many of us would be tempted? Greed we understand.

Each time the money ran down in the Halifax accounts, the threats became more aggressive and strident. Growing frustrated and tired of the excuses, the blackmailer made a telephone call to a supermarket in Basildon, Essex, on 6 December. A male voice instructed office staff that a tin of Pedigree Chum had been contaminated.

The tin had been cut open, spiked with broken razor blades and resealed before being placed on the shelf. Mercifully, it was clearly marked 'contaminated'.

There were two more contaminations before Christmas at supermarkets in Royston, Hertfordshire and Heyford Hill near Oxford. Again there were warning calls to the store and the police.

I found this interesting. Often in a protracted campaign the blackmailer gets tired of waiting and negotiating and simply goes away; or he gets sloppy and makes a mistake. When control is slowly wrested away from him, he can feel less powerful than he first imagined and decide to pull out. There was no sign of any of this in our man. Almost as if challenging the various scenarios, the blackmailer turned up the heat just when the police thought they had his measure.

'It's part of his battle for control,' I told a difficult management committee meeting.

'But you said we'd stop him contaminating,' said Pedigree's PR man.

'And we have, until now. Right from the very beginning this man has had each step of the escalation prepared. He knows that Pedigree respond to the commercial threat. He thinks that he can wear you down and you'll give him everything he wants.'

John Simmens looked disconsolate and I knew they were tired.

'Eventually, he will move on,' I said. 'When he gets frustrated with not being able to get large amounts of money and bored with travelling all over the country, he'll find a new target. Right now he's thinking, "The plan works and I can do it to anyone."'

Shortly before Christmas the stakes rose further when the blackmailer demanded that unless the full £500,000 was paid immediately, he would disclose to the media the incidents of contaminated food on British supermarket shelves. For the first time Pedigree realized it was in the centre of a storm. Do they go public or maintain the secrecy? Do they pay the money or continue to drip-feed the accounts?

I tried to be reassuring. 'He's always had the power to do this; it's a prepared demonstration. I think you should stay with him. He's not going to carry out his threat unless you say, "Get lost, you're getting nothing." The moment you do that, he may do it for real with no warning calls.

'If you don't withdraw the product and you don't go public, he'll think he still has the control and will push for the money.'

Pedigree held its nerve.

Meanwhile, the daily withdrawals continued, each of them picked up by the building society's central computer. In London the spread of withdrawals were mostly north of the Thames and stretched from the West End to commuter-belt towns in Essex such as Gillingham and Southend. Studying it closely, I reasoned that the blackmailer probably lived in the centre, so I ran a basic mathematical analysis of the withdrawal points. The results put him near

Hornchurch, an area slightly to the east of London.

Operation Roach was proving expensive. Even with a massive team of detectives, working in pairs, less than half of the cash-point machines could be covered at any one time. Given the pattern of withdrawals, only the Halifax outlets in the south of England were targeted on two days a week, Monday and Thursday, from closing time until 1.00 a.m.

This carried on through January and February, costing an estimated £1 million a week, but the blackmailer always seemed to be one step ahead. Quite remarkably, he never made withdrawals from machines which were under surveillance. Every time the police were active, he'd suddenly go quiet. Why?

Why had the biggest, most expensive surveillance operation ever mounted in Britain failed to turn up a single clue to his identity? Something was wrong and I seemed to be the only person who recognized the fact.

By the beginning of March the ransom demand had risen to £1,250,000 and the number of contaminations to fourteen – each preceded by warnings. The blackmailer had withdrawn more than £18,000 and the money was running down again, but instead of more threats or contaminations he went quiet.

I think David Baker and his team had mixed feelings. On the one hand they had gained great satisfaction at having kept the blackmailer at bay while having paid him a very small amount of money in corporate terms. The company had also been protected. In fact, every goal had been achieved with the exception of one – catching the man responsible.

Now he had two choices, either he'd give up his campaign or find a new victim.

On 12 March something happened which may possibly have made up his mind. Against the advice of Leicestershire Police, a national newspaper revealed the existence of the blackmail conspiracy against an unnamed pet food company and details of the undercover operation.

The blackmailer now had confirmation that the police had been involved from the outset.

David Baker and Malcolm Cairns were furious that someone had leaked the story to a journalist. The long-running undercover operation was now effectively dead and the blackmailer would have to find a new target.

Ten days later he did just that. Arguably, only one product was certain to have more impact on the hearts and minds of the consumer than pet food and that's exactly what he chose to contaminate – baby food.

One of the world's largest food manufacturers, H. J. Heinz Co. Ltd, received a written demand for £300,000 or the company would 'be irreversibly ruined after their entire product range has been attacked with most lethal substances and boycotted by the public. There will have been many casualties before we finish with them.' Again he demanded replies through the *Daily Telegraph.*

On the same day, a jar of Heinz baby food arrived in the post at a police station in Leicester. It had been laced with caustic soda and the accompanying letter said, 'This time we will have to ensure that somebody buys the product. Then, if one casualty is not enough for you, we go again.'

The task of investigating the new threat fell to the South East England Regional Crime Squad working out of New Scotland Yard, who immediately contacted Leicestershire CID.

David Baker rang me. 'He's surfaced again and found another target – Heinz. We're going to a meeting at Scotland Yard. I'd like you to come.'

We took an early train the next morning, Baker, Malcolm Cairns, Tim Garner and myself. Having breakfast in the buffet car and discussing policy issues, Cairns was concerned that the Metropolitan Police would try to take over the investigation. Normally when inquiries involve more than one regional force, the initial team is given the lead.

'The Met are going to want to hijack it,' he said, polishing off a piece of toast. 'But we can't let that happen. It's our inquiry – we know more about this man than anyone. We ought to be the lead force.'

'The main thing is that we catch him,' Baker reminded him.

'Yes, yes, of course, but I don't want to see it hijacked. It started here. We should have the lead.'

I sensed that prestige was at stake and the feeling that the Met always assumed it was the premier division compared to the 'Wooden Tops' in the countryside.

For all the fighting talk, when we walked into the conference room at New Scotland Yard, it took very few seconds to realize who was in charge. Waiting at the head of the table were Commander Malcolm

Campbell and Detective Superintendent David Tucker. The implications were clear – we were on their territory; it was their investigation and they'd set up camp.

I sat at the far end of the table next to Cairns and Baker. Down each side were representatives of Heinz and Pedigree, who both had legal advisers, marketing men and energetic PRs. At the end of the table sat a younger man, bright, immaculately suited and attentive but saying nothing. Later I learned he was from Controlled Risks, a security firm specializing in anti-terrorism, hostage negotiation and personal protection. Heinz had employed him as an adviser.

The conference room had windows running along one side overlooking surrounding rooftops, although the view was blocked somewhat by the anti-blast coating in front of the glass. Only a fortnight earlier security forces had foiled a terrorist attempt on the life of the Prime Minister when they uncovered a cache of explosives near Scarborough where Mrs Thatcher was due to speak at a Conservative Party central council meeting.

Commander Campbell made the introductions and invited Baker to detail the entire Leicestershire operation. Not surprisingly, the Pedigree team seemed far more relaxed and Heinz particularly cautious. Whenever questions touched upon commercial concerns, previous threats or security measures, the businessmen grew rather reticent, particularly Heinz.

I realized there were two sets of tensions in the room, between the police at opposite ends of the table and, much more interesting, between the two companies facing each other. It was like being in a group therapy room. Something was wrong but no-one wanted to talk.

Finally, I'd had enough. 'Excuse me. Is it just me or does everyone see that we've got a problem? There's an issue here – I don't know what it is – but we're wasting our time unless it's sorted out.'

There was silence around the table.

John Simmens spoke. 'He's right.' He looked across at his counterpart from Heinz. 'The problem is that my parent company competes in many important areas with Heinz. I can't come here and just put confidential corporate material on the table which could be of use to one of my major competitors.'

The Heinz corner stirred. 'We have similar reservations.'

A shocked Campbell looked ready to bang a few heads together but held his temper in check. 'Gentlemen, we're dealing with a very serious offence here. These people have already been through this,' he motioned to the Pedigree team, 'things have gone extremely well; they know this man as much as anyone can. Now he's threatening to poison babies and, much as I appreciate the delicacy of corporate rivalry, I can't let anything stand in the way of this investigation because lives are in danger. If this goes wrong then we'll have dead babies on our hands and unless I get complete co-operation you're going to have to take some responsibility for that.'

Such a stern warning would normally be calculated to have an immediate effect, however, these were international businessmen who had reached the very top of the pile. They were assertive, intelligent, analytical, very motivated people and risk assessment, in the commercial sense, was their daily bread and butter. They had yet to be satisfied that the rest of us at the table weren't overreacting to a paper tiger. From their point of view, it was easy for the police to say, 'Clear the shelves. Hold a press conference. Put your hardest won corporate intelligence on the table.' But if we were wrong then thousands of jobs were at risk and millions of pounds would be lost.

It fell to me to break the deadlock and over the next few hours a compromise was thrashed out. Thankfully, with the most senior company personnel in the room, decisions could be made on the spot. Finally each side entered into a gentleman's agreement to pool whatever commercial knowledge and resources both companies had which could help in the inquiry. In return, nothing provided would be used to gain a commercial advantage.

Finally, the meeting returned to the real issue. The Heinz team didn't know me. I was an NHS psychologist telling them to take the threat seriously but why should they believe me? They had their own advice from Controlled Risks and had probably encountered many attempts at blackmail, mostly cranks and non-starters.

But security consultants get paid thousands of pounds a week solely to protect their client, no-one else. I had no such master and had been asked to look at the whole picture.

Running through the various options, I suggested that similar tactics should be applied as before and we should appear to give just enough to keep this man in the field while aiming to move control away from him. Already we knew far more about him – his likely age, where he lived and his movements.

At about 6.00 p.m., the meeting ended and the company men drifted out to the lift. Although co-operating, I couldn't imagine them going for a beer together at a local pub. Downstairs, chauffeurs were probably waiting to whisk them away.

Commander Campbell invited us to his office where he opened a cabinet and produced half-a-dozen glasses and a very pleasant bottle of Scotch. At the ragged end of a long day, we sat in silence and sipped our drinks.

I had something to say that I couldn't have revealed in front of Pedigree or Heinz because of the implications.

'Get it off your chest,' said Campbell, leaning back and resting the glass on his knee.

'It's about our man. I think he is, or was, a police officer.'

The silence took on a new meaning. Tucker shook his head.

'That's quite a call,' said Campbell, dubiously.

I went on, 'Everything about his actions suggests a detailed knowledge of the way police investigate crimes – how they can monitor account withdrawals, trace telephone calls, identify where products are bought. He uses commonly available paper, photocopies the letters first, he hasn't left so much as a fibre. More importantly, every time a major surveillance operation is organized he goes to ground. It's as if he knows which days and what machines are being watched. How could he know that?

'The only other known blackmail attempt that used cash-point machines to collect the money was kept secret by the trial judge to prevent copycat crimes. Now it's possible that our man just happened to come up with the same idea – or as a policeman he's more likely to know the details.'

I could see they weren't entirely convinced. A great deal of loyalty exists within the police force and it can't be easy accepting or contemplating that one of your own might have turned. To his credit, Campbell encouraged me to go on and tell him more of my theory.

'At some stage he was metropolitan-based and more than a PC,' I said. 'He is demonstrating a deep understanding of both crime and the investigation of crime. For him it's a way of making money but he also really enjoys putting it together. It's almost an artistic form of self-expression.

'He's tenacious but hasn't done well in the police service. He thought he was going places but his career stalled and he blames his superiors. By putting this operation together on a national canvas he's demonstrating just how good he could have been.

'He knows there is no way back – the police are involved. He knows there is a major operation underway; he knows that he has to be so careful because his police experience tells him that you only need a single thread to follow him home.

'But he doesn't plan to get caught. He's going to put together this wonderful series of offences against the largest corporations in the world and it's going to make him famous. No-one will ever know his name but his old colleagues and his superiors are going to talk for ever about this master criminal with a delicate touch who left no footprints.

'Given his movements, I'd say he's possibly retired, on suspension or on sick leave; however, he seems to know so much about what's going on, you have to look at someone who has an inside contact.'

'Christ,' said a voice nearby. Campbell's face gave nothing away.

I knew I was right – all the facts supported me but it was an embarrassing scenario coming from an unlikely source.

Even as we spoke, contaminated food was already on supermarket shelves. A farmer's wife from near Chelmsford in Essex burnt her face and fingers on sodium hydroxide (caustic soda) as she opened a jar of baby food that she'd purchased from Sainsbury's supermarket in nearby Raleigh on 8 April. Later tests showed the jar had been laced with twenty-seven times the lethal dose for a child along with two brass drawing pins. A message inside, punched on a Dynotape, warned: 'POISON. Three more unmarked jars in the store.'

Two days later, Helen Coppock of Cowley, Oxford, was feeding her nine-month-old baby daughter yoghurt. She told police, 'I glanced down at the jar and I saw what appeared to be shavings of metal in there. When I looked at Victoria she appeared to be chewing something. I opened her mouth and found what looked like a piece of metal on her tongue which turned out to be from a razor blade.'

Victoria's mouth was bleeding and she was taken to hospital. While waiting in casualty, Mrs Coppock noticed a Dynotape message in the jar saying, 'Poison also in Heinz beans and soup.'

Heinz immediately cleared the shelves at the supermarket branches where the products had been purchased. If the company had pondered the seriousness of the threat before, it was now in no doubt.

Another meeting of all parties was arranged, this time at Leicestershire Police Headquarters. What I remember most about it was that Heinz was unwilling to adopt the same strategy that had worked for Pedigree. It was impatient and didn't relish the prospect of several months of playing cat and mouse with the blackmailer. It was a variation on the theme, 'we don't bargain with terrorists'.

Again and again, I was asked, 'How serious is he? If we don't do as he says, what will he do?'

So far every contamination against Pedigree and Heinz had been flagged with a warning message and telephone calls giving the stores a chance to intervene.

'Will it always be the case,' I was asked, 'or is he likely to escalate?'

I could sense the frustration around the conference table. 'Yes,' I answered. 'His behaviour is in direct response to yours. If you decide to face him down and pay him nothing, then he'll feel that you're giving him no alternative. His sense of pride and investment won't allow him to do nothing.'

I recommended the same strategy as before but Heinz seemed adamant that it wouldn't negotiate.

'Then you have to go public,' I said. 'If you slap him in the face and he carries out his threat a child dies, two children die . . . where does that leave you? This man is not about to waste his time.'

The police agreed with me. Their overriding concern had to be for public safety, although none of them was cavalier about the damaging impact disclosure would have on Heinz. The company's team took a very forceful view. They knew about the marketplace and the potential losses they faced, running into millions of pounds.

'This is a major undertaking. We have to be sure.'

'I'm sure,' I said.

Newspapers had already reported several of the contaminations but these had been labelled as being unrelated. It wasn't until Wednesday 26 April that the extortion attempt exploded into the headlines: TERROR OF BABY FOOD BLACKMAIL wrote the *Daily Mail*, while the *Evening Standard* reported, MORE DANGER JARS FOUND.

Scotland Yard released the bare minimum of information for 'operational reasons' but the publicity quickly triggered a wave of contamination reports. That afternoon John Patten, the Minister of State for the Home Office, told the House of Commons that 'British shoppers were at risk from a new and frightening threat "consumer terrorism" . . . It is difficult to imagine the twisted minds that could mount such a vicious attack on defenceless babies.'

Mr John Hinch, managing director of Heinz, warned mothers to be particularly vigilant and said the company would withdraw products and replace them with fresh stock only where contamination was reported.

'Withdrawing products doesn't solve the problem. This man could come back tomorrow, the next day or the next month and do it again.'

Unusually for me, I followed events in the newspapers and nightly television bulletins. It almost seemed surreal as the story snow-balled. Within twenty-four hours, the number of reported contaminations had risen to forty, not just affecting Heinz but also baby food rival Cow & Gate. By the weekend the reports had risen to 300 and three people had been arrested for wasting police time and money.

Police believed that the blackmailer was responsible for only two of these cases – each of them clearly flagged – while the rest were the work of copycats, hoaxers or were false alarms. Sadly, people were trying to cash in on the panic, hoping to extort money, gain notoriety or claim insurance payouts. This had been a major concern expressed by both of the companies and investigating teams, but was accepted as an inevitable price for alerting the public.

A £100,000 reward was posted by Heinz and Cow & Gate, while the Home Office called an emergency meeting with the police and manufacturers to discuss future strategy. Officials from the Ministry of Agriculture and Fisheries and the departments of Health and Social Security were also present.

One by one, various retail outlets decided to remove Heinz products from their shelves, unwilling to take the risk. The company stood firm and planned to replace all of its jars with tamper-resistant containers. The change-over took time and was costing millions of pounds.

Meanwhile, the police came under attack from parent and consumer groups who were critical of the delay in alerting the public. Anger increased when it was revealed that the blackmailer had been trailed for seven months.

A team of executives from Heinz flew from the US to mastermind the company's response. Mr Ted Smyth, director of corporate affairs, stepped from his Concorde flight at Heathrow and branded as 'thugs and terrorists' the people who were contaminating baby food. He vowed that Heinz would not pay any money to the blackmailers. 'I'm absolutely outraged and disgusted,' he said. 'These people are attacking the most vulnerable sections of our society – babies.'

The wave of copycat contaminations and hoaxes spread across Europe and similar cases were reported as far away as Australia and

America. Three supermarkets in Illinois removed Heinz products from the shelves after a babysitter reported finding pins in two jars. The company was reported to have lost £25 million in a single week and, despite its best efforts, the first tamper-resistant jars wouldn't be in supermarkets until 15 May. Later it was reported that the senior executives actually put a plan to the US board proposing to close the entire UK operation of Heinz which employs 5,000 people. Only political intervention saved their jobs.

Heinz continued to insist that it wouldn't 'give in' by recalling goods or paying the ransom. Angered by this, the blackmailer made anonymous telephone calls to supermarkets, police stations and the media about forthcoming contaminations to increase the panic caused. His letters grew more threatening.

'You should know by now that we do not bluff. An infant's death will be another statistic as far as we are concerned, but at least we will not be ignored.' Another message warned, 'Babies will not be able to inform their parents that the product does not have its normal flavour. Their systems are also much less resilient.'

At the same time, his demands grew. Instead of the one-off payment of £300,000 he now wanted annual payments over five years that totalled £1.2 million.

By the end of June he was known to have spiked jars and tins that were put on the shelves of supermarkets in Luton, Tunbridge Wells, Rayleigh, Basildon, Oxford, Croydon and Royston. In each case the store and local police were telephoned but one woman almost ate Heinz Weightwatchers minestrone soup saturated with more than five times the fatal adult dose of caustic soda.

Finally, the company accepted a change in tactics. As ordered by the blackmailer, eight accounts were opened with the Woolwich and National Provincial building societies in the names of Ian and Nina Fox. The cash-point cards and PIN codes were to be sent to several accommodation addresses in South London.

These were put under round-the-clock surveillance by the South East London Regional Crime Squad in an operation code-named Stab. It also involved the longest media blackout ever requested by Scotland Yard. The blackmailer didn't collect his mail and the operation was effectively blown when he next contacted Heinz on 5 September.

Pretending to be another party, the blackmailer wrote a letter that contained deliberate spelling mistakes such as the word 'syanide' so as to appear to be an illiterate informer rather than the extortionist. The 'informant' said he knew the identity of the blackmailer but couldn't reveal it straight away because the man concerned was 'a bent cop'. If the company paid him £50,000 he'd name names.

The letter contained intimate details of the police investigation and referred to 'Operation Stab' and the most senior officers involved.

Now there could be no doubt that the blackmailer had inside knowledge. He could even be in league with a policeman close to the heart of the investigation.

In an unprecedented move, Scotland Yard set up a covert 'operation within the operation' designed to stop the leaks. Deputy Assistant Commissioner Simon Crawshaw, head of the Yard's serious crimes branch, took charge of the 'leak-proof' inquiry, setting up a secret headquarters outside of Scotland Yard. He took with him three trusted officers, ostensibly on compassionate or sick leave, and another forty were drafted in from Special Branch.

Effectively there were now two investigating teams, but the blackmailer would hopefully only know about one of them.

Meanwhile, Heinz paid £19,000 into two building society accounts that had been nominated by the 'informant' and daily withdrawals began in early September. Five weeks later, the money was disappearing fast and the police were still no closer to identifying their target.

In mid-October, Friday the thirteenth, a last-ditch surveillance operation code-named Agincourt was mounted by DAC Crawshaw. He selected fifteen Woolwich machines in and around London and had them continually watched outside business hours. The Special Branch teams were detailed to stay close to the machines but out of sight. When the blackmailer's cards were inserted, a computer would pick up the transaction, alert the incident room and the surveillance team would be informed by radio to move in.

Despite the technology, the withdrawals continued and £14,000 had been taken by the morning of 20 October when the blackmailer made his fifty-sixth withdrawal from the Enfield branch of the Woolwich.

That night the operation ran into difficulties – a severed electricity cable had brought down all the cash-point machines in the London area. Crawshaw and Detective Chief Superintendent Pat Fleming decided to maintain the surveillance and shortly after midnight two Special Branch officers posted near a machine in Enfield, North

London, saw a burly, grey-bearded man park his car nearby.

He approached the cash-point machine, realized it was out of order and retraced his steps.

Why is he carrying a crash helmet? thought one of the officers and they moved in.

When challenged, the man said, 'No problem, guys, I know what this is about, but I am innocent.' Then he fainted.

The following day's headlines announced that it was over.

'POISONED FOOD ARREST – Ex-detective quizzed over blackmail plot,' trumpeted the *Daily Mail*. 'Ex-CID man is arrested over poisoned food' declared the *Daily Telegraph*.

It went on, 'A former detective was arrested yesterday in connection with an attempted £1.5 million campaign of extortion and food contamination against the Heinz and Pedigree food companies.

'The man was once a member of the London-based Regional Crime Squad which has been investigating the blackmail plot since August last year. He is well known to the officers who arrested him in Enfield, north-east London, and before his retirement on health grounds he was for a time under the command of Det Chief Supt Patrick Fleming who is in charge of the blackmail inquiry.'

Rodney Whitchelo, aged forty-three, was taken to Paddington Green police station for questioning. The blackmail cash-point cards were found in his wallet and a search of his home revealed papers relating to the accounts, a syringe, drill and caustic soda. As I'd predicted, he lived in Hornchurch, Essex.

From the very beginning Whitchelo refused to co-operate and, given his knowledge of interview techniques and police procedure, the inquiry team had to make sure every loose-end was tied up. Slowly the life and times of the 'baby food blackmailer' unfolded.

Born in Hackney in 1947, he passed six O levels and was studying for his A levels in chemistry, physics and maths at Hackney College when he left school in the middle of his course. He joined the electronics firm Plessey in 1967 and by 1976 had reached the position of electronics engineer grade one.

At the age of twenty-nine, seeking a new challenge, he joined the Metropolitan Police Force and proved to be an impressive recruit, finishing top of his class at the Hendon training college and quickly passing his exams for the rank of sergeant. Later as a detective based at Gerald Road police station, he was involved in the inquiry into how

Michael Fagan was able to break into Buckingham Palace and make his way unchallenged to the Queen's bedroom.

It was a flying start to his police career and soon afterwards he joined the Regional Crime Squad, based at Barkingside, East London. Unfortunately, things then stagnated. Whitchelo believed he was better than most of his senior officers but felt he was being held back because he wasn't a Freemason.

In July 1986, he attended a training course to learn advanced techniques for police surveillance work. It included a case study of the extortion attempt made against Bernard Matthews, the poultry producer, by William Frary, twenty-three, a microbiologist and struggling businessman.

This is how Whitchelo had learned of the previous extortion. All the details were laid out in front of him, including the mistake that Frary made in not casting his net wide enough when he came to withdraw the ransom from the building society accounts. Inspired by the plan, Whitchelo knew he could improve upon it. He'd open more accounts, make withdrawals from all over the country and keep track of the police investigations by using his mates in the Regional Crime Squad.

He returned home to Hornchurch, Essex, and began opening building society accounts under false names. Two years later, in August 1988, he sent his first letter to John Simmens of Pedigree while still serving as a detective sergeant. In October he retired on health grounds, thus giving himself the freedom to travel the country withdrawing money.

Meanwhile, he drank in the same pubs as his police mates and went to their Christmas Party. Occasionally, he dropped into the Regional Crime Squad office and glanced up at the white-boards dealing with Operation Roach. At one stage, when two of his mates were staking out a building society, Whitchelo sat chatting to them in the back seat of their car.

His attempt at committing the perfect crime with total extortion demands amounting to £3.75 million had netted him just £32,000. In all, he was linked to seventeen contaminations.

I heard nothing from the inquiry team until midway through 1990 when I received a visitor at Arnold Lodge. A senior policeman explained that the trial was approaching and the prosecution were tying up the final details of their case against Whitchelo.

'Given that your advice was so accurate in describing the offender and managing his behaviour in the field, counsel feels it would be extremely useful to have you give evidence,' he said. 'We want you to explain how you came up with your offender profile.'

The officer had brought with him a considerable amount of material, much of it found in Whitchelo's house. Apart from business-related papers, there were letters that he'd written to women after advertising in sex contact magazines for bondage partners. He was aroused by domination games and constantly looking for like-minded women.

Although living at home with his widowed mother, he travelled widely for sexual liaisons and some of the building society withdrawals matched the locations that he'd visited.

Other statements also supported my original conclusions that the blackmailer would tend to be fanciful and grandiose. He'd told a former girlfriend that he'd gone undercover to infiltrate the IRA. He also started a pen-pals club for sadomasochists using bondage magazines but the club flopped because not enough women joined.

Similarly, a journalist acquaintance, George Webber, a former night news editor of the *Daily Mirror*, said that Whitchelo had suggested they co-write a book about the perfect crime. Several of the completed chapters contained details of accommodation addresses and building society accounts used in the extortion, although Webber had no idea they were real.

Nothing that I read surprised me; it simply filled in the subtle colours of Rodney Whitchelo. I'd never seen his photograph or heard the sound of his voice, but I knew what went on inside his head.

Even so, I felt uncomfortable about giving evidence at the trial because I didn't think I could move the prosecution case forward. I explained, 'When I gave the psychological profile I talked in general terms about the person responsible – I couldn't tell you his birthdate, or the colour of his eyes, or whether he's got good teeth. I dealt in strong probabilities, not absolutes. I'll give you an example. When I'm asked about what degree of probability I associated with, let's say, my belief that he was a policeman, I'd have to say ninety per cent. That automatically leads to the next question, "So Mr Britton, you're saying there is at least a ten per cent probability that he was something else?"

'So you see, it doesn't strengthen your case. If counsel wants me to give evidence, I will, but I think you either have the evidence against this man or you don't. Nothing I can say will help your cause.'

The senior officer returned to London and a few days later he telephoned to say that senior counsel had agreed with me. I was relieved because I didn't want to publicize my involvement. Until then, my work for the police had been entirely confidential. Not even my superiors at the Leicestershire Health Authority knew of my extracurricular activities, although the time was coming when this had to change.

After a three month trial at the Old Bailey in London, Rodney Whitchelo was found guilty of six counts of blackmail, making a threat to kill Heinz customers and two charges of contaminating tins of Pedigree Chum. He was sentenced to seventeen years imprisonment.

Yet the impact of his crimes will endure for much longer than his incarceration and touch all of us each time we shop in a supermarket. Thousands of foodstuffs are now packaged in special tamper-resistant shrink-wrapping. We now pay two or three pence more for every jar of baby food, jam, soup and sauce etc. that we buy.

It also led to changes in how people open bank and building society accounts. Police called for tougher restrictions on the opening of accounts, still shocked by how easily Whitchelo had set up his plot using bogus names and never having to set foot into a branch office.

Equally, having become instant experts in how computer transactions worked in the banking system, detectives were horrified by the potential for fraud and extortion. High-level meetings were held with financial regulators to discuss the implications.

Back at home the Pedigree Chum went back into the cupboard and Jess showed no sign of having been deprived.

6

THROUGHOUT HISTORY THERE HAVE BEEN THEORIES AND STUDIES that have tried to identify and understand the criminal mind. In hindsight, some of these seem quite bizarre. The French prison surgeon Lauvergne made plaster casts of his patients' heads to demonstrate 'degenerate' features of the skull; and Professor Cesare Lombroso, an Italian doctor, devised a whole range of strange measuring instruments to support his theories that various classes of criminals had very particular 'faces'. For example, assassins had prominent jaws, widely separated cheekbones, thick dark hair, scanty beards and pallid faces.

Modern research into 'criminal man' is rooted on more precise scientific principles. Forensic psychology is an area of expertise that emerged from two separate strands – from the prison system, where psychologists have worked for many years both with individual prisoners and also to find the most effective regimes for running the prisons themselves, and also from the special hospitals and regional secure-units where people who offend as a consequence of mental abnormality are detained, assessed and treated.

This task of clinically interviewing, assessing and treating people has always been at the heart of my work, but it soon became important to me to understand the broader psychological aspects of offending and offenders. What could make a person abduct, rape, kill, torture or abuse another human being? What were the developmental processes that moulded them and sent them along this particular path?

When I first described to David Baker the psychological characteristics that later proved to match Paul Bostock and Colin Pitchfork, my analysis arose from an understanding of both sexual dysfunction and sexually deviant personalities. This understanding came from the psychological literature and my own direct clinical experience. Although sexual psychopaths are relatively rare in the general population, there are quite a number of men like this within our prisons, special hospitals and regional secure-units. Some prey on children, others stalk and rape women, a few target men. Some are responsible for murder. Mercifully, many are identified early in their 'careers' before they have caused maximum damage. As each of these people is caught, more is learned about their backgrounds, psychopathology and especially their motivation.

In painstaking clinical interviews their life-stories are dissected – their childhood, schooling, employment, accommodation, hobbies, sexuality, relationships and offending sequences are probed over and over again. Of course they lie, not only to the clinician, but also to themselves. Nothing can be taken at face value, the facts have to be winnowed from the rationalization. Their accounts are checked and rechecked with other sources such as family, social workers, teachers, friends and court and medical records. It is a continual contest that we can't afford to lose.

Eventually in this process, a series of pictures emerges of a person at various points throughout his or her life. These personality structures and motivations are then compared with those of others who may not yet have killed but who share many of the same characteristics. Comparisons are also made with ordinary men and women, who have developed in a normal way, so that we can determine what factors may separate them from each other. By exploring these things in minute detail, we have an even bigger database to work on.

When I first sat down to draw up a psychological profile, this was the knowledge that underpinned my conclusions. There are thousands of deviant personality structures, all of them individual, but many of the core elements are the same. It's like looking at different houses yet knowing that each one is going to have a bathroom, a kitchen and a lounge.

When profiling an offender, the details of their crime are set against this bedrock of knowledge. Everything about it, the location, timing, weapon, victim, ferocity of the attack and degree of planning, says something about the person responsible. It's all in the detail. If you miss it, you are lost and if you don't understand what you're looking at, you won't see it anyway. It is like going into an Egyptian tomb and seeing the walls are covered by hieroglyphics. Knowing the language, syntax and the grammar you can read the messages and understand more about the people who built the tomb. But if you don't know how to read the writing, the carvings are just pretty pictures on the wall, with no relevance whatsoever, or worse, are misinterpreted and lead to completely the wrong conclusions.

Perhaps a better analogy is that of a jigsaw puzzle. Take, for example, the four questions I ask myself at the start of every investigation – what happened, how did it happen, who is the victim and why did it happen? Only when I have these answers can I tackle the most important question – who was responsible?

To find the answers, I have to sift through an enormous amount of information and decide which pieces I can rely upon and which are less certain, or can be totally ignored. It's like working on several jigsaw puzzles at the one time. One puzzle will tell me what happened, another will reveal how it happened, a third will tell me about the victim and a fourth will show me the likely motivation of the offender. When completed, each of these puzzles then becomes a vital piece in a much larger jigsaw that will help me identify the psychological characteristics of the offender.

Despite having advised in numerous cases by 1990, I had very little interest in the history of psychological profiling or, as it was better known, offender profiling. Wrapped up in my clinical and consultancy work, I had little time or inclination to look at what was happening elsewhere. My police work had been done in my spare time, entirely unpaid. My only stipulation had been that I remain anonymous.

This changed in the middle 1980s, when out of the blue I received an invitation to attend a meeting at the Home Office hosted by John Stevens, a law graduate and chairman of the Association of Chief Police Officers (ACPO) Crime Sub-Committee on Offender Profiling. John had first hand experience of investigating major violent crime having reached his ACPO rank by way of the CID, serving for some years as a Detective Chief Superintendent in the Metropolitan Police.

ACPO is one of the most powerful bodies in British policing as it brings together the most senior police officers from the forty or so forces in England, Scotland, Wales and Northern Ireland.

Accepting the invitation, I found myself sitting around a table with various senior police officers, civil servants, psychologists and mental health professionals. The meeting had been called to discuss 'offender profiling' and to explore its future development. Independently, others had been working in this area and it had been recognized that the early results looked promising and it was time to clarify exactly what should happen next.

Everyone around the table introduced themselves and had their say – some more assertively than others – and when the meeting broke up it had been agreed that a strategy should be developed for the future that would expand the understanding and use of offender profiling.

I heard nothing more about this for several years when I received a telephone call from Detective Superintendent Ian Johnston of the Police Requirements Support Unit (PRSU). Set up originally as a link between the Home Office and the police service to ensure that the police had what they needed, the PRSU had also taken on a research and development role, looking at advances in law enforcement around the world in training, equipment and technology. One of the areas that had come under scrutiny was offender profiling.

Johnston wanted to come and talk to me and we eventually met in an old professorial office at Leicester University after I'd given one of my regular lectures on forensic clinical psychology to third-year students. A vastly practical and entertaining man, Johnston was the archetypal battle-hardened, rugby-playing Welsh policeman. He had a college-boy haircut, a stocky build and plastic-framed glasses that almost looked like a Clark Kent disguise.

He tiptoed cautiously around the subject of his visit until revealing that the PRSU wanted to research and evaluate offender profiling and he wanted to discuss how he might do this. In particular, he wanted to follow up all the work that had been done over recent years to see if it was proving useful to police.

We chatted generally about the issue and then he revealed that several years earlier the Home Office had committed a significant amount of research money to the construction of a database to contain information about sexual murders and rapes and the sort of people who commit them. This was to deliver an operational service, whereby police from around the country could contact the project and obtain offender profiles based upon the database.

The money had led to the creation of the Offender Profiling Research Unit in the psychology department of Surrey University under the directorship of Dr David Canter. I had met Dr Canter at the Home Office and learned of his profiling work with Surrey CID – in particular the case of John Francis Duffy, 'the Railway Rapist', who murdered three women and raped at least twenty others before being captured in 1987.

Since being established, the Offender Profiling Research Unit had reportedly been involved in more than fifty rape and murder investigations and helped jail a dozen dangerous criminals. However, according to Johnston, this success hadn't been verified and, having funded the project, the Home Office wanted to make sure it was getting value for money.

Obviously, the simplest way of gauging the success of an offender profile is to match it against the outcome of the case. How accurate is it? Did it lead to the offender being arrested and charged? Did it positively influence the direction of the inquiry?

Johnston agreed, but unfortunately he was having trouble getting hold of the profiles from the Surrey project. So instead he wanted to tackle it from the other direction by sending out a questionnaire to the various police forces, asking about their experiences with profilers.

'If I draft a questionnaire and send it to you, would you look it over?' he asked.

'Of course,' I said, assuming this would take him some time. Surprisingly, it arrived within two days.

After giving my opinions, I heard from Johnston regularly over the next year on a whole range of issues. His analysis of offender profiling seemed to stall and he asked me to evaluate various research proposals and independent reports prepared for the PRSU, including studies into stress and sickness rates in the police force and the impact on emergency personnel of disasters such as the Lockerbie terrorist bombing and the Piper Alpha oil-rig fire.

At about this time an organizational review within the Home Office led to the formation of the Police Research Group, which would eventually take over many of the key areas of investigation and development formerly handled by the PRSU. During this changeover I had a call from a middle-ranking mandarin in the Home Office saying that the department wished to formally review offender profiling.

In a wonderful blend of diplomatic-speak that was couched with sub-clauses and provisos he told me that the whole area had to be independently reviewed because the Government had been asked to put another significant amount of money into offender profiling, but had been unable to find out if the investment already made had been worthwhile.

He came to see me in Leicester and asked me how I thought such a review should be undertaken. We spent a long time talking and I told him what quality checks were needed. In due course, he came back and said, 'Would you carry out the review?'

I didn't anticipate this.

'What do you think?' he asked.

'I think the idea is very worthwhile.'

'Well, come to London and we'll talk about it.'

I think they chose me for several reasons. Importantly, I wasn't part of any previously funded initiatives and had never been paid for my profiling work, so there was no question of me having a financial stake in its future. At the same time, my own work in this area had been effective.

In London I met with the head of the Police Research Group, Dr Gloria Laycock, previously a psychologist who had worked in the prison service for many years. There were to be several elements in the review. On the one hand, it was a user survey – what did the police want from offender profiling? This would mean interviewing senior policy-making police officers such as John Stevens and also senior practising detectives from around the country.

It also had to look at the product and see what had happened so far. How accurate and valuable had existing offender profiles been when compared to the outcomes of cases? At the same time, it was important to see what work was being done elsewhere, by the FBI in America and European police forces.

'How long do you estimate that it will take?' Dr Laycock asked me.

'Two years.'

She flinched. 'It can't be two years. It has to be done much more quickly. The most we can give you is seventy-five days.'

'That's impossible,' I uttered, 'think of the people who have to be interviewed and the literature that must be reviewed – not just here but overseas.'

Dr Laycock understood the scale of the task but explained that the review was long overdue and had virtually been dropped in her hands. 'We're not happy with what we see and we need to have some answers quickly.'

'Based on your time scale all you'll get is a very sketchy impression,' I said.

'I appreciate that. Give us the overview so we can make some decisions.'

The Home Office wanted a report based on just seventy-five days' work but I had a full-time job as well as the growing number of requests from police to assist in operational inquiries. This meant having to squeeze out the time from my annual leave entitlement, as well as using weekends and bank holidays. It took a year and in that time I interviewed a great many individuals and most institutions which had something relevant to say about offender profiling.

The questionnaire that Ian Johnston had first wanted to send out to Chief Constables and Heads of CID now proved vital in identifying psychologists and psychiatrists who had assisted police with major inquiries. Detectives were asked why a profiler had been called, what were the case details and how accurate had the profile been?

At the same time, I interviewed psychologists involved in areas of research that had a bearing on offender profiling and looked at developments such as CATCHEM, the largest complete database in the country dealing with child murders, abductions and missing children. It had been established in the wake of the Hogg, Maxwell, Harper murders – three schoolgirls taken from different counties but killed by the same man. Set up in Derbyshire in 1986, the database held details of child-related crimes dating back to 1961 and I saw that, properly enhanced, it would be a strong element in a future offender profiling system.

Ian Johnston and Detective Inspector Jon Dawson arranged appointments and acted as my liaison as I met with senior policemen and selected detectives up and down the country, travelling thousands of miles. They were my most important guides as I studied the detective process.

The picture that emerged came as a surprise. Opinions differed enormously. Some experienced investigators were outright hostile, claiming that offender profiling was nothing more than 'a load of psychological bullshit' and they would never use it again. Others were impressed and could see real benefits.

The number of bad experiences caused me concern. When I started the review, I thought I might find an occasional offender profile that proved to be less than accurate, but for the first time I discovered the potential for damage to an investigation, and it frightened me.

Officers told of profiles that were so inaccurate that if relied upon they would have seriously misled the inquiry team. If this had happened in a murder or rape investigation, then someone else could have died or been attacked.

As the data accumulated the picture didn't improve. Instead of being a great advance in crime detection, offender profiling in Britain was at risk of being stillborn.

Modern offender profiling began in America with the FBI and it was impossible to do an international review without looking at what had been achieved across the Atlantic.

In Bureau folklore they tell a story about when it all began. A 'Mad Bomber' had been terrorizing New York City for more than a decade, sending taunting letters to newspapers and blowing up prominent landmarks. In 1956 American psychiatrist Dr James A. Brussel studied the crime scenes, messages from the bomber and other information, and then told police they were looking for an unmarried, middle-aged Eastern European immigrant, who was a Roman Catholic and lived with his mother in a Connecticut city. He was impeccably neat, hated his father and when arrested would be wearing a double-breasted suit, buttoned to the neck.

When arrested, George Metsky had indeed been wearing a buttoned double-breasted suit. He fitted the profile almost perfectly except for the fact that he resided with his unmarried sisters rather than with his mother.

When asked how he managed this, Brussel explained that he normally examined people and tried to predict how they might react in the future. Instead he reversed the process and by looking at the deeds, tried to work out what sort of person would have done them.

From such celebrated beginnings, profiling fell out of favour during the 1960s but picked up again when the landscape of violent crime in America began changing in the 1970s as the murder rate soared and a growing number were committed by strangers.

In the early 1970s, the Bureau had opened the new FBI Academy at Quantico, Virginia, which included a fledgling Behavioural Sciences Unit. The officers involved were mainly occupied with teaching but occasionally they analysed violent crimes and 'profiled' likely suspects.

None of them were trained psychologists although some had studied the literature and, like many investigators, they relied heavily on their detective expertise and knowledge of past cases. Within a decade, this behavioural approach to crime had led to the establishment of the FBI's National Centre for the Analysis of Violent Crime (NCAVC) and the Violent Criminal Apprehension Program (VICAP).

The latter is a reporting system where crimes are summarized in a sixteen-page questionnaire filled out by homicide detectives. The primary aim of the scheme was to link unsolved murders that stretched across state borders but it soon became a vital tool in offender profiling.

Because of America's vast size the FBI didn't have enough experienced profilers available to travel the country, studying crime scenes. They could use the details gathered by local police to classify crimes into broad categories and draw up offender profiles. Although much of this work had been computerized, profiling still relied heavily on a brainstorming approach by experienced FBI agents, together with psychological background research. This had proved effective and their success rates compared favourably to anywhere in the world.

Obviously, one of the first people I went to see when I began the review was Dr David Canter of the Offender Profiling Research Unit at Surrey. I wanted material from him so that I could check on the success of his database and the offender profiles it had generated. The Home Office had found it difficult to get this data, but I assumed that Dr Canter and everyone involved would be interested in working together and making sure the review succeeded.

I went to see him several times and explained that I looked forward to his co-operation and participation. However, on a subsequent visit Dr Canter explained that he didn't think it appropriate for the Surrey profiles to be included in the review because he didn't agree with the method of evaluation. I was surprised. How else were offender profiles to be judged, if not by their accuracy and value?

He told me that operational profiling didn't really interest him and he couldn't understand why police officers kept coming to him and asking him for profiles. I suggested it might have something to do with the name he'd given his project.

The review moved forwards until eventually I awaited only the material from the Offender Profiling Research Unit. It would have been unthinkable to complete my work without input from a body that had actually been funded by the Home Office and set up specifically to provide an offender profiling service for the police.

It led to a crunch meeting at Surrey Police Headquarters, when Dr Canter agreed to provide copies of the profiles. He also made it clear that none of them had been generated by the database of sexual murders and rapes that had been portrayed as the scientific bedrock of his profiling work. Instead, Dr Canter and his team had adopted a brain-storming approach of bouncing ideas around until they agreed on the offender's details. This is a method which I had understood Dr Canter to have earlier argued was not the way forward.

Eventually, I received thirty-six of the promised fifty profiles from the Surrey project and the results were disappointing. Because of the questionnaires filled out by the various police forces I already had a reasonable idea of what to expect. There was little evidence that the profiles were accurate or that they had contributed to arrests being made. Two particular cases had been put forward by Surrey as examples of successful work. In the first, a serial rape inquiry, senior detectives reported that if the team had acted on the guidance of the profile the investigation would have been seriously hindered or misled. In particular, they drew attention to the fact that two separate series of rapes were being perpetrated, but had not been identified in the original profile advice, and that this was only recognized by police sources later in the investigation, which in turn led to the production of an amended profile. The area in which the profile predicted the single rapist would live, and by implication where the police should look, was at the opposite side of the investigation area to where he actually lived. They felt that other aspects of the profile had simply been a repetition of information provided by the investigators.

In the second case, the murder of a prostitute, a senior detective reported that the profile had been wrong in most respects, including having indicated a single male offender (three were convicted); that the offence had been sudden, disorganized and impulsive (it had been planned); the offender would come to police attention due to sudden violence or associated lack of control (they didn't); he would possibly be mentally disturbed (they were not); he would live more than one mile from the scene (they lived within a short walking distance); and he would show considerable remorse for his crime and would admit it if 'firmly accosted' (there was no evidence of remorse in those convicted and no admissions were made during the interrogations).

This effectively marked the end of the further government funds for the Surrey database profiling exercise, although the M.Sc. in Investigatory Psychology has continued to be popular.

In June 1992, I delivered my report to a small executive meeting at the Home Office and then to the ACPO Crime Sub-Committee. Not surprisingly, many people felt let down because it proved to be such a damning report, yet I told them to look past the rhetoric and disappointment and they would see the gold.

They had to look at what was being done elsewhere, particularly with CATCHEM, and at Broadmoor, and, for methodology, at Cambridge. The Dutch had begun experimentally adapting the FBI system to a European setting and there was sound evidence of successful work by individual NHS and university psychologists associated with offender profiling. From all these solid, continuous and positive sources, it was possible to see a future for offender profiling but there had to be a far better method of evaluating its success and securing its development.

I made a series of formal recommendations as to how this might be achieved, the major point being that any future offender profiling service had to be entirely owned and guided by the police. No-one with a financial or a reputation-enhancing interest should be involved in the management. Every profile had to be followed up for accuracy and if it wasn't there, they had to look carefully at where it was obtained.

I set out a blueprint that included a police-run computer-based support system, guided by artificial intelligence principles, that could eventually take out a lot of the donkey work by looking for the presence of certain factors in a crime and drawing particular conclusions from this. I thought it highly unlikely that computers could ever replace experienced psychological profilers in crime analysis but they could save time and act as an early guide for investigators.

Equally, having carefully explored the processes used by detectives in their investigations it was clearly possible to teach police officers to look for psychological clues at a crime scene. One of the major points that came across in my interviews with senior officers was that, despite problems with the accuracy of some profiles, many of them were very enthusiastic about the impetus that profiling had brought to their investigations. A new perspective had been gained by officers when they looked at a crime scene and they took this to their future investigations.

Summing up, I said that the clear goal of my recommendations was to make the UK the major European centre of excellence for offender profiling within two to three years.

With very little discussion and a sense of genuine excitement, all of the recommendations were accepted.

7

MILLGARTH POLICE STATION IN LEEDS LOOKS LIKE AN ENORMOUS modern red-brick building block that someone accidentally dropped into the middle of the last century. The result is totally incongruous with the Victorian working-class terraces, workshops and garages that fill the surrounding acres and represent older Leeds.

The station had the largest incident room I'd ever seen, an enormous open-plan office which had been zoned into sections for house-to-house inquiries, vehicle tracing, intelligence, known associates and the other specialist fields of major investigations that rarely come to public notice.

Detective Chief Superintendent Bob Taylor gave me the tour. A bear of a man, solid right through, he looked like a Celtic warrior with his dark hair and bushy moustache. I'd never met Taylor before and don't know how he got my name or telephone number.

Looking me straight in the eyes, he spoke frankly. 'I have a very difficult and complex murder inquiry. To be honest it's a bloody nightmare because nothing makes sense. All we have are questions.'

He paused to shrug off his jacket. 'Have you read about the murder of Julie Dart?'

I shook my head.

'Well, for operational reasons we've been careful about releasing details. Let me give you the whole picture. Julie disappeared from Leeds on the ninth of July [1991]. We found her body ten days later in a field about eighty miles south of here, near Grantham. She'd been battered to death with a hammer or a brick.'

'How long had she been dead?' I asked.

'Eight, possibly nine days.' He drummed his fingers on an unopened packet of cigarettes. 'Let me start right at the beginning.'

Taylor explained that two days before Julie's disappearance, she and her boyfriend had a violent row and both of them were admitted to St James's Hospital in Leeds in the early hours of the morning. Julie had head and facial injuries and her boyfriend, Dominic Murray, suffered a broken ankle. Against medical advice, they discharged themselves from hospital seven hours later.

Julie, aged eighteen, normally lived at home with her mother at a council house in Oakwood, Leeds, although she spent much of her time staying at Dominic's flat on the St Wilfrid's Estate at Gipton. According to neighbours, she and Dominic had a stormy relationship that swung between stand-up fights one day and open displays of affection the next.

On 9 July she left Dominic's house at 7.45 p.m., saying that she was going to her job at the Leeds General Infirmary where she worked as a laboratory assistant several nights a week.

'Only there was no job,' said Taylor. 'We've checked and rechecked. No-one at the Infirmary knows her.'

'So where did she go?'

'Good question.'

Taylor handed me a letter in a clear plastic envelope. 'This arrived at Dominic's house three days later. We're ninety per cent certain it's Julie's handwriting.'

> *Hello Dominic,*
>
> *Help me please. I've been kidnapped and am been* [sic] *held as a personal security until next Monday night. Please go and tell my mum straight away. Love you so much Dominic.*
>
> *Mum phone the police straight away and help me. Have not eaten anything but I have been offered food. Feeling a bit sick but I'm drinking two cups of tea per day. Mum – Dominic, help me.*
>
> [Then a paragraph appeared to have been written by another hand, giving her mother's telephone number. The letter ended:]
>
> *Love you all,*
>
> *Julie.*

The handwriting seemed quite immature, but certain phrases didn't seem to fit with the little I'd been told of the girl. It struck me as unlikely that Julie would use a term such as 'personal security'.

But the next phrase, 'Love you so much Dominic,' did sound like something she might have added. It suggested that for at least part of the letter she was writing words that someone else had dictated to her.

A very neat construction ensured that a considerable amount of information and instruction had been conveyed in only three paragraphs, but with no explanation of why the letter had been sent. There was no demand for money from Julie's family. Instead, her mother was told to ring the police. Why would an abductor want the police involved?

Taylor had another letter in his hand, this one type-written.

'This arrived on the same day, July the twelfth, addressed to "Leeds City Police". Both letters were posted in Huntingdon, Cambridgeshire, the day before.'

On the envelope the word 'headqarters' (sic) had been misspelt and Taylor pointed out that there was no longer a force called 'Leeds City Police'.

All spelling and grammatical errors are the blackmailer's.

> *A young prostitute has been kidnapped from the Chapeltown area last night and will only be released unharmed if the conditions below are met. If they are not met then the hostage will never be seen again also a major city centre store (not necessarily in Leeds) will have a fire-bomb explode at 5am 17 July.*
>
> *1) A payment of £140,000 is paid in cash (one hundred & fourty thousand).*
>
> *2) £5,000 is put in two bank accounts, 2 cash cards and P.I.N. issued, these two bank accounts to allow at least £200 per day withdrawal.*
>
> *Next Tuesday 16 July a WPC will drive to Birmingham New Street station with the money, and await a phone call at the Mercury phone terminal in the waiting room on platform 9, she must wear a lightish blue skirt with the money in a sholder bag.*
>
> *She must be there by 6 pm and await the call at 7pm, she will then be given a location of the next phone call, (after receiving the call she must drive north out of the city on the A38M Aston Expressway to join the southbound M6, this information is given to avoid her getting*

lost in the city.) She must have enough petrol for at least 200 miles driving, and a pen and pad may also be carried, but no radio or transmitter,

All phone calls will be prerecorded and no communication will be possible or answered. No negotiations will be entred Into. Any publicity or apparent police action will result in no further communication.

The monies must be in equal quantities of £50/20/10 used notes and the cash cards to have their P.I.N. marked on them in marker pen. The money to be wrapped in polythene of at least 120 microns then taped with parcel tape the bank cards to then be taped to the polythene then the package to be wrapped in brown paper and tied by a nyolon cord with a looped handle. The whole package to be no more the 350mm X 350mm X 90mm.

Once the money has been received, Leeds will receive a phone call at around midnight of the name and address of store with the firebomb in five hours should be ample time to gain entry to the store. The hostage will only be released when all the monies have been withdrawn from the accounts.

The hostage will be well fed and well looked after in a home rented for the purpose, she will be guarded 24hrs a day by P.I.R. detectors connected directly to the mains. Once the monies have been withdrawn you will receive the address of the hostage, BEFORE ENTERING HOUSE THE ELECTRICITY MUST BE SWITCHED OF FROM OUTSIDE before opening the door or any movement will activate the detectors.

No attempt must be made to follow the WPC and as she will be followed over very quite roads which can easy be checked, aircraft can be heard.

Tuesday the WPC will at al times carry the only packages with her. She will bring it to various phone boxes for phone messages. At one box a small plastic box with a small green L.E.D. illuminated will be inside the box, this must be picked up and placed ontop of the instrument panel of the car dashboard and must be visible through the front windscreen, this box will also have a large red L.E.D. (Antitamper) and a large amber L.E.D. (Transmitter detector) if either of these two illuminate then no further messages will be received. The money package as I said must be carried at all times and at one destination it must be clipped to a dog type clip that will be hanging from a tree, no downward pull must be made on the rope. The WPC must then return to the car which will be some 300 metres from this point within 60 secs and drive a further 800 metres before removing the plastic box with the L.E.D.s.

The money will be picked up by some-one unconnected with the writer but will be the only person who parks down this 'lovers lane' each Tuesday for a few hours, his female companion will be held hostage until the money is picked up from him, he will have a short range two way radio which I can direct him. Should anything go wrong these two hostages will not be harmed.

This action has been planned for some time, but obstining a small hand gun plus ammunition took longer than antisipated. If anything goes wrong or the ploice are not able to meet the demands then the hostage will never be seen again, plus the store will be fire bombed, the action will then begin again next time an employee of say the Electric/Gas/Water companies will be used, to kidnap them in course of there work will make the company pay the ransom.

No publicity must be given until the money has been received then a press statement may be released but must mention that no monies were handed over.

The extra £5,000 must not be added in cash with the main money, as the main package will be buried for a long while so that serial number will not be traced, serial number in cash dispencers cannot be traced.

A great deal of information and a complex set of instructions had been encapsulated in just a few pages. The author had obviously gone to considerable effort yet, strangely, had managed to put the wrong address on the envelope and make a number of spelling mistakes and grammatical errors. Were they contrived or genuine?

'The dimensions he gives for the package of money . . .'

'They're perfect,' said Taylor.

'And the directions out of Birmingham?'

'Totally logical.'

What remarkable details, I thought, yet none of them made sense in the context of a straight forward extortion. Why send a blackmail demand to the police, making the very people who have to investigate the crime into the primary victim? And why ask for such an unusual amount of money; £140,000 was almost small beer when compared to the time, effort and, above all, the risk that would have to be taken to collect it.

Julie's family and boyfriend insisted that she wasn't a prostitute, but within twenty-four hours police had linked her with the Chapeltown red light area of Leeds and several known prostitutes confirmed seeing her on the night she disappeared.

I asked Taylor what had happened on the Tuesday. He said that a WPC had been waiting for the call at Birmingham New Street. The telephone rang but when she picked it up no-one answered. Three days later Julie's body was discovered.

'So the first two letters must have been posted after she'd died,' I said, thinking out loud.

Taylor nodded.

I began flicking through the photographs showing how Julie's body had been found wrapped in a sheet lying at the foot of a tree. The field could be entered from a farm track that ran in the direction of the A1, The Great North Road, a few hundred yards away. The only other notable feature was a grassed-over disused railway line not far from the tree under which she'd been left.

The post-mortem report indicated no evidence of sexual assault. Two injuries to the back of her head were inflicted by a heavy blunt instrument, possibly a hammer, which had fractured Julie's skull. A series of bruises on her right ankle were consistent with a rope or chain having been tied around it. Julie had been dead for at least a week. The rapid deterioration indicated that her body had been kept in some container sealed from easy air flow and exposed to warmth.

Julie had been an attractive girl, five foot nine inches tall with brown eyes and shoulder-length curly brown hair, normally tied back. She had a distinctive chipped front top tooth and had last been seen wearing a black and mauve suit jacket, black shirt, suede shoes and carrying a black shoulder bag.

'How long had she been a prostitute?' I asked.

'Not long and probably only part-time. She had no convictions or cautions.'

She'd also been in the habit of using different names, sometimes going by 'Atkins', her mother's maiden name, or 'Hill', her natural father's surname. At school she'd been a promising athlete, winning dozens of medals and trophies. She carried on running after she left, aged sixteen, and got a job at a High Street chain store. According to friends, she enjoyed karaoke nights and going out for a drink and was well-known in the pubs and clubs of central Leeds.

Three days after Julie's body had been found, another letter had arrived at Millgarth Police Station.

> *Words will never be able to express my regret that Julie Dart had to be killed, but I did warn what would happen if anything went wrong, at the time of this letter there has been no publicity, if you do not find the body within a few days I will contact you as to the location, it will have to be moved today as it appears to be decomposing.*
>
> *She was not raped or sexually abused or harmed in any way until she met her end, she was tied up and hit a few blows to the back of her head to render her unconscious and then strangled, she never saw what was to happen, never felt no pain or know anything about it.*
>
> *The fire bomb was not left as promised as the selant around the combustables must have got knocked in transit and smelt badly, so it was never placed. Owens furniture store in Coventry was to be the target.*
>
> *The mistake I appear to have made is that I did not know the voice at the end of the phone . . . I still intend to carry out this campaign until I receive the monies no matter how many people suffer. In two weeks or so I shall demonstrate my fire bomb.*
>
> *I still require the same monies as before under the same conditions if you want to avoid serious fire damage and any further prostitutes life, to contact me place an ad in the Saturdays 'SUN' newspaper personal column and a phone call will be made to the box at Leicester Forest East northbound services, the box nearest the R.A.C. box. On the following Tuesday at 8.30 p.m. The courier to be the same W.P.C. as used last time (I presume it was her of course that was at Birmingh New Street) and when answering the phone must say, 'Julie speaking' she will once again be given instructions, a little clearer next time, if she misses the instructions a reaet phone call will be made straight away, she must pick it up a second time if she has got it the first time*

as only one repeat call will be allowed. If any phone box is occupied then a call will be made as soon as available. The calls as before will be recorded, this time by a hostage picked up on the Monday evening in other cities red light district.

The ad in the Sun to read 'Lets try again for Julies sake'. If no message is seen on Sat 27th or Sat 3 August then the fire bomb will definately be placed on Tuesday 6 August. No prostitutes will be held until the message is received or until the fire bomb fails to bring any response.

A Home Office pathologist immediately re-examined Julie's body and found a compression mark around her neck indicating that a ligature had been applied. The cause of death had been strangulation – something only the killer could have known.

In the wake of this letter, the Regional Crime Squad and murder inquiry team began planning a full operation to trap the blackmailer. On Saturday 27 July, as demanded, they placed the advertisement in the *Sun*. It prompted a fourth letter posted from York and found on Tuesday morning at a sorting office in Leeds.

This time it had been handwritten in upper-case letters and obvious attempts were made to disguise the writing, perhaps by holding the pen in a different hand. It listed the final details for the ransom drop that night.

A policewoman was to wait for the call at 8.30 p.m. at the Leicester Forest East service station on the M1. She would answer the phone by saying, 'Julie' and give her car make and colour. She would then be given the name and place where another 'prostitute-hostage' had been picked up during the previous two days. The WPC was then to follow the tape-recorded directions to the location of the next call.

In addition, the blackmailer wrote that a young couple would be picked up from a lovers' lane and also held as hostages during the ransom drop. The male hostage would be sent to pick up the money to thwart any police marksmen who may be waiting.

The letter then drifted into a rambling one-sided debate, listing the possible outcomes of his plan, but in each case giving the reason why he believed he would succeed. He was showing the police how clever he was and how he'd thought of absolutely everything. He was telling them to forget about the road blocks, bugging devices, helicopters, satellite observation, marker dye and transmitters – he'd covered them all.

Quite pointedly, he criticized the headlines that he'd seen in the newspapers.

> *Julie was not bludgeoned to death (Jim Oldfield, Daily Mirror) she was rendered unconscious by three or four blows to the back of the head and then strangled. She never felt a thing.*

That night, the operation went ahead at 8.31 p.m. when the phone rang at the service station. However, it faltered immediately when the WPC was unable to hear the tape recorded message.

As he finished bringing me up to date on the inquiry, Bob Taylor looked in dire need of a cigarette. I could sense his frustration. He didn't know if he had a killer who was trying to cash in on a girl's death; or a blackmailer who accidentally killed his hostage; or a scam involving Julie that had gone badly wrong. Not a great deal made sense.

I liked Taylor's directness and we made arrangements to meet again in several days.

At home over the next two nights, I immersed myself in the details of Julie's death and the blackmail letters. People often talk about 'reading between the lines' but my analysis had to leave the page and step into the mind of Julie's murderer. To know him, I had to see the world through his eyes and to hear the sounds that he heard, even if it meant 'watching' and 'listening' to the screams of a terrified young hostage.

Julie was obviously relatively new to prostitution. Being inexperienced, she was perhaps more vulnerable because she hadn't encountered the focussed sexual violence and hatred that plague women who regularly work the streets.

On 9 July she'd left Dominic's house and travelled into the centre of Leeds where she shared an address in Spencer Place with two other prostitutes. They worked together that evening, soliciting on the street outside, before leaving Julie alone at about 11.30 p.m.

Few prostitutes in Leeds are still on the streets after the pubs empty and business dries up. Apart from the lack of trade, it's less safe because the girls can't keep an eye on each other. For some reason, perhaps inexperience, perhaps because she had debts to repay or wanted to save money before accepting an offer to join the army, Julie continued working.

That night someone had watched her from a distance and thought to himself, is she the one? He'd been out trawling before, waiting for the right victim. She had to be on her own so that no-one would see her stepping into his car.

A prostitute suited his purposes because she was easier to acquire and more anonymous than most. Her disappearance wouldn't create the same headlines as abducting, say, a schoolgirl who is expected at home. Scores, maybe hundreds of women who work as prostitutes disappear, sometimes for days or weeks, from some habitual red-light area only to turn up later working in another. They are usually driven by trade, by whimsy and by fear. Some, far too many, never turn up again, or, if they do, have to be entered in the growing file marked 'Unsolved Prostitute Murders'.

From her killer's viewpoint, Julie suited his purposes because he wasn't seeking headlines or demanding ransom from her family; he wasn't interested in her as a person, he needed her only as a manageable hostage.

He pulled up alongside her and she leaned in the window, quoting a price. She had a room nearby but he wanted to do it in the car. That'll be more, she told him as she slid into the passenger seat. It may have happened more violently than this because he had the strength to drag Julie inside and disable her quickly, but this would have risked attracting attention, something which didn't happen.

In all likelihood, he secured her by tying her hands and feet and then drove her somewhere that had been prepared in advance. He planned to keep her alive, at least until she wrote a letter to her boyfriend. The other letter, detailing the ransom, had been written in advance ready for posting.

But why demand money from the police? Why give complex instructions saying that no-one should follow you, or use radios, or tracking devices, when the very people you're blackmailing have no option but to do exactly the opposite?

The answer became clear. His main motivation wasn't money. All the meticulous detail and elaborate camouflage pointed to a man set on challenging the police, inviting them to play a game with him. His letters read like shopping lists of demands, specifying how the money should be wrapped, the thickness of the plastic and exact dimensions of the bundle. Why be so specific? Does it matter? Only if you want to exert control, making your opponent jump through as many hoops as possible.

The demand for £5,000 to be lodged in bank accounts was all part of the game. He knew withdrawals could be traced and was obviously inviting police to 'track me if you can'.

Similarly, the overall demand for £145,000 was too small in the context of what he'd planned. If he'd asked for a million pounds or two million, then the planning and risk might be worthwhile. The only other explanation was that he had a specific debt that needed paying for this amount, such as a mortgage or a business loan, or believed that some earlier injustice had cost him exactly that amount.

The blackmailer knew he was clever and now he wanted the police to show him some respect. Maybe they hadn't respected him before and had treated him like scum or some petty criminal, but now he was going to show them. He was going to prove to the world how much better he was than life's opportunity had shown. All the failure and disappointments would be forgotten and people were going to be impressed. He might not have some fancy degree from university but he had brains and was far too clever to be caught.

The letters contained no evidence of loss of control or anger, but clear signs of a quiet excitement. It must have taken him a long while to plan it all – every hour enjoyable.

He probably kept Julie alive until the next morning, I thought, which meant he needed somewhere to keep her – a garage, basement or workshop – where he wouldn't be disturbed. He had to kill her, of course. He wanted to be taken seriously by the police and for that to happen he had to make it absolutely clear that having killed once, no boundary could be taken for granted.

It wasn't a sexual murder and he probably regarded Julie's death with indifference – as partly a matter of good housekeeping or the clever use of an exclamation mark instead of a full stop. If he did feel pleasure from the act, it was like picking cherries from a tree as you walk past. Yet he clearly didn't want to be regarded as a cold-blooded murderer, so his third letter didn't gloat.

He wrote instead, 'Words will never be able to express my regret that Julie Dart had to be killed . . .' and stressed how painless it had been. It was to do with image management. He wanted to be seen as a Raffles-like figure, a clever rogue whom the public would admire and the police grudgingly respect.

I delivered my psychological profile to the crime management committee which consisted of about a dozen officers, Tom Cook being the highest ranking. We took up a conference room at Millgarth Police Station, sitting around a large table. The meeting began with a briefing from each of the officers responsible for various aspects of the inquiry. Certain teams were tracing Julie's last known movements, talking to her family and friends; others were going door to door asking if anyone had seen her on that Tuesday night. Detectives were also checking dozens of hotels and boarding houses in the Huntingdon area of Cambridgeshire.

Meanwhile, everything about the letters was being analysed – the brand of stationery, where it was sold, the typewriter (an old Olivetti with a faulty 'f') – and every person who had handled the letters, right back through the sorting office and postal collection had to be fingerprinted to perhaps isolate the blackmailer's prints.

One lead involved an unusual laundry mark on the sheet wrapped around Julie's body. The tag was printed with the letters 'MA143', which dated back to the late 1940s and had been traced to a shop in Mosley Avenue, Coventry, which twenty years earlier had been a laundry.

Similarly, his second letter, postmarked in Leeds, yielded another possible clue. The first-class stamp, depicting the head of a teddy bear, was quite unusual and had only been released in a presentation pack containing ten different stamps. It might be possible to trace the people who bought them.

Bob Taylor introduced me to the management committee and made it clear that everyone should listen carefully and they could ask questions afterwards.

'The man you're looking for is in his late forties or early fifties,' I said, glancing at my notes. 'The methodology and tone of the letters has a maturity about them that wouldn't be found with a younger offender.

'He's of above average intelligence, probably consistent with university entrance but his formal education is to secondary level, not to degree standard – the quality and structure of the language support this.

'It's quite likely that he has continued self-improvement since leaving school, possibly attending some formal courses. He will be familiar with electrics and machinery, perhaps in his job, but his theoretical knowledge is much better than his ability to implement it.

'He's not a senior employee in a large organization – there isn't the conceptual lay-out and complexity of language in the letters. They've been written by someone who is familiar with typewriter keyboards but is probably only a two-fingered typist.

'He's likely to have been married but won't be able to sustain a marriage over any length of time.

'He's a very strong planner, look at how carefully he's thought things through. He needed time to prepare, it didn't happen spontaneously, and he has probably rehearsed a lot of his plan.

'He's likely to have a previous history of offending but this will be for things like property offences, deception, fraud and misrepresentation,' I said. 'His plans are well debugged and he clearly has some knowledge of police procedure that suggests he's been through the system before, although I see nothing to indicate that he has killed before.'

One avenue that I suggested checking was anyone who might have a personal or family grudge against the former Leeds City Police.

'This person could be projecting responsibility for their own troubles onto the police,' I said. 'You'll need to check back quite a long way because thoughts of revenge can simmer for a long while before boiling over into action. This man or his family would have been in touch at the time, demanding justification. This means that somewhere there'll be a written record of a complaint and that should narrow the search.'

At the same time, I warned about placing too much emphasis on this strand of inquiry. Although it had to be followed up, I was intrigued by the spelling errors and antiquated address on the first letter to the police.

'These details aren't likely to have just drifted past this man's planning processes. He's almost certainly creating blind alleys for you and will be hiding behind a welter of smokescreens and diversions. It's precisely in these that he'll overreach himself and allow us to turn them back on him, and then we'll find him.'

Now I reached a point that had particular resonance as far as I was concerned. 'Julie Dart was always going to be murdered. This man wants to be taken seriously by the police and in order for that to happen he had to kill her. And, if necessary, he'll go on killing until he feels that he's got your attention.'

Understanding this was vital. Julie didn't die in a botched kidnapping or while trying to escape – two of the theories being bandied about. Her killer wanted a contest, he was constructing games and issuing challenges. He wanted to be highly regarded as an adversary by the police so his plans and demands were designed to be thorough and most of all to be very impressive.

'He's primarily a games player. This is, for him, the most thrilling, exciting, self-fulfilling thing that he's ever been engaged in,' I said. 'He's now playing on a national canvas and the intensity of his feelings of satisfaction, control and pleasure is difficult to convey. He's hooked on this. Even if he gets his fill for the moment, after a while he'll want it again and come back – he won't be able to stop.'

Tom Cook asked if I had an opinion on the blackmailer's home turf. Looking at the chronology and maps, a large triangle had emerged with Leeds, Birmingham and Huntingdon forming the apexes. He knew Leeds well enough to locate and take Julie without being seen; had posted the first two letters in Huntingdon and had chosen a particular phone in the heart of Birmingham railway station for the first ransom call. All of the prominent locations were connected by good road and rail links.

'He has strong geographical connections with the West Midlands and I think he'll live somewhere inside the triangle,' I said. 'If you want me to put my neck out, I'd favour the right-hand corner closer to where Julie was found.'

When I finished, we took a break. I wondered what the police were thinking. Some of them were probably sceptical about the profile, others undecided although they didn't let it show. The next stage, discussing strategy, would be more delicate because I had to be careful not to tread on professional toes or suggest the inquiry was heading in the wrong direction.

In my view they had five options.

1) Follow all existing lines of enquiry, but ignore the threats and refuse to negotiate. Not wise. Julie had died to attract police attention and if they ignored him I had no doubt there would be dead prostitutes up and down the country.

2) Launch a major press campaign, making all the details public, and hope that someone out there could identify him. A very slim possibility, but more likely to send him to ground for a few months. Then he'd be back, perhaps killing again to reintroduce himself.

3) Give in to his demands, pay the ransom and trust that he just goes away. Not an option for the police.

4) Put out a false profile suggesting, for example, that the blackmailer was psychotic, of low intelligence and sexually immature. Although I included this, for the sake of completeness, as a way of

drawing the blackmailer back into contact, I quickly discounted it as being too dangerous because it could also goad him into killing again solely to punish the police for insulting him.

That left option five – playing the game. If the management committee accepted that his deep motivation wasn't just money but was the contest itself, then this had to become the central organizing motif of the entire investigation.

By drawing this man into the field on our terms, to the extent that this was possible, and understanding the options open to him at each point, we could keep his need for the game satisfied and so begin to channel his behaviour to stop him killing again. At the same time, we could move him closer to a position where he would disclose enough information about himself, or become over-confident and drop his guard, making an operational mistake that would lead the police to him.

Just as with Rodney Whitchelo, each new contact increased our chances of catching him and each letter told us something more. We had to let him think he could win and then prepare to beat him.

The last option, option five, was accepted and planning began for his next contact and the inevitable demands. The team had to be ready to respond to whatever situation he engineered rather than waiting until it happened and then reacting instinctively. Part of this involved choosing and rehearsing a courier. A massive murder and extortion investigation involving scores of officers and specialists would, for a brief period, funnel down and rest on the shoulders of a lone policewoman. For that time she carried the weight of the entire operation and we had to make sure she could handle the pressure and deal with the unexpected.

Such outside operations are co-ordinated by the Regional Crime Squad, in this case No.3 unit based at Wakefield, and a senior officer came to see me at Baverstock House in Lincoln where I conducted an out-patients clinic once or twice a month. We discussed the attributes of a successful courier/negotiator – someone bright, fast on her intellectual feet and able to deal with rapidly changing situations. She had to be able to maintain her role and not give way to disabling fear even when she felt totally alone and at the mercy of a calculating and very deceptive killer.

The blackmailer would deliberately attempt to use his words, his vocal tone and pace to control and intimidate her, perhaps even trying to make more direct physical contact.

'She has to be rehearsed over and over again,' I said. 'I don't care how confident she says she is, she won't have experienced anything like this. When that man speaks to her, everything will freeze.'

Several days later, the officer introduced me to a detective constable in her late twenties who looked me straight in the eye as she shook my hand. Anna (not her real name) had solid police experience but had never acted as a ransom courier. A question remained over her appearance. The blackmailer had stipulated that the police use the same WPC as before. Would he recognize the change? That depended upon how close he'd got to the first courier. What would he do if he discovered the deception? Perhaps take another life or set a store ablaze. How could we prevent it? I thought about this and suggested a cover story. We could tell him that the first policewoman had gone on sick leave suffering from stress. It would appeal to his sense of control and need to intimidate.

Anna sat in my room at Baverstock House listening to my description of how the blackmailer would try to manipulate her. Finally I had her pick up a nearby phone and I stood behind her out of sight.

'Hello, Julie speaking,' she said, a little self-consciously.

'Switch off your radio – NOW!' I yelled, with all the venom and authority of the extortionist.

She flinched. 'I . . . I haven't got a transmitter.'

'Don't insult me,' I spat. 'I've got a radio detector hidden near the phone box. I know you've a transmitter open. Switch if off!'

There was a long pause as Anna went over our earlier briefing in her memory. 'Look, we're trying to do what you want, honestly, but please, why do you have to do this—'

'I'll ask the fucking questions. Get that transmitter off!'

'OK, OK. I'm doing it now.'

Anna indicated that she wouldn't turn off the radio, anticipating that the blackmailer was bluffing about having a detector. If he did have such a device, she'd say that she fumbled the switch in a panic.

'Now try something else,' I said. 'Even though he threatens, sneers and abuses, don't challenge him or confront him yet – just build a rapport, let him truly think that you are trying to do things his way. But remember he has to learn that you are just a messenger, he can't win policy concessions from you. Make him see that although you might want to go along with his demands, you're just a cog in the wheel. Use your vulnerability to satisfy his need for control.'

Again I stood behind Anna as she picked up the telephone.

'Unscrew the light bulb in the booth,' I said, 'then wait no more than twenty seconds and walk behind the bush by the kiosk, get into the blue Ford car that is parked there and drive off immediately, straight ahead. Take the first lane on the left, travel at precisely forty-five miles per hour, and stop at the phone box in a lay-by a mile and a quarter on the nearside. Go into the phone box and wait for my call. It's timed exactly, if you're not there within six minutes I'll know that you're not taking this seriously enough. Oh, you must have got rid of your watchers and backup or it's all off anyway. START NOW!' I shouted.

Anna said, 'I can't do that. I can't make that decision.'

'No, try again,' I said, 'don't just dismiss it, offer him some reason.'

'I'm trying to do what you want, but I can't twist the bulb.'

'I don't want excuses.'

'I know you're very serious, but I'm frightened that there isn't enough time for me to get there.'

'Unless you start now another one will be dead tonight and it will be your fault. It's not me – she lives or she dies depending on what you do now.'

The conversation continued as we practised and honed Anna's responses over and over again until she was able to deal fluently and naturally with a broad range of threats, demands and tricks. Eventually, I was confident that if this stage of the operation went wrong, it wouldn't be because the courier fell apart.

On Tuesday evening, 6 August, the ransom drop began again and Anna waited at the telephone box at Leicester Forest East. An hour after the deadline passed, all units were stood down. The blackmailer had failed to make contact.

Two days later another letter was found at Leeds sorting office, postmarked from Nottingham. Bob Taylor faxed it to me.

Re Julie,

Could not make it Tuesday evening due to the fact that there was no suitable hostage in the Huddersfield red light area on Monday evening, also our young lovers are not down the lane on Monday evenings, the latter are more important than the prostitute, as a prostitute can be eliminated any time should the police no co-operate. But another suitable couple have to be located but the day will have to be changed to Wednesday. This being the case, a phone call will be made to the usual box on Wednesday 14 August at 8.15 p.m. (not 8.30 p.m.). The extra 15 min being needed due to location change.

Also this time your W.P.C. will need a Stanley type knife, with a sharp blade, she will not now be travelling to the box where there is one located. this will be the last time you will receive a call at the usual location, should anything go wrong, then you will not be given the location of the incendiary device or the location of the prostitutes body, mind you, you found Julies within 24 hours. I did think of hiding her body till it was all over but felt sorry for her, she was only killed because she saw where she was, but this time the second prostitute will need to be kept for 24 hrs so there should be not problems if nothing goes wrong.

I will also need to know the phone number of where you want to be told the location of the incendary, this phone number must be given at the second box not the first box at Leicester.

Again he apologized for missing the appointment – almost suggesting that 'if you play it straight with me, I'll be straight with you'. He wanted the police to admire him as an honourable opponent. Another handful of misleading clues were added to the pot like a pinch of salt or dash of pepper. The Stanley type knife? The extra fifteen minutes he needed? The lovers in the lane and the change of days? He loved stirring the pot and watching it bubble.

As instructed, the operation began again on Wednesday 14 August and this time the telephone call was made at 8.16 p.m. The blackmailer said that he'd taken another hostage, a prostitute from Ipswich called Sarah Davis or Davies and he instructed Anna to take the M1 northbound to junction 40, then take the A638 to Wakefield. After an eighth of a mile, on the right-hand side near a bus stop, she'd come to another telephone box. She had ninety minutes.

At the control centre, detectives scrambled to establish if any woman had been reported missing in or around Ipswich. A convoy of unmarked police cars shadowed Anna to the next contact point where she discovered there was no telephone box an eighth of a mile down the road. Two possible boxes were found nearby and a quick decision made to put a second female officer into the field, so both phones were covered.

Anna didn't get the call, it came to the other policewoman. As she picked up the receiver she found the cradle had jammed. Struggling to free it, she heard the blackmailer say that he'd call back in half an hour. No call arrived and at 11.30 p.m. the operation was stood down.

When Bob Taylor told me what had happened he couldn't hide his frustration. He cursed British Telecom and cursed the blackmailer. The cradle had jammed – a simple fault – and now he feared the police were going to be punished for this with the death of another woman.

Checks with Ipswich police indicated that no-one had been reported missing and the street name given for the abduction didn't exist. Despite this, telex messages were sent to all heads of CID throughout England and Wales informing them of the possibility of another hostage being taken.

Later that morning, 15 August, a road cleaner on the M1 motorway, south of junction 37, spotted a white-painted brick lying near a disused railway bridge that crossed the carriageways. Attached to the brick was a brown envelope and nearby lay a silver tin with two red lights, one of them illuminated.

The South Yorkshire police were unaware of the blackmail operation and, fearing the package was a bomb, they called in an army bomb disposal team which used a remote controlled robot to destroy the suspect device. The envelope survived and contained a stencilled message directing police to another bridge used by pedestrians further along the motorway where a second white-painted brick was discovered but no letter.

Despite the missing pieces, a picture began to emerge of the ransom trail. The blackmailer had planned to direct the courier beneath the pedestrian bridge. He would then drop a length of rope from above and she would attach the package using the dog clip. He would then pull it up and make his escape, perhaps along the disused railway line.

The railway connection interested me. New Street Station had featured in the first demand; Julie's body had been dumped near a disused stretch of track and now the latest ransom drop involved the Dove Valley Trail, another disused line. Meanwhile, all of the letters had been posted from towns or cities that were linked by the rail network and often put in post boxes within a few hundred yards of the station.

If you dropped a pebble on a map, how many times would it land close to a disused railway line or bridge? I asked myself. Occasionally, yes, but not three times out of three. Railways were obviously an important part of this man's life and his planning. He didn't necessarily work on the trains but he had more than a casual interest in them.

Six days after the failed ransom drop, a seventh letter arrived in Leeds, having been posted on 19 August in Grantham. Littered with spelling mistakes and grammatical errors, it revealed a great deal about how cunning and manipulative the author could be.

No prostitute had been kidnapped from Ipswich. Instead, he claimed it was all a ruse to let him watch how the police would react and counter him. He was merely gathering information for a later, greater ransom demand.

He wrote:

> *Game is now ababdoned, Crimewatch U.K. will tell me most of what I wanted to know, but what I was realy looking for was the package, I never envisaged any money in the package, but had made arrangements for the bug/transmitter would have been in, to be made inoperative, I wanted a sample of the type police would use . . .*
>
> *You will have to file your papers until I try again, which is what this was all about, as you know I never picked anyone up in Ipswitch or planted and devise, I didn't need to following Julies unfortunate death, you would co-operate in anthink I said.*
>
> *For your records Julie was picked up on Tuesday the 9 July 11.30 p.m. just off Roundhey Road and was wearing jeans not a skirt, I believe I mentioned last time the date and reason she died. The reason the body detiated so quick, was that it was kept in a wheely bin in a greenhouse for two very hot days, I thought this was the best way to keep the body . . . The wheely bin was used to transport the body to where you found her, although you will know that by the tracks.*

Much of the letter was an explanation of how messages had been left and how clever the plan had been, but everything he wrote had to be questioned. Part of his smokescreen was to drop in truthful details among the lies, trying to disguise his true plans. The letter also confirmed that Julie Dart had died as a demonstration rather than by accident, although he still attempted to dress up his motivation as being less brutal.

On 21 August the blackmail threats finally became public and the *Yorkshire Evening Post* ran the front page headline: PAY UP OR I KILL AGAIN.

The management committee had decided to go public because a graphite test had discovered a message imprinted on one of the envelopes sent by the blackmailer. It had probably been beneath a sheet of paper as someone jotted down the words, 'Mavis, will not be in Tuesday, Phil.'

There was no way of knowing if this was fabricated or genuine but Bob Taylor went public hoping that somebody would recognize the names and call the police. It triggered thirty new leads that had to be followed up.

Meanwhile, the blackmailer had gone quietly to ground, although I knew that he'd be back. He loved the game too much to let it die. Throughout September I had regular calls from either Taylor or one of his sergeants. I actually bumped into a couple who were trying to trace a particular car.

Several new leads were being followed, including the sighting of a suspect red Suzuki car in a lovers' lane in Barnsley. Detectives were also tracing the origins of the white-painted bricks used as markers on the ransom trail and had linked them to a now defunct brick company.

The silence was broken on 15 October when a letter addressed to British Rail arrived at Euston Station in London. A second envelope inside was marked, 'For the attention of a senior executive only.'

> *Unless we receive a cash payment of £200,000 we shall cause the derailment of an express train, either the D. T. V. of an East coast 225 or the D. T. V. of a West coast push-pull. A high speed section has been selected and some materials already concealed nearby, below is a drawing of how we intend.*
>
> *We are extreemly serious about the course of action should you ignore this letter or no money is forthcoming. We expect you shall cal the police, but any publicity or visible police action will result in us not communicating again. Should you ignore this letter then you will be able to see how serious we were.*
>
> *Should you also pretend to go along with our demands but do not deliver any money then this will make us even madder than ignoring the letter . . .*

It went on to give precise instructions on denominations of money and how it should be bundled, packaged and eventually put into an unlocked case. British Rail was to insert an advertisement in the personal column of the *London Evening Standard* on the following Monday, which would read, 'The train is ready to depart.'

Two days later, on Wednesday 23 October, two female employees of British Rail had to drive to Crewe Station with the money. One woman was to stay in the car at all times while the other waited for a phone call on platform three at about 7.00 p.m.

She had to answer, saying, 'This is Amanda speaking' and would be given the name of another railway station that she had to travel to and await further instructions.

> *The person receiving the calls must wear a skirt and shoes with heels, we want no Olympic sprinters in trainers, the women must have a good road atlas and have good road direction sense . . .*
>
> *Note. As security against a police ambush we have an ace card to be played at the time the money is picked up, this you will learn of later. But your females will not be harmed in any way if they attempt no heroics, there will be a firearm trained on the driver at the time of the pick up, but she will not see anyone.*

The letter was initially investigated by British Rail Transport Police and then handed to Scotland Yard. An old acquaintance from the Heinz baby food investigation, DCS Pat Fleming, was put in charge and had to decide if the threat was genuine and how to react. At that stage, he had no idea that West Yorkshire police were tracking a killer and blackmailer.

Meanwhile, Bob Taylor also had a letter, this one addressed to 'The Chief Constable West Yorkshire Police, Millgate, Leeds'. The misspelling of 'Millgarth' would later become a vital piece of evidence.

> *Re Julie (with no hair)*
>
> *As you are no were near on my tail the time has come to collect my £140,000 from you. I do not get any bigger sentence for 2 murders and prostitutes are easy to pick up but as this time you know I mean business I don't need to pick one up until Monday & I have purfected the pick up. The money to be the same as before.*
>
> *On Wed 21 Oct the same WPC will be at the phone box on Platform 3 of Carlisle Station (bottom of ramp) at 8 p.m. for message (recorded) at 9.15 p.m. approx.*

I believe you will deliver the money as you will not risk life of WPC or prostitute . . .

Within days Scotland Yard and the Leeds murder team had established the link and I compared the letters. I had no doubt that they were written by the same man, despite his attempts to conceal the fact. There were numerous clues – the poor grammar, addresses written in upper-case, the relatively small cash demands, the use of railway stations and the shopping list of precise instructions about how the money had to be bundled and packed. These far outweighed the dissimilarities.

The second letter specified an incorrect date – 'Wed 21 Oct' – for the ransom drop. The Wednesday fell two days later on the twenty-third, the same date as the British Rail drop. Was it a deliberate mistake or, more likely, an attempt by the blackmailer to stretch police resources by forcing them to run two different surveillance operations simultaneously 150 miles apart. Hundreds of policemen from different Regional Crime Squads would be tracking the same man and risking arresting each other in the mayhem that followed.

I suggested a third possibility – he wouldn't call either courier. Maybe he simply wanted to sit back and laugh, knowing that each time the police were frustrated and disappointed, their enthusiasm and resolve would be worn down.

The BR threat included a drawing of how the high speed express would be derailed using two rigid steel joists (RSJs) dug into the tracks. An expert confirmed that such a device could indeed lift an express train off the rails and send it hurtling into the air at more than a hundred miles per hour. Multiple fatalities were almost inevitable.

Pat Fleming then made a brave call and chose not to follow the demands. He wanted to stall for time and to hopefully communicate with the blackmailer through the newspaper columns. At the designated time, WPC Susan Wooley answered the call at Crewe Station but instead of saying, 'This is Amanda speaking', she pretended to be a commuter who simply picked up the phone when it began ringing. Meanwhile, at Carlisle station, Anna waited in vain for a call and the surveillance operation was stood down.

On 28 October a second letter arrived at Euston Station.

Congratulations, you have now qualified for retribution. Within a week or so a small penalty will be imposed in the form of the removal

> *of an electric locos pantagraph, and with a little luck the downing of a section of line, a suitable place has not yet been located, but studies are under way. This is the small demonstration I wished to perform initially to prove our determination.*

Five days later a British Rail track inspector on the main West Coast line at Wolverhampton not far from the village of Millmeece, found several blocks of sandstone lying directly under a railway bridge. The words, 'To the chief executive of BR' had been written on one of the blocks. Close examination showed that the sandstone had been drilled with holes and had initially been suspended using rope and wire from the bridge.

It was a booby trap designed to destroy a train's pantograph – a device that extends from the cars to the overhead electricity lines. At best such damage would simply stop the train within a few hundred yards; at worst it would bring down the high-voltage cables and risk electrocuting passengers. In this case the device had failed because the draught generated by the train had probably blown the suspended blocks out of the way and sent them crashing onto the track.

However, the blackmailer had again illustrated his knowledge of trains and his potential for destruction. He wasn't just a trainspotter with a bad attitude, the railway system was like a framework that rumbled beneath all his plans.

It had been nearly four months since Julie's murder and the police felt they had come close to catching her killer at least twice. All they could do until he began playing again was to follow up every lead and gather the forensic evidence that might one day help to convict him.

8

AFTER A TYPICALLY QUIET CHRISTMAS WHEN THE SNOW RARELY threatened and the mist didn't lift off the hills around the village, I returned to work at Arnold Lodge. On 24 January I was conducting an out-patient clinic at an old gatekeeper's house that formed a small outpost of the forensic unit, when Diane my secretary interrupted.

'A Detective Chief Superintendent Mike Jenkins from West Midlands CID wants you to call him straightaway. It's urgent.'

The note in my diary for that afternoon reads: 'West Midlands – some sort of crisis'.

Jenkins told me that a young estate agent, Stephanie Slater, had been kidnapped and a ransom letter received. As he spoke, the image of Julie Dart bundled up, dead in a muddy field, immediately flashed in front of me. He's back, I thought.

Throughout the drive to Birmingham, although I didn't know Stephanie, I kept imagining a young woman imprisoned somewhere, probably exhausted, possibly injured and almost certainly overwhelmed with fear and disbelief. The sense of immediacy this created was unlike anything I'd confronted in past cases. Someone's life was in immediate danger and depending upon which way the police reacted, Stephanie could live or die.

It was 5.30 p.m. when I arrived at Lloyd House in Birmingham to be met by Jenkins, an old-style copper who had risen through the ranks, and the Assistant Chief Constable (Crime), Phil Thomas. I'd interviewed Thomas for the Home Office Review and found him a big and bright man with a voice that matched his frame. Since then he'd undergone some sort of throat surgery and his voice had lost much of its authority.

They outlined the situation. Two days earlier, Stephanie, aged twenty-two, had left the Shipways Estate Agent's office in Great Barr at 10.30 a.m. to show a man around a three-bedroom house in nearby Turnberry Road. The customer had given his name as Mr R. Southwall of Wakefield when he rang the agency a week earlier to inquire about buying a house and also when he dropped in to collect the details of twenty vacant properties.

Several neighbours saw a man waiting near the door of the vacant house before Stephanie arrived and described him as being in his forties, around five feet eight inches tall with dark collar-length hair and wearing black-rimmed Michael Caine-style glasses. Half an hour later one of them saw a bright red van in an alley behind the house. A sign along the side windows said, 'BLOCKED AND BROKEN DRAINS'.

At midday, Sylvia Baker, another employee of Shipways, took a telephone call for the manager Kevin Watts. The male caller said Stephanie had been kidnapped and a ransom letter would arrive in the following day's post. He ended with the warning, 'Phone the police and she'll die.'

The agency quickly established there was no Mr Southwall at the address supplied and the telephone number he'd given was a phone box on the A1 in Nottinghamshire. Stephanie's car was found outside the vacant house and inside, at the top of the stairs, was a small spot of blood on the wall.

'Let's get you over to the incident room,' said Jenkins. 'Then you can see the maps and photographs of the scene. You can also talk to the lads on the ground.'

We drove in a fast but discreet car from the brightly lit city centre through a tangle of residential and commercial areas until we squeezed into a small overcrowded car-park behind the two-storey police station in Nechells Green. Behind the blinds every light was burning and each room in the building had been temporarily labelled for some particular use by the task force – SIO, Briefing Room, Incident Room, etc. – all the specialist functions employed by a major inquiry.

Having introduced me to the SIO and the other senior operational detectives, Jenkins handed me a photocopied page. 'We intercepted the ransom letter and a cassette tape at the sorting office,' he said.

Again, the spelling and grammatical errors belong to the abductor.

> *Your employee has been kidnapped and will be released for a ransome of £175,000. With a little luck he should be O.K. and unharmed, to prove this fact you will in the next day or so receive a recorded message from him. He will be released on Friday 31 January 1992 provided:*
> *1) On Wednesday 29 January a ransome of £175,000 is paid, and no extension to this date will be granted.*
> *2) The police are not informed in any way until he has been released...*
>
> *The money must be carried in a holdall and made up as follows precisely: £75,000 in used £50. £75,000 in used £20. £25,000 in used £10 packed in 31 bundles. 250 notes in each.*
>
> *Kevin Watts (if not the hostage) must be the person to receive all messages and carry the money to the appointed place. However, please note that all messages will be pre-recorded, and no communication or negotiations can be made.*
>
> *YOU HAVE BEEN WARNED. HIS LIFE IS IN YOUR HANDS.*

A plain audio-cassette was clicked into a machine on the desk. Stephanie's voice filled the room sounding apprehensive but not fearful. She recited a prepared message from the kidnapper. In the silence that followed I could almost hear the questions before they were asked. However, before I could answer them, I needed a quiet space to look for the writer behind the letter.

I knew that each hour that passed increased the risk to Stephanie and made the news blackout more difficult to sustain, yet I couldn't afford to rush. The experience of others had already shown me the dangers of giving advice to the police that was so wide of the mark that it could point them in completely the wrong direction. Even a small error at this point could lead to Stephanie being murdered.

Unwilling to take such a risk, I sat down and began studying the letter, confident that the author would reveal himself, not only on the page but in the structure of the crime itself. I had to absorb his method in as much detail as I could, and map it onto the psychological understandings we have of personality and motivation. It took several hours, going over the chronology again and again but finally I was sure. I had met this mind before. The author was the same man who had murdered Julie Dart and tried to extort money from British Rail.

It was flagged by the same degree of planning, intelligence and arrogant tone. The spelling and grammatical mistakes in the letter were similar, as was the careful way the money had to be packaged. Clearly, the abduction had been set up over time and scrupulously planned with a richness of behavioural colour. The suggestion that a male employee had been his intended victim was an attempt at camouflage, but not good enough. It was inconsistent with the other detailed aspects of the planning. In both cases, Julie and Stephanie had been forced to send messages to confirm the kidnapping.

'You're sure it's the same man?' asked Jenkins.

'Virtually certain. I'd say better than ninety-five per cent.'

'Is he serious?'

'Very serious.'

'Will he kill Stephanie?'

'If he thinks it's necessary. He killed Julie Dart to make just that point, and he's already taken a greater risk this time. He let himself be seen at Shipways when he made the appointment.'

'Could Stephanie be dead already?'

'No, he'll try to keep her alive for proof of life; to record another message.'

Thomas asked, 'Does that mean he plans to kill her in the end?'

'That depends on what you do and it depends on Stephanie. He knows the police will get involved and he knows that Stephanie will be able to identify him.'

I explained that a great deal hinged on how she reacted to her abductor. Some people become very compliant when shocked and if Stephanie had been passive and respectful it could appeal to him and make it less likely that he harmed her.

These were only preliminary comments and I needed to learn far more about Stephanie to better predict her behaviour and establish if there was any particular reason why she had been chosen.

Although there was a hunger to lay hands on the kidnapper, everything gave way to two main priorities – keeping Stephanie Slater alive and getting her back safely.

When I called Marilyn I couldn't tell her what had happened because of the news blackout.

'What about your food?' she asked.

'We'll manage,' I said, eyeing an unappetizing plate of sandwiches.

'When will I see you?'

'I'll call you.'

* * *

Over the next few days I got to know the incident room well, staying until late at night. My main contact was Superintendent Tom Farr, who kept me briefed about the various leads being followed.

On Sunday afternoon, Stephanie's father, Warren, received a telephone call at home. In a recorded message his daughter said she was unharmed and she gave the score of a soccer match played the previous day. Then she said, 'I want you to know I love you. I'm not to say too much, and, whatever the outcome, I'll always love you. Look after the cat for me.'

Only four days remained before the ransom had to be paid and talk now turned to what the police should do. Shipways' parent company Royal Life Estates had happily provided the money but questions still had to be answered. With a young woman's life at stake, there was no talk of heroics or jeopardizing her safety. The police would follow Kevin Watts on the ransom trail, make the drop, and then follow the extortionist back to his hideout and to Stephanie.

There was discussion about putting tracing devices with the money but the police had no way of knowing if the kidnapper was bluffing about his technical knowledge or use of gadgetry to scan for such devices. It wasn't worth the risk. Other ideas included replacing Kevin Watts with an undercover officer, or hiding detectives in his car. One by one these were ruled out.

From what I knew of this man's planning and expertise, it was possible that he'd construct a bargaining lever in case of capture such as claiming that Stephanie had only a limited air supply or no warm clothing. Weighed against this was my belief that he was so cocky and self-assured he wouldn't even consider the possibility of being caught.

It was agreed that Kevin Watts would make the drop, travelling alone. He'd be wired with a radio transmitter and more than fifty RCS officers would shadow his every move from the air and the ground.

Thomas asked me what the courier could expect. There were several possible scenarios, but the most likely was that the extortionist would give him a complex set of instructions taking him through hoops and roundabouts, from phone box to phone box, stretching police manpower to the limit.

One of two things would then happen – either the extortionist would intervene very quickly in the process, hoping to catch the police off guard, or he would take them on the long run, dragging them backwards and forwards over a considerable distance. Traffic around

Birmingham and the West Midlands was normally quite heavy and travelling times unpredictable, so I reasoned that he'd take the second option – the long run.

Looking at a map of his past movements, I thought the drop would be in the northern part of the triangle, a less populated area. Once he felt that the police had been lulled into a pattern of going from one phone box to another, he would intervene suddenly in between two sets of instructions. He'd create a diversion, block a road or force Kevin's car to pull over.

One of the last things I said was, 'Remember the bridges and disused railway tracks.'

At 3.35 p.m. on Wednesday 29 January, Kevin Watts picked up the telephone at Shipways Estate Agents. With the money in a holdall in the boot of his car he drove north along the M6, by-passing Manchester and then taking the A57 to Glossop railway station fifteen miles east of Manchester. At 7.00 p.m. a telephone call directed him to a nearby kiosk where an envelope had been taped under the shelf.

I was at home but my thoughts were with Kevin on his lonely drive. He could talk to the police in Birmingham on a two-way radio, relaying the instructions which were then passed on to the various cars and motorcyclists discreetly following him.

But there was a problem. Fog had rolled in and was growing thicker by the minute. Travelling the unfamiliar back-roads, Kevin had to cut his speed to a crawl. With difficulty, he found the various telephone boxes, each time collecting new instructions that finally led him to a remote Pennine track near Oxspring in South Yorkshire.

The radio link was breaking up due to the fog and Kevin recited the various messages, hoping the police could hear him. Visibility was down to five yards when, following instructions, he stopped at a red and white traffic cone and transferred the money into a waiting holdall. A message inside gave directions to take it to another telephone box, but this was merely a ploy.

Within a hundred yards, Kevin spied another traffic cone in the centre of the track and a large cardboard sign.

STOP
60 secs allowed.
On wall by (4) sign > wood tray > do not move tray sensor

inside > put money & bag on tray > if buzzer does not sound leave money there > remove cone in front of car and go > money will not be collected until you have left.

Leaving the money on a wooden tray resting on the parapet of a bridge, Kevin drove away still desperately trying to make radio contact with the police. The trailing police cars had no way of knowing about the drop. By the time they arrived on the bridge all that was left was the traffic cone, a spray-painted number '4' and a thin layer of sand on the parapet where the tray had rested.

The kidnapper, hiding thirty feet below on a disused railway line, had simply pulled on a rope attached to the tray and the money came tumbling down. Then he escaped along the track on a motorcycle. The tortuous 110-mile, four-hour surveillance operation had been a disaster. The fog had fouled up everything.

What would happen to Stephanie Slater?

Four hours later, a thirty-two-year-old spray painter who lived with his wife and two children in Bowstoke Road, Great Barr, heard a car pull up outside his house and the engine revving. Looking out of the bedroom window he saw a vermilion red Mini Metro with a couple inside. A woman got out and stumbled up the road, looking drunk and disorientated.

A few minutes later Warren Slater opened the front door and Stephanie stumbled into his arms.

I was telephoned that morning and told of the ransom drop. The initial panic and sense of shock of having lost the blackmailer had dissipated because Stephanie was home safe and well. The police were thrilled and I shared their sense of relief. Yet when I heard how the kidnapper had collected the ransom, I cursed myself and promised that if it ever happened again I would insist on being in the control room.

The fog couldn't have been predicted but I knew about the bridges and disused railway lines playing an important part in this man's planning. If I had been there I would have suggested to the police that they compare each new set of instructions with maps that showed nearby railway bridges and disused railway lines. Surveillance teams could have staked them out and, perhaps, picked up the kidnapper despite the fog.

The important thing now was to debrief Stephanie to discover every detail of her time in captivity. Psychologists often use a process known as 'cognitive interviewing' which is designed to slowly take the subject back and put them at a scene, asking them to describe the events in different sequences, exploring the minutiae of sights, sounds, smells and textures.

Although I wasn't asked to interview Stephanie, a few months earlier, I'd used the process with a twelve-year-old girl who had been abducted and brutally raped as she walked home from school.

The local CID had asked for a psychological profile of her attacker, but when I read Chloe's original statement there wasn't enough information to draw any firm conclusions. I needed to know everything possible about her assailant, his vehicle, the journey, what was said and what was done.

But how could we access this? Chloe was obviously traumatized and we had to balance her interests with those of the inquiry. This pervert could attack another girl and next time might kill her.

Her mother and father disagreed on what should be done. Seeing her pain, one of them wanted Chloe to be left alone, while the other could see great strength in her and was determined to catch the man responsible. Finally, it was agreed to go ahead and I chose to interview her at her home to give her at least some feeling of security.

The technique I used involved cognitive interviewing combined with deep relaxation and as Chloe lay on the settee with her eyes closed and her hands in her lap, I explained that I was going to take her back to what had happened; that I knew it hurt very, very much but that I'd try not to hurt her any more.

'If I ask you to tell me something that makes you feel upset or frightened, you should lift the fingers on your left hand, like this, and I'll stop and give you some time.' I showed her. 'If I go too quickly or make you feel confused, you should lift the fingers on your right hand and I'll go back over things more slowly.'

We practised relaxation and visualization for a while, until she grew comfortable with the knowledge that she had control of the interview. It wasn't a question of me saying, 'Now, be a brave little girl and tell me what the bad man did to you.' We tackled it together, overcoming some of the hurt, skirting the obstacles and piecing together memories that she had tried to block out.

We began the journey together. The first trawl was hers, without interruption. Inexperienced interviewers are tempted to enter into the narrative flow too soon with questions or requests for more detail. By letting her establish the full area over which the story ranged we found new information which direct questioning had missed. Only when she froze with stress did I use the gentle prompt, 'It's all right to be frightened, anyone would be. Just rest for a moment before you carry on.'

Later, on other more detailed trawls, the horror was replayed in front of me. She had been blindfolded, but ineffectively and was able to see beneath it.

'You said that he hurt you when the car had stopped and he came round to the boot. Can you try to say how he hurt you?'

'He held my tummy with one hand and rubbed and squeezed my bottom and, and . . . then . . . he . . .', she stopped, all four fingers on her left hand raised. Her small body stiffened and I could see her heart was racing.

'Chloe, you're safe at home now, Mummy and Daddy are in the kitchen, they won't let anyone else hurt you. Just rest with your eyes closed for a moment. When you feel better raise your fingers again, and, if it's all right, we'll carry on. But I'm not going to ask you again today to remember what the man did to you, I want you to look out from under the blindfold and tell me about his hands. Were they smooth and soft, were they scratchy and rough or were they in-between?'

She settled, moments passed. I wasn't sure if she had blocked it all out and cut herself off from me. Then, so very quietly, 'They were soft, with ginger hair on the back.'

'Please look carefully, does he have any rings on his fingers?' I can only use the tone of my voice to comfort her, and make sure that I keep the full length of the room between us to reduce any fear that being physically close to another man, so soon, might elicit. Yet I must not offer any cue which might guide her answer. Unless I can hold her there between the sensory re-examination of her ordeal and the cocoon of safety at home, the opportunity will be lost and her repeated discomfort without purpose. Again a long wait.

'Yes, one like Daddy's.'

Slowly the sequence became clearer and much more detailed. Eventually she was able to hear tyres running over gravel. Through a gap in the boot she could see a row of street lights and place these in relation to periods stopped at traffic lights and a remote lane close to motorway traffic. She was able to give a description of the rear-light assembly on the car which allowed the make of vehicle to be narrowed down significantly. Finally her description of her attacker developed to include which hand he favoured, his eyes, lower face, vocabulary and a more accurate placing of his accent.

The same level of detail had to be gleaned from Stephanie Slater. If she didn't see his face did she see his hands? How long did the journey take, were the roads windy or straight? Something as outwardly insignificant as the hour pips on a radio or the inflection of a spoken word, could prove vital.

Over the next week, police motorcycle couriers delivered material to my home almost daily. Stephanie proved a brilliant interview subject and could remember the black hairs on the back of her kidnapper's hands and the way he pronounced the Ks and Ts at the end of words. Although blindfolded throughout, she knew that her prison had an old-fashioned dial telephone and a radio tuned to BBC Radio. The doorbell sounded like a cash register ringing.

Because she'd seen her attacker when they met at the house, she could also give a police artist a good description of what he looked like and what he'd been wearing. There was a train motif on the breast pocket of his duffel-type coat.

She'd been attacked while showing him the bathroom upstairs. Turning, she saw him holding a knife in one hand and a sharpened file in the other. 'I panicked and started to scream and it all happened very quickly. It was very frightening and I was just shouting and screaming,' she said.

He pushed her into the bath, tied her hands, put black plastic glasses on her eyes so she couldn't see and bound more rope around her throat. Then he led her like a dog downstairs and outside to his car which had the passenger seat fully reclined.

When she arrived at their destination, possibly after dark, she was taken from the car, into a building and tied to a chair. After feeding her chips, the kidnapper made Stephanie change into clothes that he provided and then put handcuffs secured with chains on her legs and hands.

'I hope you're not claustrophobic because you're going in a box within a box,' he said and then made her slide into the coffin-like container. It was very tight and she had to turn sideways to reach the bottom. He told her that there were boulders on top of the box and that if she moved they would come down on top of her. He said he had also placed electrodes around the sides so that if she tried to escape she'd be electrocuted.

This had been Stephanie's prison for the next seven days.

Reading through the interview transcripts, I was quite confident that there were two things which had kept Stephanie alive. This man didn't have the Raffles-like image that he wanted to convey; he'd come across in the press as being a cold-blooded killer and he didn't care for that. Secondly, Stephanie had been so shocked by what happened to her, she became passive and yielding. This made her more attractive to a man who got a buzz out of being in control. Without these two factors, I'm sure that another body would have been found dumped in a field.

After Stephanie's return, Tom Cook asked me if she was still in any danger or if the kidnapper was likely to make contact with Shipways again. I said there was a very good chance he would. Stephanie had become important to him and we could never forget his primary motivation. Even if he went quiet for while, he'd come back because he loved the game.

When the media blackout was lifted, the headlines proved embarrassing for the police and I was surprised at how the media reacted and at the criticisms that were made. After all, Stephanie was safe and that had always been the top priority.

At a press conference in Birmingham, ACC Tom Cook, who had overall charge of the joint inquiry, revealed the link with Julie Dart's murder. He described several of the similarities between the crimes and mentioned that the man's main motivation had not been the money.

When pressed further, Cook said, 'Well, we'll have to see what Paul Britton has to say about that.'

It was the first time my name had ever been publicly mentioned in relation to any criminal investigation. The reaction was immediate and Cook realized that he'd made a mistake. As more questions followed, the leak couldn't be shored up.

That afternoon a press officer from Leeds telephoned to apologize. 'We're awfully sorry,' she said. 'We made a mistake during the press conference.'

It didn't take journalists long to track me down and by that evening the telephone was ringing and didn't stop. Psychological profiling became a new angle on the hottest story of the year and my carefully guarded anonymity was shattered.

Each time I was asked to give a comment or an interview, I politely declined. 'Perhaps when he's been caught and convicted,' I said, hoping to fob them off. Meanwhile, the newspaper accounts portrayed me as being locked in a battle of wits with a madman. I cringed and gave up reading the papers.

The inquiry had fresh impetus thanks to Stephanie's amazing recall and slowly the police began closing the net. A very good artist's impression had been drawn up and, if necessary, they had tape recordings of the killer's voice.

During the drive back to Birmingham, although blindfolded, Stephanie had talked to her kidnapper, who counted down the miles and told her when they were getting close. Based on the descriptions and times involved, they had narrowed the offender's territory to a small triangle of A-roads in Lincolnshire. A team of detectives moved into a small hotel just over the Nottinghamshire border, ready to move quickly.

On 7 February a letter posted in the Sheffield area arrived at Millgarth Police Station in Leeds. Copies had also been sent to West Midlands police, Mrs Lynn Dart, the *News of the World*, the *Sun*, Yorkshire TV and BBC TV.

The three pages read like a plea of mitigation or the beginning of a killer's defence.

The facts.

I, being the kidnapper of Stephanie Slater, am not the killer of Julie Dart. It is impossible that there can be any positive connection between the two cases.

I am also not the person who idiotically tried to blackmail B.R. the idear was a variation on an idear I had discussed with another, I now believe that he may have used my word processor to make his demands. The reason for the sudden cessation of communications between B.R. and the other, was my intervention when I learned with horror that he was to use my idears about picking up the ransome monies.

It could have been to my advantage to allow the police to continue to believe that the cases are all connected, but my concers are for Stephanie and her parents, and how they must be now feeling after reading the reports. I promised and gave my word to Stephanie on a few things, and with only one exception I kept them. Some of the promises were; a) I had not killed before, b) Provided she did not remove her blindfold she would be released and not harmed in any way, both at that time or any time in the future . . .

> *The fact that I knew, could, and did carry out the crime extremely successfully is my only satisfaction, I am ashamed upset and thoroughly disgusted at my treatment of Stephanie and the suffering I must have caused to her parents . . . even now my eyes still fill with tears, I wake up during the night actually crying, with a little luck Stephanie will get over it shortly. Myself? I do not think I ever will.*
>
> *Sorry Stephanie. Sorry Mr & Mrs Slater . . .*

The letter ended with the bold statement: 'This case will never come to court as I have contingency plans should the police be two steps behind.'

Clearly he felt threatened; the artist's impression had scared him and suddenly he feared for his freedom. He didn't want a murder charge yet even his plea of innocence contained damning evidence that he was Julie's killer. In the letter to West Yorkshire police he'd written 'Millgate' instead of 'Millgarth' – exactly the same mistake that had appeared on the letter sent to Leeds the previous October which began 'Re Julie (with no hair)'.

There were also similar grammatical errors and spelling mistakes.

Psychologically, he was feeling hunted and feigning contrition as if constructing a defence for himself. He hadn't expected Stephanie's kidnapping to create such enormous publicity or for detectives to link him with Julie Dart's murder.

The pressure continued to tell and on 20 February he made a call to Shipways and asked to speak to Sylvia Baker. On hearing the voice, she pressed a button alerting the Nechells Green police station.

The kidnapper said, 'I'm the person who kidnapped Stephanie. Stephanie and you are the only two persons that can identify me and Stephanie won't because she knows what will happen. Do you understand?'

That same evening *Crimewatch UK* and the ITV late evening news were both planning to broadcast a tape-recording of the kidnapper's voice. It would be heard by an audience of more than fifteen million viewers, who would also hear details of where the man was believed to live and what car he drove.

Fifty telephone lines had been set up in three adapted incident rooms to take the expected flood of calls. Among them was a message from Susan Oake of Keighley, West Yorkshire, who had videoed the programme and watched it when she returned home that night.

She phoned the incident room, convinced she recognized the kidnapper's voice. It was her ex-husband Michael Sams who ran a power-tool repair business from a workshop in the Swan and Salmon yard at Newark.

This news was flashed to Bingham Police Station and a surveillance operation began the following morning. Background checks confirmed that Sams owned an orange Austin Metro, had minor convictions for deception and fraud and was a keen trainspotter and railway enthusiast. In fact, Sams, fifty-one, seemed to have only one major drawback as a suspect – he had only one leg.

Shortly before midday on 21 February, four officers walked into the workshop and, with only the briefest glimpse of the interior, they knew he was their man.

The picture that emerged of Michael Sams fitted almost perfectly with the psychological profile that had been drawn up many months earlier. He was *the nearly man*, who never quite made it. A promising athlete in his youth, he had had to have his leg amputated because of cancer. All three of his marriages had failed, as had his numerous business ventures. Every time he became successful, a poor decision destroyed the hard work.

Intelligent and good with his hands, he spent three years in the Merchant Navy before leaving and doing a variety of jobs such as installing lift equipment and central-heating systems. He was sentenced to nine months in jail in April 1978 for deception and fraud after stealing and respraying an MG Midget and putting on false number plates. Cancer was diagnosed in prison and surgeons took off his right leg below the knee.

He resented how life had treated him and knew he was capable of much more. Who was to blame? Certainly not himself. With money being tight and his third marriage in trouble, he began planning how to show his talents.

Upon his arrest, Sams was taken to Newark Police Station and Tom Cook decided that West Midlands would have first crack at interrogating him because Sams readily admitted to kidnapping Stephanie. Then it would be West Yorkshire's turn to probe the murder of Julie Dart.

Meanwhile, forensic experts began stripping the workshop and their discoveries would later prove vital in linking the suspect to all of the crimes. Fibres from the navy trousers he was wearing when arrested matched those found in a blackmail letter sent to British Rail. Fibres in the workshop also linked Sams to the rope and sheet used to wrap up Julie's body and diluted blood on an old curtain almost certainly came from her.

From the outset it was clear that Sams hadn't given up playing the game. The smoke, the lies, the false trails and exaggerations were on display as he pulled interviewers one way and then the other. He picked up on every ambiguity in the police case and played on the weaknesses, inventing scenarios which involved an accomplice who had supposedly been paid £20,000.

How else did I do it? challenged Sams, pointing to his artificial leg. He claimed his motor scooter didn't fit in the Austin Metro and that he couldn't have left all the ransom notes in the given time. Of course, he wouldn't name the alleged accomplice and it was clearly another ploy designed to confuse and exasperate.

He even played games within games, jotting down numbers on scraps of paper and making sure the police found them. Hours were then spent questioning him about whether these were map references for the buried ransom. Sams would smile and say nothing.

By the time he was transferred to Millgarth Police Station, Bob Taylor and his team knew the difficulties that confronted them in interrogating him in connection with the murder of Julie Dart. Taylor asked me to look at the videotapes from Birmingham, to see if I could suggest an interview strategy. They had three days before Sams had to be produced in court again.

I arrived late in the evening and had dinner with Bob Taylor and the interview team in the police canteen, sipping tea from cups embossed with the West Yorkshire coat of arms. Talk shifted to whether Sams was likely to make any admissions about Julie.

'He's not going to make a confession,' I said, 'at least not before he's convicted. He's still playing the game and thinks he's cleverer than you are.'

It didn't come as a surprise. Afterwards we gathered in a small stuffy room crammed with technical equipment such as video and audio machines. Someone slid in an interview tape from Birmingham and Michael Sams flickered into view. I'd known him for a long while, but this was the first time I'd ever seen his face.

The time-coded video image showed him sitting casually in the interview room, dressed in a white open-necked shirt and trousers. He didn't look particularly confident but neither was he anxious. The initial shock of having been caught was still evident – he didn't think the police were capable of catching him but had been proved wrong.

His pale face was relatively expressionless but he sat in a posture consistent with trying to hold things in, rather than completely laying them out. He continually denied killing Julie Dart or blackmailing British Rail and I could see him working hard to create an intellectual space for himself so that he could take control of the game again.

Sams didn't want to be seen as a cold calculating killer; he wanted to be the intellectually dazzling and successful villain, like Cary Grant in *To Catch a Thief.* The only way he could account for the bloody evil was to say that somebody else was responsible.

This, however, created problems for the interviewers. How did they counter someone who constantly tried to lay the blame on an accomplice?

'Understand that this is a fiction,' I said. 'But you can let him maintain it because in doing so you can still draw out all of the details that could only be known by the person who killed Julie Dart. When you have all of these, then you can work on destroying the accomplice theory.

'He will never admit that he's lying but unwittingly he will give you the details that you can put before a jury. Then they can decide how this man has all this intimate knowledge.'

I warned that Sams would try to control the interview by acknowledging that he abducted Stephanie Slater and talking of his remorse, while at the same time repudiating entirely that he had anything to do with Julie's murder. They had to keep him on track but not with aggression or anger.

'Status is important to Sams. He has to believe the people on the other side of the table have the intellect to understand and play the game. If he thinks you're worthy of him, he'll be far more forthcoming but if he feels you lack confidence or are simply going through the motions, he won't play.'

For any of this to work the preparation was of almost exquisite importance. It was *the* single factor that would determine whether Sams would convict himself or not. The interviewers needed to have an intimate knowledge of the crimes and the inquiry; they had to prepare themselves not just in rough outline terms, but with the actual questions they were going to ask. And then for each of his likely answers they had to have more questions and so on, and so on. They were collecting a web of detail that would eventually snare their suspect.

In the meantime, forensic experts were tying up every loose end. Reconstructions were filmed to show that the motor scooter could fit in the back of Sams' Austin Metro, as could the large wheelie bin used for transporting Julie's body. Traces of paint were found that confirmed the scooter had been in the car.

Sams wrote his later letters to the police and Shipways on a word processor rather than an old Olivetti typewriter. He had deleted the files but failed to realize that they could still be retrieved from a 'limbo' section of the computer's memory. He had also tried to create an alibi for himself for the day Julie disappeared, claiming he was trainspotting at a rail marshalling yard near Nottingham and cataloguing photographs to support this. However, a check of rail time-tables showed that the trains he'd photographed were not in the yard that day.

Three days after being transferred to Leeds, Michael Sams was charged with the kidnap and murder of Julie Dart. One final mystery remained: where had he hidden the ransom money?

9

ON THE MORNING OF 28 JULY, 1992, I FOUND A MESSAGE ON MY DESK. 'Paul Britton, Please call Superintendent John Bassett, Wimbledon police station.' Underneath, my secretary Diane had written: 'Does this mean I clear your diary for tomorrow?'

I slid the note into my jacket pocket and bemoaned my crowded life. How would I find time to go to London? Already my day-to-day NHS work had backed up and it would take a month of weekends to clear. I also had two court reports to finish for the Crown, a solicitor waiting on a psychological analysis of his client and a particularly distressed young woman who needed treatment.

'If you want something done, give it to a busy man,' is how the saying goes. Somehow, I had to try and squeeze a few extra hours out of most days.

When I met John Bassett, I was immediately struck by his quiet voice and gentle face. His hair had long ago turned silver, leaving his eyebrows a bushy black. Typically, he wore a dark suit and plain white shirt with a wide floral tie that might have been a Father's Day present.

The incident room at Wimbledon Police Station was barely larger than an average sitting room, crammed with telexes, phones and computer terminals. White boards lined the walls, listing the names of investigating officers and the computer codes that showed what leads they were following up. Nearby, a large pictorial map of Wimbledon Common was covered with sticky yellow notes.

The first seventy-two hours of a murder investigation are usually the most important, but when the killer is a stranger, or the planning is particularly complex, the search is destined to be far more difficult. Thirteen days had now passed yet there was still an amazing sense of purpose in the room. Stained coffee cups competed for space with well-used ashtrays and take-away sandwich wrappers. No-one seemed to want to go home.

Bassett led me down a hallway, stopping to pick up a cup of tea. Detective Chief Inspector Mick Wickerson appeared at his shoulder. Younger and less careworn, he was one of the first officers to arrive at the murder scene and wasn't likely to forget it. There are some bodies that you never get out of your mind.

John Bassett set down his tea and leaned against a desk. Wickerson found a chair near the window.

'The victim was a twenty-three-year-old woman, Rachel Nickell,' Bassett said, toying with his tie. 'She's a very beautiful girl, murdered in a horrible way. The public response to this is something I haven't seen before. I'm surprised you haven't seen the papers.

'Rachel lived with her boyfriend, Andre Hanscombe, in a two-bedroom flat in Elmfield Mansions, Balham. He's a motorcycle messenger in the City and left for work at eight-thirty a.m. on Wednesday the fifteenth of July.

'Rachel left the flat fifteen minutes later to take her son Alex and their pet dog for a walk on Wimbledon Common.' He glanced at Wickerson. 'How old is the young one?'

'Barely two.'

He slid a map across the table. 'The Common is about a thousand acres of open fields and woodland. It's public parkland – used for walking, golf, picnics, horse-riding, you know the sort of thing.

'She was an attractive girl,' pondered Bassett, almost to himself. 'She only recently started using Wimbledon Common because she'd been approached by men on Clapham Common and Tooting Bec which are closer to her home. She thought Wimbledon would be safer.' The irony in his voice was obvious. 'She went there about four times a week; letting Alex play outdoors and giving the dog some exercise. On this morning she was wearing blue jeans, a grey t-shirt and brown boots.'

Using a pen, he pointed to a windmill on the eastern edge of the Common. 'This is where she parked her silver Volvo estate some time before ten a.m. At some point she began walking along this path. We have a witness who says he saw Rachel and Alex at exactly ten twenty a.m. walking between the car-park and Windmill Wood. That's where the attack occurred, about five hundred yards from the car-park – where the pathway runs through a lightly wooded area. It's not exactly hidden but it does provide privacy from long-range view.

'Her body was found about twelve feet from the path . . .'

Mick Wickerson interrupted, 'He went berserk . . . he must have thought he almost took her head clean off. What sort of . . . ?' He didn't finish.

Bassett glanced at the photographs. 'As you can see, there was no attempt to hide the body. The next person on the path found her.'

'What about the little boy?'

Bassett replied, 'He wasn't hurt but we think he witnessed the attack. He's barely uttered a word since they found him at ten thirty-five a.m. trying to wake his mother up.'

'He's going to need help,' I said.

'Yeah. He's getting it.'

A ring-bound set of photographs slid across the desk towards me. The colour prints ran in a sequence of wide-angle shots starting with long range views of the woodland copse. Rachel's body was barely visible – showing up as a splash of white amongst the trees that could have been a discarded shopping bag.

Finally the lens moved closer, zeroing in and revealing it from every conceivable angle. There could be no dignity or privacy about the process. Rachel Nickell, lifeless and near naked, was captured by the camera. No matter how much was done later to restore her dignity, for the next few days or weeks she became the most important piece of evidence in the investigation.

I knew the procedure. Every square inch would be photographed, scraped, swabbed or cut open. Body fluids, fingernail dirt and pubic hair would be sealed in plastic or glass and then be passed, hand to hand, along the evidential chain; from pathologist to the laboratory, to the prosecution, to the court and to the jury. Violent death becomes a very public event.

'What's this?' I asked, pointing to a close-up photograph of Rachel's face. A piece of paper, folded once, was lying on her right temple.

'I was hoping you could tell us that,' said Bassett. 'It's a bank notification giving the PIN (Personal Identification Number) for Rachel's account. Maybe she was carrying it with her, but we can't work out how it finished up where it did. We don't know what it means.'

It didn't make sense. Even if the note had fallen out of Rachel's jeans during the struggle, how did it get on her face? The attack was so swift and violent, it was almost impossible for it to have fluttered there accidentally. It stood out as a deliberate act, but why?

'SOCO (the Scene of Crime Officer responsible for logging any physical clues) found nothing that the lab could work with,' said Bassett. 'No blood, semen, saliva, hair samples . . . nothing. The murder weapon was probably a single-edged sheath knife with a brass hilt. We haven't found it.'

'So he left no evidence of himself?'

Wickerson replied, 'There was a shoe-print in the mud that could be important; also a few interesting witness statements. There were about a hundred people in the general area at the time. We're working through them and so far two people recall seeing a man washing his hands in a stream about a hundred and fifty yards from the scene.'

'Tell me about him?'

'It was by Curling Pond,' he said, pointing to the map. 'He's in his twenties or thirties, something like five feet ten inches tall, with short brown hair . . .'

I interrupted, 'Don't worry about the physical details, they're your department. I want to know how he looked? Was he running, was he frightened, was he anxious?'

'I'd say agitated,' said Bassett. 'He was carrying a bag and washing his hands. Another witness saw a man running towards a council estate in Norstead Place, in Wandsworth. The description is different – he might have been a jogger.'

'Tell me about the shoe-prints?'

Wickerson said, 'We took a single print from the path.'

'Do you have anything matching Rachel or Alex?'

'No.'

'What about elsewhere – in the grass – are there any other prints that don't show up in the photographs that take us from the path to the body?'

Wickerson shook his head.

'OK. You said Alex wasn't hurt. No bruises or scratches . . .'

'He was covered in mud. We think he may have been pushed to the ground.'

I began flicking through the post-mortem records.

'The bastard left us bugger all,' said Bassett.

'Sweet F.A.,' echoed his colleague.

I understood their dilemma. They had a killer who had left very few clues behind and a crime that had outraged the country. The newspaper stories were florid in detail and not always correct. Women were terrified to use Wimbledon Common and other public parks. So much so that one local women's group had actually offered a donation of £400,000 to help fund the investigation. The money could have been well spent but, of course, the police had to turn it down.

The investigation team had, however, enlisted the help of HOLMES (Home Office Large Major Enquiry System) a computer facility for classifying, storing and cross-referencing the tens of thousands of pieces of information collected during such an inquiry. The system had only been available since 1987 when the hunt for the Yorkshire Ripper had exposed the dangers of important information being buried under a mountain of paperwork. It became clear that the Ripper, Peter Sutcliffe, would have emerged as a strong suspect much earlier if there had been a computer system that highlighted the numerous points at which his name appeared in relation to the murders.

'Tell me about Wimbledon Common?' I asked Bassett.

'What can I say? We get flashers and nuisances, but nothing like this . . . not until now. We're looking at the usual categories – sex assaults, voyeurism, flashing. Also any complaints from the Common, and sex offenders with a history of using the park who might recently have been released from prison.'

'What about the surrounding area?'

Wickerson raised an eyebrow.

'I need as much detail as possible – not just from the Common but outside it. Look for odd events or strange complaints.'

Bassett said, 'We'll do that for you.'

Over the next hour I listened to a day-by-day account of the investigation and collected copies of statements, photographs, the post-mortem, maps and a home video of Rachel. These I would study later. John Bassett was clearly fascinated by the principles of psychological profiling. I learned that his interest dated back to an earlier case when he led the hunt for a baby abducted from St Thomas's Hospital in London. He had reasoned that the abductor would have a link with the hospital – either as a nurse or an out-patient. The assumption proved correct and the baby had been found safe and well.

That was one of the happier cases. Although he'd handled dozens of investigations over thirty years, few were as brutal as Rachel Nickell's murder. Now only a year away from retirement, Bassett badly wanted to close the file on this one. There were no promotions on offer or points to be scored – he simply wanted a killer off the streets.

He cleared his throat. 'I'm always optimistic, Paul, but my pool of suspects is seventeen and a half million – every male over twelve. We have to narrow the field.'

'All right,' I said. 'Firstly, I need to learn everything I can about Rachel, herself. What sort of person was she? Did she have a job? What were her routines? Was she streetwise and perceptive or was she naive? When confronted by a stranger would she tend to be reserved or would she smile and make eye contact? Was she likely to resist if threatened or attacked? Was she aggressive and likely to ridicule people? What relationships did she have? Did she have any other boyfriends? Did any previous affairs end badly? Did she ever work as a prostitute or was she sexually promiscuous . . . ?'

These were routine questions.

'She was a lovely girl,' said Bassett, a little defensively.

'What difference does it make?' asked Wickerson. 'She's dead. Haven't we got enough in the statements we've already taken?'

'No. I need to know Rachel as though she were sitting in the chair opposite. What's she going to say; what's she going to think; how's she going to respond to any given situation? Only when I know her, do I move a step closer to knowing her killer.

'Take, for example, a young woman who tends to be sexually provocative – not deliberately so, but unwittingly. She may draw sexual attention to herself due to her appearance and mannerisms. She may enjoy the feeling and when she walks past a strange man who takes an interest, she giggles and says, "Hello". This has very different implications than if the same young woman tends to be self-effacing and tries not to attract attention to herself or make any contact.

'Different women present different levels of vulnerability. Was Rachel a high-level risk victim or a low-level risk victim? If I know that, then I can begin to know how particular the killer was in choosing her.'

Bassett said, 'We haven't got all those answers.'

'Then please send someone to talk to her family and friends – particularly her parents and her boyfriend. Be careful of their bias; they will have filtered out any negatives. I want to know everything about her, but in fine detail – that's what makes the difference.'

Bassett said, 'You list the questions, I'll get the answers.'

Outside the heat shimmered off the concrete and asphalt. Pedestrians moved in slow motion amid the exhaust fumes and broken shade of shop awnings. The murder squad had provided me with a car and driver – a young detective who explained some of the local landmarks as we edged through the sluggish early afternoon traffic.

Pulling into the car-park beside the windmill made famous by Baden Powell, founder of the Boy Scouts, I gazed across the undulating fields and leafy woodland. Mick Wickerson took the lead and, with my jacket slung across my shoulder, I followed him along a dirt path baked dry in the heat. On the morning of the murder it had been muddy. Shuffling down a slight rise, we crossed open ground where every clump and hollow had been searched by police.

As I entered the shade of an enclosed woodland glade, I immediately noticed a deliberate misdirection. Detectives had identified a false murder location about thirty metres from the real scene, in order to keep the media and mourners at bay. Apart from the floral wreaths and cards left at the base of a nearby tree, it looked like a perfect picnic spot, dappled by sunshine and fanned by a slight breeze.

The glade had the feel of a marquee in a garden, cool and enclosed, and was far more private and secluded than I expected after having seen the photographs. It could never be exactly the same as it was on the morning of the murder – undergrowth had been cleared, along with leaf-litter and foliage during the search. This, of course, made the crime scene photographs vital because they were the abiding record of the scene.

A grassy hummock that overlooked the area was closer than I imagined. I didn't know if it was important, but it was definitely an ideal observation point where a person could sit, waiting and watching, as someone came down the path into the glade.

Mick Wickerson pointed things out to me, indicating where Alex's t-shirt had been found and also the shoe-print. Several times I walked down to the stream where a man had been seen washing his hands. How soon did a person become lost in the trees, I thought, as I watched detectives moving through the glade.

I was looking for the various potentials of the place; where the trees and undergrowth provided cover or vantage points. Depending on the motivation – be it the most innocent courting couple seeking privacy, or voyeurism, stalking, rape or murder – I could understand to what extent it was a suitable venue or otherwise. What I couldn't do – not yet, anyway – was to see it through the eyes of the killer and a terrified young woman about to die.

On the drive home I listened to the Radio 4 news which was dominated by Royal stories and the High Court libel trial involving journalist Jani Allan who was suing a TV station over claims that she had an affair with South Africa's neo-Nazi leader Eugene Terre Blanche.

Rachel didn't get mentioned. Her murder had been shunted to the back news pages, but not forgotten. Rarely has a crime generated so much publicity. A week before her murder, another young woman, Katie Ratcliffe, was stabbed to death in Hampshire. Two women, two stabbings – yet one captured the headlines and the other had barely been mentioned.

I could understand this. Rachel's attack had happened in daylight, in a public place used by hundreds of women and children every day. The only witness was an innocent child who would probably carry the mental scars for ever. A less obvious, but potent influence was the televising of home-videos showing Rachel laughing, smiling and playing with her baby. She came to life in people's awareness far more vividly than if her face had only appeared as a photograph in a newspaper.

Something else had elevated the murder above other crimes. It struck me the moment I heard where Rachel had died. Wimbledon Common has a special place in the minds and hearts of mothers and children. It's the fictional home of the Wombles – those lovable creatures of storybooks and TV – who made the Common a magical place for thousands upon thousands of people, young and old. Rachel's killer didn't just slaughter a young mother, he destroyed for ever the home of the Wombles; he defiled a piece of all our childhoods.

I thought about little Alex. Although barely two years old, he wouldn't suffer from total traumatic amnesia which would cloak his pain. He would remember his mother's screams and the sudden silence, but whether he would ever be able to retrieve this fully and put it into words was entirely another matter. The danger in drawing it out of him was that it could do further damage to his fragile mind.

That fact that he hadn't been killed or harmed was an important indicator. It demonstrated that Rachel had been the specific object of the attack.

Other questions plagued me, however. What on earth was the significance of the folded piece of paper on Rachel's temple? Why was it placed there and by whom? Had Rachel brought it with her, or did the killer have it? Was it left as a calling card, or a jest, or as part of some ritualistic need? It didn't fit.

Yet the biggest unknown was whether we were dealing with a repeat killer who would strike again. The chances were high. Even without a detailed analysis, it didn't look like a domestic murder dressed up, or an argument gone wrong, or a one-off episode caused by a psychotic disturbance that wouldn't happen again.

Assuming the worst case scenario, we were dealing with a violent sexual psychopath. But what time cycle did he operate on, a year, a month, a day? The clock was running and we had to get to him before he got to someone else.

Until John Bassett could answer my questions about Rachel there was little I could do but wait. In the meantime, I had to give evidence in a High Court case where a young woman claimed that she'd suffered a series of sexual assaults at a hostel in Derby.

The hostel employee had been arrested, interviewed and charged, however his principal defence argument was that Josephine, aged twenty-two, wasn't competent to give evidence before the court because she was severely handicapped and therefore no trial should take place. Her parents and the staff at the hostel were outraged – they couldn't accept that because a young woman was mentally handicapped she had no rights to make an allegation that she'd been raped. They argued, that if this was the case, then it was virtually an open licence for anybody to sexually abuse the mentally handicapped knowing that the law couldn't touch them. They even contacted their local MP Edwina Currie seeking help.

Eventually the police on behalf of the Crown Prosecution Service contacted me and asked me to examine Josephine so I could advise the court as to her competence or otherwise. I had to answer three questions: Could she distinguish right from wrong? Did she understand the concept of God, because she had to be invited to give an oath? And could she follow the process of a trial and instruct counsel?

My understanding was that if any of the answers were no, there could be no trial regardless of the evidence. But it wasn't my job to find her competent; my role was to advise the court and to be totally objective regardless of the pressure from family and friends.

It proved a difficult case. For one thing, Josephine's parents wished to support her during my examination, but that's not the way I work. Similarly, with so much anger and outrage evident, there was a genuine risk that people would unwittingly contaminate Josephine's knowledge of what might, or might not, have happened.

I sat down with Josephine, using a room at the hostel because the surroundings were familiar to her. She was fretful, sitting perched on the edge of an armchair with her hands fluttering like trapped birds.

'I want my mother,' she said tearfully.

'She's not gone far. She'll be back in a little while. I just need to talk to you. I'm not going to hurt you.'

'I didn't do anything. I've done nothing wrong.'

'I'm not saying you have, Josephine.'

She was anxious and defensive – common responses for people with learning difficulties when something around them is wrong. They feel they're going to be blamed or criticized.

I needed to use focussed patience with Josephine and to create a place where there was no sense of time. It didn't matter that work was piling up on my desk; or the drains at home were blocked – the only thing that counted was this young woman who, in the scheme of things, had never rated as a high priority. Let's face it, the alleged rape of a grossly handicapped twenty-two-year-old woman doesn't make national headlines or the TV news. If she'd been the local beauty queen it would have been different.

Josephine's handicap was such that I had to somehow construct verbal exchanges that were accessible to her. She had to be able to understand and cope. At the same time, my questions had to be entirely neutral in tone and suggestibility. I had to find the answers without contaminating her memory of events.

But most importantly, I needed to keep an open mind. Without it, I may as well not have been there.

When Josephine had relaxed a little, I began by trying to discover if she understood the concept of God. The questions had to be carefully framed. I couldn't ask her, 'Who is God?' because that would have suggested that God is some sort of person.

'Please tell me about God,' I asked.

Josephine said, 'God lives in Heaven.'

(So she knew it was a place and that God was a living being.)

'Where is Heaven?'

'It's where you go when you die.'

'Does everyone go to Heaven?'

'My gran went to Heaven. She wasn't bad.'

(The implication being that you can't go to Heaven if you're bad.)

'How does God know if you should go to Heaven?'

'He can always see you. He knows what you're doing.'

(She had the notion of God being aware of what individuals are doing.)

'Now Josephine, I have to tell the judge if you know what is right and what is wrong.'

There was a silence.

'Tell me what doing something right is.'

'I'm not naughty.'

'What does someone do when they're naughty?'

'I'm not naughty.'

The questions were too abstract for her. She wasn't capable of giving a definition of right and wrong. Gently, I began again, using examples.

'Have you got a handbag?'

'Yes.'

'If you took it would that be wrong?'

'That's not wrong.'

'What would happen if someone else took your handbag?'

'Well that's wrong. It's mine. It's wrong for them to take it.'

'What would happen if you took someone else's handbag?'

'That's wrong. That's not mine. I'm not naughty, I didn't take anybody's handbag.'

It was clear that Josephine had a simple but real concept of right and wrong. It was also clear that she was extremely anxious and frightened of disapproval.

In the witness box at Queen Elizabeth II Law Courts in Birmingham, I told the judge and jury that Josephine could follow the trial but only if the court was willing to make allowances for her. Counsel must recognize her vulnerability and use tones of voice that didn't increase her anxiety. Likewise, if they talked at normal speed with ordinary vocabulary, she would be lost. They had to slow it down and use simple words.

Josephine could be cross-examined, providing she wasn't bullied or hectored. This didn't mean that she couldn't be challenged but if counsel used the sort of sniping approach applied to some witnesses, she wouldn't be able to cope and could be emotionally damaged.

She had an adequate concept of God, I told them, but it wasn't sophisticated. And she understood the importance of telling the truth, although her comprehension of right and wrong was based on concrete examples rather than abstract definitions. If the court insisted upon some higher criteria then she wasn't competent.

The judge ruled in favour of the Crown, despite arguments from the defence. As a result of Josephine being deemed to be competent by the court, physical evidence was allowed to be introduced which included DNA tests that identified semen found in her room as belonging to the defendant. He was found guilty of sexual assault and sentenced to a long term of imprisonment.

When John Bassett called again, he had most of the answers I needed about Rachel. I jotted down notes and afterwards spent time examining photographs taken of her during a holiday at the seaside. She was laughing and tossing back her blond hair that had been caught by the wind.

There was no doubt that Rachel had a natural poise, self-confidence and charm. The camera liked her. She had been a part-time model, who loved sport and outdoor activities such as tennis, swimming and walking. Having dropped out of university before completing her degree, she then happily focussed all her attention on her baby and her relationship with Andre Hanscombe.

They met while he was working as a lifeguard at Richmond swimming pool in southwest London and within months had fallen in love and moved into a flat together. A year later Alex was born. Andre, a talented semi-professional tennis player, became a motorcycle messenger to earn more money and support his new family.

Tall and elegant, Rachel was attractive but not provocative. She didn't flaunt her beauty. Although she knew that she was compelling, I thought that she was possibly unaware of the full effect of her visual impact on other people. I don't think I appreciated this at first. I saw her in death when her personality had been extinguished. Later, as I looked at the holiday snaps and home-video, I began to understand why others were so captivated by her.

After a light supper, I turned on the desk lamp in my study and spread the statements, photographs, post-mortem report and maps across my desk and on the floor. My study is quite small. Along one wall, wooden bookshelves reach almost to the ceiling, the contents leaning this way and that, seemingly in disarray but I can always find what I want so long as no-one tries to tidy them up. Opposite are several filing cabinets, all of them crammed with case notes and research papers. The tops of each are hidden beneath bundles of the *British Journal of Clinical Psychology.*

Closing my eyes, I tried to step back into the pretty woodland glade on Wimbledon Common. An image was forming in my mind. I knew how this killer functioned; I knew what drove him, because I had seen the same impulse in other people whom I'd interviewed and treated over the years. I knew that this killing was a decisive stage in a fantasy process that had been rehearsed for years before it ever became a reality.

Very few people are born to become sexual predators. The vast majority of us have a strong desire to be approved of and well regarded by others. As we grow up and become more effective in forming relationships and more confident in ourselves, we come to feel that people value us and want to hear what we have to say, just as we come to know and value them.

At the same time, we have growing and developing sexual needs. Mercifully, these two elements usually evolve together, so that the expression of our sexual desire is related to positive social values. The fantasies and mental images that naturally arise because of sexual desire and arousal, will involve consensual sex where the seduction, courting and intercourse are enjoyed by both parties.

There are, however, a small number of people who have straightforward and strong sexual needs but who haven't been able to develop social confidence and self-esteem. Maybe their early attempts to form relationships, either sexual or simply courting, have been disappointing, causing them to feel hurt, rejected, or ridiculed.

It doesn't actually have to be true that they've been discarded, they simply have to believe it's true. If so, it can lead people to spiral downwards into a life of sexual inadequacy and usually unaccompanied loneliness.

An even smaller proportion of these people will find that anger develops; a sense of bitterness and a need to blame others for what has happened. People have hurt them, they believe, and they want to punish them for that.

Because in their ordinary lives they sense that they have little, if any, control or influence over others they begin to develop a private fantasy world – an alternative place where they are powerful and they determine what happens.

When this is combined with a strong sexual need, the fantasies may come to be based upon the sexual control or sexual coercion of other people in imaginary relationships with them. Their fantasies begin to mirror their predicament; they don't value others because they themselves aren't valued. The anger, bitterness and resentment consume them and you have all the seeds of a fantasy life that can ultimately lead to sexual aggression.

Such a person often has an enormously powerful visual fantasy system – a kind of virtual reality that is so incredibly vivid that today's scientists and computer programmers have a long way to go if they hope to match it.

In the alternative world that this person creates, people behave in ways that he directs and determines. And as the fantasy system develops, it requires more and more energy and specificity of detail for it to be as rewarding as it was in the beginning.

It's an escalating process. Where a fantasy might once have involved the mild or minor degradation of a participant to fulfil sexual desire, it will need to become more and more extreme in order to maintain the same level of pleasure. This usually means increasing the degree of sexual violence and the intensity of detail. Ultimately, he will have in his mind a set of images and scenarios that are brilliantly and intensely clear.

Within sado-sexual or sadomasochistic fantasies there are a number of different domains, but the band of activities is quite narrow. Some focus on verbal interaction and degradation; others require types of constraints and bindings; others use lashes or whips; or weapons such as guns, clubs and knives. These instruments are used in combination with a particular sort of victim and setting that have been developed so that the creator of the fantasy can maximize his sexual release and reward.

Eventually, the fantasy alone is not enough and he may begin to rehearse some aspects of it in the real world. You may, for example, have a person who fantasizes about raping a woman, someone of a certain age, with blond hair or brown hair, blue eyes or green eyes. He visualizes following her home; she doesn't know he's there. He waits outside the house, looking at the bedroom window, and as she undresses her silhouette falls on the curtains. He enters the house, usually in a particular way, and goes up the stairs. Depending on his fantasy, he will either violently rape her, or she may acquiesce, or perhaps after initially resisting she becomes sexually aroused and they have passionate consensual sex.

When the pleasure provided by this fantasy begins to wane, he takes parts of it into the real world, cruising the streets and rehearsing. It sexually arouses him and gets the adrenalin pumping. Soon he needs more than this and begins to actually follow particular women. They might not look exactly the same as they do in his fantasy – either taller, shorter, thinner or fatter – but they present opportunities and he will follow them at a distance. If they are with someone such as a boyfriend or a child, he will simply blot out that person in his thinking.

Much more likely, he will find victims of opportunity, women who are alone but have some of the characteristics from his fantasy. This may go on for months as he cruises bus stops, creeps into yards or walks up and down the back of railway embankments looking into bedroom windows.

Eventually, the level of sophistication and risk-taking increases. He begins to take something to break into the house, or to tie her up, or a mask to disguise himself. He may even go through the early stages of entering a house and then run off.

What he can't predict is how she's actually going to react. While he can control how she acts in his fantasy, he can't control how she reacts in real life. Sometimes a victim is entirely passive and, depending on his temperament, this may save her life. It may also lead him to kill her because he has no reason to stop. It may be that she resists, very vigorously and with verbal abuse. This may make him kill her, or he may have been going to kill her anyway – it all depends on the blend of what happens in his fantasy and what happens in real life.

But what about Rachel Nickell?

Her murderer was a stranger – of that I was almost certain. For one thing, Alex hadn't been harmed. If it was someone well-known to Rachel, there was a fair chance that the baby would know him too. The sexual fantasy element of the attack and the location also suggested that he was a stranger. If he set out to kill a woman he knew, he would probably have known where she lived, or where she worked, or where she was going to be at a given hour so he could have selected a site that gave him more time with her.

The woodland glade was a risky place to take someone. Although it was shielded from a long view it was perfectly possible that at any moment someone could interrupt him. He was willing to take the risk.

Equally, he couldn't have known exactly how Rachel would respond; what she would say or do, but to some extent that was irrelevant. What was important was that she fulfilled the role that he assigned to her in his fantasy.

At 10.00 a.m. on Wednesday 15 July, he would have known that the only people likely to be on the Common were joggers, horse-riders and people out walking their dogs. Young women would be among them, some with children. From his point of view, a few of them would be provocative and titillating. He wants them but doesn't possess the skills to begin an ordinary conversation, or to chat them up.

But this doesn't really matter any more. He's grown angry and embittered over the years and this has fuelled his sexual fantasies. He's been rehearsing, using his fantasy as a template, stalking women and taking home the images he collects.

But today is an exception, because today his overwhelming urge and the opportunity to enact his fantasy will collide and combine in the person of Rachel Nickell.

To her Wimbledon Common is a place of rest and relaxation; of sunshine and soft green grass – somewhere she can take her dog and child in safety. For the killer it is a theatre – a place where victims are to be found, where he has hiding places, observation posts and escape routes. He may have seen Rachel previously, even loosely followed her; or more likely he is simply cruising across the Common to one of his favourite waiting places.

Then he sees her – a young woman, blond, attractive, self-assured, wearing clothes he finds arousing. She's just what he wants. Not only is she compelling but she has a confidence and naturalness about her. Ironically, the very things that make her so popular with others enhance her as a victim in this man's mind. She brings all of his past into sharp, immediate relief, focussing his bitterness and rejection. As he leaves the trees and moves towards her, he has a sense of complete omnipotence; she is going to pay the price for all of those other women.

Rachel gives him a friendly smile but he's not interested in that; he's passed way beyond looking to start a friendship or a relationship. By the time Rachel realizes the nature of her risk, it's far too late. She may look round to see if there is someone there to help but there's no-one. All she knows is that she and her child are at risk from this man and she doesn't understand why. Her terror is absolute.

She drops Alex's t-shirt – it marks the initial point of contact. He controls her with his voice. The knife, prodding at her chest, draws blood and pushes her where he wants her to go. She's in shock; this is something completely outside her experience; she will never have envisaged it, or known what it feels like.

Like many women, Rachel may have talked about what she would do if accosted by a stranger. Perhaps she said, 'I'd punch him and kick him,' or 'I'd scream at him to sod off'. But what she discovers at the moment of the attack is that she has absolutely no energy and no resistance. It's not a case of being paralysed by fear, it's a passivity that overwhelms her.

For the killer, Rachel's compliance is not enough. She has to be humiliated. He forces her away from the path, separating her from her child. He cuts her throat and she can no longer scream. He forces her down onto her knees so that she presents herself to him in the fulfilment of his fantasy as a woman wholly dominated, degraded and humiliated. Then he stabs her over and over again long after she ceases to struggle.

But he wants more than just her quick death. He pulls her jeans and pants down and either just before – or just as – she dies, he forces a smooth object into her anus. This is not a sexual act in the ordinary sense, it's an act of violation. For him, sexuality is inextricably linked with exploitation, degradation and the defiling of the woman in his fantasy. Rachel, by now, has fulfilled this role.

All of this has taken just a few minutes, probably no more than five or six. Rachel has been stabbed forty-nine times and her throat so severely cut that it appears that her head has almost been severed. Her body is left in such a way, with her buttocks prominently displayed, that anyone coming across her will see her in the most degrading position the killer could manage in the circumstances.

His exhilaration is enormous. He never knew that he could achieve anything like this outside of his fantasy. This is real; he doesn't have to put energy into holding it in his imagination, he can see the blood on his hands, he's holding the knife. Whatever else happens, no-one can ever take from him the memory of his sense of fulfilment and completion at that moment.

As the arousal and exhilaration begin to decrease, so the anxiety starts to establish itself – the guilty knowledge. He knows that he has changed himself in a way that he couldn't predict. Until now, everything has been in his imagination but he has suddenly stepped across a threshold that separates him from most of mankind. Whatever else happens, he will always be a sexual murderer.

It isn't remorse that he feels; it's the knowledge of the outcry that's coming; he will become a reviled and hunted person, using all his wits and resources to protect himself.

Leaning back, I rubbed my eyes until white stars bounced across the ceiling. I'd been concentrating so hard, it was difficult to refocus. I'd forgotten to draw the curtains and the window was dark. My study looks out over the front garden – or at least it would if I trimmed the shrubs that line the path. I couldn't remember the last time I pruned them – perhaps the previous summer.

I have no affinity for gardening. Ian and Emma call me a 'demolition gardener', saying that if everything was dug up and levelled so that it was simply brown earth, then I would be content. They're wrong but I let them tease.

Years ago, Marilyn and I decided to take a horticultural class at a local college. It was one evening a week and designed to teach beginners about various flowers and shrubs. On the first night, the elderly lady teacher was talking about lupins.

'Excuse me,' I asked, raising my hand a little self-consciously.

'Yes, what is it?' She smiled.

'Exactly what is a lupin?'

It took her some considerable time to accept that my question was serious. Afterwards, she took Marilyn to one side and said, 'Mrs Britton, do you really think your husband is going to enjoy this course?'

I can't remember going back, although I don't regard it as a complete waste of time. If there's one flower I can recognize it's a lupin.

Leaving the desk, I wandered into the kitchen and plugged in the kettle. As I spooned coffee into a cup, Marilyn appeared at the doorway in her dressing-gown. She looked at the clock, got a glass of water and padded out again without saying a word. I should have been in bed.

'All right, Paul, you know how he functions and how he got that way,' I said, sitting back at my desk. 'But what else do you know about him?'

Opening a foolscap notepad, I took a sip of coffee and scribbled, 'The offender would be aged between twenty and thirty years.'

Most sexual attacks are committed by young men. This killer was well into the practising process, but probably early in the killing process. He had had time to develop one but not the other.

'He would have poor heterosocial skills,' I wrote, highlighting his inability to relate to women in ordinary conversation.

'He would have a history of failed or unsatisfactory relationships, if any. And in addition to his sexual deviation, it would be likely that he suffers from some form of sexual dysfunction, like difficulty with erection or ejaculatory control.'

I knew this could have been an early contributor to his poor heterosocial skills and failed relationships. Perhaps an early attempt at sexual intercourse failed because he couldn't get an erection or ejaculated prematurely and he suffered ridicule. If so, there was no reason to think that the dysfunction would have improved over time.

'He would be attracted to some form of pornography which would play a role in his sexual fantasy life. Some of it would be violent and he would fantasize about similar experiences.'

Observations such as these aren't pulled out of the air. For at least 120 years psychological experimentation has been carried out on an empirical basis so that by now there have been tens of thousands of studies dealing with every aspect of human functioning and motivation. This has become specialized into different areas, including mine, forensic and clinical psychology.

This vast database of knowledge, from around the world, is vital to my work, but the most important part is knowing where to look and knowing what is relevant. Rachel's killer might not have murdered before, but he wasn't the first man to slay a stranger in a park. Nor, sadly, will he be the last. As each of these killers is caught, more is learned about their backgrounds, motivation and pathology. A number of common denominators have been identified. For example, research shows that killers with higher intelligence tend to be better organized and more methodical. They plan their crimes in detail and exert greater control over their victims. In Rachel's case the attack was brutal, frenzied and seemed chaotic, if you didn't know the script.

I scribbled, 'The offender would be of not more than average intelligence and education. If he is employed he will work in an unskilled or labouring occupation. He will be single and have a relatively isolated lifestyle, living at home with a parent or alone in a flat or bedsit.

'He will have solitary hobbies and interests. These will be of an unusual nature and may include a low level interest in martial arts or photography.

'He will live within easy walking distance of Wimbledon Common and will be thoroughly familiar with it. He is probably not currently a car user.'

All of these conclusions were drawn from what we know about men who kill women in this way.

Looking at the chain of events, I doubted that Rachel's killer had murdered before. Generally, you find that repeat killers get more and more experienced as they go on; they refine their techniques and behaviour, leaving an ever-clearer signature.

Even if Rachel was the first, there was, however, a significant probability that her killer had a history of sexual offending – not necessarily previous convictions but he could have come to notice for minor offences like indecent exposure or stealing women's underwear. I put the probability of this at 50 per cent – I didn't want John Bassett relying on it, but nor should it be discounted.

It may seem like a huge physical and psychological leap from showing a naked penis to an unsuspecting woman to murdering someone, but this killer would have made that journey in his mind long before he did it in reality. He rehearsed it in his fantasies – not every detail because he didn't have a precise victim or location in mind. Rachel was chosen by opportunity and killed because of the strength of his impulse on that day. There was no caution, no sign of self-preservation, no place prepared.

Afterwards, he would have been excited and agitated but this will have passed within a few days. Mercifully, the combination of the sexual buzz together with the shock and fear of discovery was likely to keep him quiet for a while, but eventually his urges would return and he would be drawn out again.

I scrawled a final point at the bottom of the page: 'In my view it is almost inevitable that this person will kill another young woman at some point in the future as a result of the strong deviancy and aggressive fantasy urges as already described.'

It rained overnight and as I drove to work next morning, pools of water filled the ditches and raindrops clung to leaves. Passing through the village of Kibworth, I glanced at the local church that was famous for having two front doors, one on the east and one on the west.

In the old days there had been two separate villages, Kibworth

Beauchamp and Kibworth Harcourt, and they shared the same church. I had been told that the leading family from each village had argued over who should get precedence and enter the service first so the problem was solved by having two front doors allowing both families to enter at the same time. If only all of life's obstacles could be solved so simply.

In Leicester, the footpaths bustled with office workers who walked with their heads down, bent under umbrellas and dodging the spray from passing cars.

What more did I know about him? I asked myself, unable to get Rachel's killer out of my mind. Bassett had spoken of having seventeen and a half million suspects. A psychological profile would help narrow the field, but there are practically thousands of lonely men with poor social skills, who are unattractive, isolated and unhappy. It doesn't make them murderers.

Rachel's killer was flesh and bone; he ate, drank and slept like any other man; he had a birthday and had a roof over his head. But just as Rachel Nickell was a real-world person, with an inner-life that determined her relationships and how she became who she was, her killer also had an inner-life.

During the day, I had to interview a twelve-year-old boy who was lighting fires in the Midlands. Sitting opposite him, I glanced down at the front sheet of his file and saw his name, age, address, marital status and nature of the offence. The details gave me only a brief portrait, they didn't tell me what was inside the file or who the boy really was. I knew that he was much more than a few lines on a page, just as Rachel's killer was far more than seventeen points in a psychological profile.

But who was he? What was it about this man that made him virtually unique?

An answer came to me over lunch at the Towers Hospital canteen. Unlike in mystery stories or thrillers, I didn't see a face in the clouds or in the rain-streaked glass; the physical characteristics of an offender are normally irrelevant to me. Rachel's killer could have been sitting opposite, borrowing my salt and pepper, and I wouldn't know him or recognize him. It's his mind that I look into, not his eyes.

By the same token, if he came into my consulting room and I learned all of the details of his sexuality, I would know immediately that he was likely to have killed Rachel Nickell, without him mentioning it.

What set this man apart was the deviant sexual fantasy that drove him. This is what made him different. Back at my desk, I wrote a single page analysis of the killer's fantasies, hoping it might help the police understand him. I'd never done this for an investigation before, but it seemed logical and a positive step forward.

After examination of the source material, I am of the opinion that the offender has a sexually deviant-based personality disturbance, detailed characteristics of which would be extremely uncommon in the general population and would represent a very small sub-group within those men who suffer from general sexual deviation.

I would also expect the offender's sexual fantasies to contain at least some of the following elements:

1) adult woman

2) the woman would be used as a sexual object for the gratification of the offender

3) there would be little evidence of intimate relationship building

4) there would be sadistic content, it would involve a knife or knives, physical control and verbal abuse

5) submission of female participant

6) it would involve anal and vaginal assault

7) it would involve the female participant exhibiting fear

8) I would expect the elements of sexual frenzy which would culminate in the killing of the female participant

I should emphasize that I would expect his fantasies to include some of the above points but not necessarily all of them and there is no point to expect that his masturbatory fantasies would be confined solely to those points.

The police received more than 2,500 calls within the first month of Rachel's murder. The enormous publicity continued but it was double-edged. Almost everyone who was anywhere near Wimbledon Common on 15 July came forward but the result was that police found themselves drowning in paperwork and no closer to identifying the killer.

So far as I was concerned my involvement had ended after the offender profile and fantasy analysis were faxed to Wimbledon but I read that more than a dozen suspects had been detained for questioning and then released without charge.

The lack of success was particularly hard on John Bassett, who was due to retire in November. About once a week, he would return to the Common, parking his car in the spot where Rachel left her Volvo and standing in silence in the woodland glade. For the former Flying Squad officer it was one of the saddest murder inquiries of his career. He took it personally. 'I've got to hold myself responsible for nobody being arrested and charged,' he told a journalist. 'I have to be realistic and know that as each day passes my chances of catching this man are diminishing. I think it reflects on me when I cannot arrest someone and charge them with this atrocious crime.'

It reminded me of a famous case during the 1950s, the Witchcraft Murder at Meon Hill outside Stratford, one of only two killings that Fabian of the Yard had been unable to resolve in his career. He would visit the scene every year afterwards, hoping for the inspiration to crack the case.

The breakthrough for Bassett came on Thursday, 17 September, when *Crimewatch UK* broadcast a reconstruction of the crime and released two videofit pictures of men police wanted to question. One related to the man who had been seen washing his hands in the stream. He was described as being in his twenties or thirties, about five feet ten inches tall, with short brown hair. He was dressed distinctively with a belt over his white shirt and was carrying a bag.

The second videofit was of a man seen running towards a council estate in nearby Norstead Place, Wandsworth. He was described as six foot, skinny with shoulder-length grey or blond streaked hair tucked behind his ears. He was wearing grey or petrol-blue boxer shorts.

Although I'd been asked in the past whether details of my work could be referred to publicly, I had always said no. This time I agreed to let my psychological profile form part of the programme because of the particularly high risk of reoffence. The day beforehand, I spoke to Nick Ross of *Crimewatch* and explained exactly how the material should be used. A brief outline was eventually given on the programme.

Within four hours more than 300 calls were received and twenty were given top priority. One name in particular came up four times – Colin Stagg, an unemployed bachelor, living alone in a housing estate less than a mile from Wimbledon Common.

Stagg had been interviewed once before. He was stopped by a police constable at about 12.30 p.m. on the day of the murder as he walked towards the common with his dog. When told that the park had been sealed off, Stagg mentioned having been on the common between 8.15 and 8.50 that morning. He said that he'd walked his dog by the Curling Pond and then returned home. The officer jotted his name and address in his notebook.

The twenty-nine-year-old had lived on the Alton Estate for years and was a well-known face to local residents. He had shared a flat with his father, who died of cancer in 1986, and later lived alone. Lillian Avid, who also lived on the estate, recalled seeing Stagg in the street a few hours after the murder and said he looked strangely excited. He was wearing a white t-shirt, white shorts and his hair had just been washed. Colin told her that he'd been on the common just ten minutes before Rachel died and explained that he used to stand at a spot that overlooked where it happened. Mrs Avid asked herself how he could possibly know where the murder took place, the common had been sealed off.

Hours after *Crimewatch UK* broadcast the videofits, detectives arrested Stagg at his flat on the Alton Estate in Ibsley Gardens, Roehampton. The media was quick to mention that the front door had a painted pair of ice blue eyes and a sign warning, 'Christians keep away, a pagan dwells here'. Inside there were various pornographic magazines and books on the occult.

The clock began ticking. Detectives had three days to interview their suspect before they had to either charge him or set him free.

Back at my desk in Leicester, I thought little more about the Rachel Nickell investigation because I assumed my role was over. In the meantime, there was still the question of where Michael Sams had hidden the ransom money after releasing Stephanie Slater. More than £155,000 in various denominations had not been recovered.

The initial police search had come across an empty hole in a field near Sams' cottage at Sutton-on-Trent. At the same time, traces of soil were found on a red metal box in his workshop, suggesting that the money had been buried at some stage.

Sams was such a games player that my first reaction was to say, 'Keep digging in the same hole.' One of his ploys had always been to rely upon people making assumptions and perhaps he wanted the police to assume he'd moved the money when in fact he'd simply buried it deeper.

The mystery surrounding the ransom excited him and he used it to support his claim that he had an accomplice who was now merrily spending all the money. The evidence to counter this was exceedingly strong but the police wanted to tie up the last of the loose-ends.

After months of vainly searching, a meeting was arranged at Tally Ho, the police training centre in Birmingham. I joined the combined investigating teams from West Midlands and West Yorkshire, who had assembled in a banked lecture theatre to discuss the latest developments. An SAS colonel who had established much of our current expertise in search techniques had been consulted. It was hoped that his success in finding IRA arms caches in Northern Ireland could now help in pinpointing the missing cash.

The theory was quite fascinating and based on the belief that the IRA wouldn't use permanent or more obvious sites such as a layby on a road or the corner of a field to hide weapons. Instead they would look for sites that could be relocated using landmarks that were not necessarily prominent unless you specifically knew to look out for them. For instance, instead of using corners of fields, 'hides' would be located beneath the fifth fence-post, cross-referenced with the third lamppost on the opposite hedgerow.

The key question in this case, however, was where to start looking? We went through a review of the life and times of Michael Sams, discussing his known habits, prior history and what letters and numbers might be important markers at the location.

There were many possibilities and, as expected, Sams had left numerous false trails, but eventually the discussion centred on Stoke Summit, an area south of Grantham and only 1.7 miles from where Julie Dart's body had been found. Other factors linked Sams to the area. A local farmer had reported seeing an orange-coloured car similar to Sams' Metro on the day Julie was dumped. A railway line ran through the site and a viaduct crossed over the line and provided an ideal vantage point to look at trains.

Sams had probably relocated the money in a panic so it had to be somewhere that he knew and felt comfortable with – somewhere that he'd been before. In September, the police had mentioned Stoke Summit during an interview and Sams talked of visiting the area quite often. He let slip that the last time was on a wet Wednesday in February.

The money had to have been buried some time between 30 January when Stephanie Slater was released and 21 February when Sams had been arrested. A meteorologist confirmed that it had been raining on 19 February in the Grantham area. This was also the day that Sams had phoned Shipways and threatened Sylvia Baker to keep her mouth shut – an act that suggested he was under pressure because he knew that twenty-four hours later his voice would be broadcast to millions of people.

The SAS colonel looked over Stoke Summit and gave pointers as to natural hiding places. Preliminary searches revealed nothing but the application of a ground-probing radar to the sites revealed signs of a disturbance. Eventually, £120,000 was recovered from two separate hiding places on a railway embankment.

The 'accomplice defence' that Sams had tried to construct now lay in tatters but I did not doubt that he would invent another story to explain the new circumstances. It had been ten months since his arrest and another six would pass before he faced a jury at Nottingham Crown Court.

10

I WAS MILDLY SURPRISED TO HEAR FROM JOHN BASSETT AGAIN when he telephoned late in September. One of his officers had a request, he said, and then he introduced Detective Inspector Keith Pedder.

Pedder chose his words carefully. 'I've spent about fourteen hours interviewing a man whom we have reason to believe might be able to help us in connection with the Nickell murder. Now I don't particularly want to reveal the details, it might colour the way you see it. What I need to know is if there is anything in the interviews that would allow you to say, categorically, that in your opinion this man could not be responsible for the murder of Rachel Nickell, based upon the offender profile and deviant sexuality analysis that you gave us.'

'Can you get me the tapes?' I said.

'I'm arranging it now.'

That night I started listening while Marilyn plied me with coffee, closing her ears as she opened the door and gently shooed cats away from her feet. I didn't mind burning the midnight oil; perhaps it is a legacy of my marathon, all-night crams for university exams and essays. I don't know if Marilyn saw it in quite the same way; she thought those days were long gone.

The tapes consisted of a series of police interviews with Colin Stagg at Wimbledon Police Station. He was quizzed about his movements on the morning of the murder and also asked about his lifestyle, history and habits. Almost immediately it became clear that he had an extraordinary knowledge of the Common, using the proper names for the various hills, paths, ponds and woods. He walked there two or three times a day and occasionally visited his father's grave at the adjacent Putney Cemetery.

Stagg said he remembered the day of Rachel's murder because he had been suffering from a painful headache and from cramps in his neck. He woke at 6.30 a.m., delivered papers for a local newsagent and then took his dog Brandy for a walk on the common at 8.30 a.m. He showed the police his route on a map and explained that it had been a shorter walk than usual because of his headache.

'I wanted to get back to get some sleep,' he said. 'I felt really drowsy.'

He said he went back to Ibsley Gardens, ate several crispbreads and fell asleep on the settee watching a game show on the television. He couldn't remember which one. Later he was woken by the sound of a police helicopter overhead. A local shopkeeper had told him about the murder on Wimbledon Common and he'd read the stories in the newspapers.

When asked if he'd ever seen Rachel on the Common, Stagg remembered seeing someone who could have been her about two years earlier. She'd been pushing a baby in a buggy and lying by the pond.

'She was a nice-looking girl. I saw her take her top off and sunbathe in a bikini. I stayed for quite a while,' he said. He went back to the common the following day, hoping to see her again.

When asked if the police could examine the shoes he'd been wearing on the day of Rachel's murder, Stagg said, 'I threw them away two days ago . . . They went into the bins in the block.'

Admitting to still being a virgin, Stagg described having had several girlfriends but his efforts at intercourse had failed because he 'just couldn't get it up'.

Throughout the second day of interviews, Stagg maintained that he knew nothing about Rachel's murder. He claimed that the policeman that he'd met at the A3 underpass had told him the murder victim was a young woman. He denied being the man seen near Curling Pond carrying a black bag or wearing a belt around his waist. He would also never wash his hands in the stream which he said was polluted and smelled.

Keith Pedder and I spoke several times over the next few days as I worked my way through the tapes. I discovered that Pedder had previously had a somewhat 'open mind' about psychological profiling, bordering on scepticism, but this had altered when he went to arrest Colin Stagg at his flat because the similarities between the profile and the suspect were so great. Now he was keen to learn more.

'On what basis could you say, "Yes, he's eliminated himself from the investigation"?' he asked.

'Well, for example, if he said he'd been happily married for two years and has a baby, that wouldn't be consistent with the killer. Or if he had a long-term occupation that required a high level of intellect; or if he demonstrated that he had had successful, stable relationships with women. These things would eliminate him.'

Having explained all this and listened carefully to the tapes, I told Keith Pedder that I found none of the factors that would definitely eliminate Colin Stagg from the inquiry. It didn't mean in any sense that he was guilty, only that he should not be disregarded.

The tapes also contained a surprising confession. Mr Stagg admitted that he had indecently exposed himself on Wimbledon Common in the days following Rachel's murder. A woman exercising her dogs on the playing fields had seen him lying completely naked apart from sunglasses with his clothes piled nearby. As she passed him, she claimed that he opened his legs and smiled.

Stagg was charged with indecent exposure and fined £200.

Throughout three days of questioning, Stagg's denials were persistant and emphatic. Yet despite the lack of physical proof he remained an important suspect for the police.

This was reinforced a month later when police were handed a letter written by Stagg to a woman who had placed a lonely hearts advertisement in *Loot* magazine. Julie Pines had initially corresponded with Stagg but had broken it off because she said his letters became too obscene.

Two years had passed but she recognized his name in the newspapers following his arrest. She contacted the incident room and provided police with one of Stagg's letters which she'd kept hidden away. In it he imagined sunbathing naked in a local park and beginning to masturbate. An attractive woman surprises him and, instead of being horrified, she invites him to have sex with her outdoors.

I knew nothing of this until late September 1992, when I was contacted by John Bassett who came to my office at Arnold Lodge in Leicester, with Mick Wickerson and Keith Pedder. I was intrigued. Why would the three leading figures in a murder investigation drive two hours out of London to see me?

We sat in the seminar room and I noticed that no pads or pens were produced. Bassett was first to speak.

'Paul, I want to ask you a hypothetical question. I need to sound you out on a few things. Based upon your analysis of the murderer's deviant sexuality, is it possible to design a covert operation that would allow us to either eliminate a person from the inquiry or in which a person might further implicate themselves?'

I was surprised. It was a question nobody had ever asked me. All three detectives were silent.

'You mean an operation where knowing the particular sexual deviancy of the murderer can be used to give someone the space to reveal their involvement in the killing by letting them build up some sort of relationship with someone who they feel safe with?'

They nodded.

I thought about this for a long while. 'Yes, it's possible.'

'Fine,' said Bassett. 'That's the first hurdle . . .'

A notebook was produced.

'There are several ways to do it, but it would mean that someone would have to get close to the suspect.'

Pedder asked, 'An undercover policeman?'

'Or a woman. Basically, the covert officer would make contact and allow the suspect to befriend them. This relationship would be designed to create an escalating pathway of revelation whereby the suspect might eventually choose to disclose aspects of their sexual functioning. There would be lots of cut-outs along the way – decision points where the suspect could choose to go in several directions. Only if he chose the previously specified and very particular pathway would there be any basis for the operation continuing. If any other pathway was followed then the operation would end because the suspect, from my point of view, would eliminate himself.'

No names were mentioned. It made no difference to me. My analysis of the killer's powerful and violent fantasies had been written before anybody had come under suspicion. Nothing had happened since then to change my opinion.

Pedder asked, 'So how would it work specifically?'

Using a white-board, I outlined two hypothetical covert operations designed to exploit the powerful deviant psychosexual functioning of Rachel's killer.

'Let's assume that communication is established – based on a chance meeting or perhaps an exchange of letters for example. In the right circumstances and with the right confidante – someone with a specific history and personality – the offender would begin to reveal the fantasies that demonstrate his need for extremely violent non-consensual sexual activity.

'These would include the use of a knife to stimulate, penetrate and control the woman in his fantasy; also the degradation and extreme domination of her to the extent of dehumanization. At the same time, he would become sexually and aggressively aroused.

'As he reveals more, the fantasies would increasingly come to feature a venue that closely resembles the woodland in which Rachel was murdered. At their highest intensity they would replay important aspects of the killing itself, and the offender would derive potent sexual gratification from recounting them. This isn't for intellectual stimulation, it's his most powerful aid to masturbation.'

'And this can be done by letter?' asked Pedder, referring to the operation using a female officer.

'In the initial stages yes but the murderer would quickly try to progress the relationship from written correspondence to personal meetings and an intimate relationship. He will want to present himself as a person attractive to the confidante and is likely to fabricate whatever story he thinks is necessary to secure physical intimacy in the early stages of the relationship.'

Bassett asked, 'He'd invent things?'

'He won't immediately implicate himself in the murder – remember, he has a strong sense of caution and self-preservation. But as his deviant sexual arousal intensifies this would overwhelm his caution and could lead him to reveal knowledge of the circumstances of Rachel's death that would only be known by the killer.'

I explained that the behaviour of the offender and the course of the relationship could be influenced by external events, such as media coverage of the case. 'The murderer is cautious. As long as he believes the police investigation is getting nowhere and public attention is shifting away, then he'll be less concerned for his safety – he'll think he got away with it. But if he has reason to suppose that the police have a continuing, high-level interest in the case, then he's going to be more cautious and suspicious of any relationship.'

Bassett and Wickerson exchanged glances.

'Nothing like this has ever been done before,' said Wickerson.

Pedder replied, 'Yes, but Paul says it's possible.'

'If it's approved,' said Bassett, 'would you be willing to flesh out a design for us and act as a consultant?'

'I've got a few questions first,' I said. 'You say it's never been done before – would it be legal? I'm not a lawyer, I don't know very much about the legal aspects of something like this. Would the Crown say, "Yes, it's all very interesting but it's inadmissible; it amounts to an interview not under caution; or even entrapment."'

'That's not an issue,' said Pedder. 'The lawyers are going to go over this one with a fine-tooth comb. There's no point in going ahead if the CPS (Crown Prosecution Service) say it's illegal and won't stand up in court.'

Bassett agreed, 'This has to be the whitest of white operations; it has to be completely pure. We know that and so does the Met.'

I nodded. 'OK, if that's the case, it will have to be run under very strict conditions. I can design an operation along the lines I've explained, but it will require a suspect to actively climb a series of ladders whereby he either eliminates or implicates himself by his own choices. I am not willing to design an operation that is the functional equivalent of putting a person on the edge of a slide and giving him a nudge so he has no choice where he goes.'

They all agreed. No-one wanted the wrong person charged and the real killer left out there to kill again.

Over the next few days, I drew up a list of the specific requirements needed by the undercover officers and then phoned Keith Pedder, giving him two alternatives, a man and a woman. Either would do, or they could be used in combination.

The first was a white male, aged twenty-five to thirty and of fit appearance. He had to be quite intelligent but should slightly downplay this and be comfortable describing a range of sexual fantasies and actions that are similar to – but fall short of – those attributed to the murderer of Rachel Nickell.

It was important that the undercover officer's background story included examples of him either having successfully dealt with police in an interview situation or never having been interviewed because the police hadn't been able to get close enough to him. He had to be self-sufficient; cautious in the early stages of the relationship and surprised or impressed as the subject began to disclose his own activities. They would be forming an exclusive club with their personal exploits being the criteria for admission.

As their mutual trust seemed to grow, the officer would gradually disclose more of his history which would include serious violent sexual crime. This would help to create an environment where the suspect could feel safe and even boastful in revealing his own background, without any mention of Rachel Nickell or formal shaping of his choices by the officer.

The second confidante was a white female, aged between twenty and forty, with blond or fair hair, shoulder-length or longer. She had to be attractive in a traditional or glamorous sense. She should appear to be sexually knowledgeable but not promiscuous and be attracted to 'interesting' or experienced men who are able to live by their own rules.

She had to be able to respond to any cues given by the suspect and acknowledge being sexually aroused by coercive activity in which she is, preferably, slightly passive but often active. She should be willing to indicate her previous enjoyment of sharing experiences with men who have taken her through sexual fantasy which has progressed from romance into violence and have shared their exploits with her.

An interest in occult religion would be a useful element in her background and she should be impressed by men who indicate they're willing to achieve their desires in action, even when these clearly conflict with the accepted range of social behaviour.

I didn't know that Colin Stagg was to be the subject of the covert operation, although I knew he remained a suspect. It was irrelevant to me; I was designing an operation based on the deviant sexuality analysis that I drew up of Rachel's killer months before Mr Stagg ever came under suspicion.

Pedder and Wickerson came to see me a fortnight later bringing two undercover officers to Arnold Lodge, a man and a woman. As I greeted them at the front gate, I could have sworn that I'd met them before. They'd even managed to find a blue-eyed woman, just like Rachel.

Lizzie James and Robert Harris (not their real names) had been briefed in a general sense and knew that the operation could put them at enormous risk. If the suspect they befriended was subsequently proved to have killed Rachel Nickell, they would have put themselves in danger, particularly Lizzie.

Both were from Scotland Yard's covert operations unit, SO10, one of the most secretive units in law enforcement. The squad is at the very heart of undercover crime detection and performs some of the most hazardous tasks in policing, such as infiltrating gangs, protecting vulnerable juries and posing as contract killers. They were experienced and had a relaxed and easy confidence, yet neither had participated in this sort of operation and it was important to discover if they had what it takes.

Colin Stagg's 'lonely hearts' letter to Julie Pines automatically suggested a means of introducing the undercover policewoman. If a friendship blossomed and the suspect remained in the picture, this was likely to progress into telephone conversations and then personal contact. I described to them in clear detail the type of fantasies and deviant behaviour I would expect them to face if they encountered the murderer of Rachel Nickell.

'You can't tell me there are people out there like that,' said Lizzie, shaking her head.

'That's exactly what I'm saying. Rachel's killer isn't going to come across, at first, as a monster. You won't be able to see what goes on behind his eyes. He may present himself as a lonely young fellow looking for companionship, but you must understand that the true killer will be exploiting and manipulating you all the way. What is happening inside his mind is something you have never come across before.'

After several meetings at Arnold Lodge, the murder squad decided to use just one undercover officer, Lizzie James, and I concentrated on getting her ready. No-one could predict every sentence she was going to hear, so a lot depended upon Lizzie being able to make the right decisions quickly. She would possibly be dealing face to face, for a long period of time, with someone who might be a killer. Did she have the courage, the intelligence and the quickness of mind to cope? Could she be self-effacing and passive but sexually open to ideas and fantasies?

Sitting very close to her in the seminar room, I invaded her personal space and whispered, 'You've got lovely blue eyes.'

I watched her body language. Would she flinch or move away? Lizzie had no idea what was happening, but she read things quickly, smiled and gave a soft laugh. It was the first of many tests that she managed to pass.

She needed to memorize her cover story – not just in rough outline but in the fine detail and nuances that every person picks up in a lifetime of experience. Her childhood, schooling, family and friendships had to be plotted out so that she could answer any question and not hesitate or slip up.

Importantly, within her history, Lizzie was to eventually reveal how she had been drawn into a witchcraft or occult group when she was between twelve and eighteen years old, where she was gradually and systematically introduced into ritual abuse of a sexual nature. This culminated in her being both a passive participant and an active accomplice in the sexual murder of a young woman. She was to have withdrawn from the group about ten years earlier in confusion and ambivalence concerning what happened. But she believed she could only enter fully into an intimate sexual relationship with a man who had had actual experiences that were very similar to her own and could consequently understand and share the extraordinary psychosexual sensations that followed.

Despite trying to form relationships since then, they had always failed because she knew they couldn't be as potent and commanding as those she had known with the group. These failures caused her considerable emotional pain so it was only with great caution that she contemplated the development of a physically intimate relationship.

The undercover operation was designed to allow a suspect to either eliminate or implicate himself in Rachel's death by showing whether he had the same sexual deviancy as the murderer. If this proved to be the case and he had killed Rachel, then perhaps he would reveal a guilty knowledge about the crime. For the operation to work, the suspect had to always make the first move; words couldn't be put into his mouth or ideas into his head. Lizzie could only react to the cues that he gave.

To begin with, Lizzie had to demonstrate her own caution about revealing details of her past, fearing exposure might place her in jeopardy. When she did talk about her experiences with the occult group, she had to release the details slowly, as if she were becoming more secure in the relationship. But something holds her back; an obstacle that prevents her from committing herself fully.

'You regard yourself to be different from ordinary people in the most profound way,' I told Lizzie, 'but you find it difficult to explain why. You're looking to find out whether this man feels the same way.'

It was absolutely vital that she didn't express any interest or knowledge of Rachel's murder in the early stages of the relationship. If the suspect mentioned it, then Lizzie had to show passing curiosity and then change the subject. If it happened again, Lizzie should continue pushing it away. Only after three or four references could she allow herself to be drawn into a conversation about Rachel and say, 'All right, tell me about it.'

Equally, it was important that Lizzie never introduce any of the violently aggressive and sadistic themes that I predicted would drive the fantasies of the killer, such as the physical control, verbal abuse, knives and the humiliation of women. She couldn't lead him by revealing new material or lines of discussion; she could only reflect back on subjects already raised by the suspect.

This was a safeguard to prevent the possibility of an innocent man being led into making untrue claims in a bid to win sexual favours from Lizzie. But it would be for others to establish and decide whether any suspect was guilty of the murder. My task was to design a clear set of procedures which would allow him to make his own decisions by which he would eliminate himself, or further implicate himself.

'He'll be devious,' I warned. 'If he is Rachel's killer, he'll try to secure sexual intimacy without putting himself at risk. He'll try to find out all he can about Lizzie James and what she desires so that he can create some scenario which he hopes will satisfy you.'

'Will he make things up?' she asked.

'Quite possibly,' I said, 'but eventually his deviant sexual drive will reach a level where it outweighs his tendency for caution and self-preservation and he may begin to reveal detailed knowledge of Rachel's murder. If this happens, you should agree to listen but indicate that you need proof that he isn't just fabricating the story to impress you and get you into bed.'

Having taken Lizzie through her cover story, I had to make sure she was comfortable with her new persona. When face to face with the suspect, she wouldn't have the luxury of time.

'How did they abuse you, Lizzie? Tell me about what happened when you were seventeen?'

'Well, they . . . um . . . you know . . .'

'No I don't know. Tell me what they did to you. I need to hear what happened. What did they make you do?'

From uncomfortable beginnings, Lizzie grew in confidence as she slipped into the role. In the real operation when the suspect revealed something of himself and asked for Lizzie to reciprocate, she had to be able to talk comfortably about having certain sorts of sex with men, even when the man opposite might be a murderer. It took quite a lot of practice.

We simulated telephone calls where I played the suspect and instructed that letters should be worded so that Lizzie didn't introduce material, themes or ideas that hadn't already been used by the suspect.

'How long will it take?' asked Pedder, aware of the cost and time pressures.

I drew him a graph plotting the likely responsiveness. 'You're looking at a journey of twenty-four to twenty-six weeks from start to finish. It should take between two to sixteen weeks for Lizzie to establish a relationship which will lead to some sort of rapport. If it hasn't happened by then, you might as well discontinue. Once the fantasy exchange has started you should have gone the rest of the way within the next two months.'

'What if he hasn't revealed any knowledge of the murder by then?'

'Then you stop and regard it as an elimination. He's either got nothing to reveal, or he's never going to reveal it.'

When all was said and done we waited for the green light.

11

A DOZEN MILES FROM WIMBLEDON COMMON, AT A POLICE INCIDENT room at Eltham in southeast London, a hunt was underway for a serial rapist who had struck at least four times with each attack becoming increasingly violent. Powerful DNA evidence linked the assaults and a special task force had been set up to investigate.

The operation, code-named Ecclestone, had been running for a fortnight when Detective Inspector John Pearse called me in early September. After several postponed appointments and a horror drive around the M25, we finally met on a Wednesday afternoon in mid-September.

'He's some picce of work,' said Pearse as he gave me a tour of the incident room. 'The level of violence is right over the top; one victim finished up looking like a bloody rag doll.' Walking and talking quickly, he seemed relaxed and confident as he introduced me to various members of the team.

'We have two rapes and two attempted rapes all linked by DNA. We have other attacks also attributed to the same man. We have strong witnesses, a solid artist's impression and a well established MO. What I don't have is a suspect.'

'What can I do to help?'

'Tell us more about this guy. Are we missing anything? How does he choose his victims? Whatever you can give us.'

He began briefing me on the confirmed attacks, beginning with the first on 10 August, 1989. Jenny, a thirty-year-old single mother had been going through her normal morning routine of letting the cat out, getting breakfast for her children and tidying up the bedrooms.

She lived in a detached house which backed onto open land near Winns Common in Plumstead. At 8.30 a.m. she was upstairs in the front bedroom drying her hair when she looked up to see a man standing in the doorway. A piece of cloth covered his mouth and nose and he carried a black-handled Stanley knife.

He ordered her onto the bed, pulled her t-shirt over her head and tied it with a belt or wire over her eyes. Frightened for her children downstairs, Jenny convinced him to close the door and told him to hurry. As she lay face up on the bed he raped her, without a full erection. Afterwards, she saw him disappearing through the broken rear fence into open land.

'How did he get into the house?' I asked.

'She left the back door open when she let the cat out. He walked right past the kids who were playing downstairs, cut the telephone lead and found Jenny.'

'Was anything stolen?'

'Nothing.'

Because the rapist's face had been partially obscured, Jenny couldn't help with an artist's impression, but she described her attacker as five foot ten inches, about nineteen years of age, medium build, with mousy hair, wearing cheap faded jeans and a brown jacket.

'It's the only attack indoors,' said Pearse. 'We wouldn't have linked it to the later ones if it hadn't been for the DNA profile.'

The next known attack was separated by nearly three years and a distance of four miles. Susan, a seventeen-year-old living at Lewisham, southwest of Plumstead, boarded a bus near her home at 8.40 p.m. on 10 March, 1992, on her way to visit a friend on a nearby housing estate. She got off on Lee High Road near the junction with Abernathy Road and began walking. As she neared the Cordwell estate she became aware of a white youth on the opposite pavement.

Turning left into the estate, she entered an open courtyard and he ran towards some garages. As Susan entered a second alley she was attacked from behind. He grabbed her right arm and stood in front of her with a knife, saying, 'If you want to live, don't make any noise.'

After dragging Susan behind garages, he forced up her jumper and bra, fondling her breasts while he tried to kiss her face and mouth. When she struggled he reminded her of the knife by pressing it against her stomach, saying, 'Shut up if you want to live.' Then for some reason which she couldn't understand he began punching her in the face. Dragging down her jeans and knickers, he pushed her to the ground, pinning her wrists above her head and began pushing his hips against hers, trying unsuccessfully to enter her.

Finally he stood up, pulled his trousers up and kicked Susan in the head six to eight times before calmly walking away.

'It was fucking mindless violence,' spat Pearse. 'He didn't have to do that.'

Semen stains had been found on Susan's clothing and the DNA profile matched the first attack.

Eight days later the rapist struck again, in open fields at Eltham, two miles east of Lewisham. Another seventeen-year-old, Leanne, had left her home after a family row and gone for a walk at 7.30 p.m. Her route took her along Eltham Palace Road and onto a footpath leading through open fields and woodland towards Eltham Palace. At about 8.15 p.m. she stopped on high ground to look across at the lights of Canary Wharf and Crystal Palace Tower.

As Leanne moved off she noticed a man nearby who appeared to be walking away from her. But as she set out for home, he suddenly appeared in front of her, holding a knife in his right hand. He discarded a black balaclava, allowing her to see his face, and said, 'Get down on your knees, I've got this and I'll use it.'

He forced Leanne onto her back and pushed a knife into her left breast making a small cut that bled and stained her bra. Now shielded by the long grass, he lifted her top and bra and began fondling her breasts before taking off her lower clothing and ordering her to hold her knees and pull them upwards. He tried to enter her but his penis was too soft. Then he started moving up and down, simulating sex and saying things like, 'Does it feel nice?', 'Are you a virgin?', 'Can you feel me inside you?'

When Leanne accidentally let her legs go, it infuriated him and he threatened to knock her out. Towards the end of the attack he achieved an erection and tried to penetrate her again. Afterwards, he put the knife at the entrance of her vagina and said, 'You could have got this.' He moved the knife back and forth from her bust to her chin.

'Good girl,' he said as he got up.

'Should I wait till you've gone?' she asked.

'Do what you like. You'll be a good girl and not make any trouble.'

Two schoolboys saw Leanne running from the scene and helped her to nearby shops where she called the police. Semen stains on her clothing produced a DNA profile and she managed to compile an artist's impression. The likeness amounted to about 75 per cent, according to Pearse, and the importance of such a figure cannot be overlooked. Artists' impressions have the potential to do great harm. If they don't have a reasonable resemblance to the perpetrator, it can mean that an important witness doesn't call.

This third attack featured a public footpath known as King John's Walk that crossed the open land where Leanne had been walking. It was part of a much larger series of footpaths that linked a string of parks and commons in southeast London and formed what was known as the Green Chain Walk. It began in two places in the London borough of Bromley and Crystal Palace and meandered northwards until it reached the Thames.

The house that featured in the first rape backed on to Winns Common – part of the Green Chain Walk – and it also figured highly in the fourth attack.

On a sunny Bank Holiday Sunday, 24 May, 1992, Cathy, twenty-two, was pushing her two-year-old daughter in a buggy along King John's Walk just before 2.00 p.m. Cathy noticed a man looking behind some grey corrugated doors beside a derelict set of changing rooms. Soon afterwards she entered a much narrower section of the footpath bordered by railings and bushes. She heard footsteps behind her and suddenly her head was violently forced back by a ligature. She let go of the buggy and was knocked to the ground by a large number of blows to her head and upper body.

The attacker removed her shorts and knickers; he must also have removed her tampon; and managed to push her top up under her armpits. Then he had forced her knees apart and removed his own shorts revealing an old fashioned pair of y-fronts. He masturbated between her legs, near her vagina and when he entered he had to hold his penis because it was still soft.

From being still inside her, he suddenly jumped up, pulled on his shorts and ran off in the same direction he'd approached from. Cathy, looking like a bloody rag doll, gathered her clothes and managed to push her baby to her mother-in-law's house where she collapsed.

Later she told police, 'I asked him not to kill me. He didn't stop hitting me. He put a rope around my neck and kept bashing me on the head.'

Pearse took a sip of coffee and muttered, 'Brazen bastard. It was broad daylight on a busy footpath; anyone could have come along.'

'He's a risk-taker – at least for the moment,' I said, studying an aerial photograph of the scene.

Cathy had also been able to provide an artist's impression which other victims described as good or fair, however her description put her attacker at well over six feet which far exceeded the estimates given by the other victims.

Pearse ran through several other attacks which he believed might also be connected, all of them linked to the Green Chain Walk. In particular an incident at Elmstead Woods, only a mile south of the Eltham attacks, which occurred on 30 August. A forty-seven-year-old teacher had been walking her dogs after breakfast when she strayed from the main footpath and turned when her corgi began to bark.

A youth passed her and then blocked the path. He began rubbing his erect penis through his trousers before grabbing a dog chain from around her neck and pulling her towards him. He pinned her to the ground against a nearby tree and then she thought her corgi must have bitten him on the ankle because he scrambled up and ran towards the clearing.

The description she gave was similar to the others and when shown the artist's impression, she replied, 'That is the man definitely.' She also described the man as a 'D-streamer', an old fashioned term used by teachers for someone with very mild learning difficulties.

Pearse described two further incidents that had happened since the special operation started. A civilian administration officer working in the Ecclestone incident room had left Eltham station to move her car from a side-street at 7.00 p.m. on 1 September. She noticed a man following her who was gripping a plastic striped carrier bag by the neck which had something long inside. He ran off as she started the car engine but she noted how closely he matched the description of the suspect.

Regarded as a genuine sighting, it prompted fears that the rapist had begun to follow publicity generated by the case and had taken an interest in Eltham police station. This theory strengthened a week later when a fourteen-year-old boy rollerskating with his friends in a nearby park was approached by a man fitting the suspect's description who opened his black leather jacket and revealed an appeal poster for the rapes. 'See that. That's me,' he said, before walking on.

Pearse had been talking as he took me through the incident room, introducing me to various members of the inquiry team. 'Now I'd better introduce you to the SIO,' he said, motioning me through a swing door.

Detective Superintendent Steve Landeryou looked so unlike any policeman I'd ever seen that I did a double-take. He wore an immaculate bespoke three-piece suit with a gold chain looping from his buttoned vest and a dress handkerchief perfectly arranged in the breast pocket.

Landeryou stayed for a brief conversation about the case and then made his excuses to leave. I sensed that he regarded my presence as an exercise in covering all the bases and that he was more comfortable with policing methods that didn't include consultant psychologists. Pearse, however, had a keen interest in psychology and had been studying aspects of it as a postgraduate student.

After giving me time to read the major statements and medical reports, Pearse and I arranged to tour the crime scenes which took most of the afternoon. The early afternoon heat made the car seem like an oven and it felt nice to stop and walk around.

I was particularly interested in the first known rape. It puzzled me because it was different from the others, so much so, that the inquiry team regarded it as almost an aberration. In his briefing, Pearse had skirted over the details quickly and hurried on to the outdoor attacks which he believed established the rapist's methodology.

Yet from my point of view the attack on Jenny held more potential clues than any of the others. The other victims were chosen and attacked out of doors, perhaps randomly or opportunistically, but something had led him to Jenny. How did he know that she was in the house? Had he been watching her or stalking her?

Importantly, there must have been dialogue between them and what they said to each other could tell me about his education, motivation and his knowledge of Jenny.

'Can she be interviewed again?' I asked.

'I believe so,' said Pearse.

'And also the neighbours. I'd like to know if anyone reported any peeping Toms or strange men hanging around the area in the weeks leading up to the attack.'

'You're talking about three years ago,' said Pearse dubiously.

'Yes. That's one of the things that puzzles me.'

'What do you mean?'

'I'm wondering whether he could have moved away from the area after the first attack. You don't expect a silence of three years between attacks. Men like this have dips in sexual need and sexual preoccupation which can keep them quiet for a few months but usually not years. Maybe there was a hullabaloo after the first rape and he took himself off for a while.'

'It had no publicity,' said Pearse.

Where was he, I wondered, in prison or in hospital? Did his family move or a relationship fail? 'Somehow we have to account for the time gap,' I said.

At the various scenes, Pearse took me over the details of where the victims had first seen the man and then where the attack had taken place. In the later attacks he allowed his face to be seen and showed little fear of being disturbed, particularly when he attacked Cathy on a busy footpath used by children, dog walkers, cyclists and joggers. Undeterred by the risk of discovery or the presence of her baby daughter, he increased his level of violence, repeatedly punching and kicking her in the head.

Pearse had shown me photographs of Jenny, Susan, Leanne and Cathy, all of them young and attractive which had suggested to police that they matched some physical picture that the rapist had in his mind. I suggested that instead of looking for physical similarities, they should look at how the victims may have appeared to the rapist. Were they likely to seem vulnerable or nervous to him because they couldn't return his gaze and looked away, etc. . . .

I also wasn't entirely happy with the attack in Elmstead Woods, involving the teacher walking her dogs. Aspects of it needed explanation. Apart from being older than the other victims, there was no sign of a knife in the attack and the teacher had described seeing a man rubbing his erect penis under his trousers. We knew from the other attacks that the rapist had trouble maintaining an erection.

She also described a man who she thought was intellectually subnormal, but I didn't think this likely of the Green Chain rapist; his control and competence were clearly evident in the other attacks. He might not have used elaborate confidence tricks or tried to seduce his victims into places more convivial to him, but he *had* proved intelligent enough to be perfectly capable of doing what he wanted.

Local newspaper coverage in South London had generated a number of leads on the Green Chain rapes and detectives were tracing the movements of known sex offenders and reports of men acting suspiciously. Two incidents were particularly resonant. On Monday 12

October, a woman reported being followed by a man on Winns Common close to the first rape. She'd been pushing her baby son in a buggy at about 10.00 p.m. when she noticed a man on a park bench. Worried by him, she asked a young courting couple in a parked car to watch her. As she passed the bench, the man stood up and attempted to follow her, changing direction only when the car headlights were turned on him.

In another incident, a man had tried to force his way into the home of a young woman who, thankfully, had a security chain on the door that managed to keep him out. Although discordant with the outdoor attacks, it suggested that the rapist might be moving back indoors.

Most rapists are perceived as preferring one or the other – an indoor or outdoor setting. This has a lot to do with their fantasy system and how they get started. Indoor rapes are often associated with a person who starts out as a burglar or a peeping Tom, whereas outdoor rapes may be traced back to early flashing offences and public masturbation. If the offender *was* moving back indoors, it meant that first rape became even more important in the search for clues.

In the meantime, I'd drawn up a profile of the rapist and delivered it to a gathering of detectives and uniformed police officers at Eltham Police Station. As Pearse introduced me I felt a sense of curiosity rather than automatic acceptance. Some of these officers were relatively junior and had never worked with a psychologist.

I began, 'There is only a low probability that he is over the age of twenty-eight years and a strong probability he is in the age range of twenty to twenty-five.'

This offender needed a certain amount of experience in the world to have gained the confidence to do what he did, but he wasn't old enough to do things in a more controlled way. The unsuccessful attempts at rape confirmed this sexual inexperience and immaturity. I also knew that places changed over time and that people normally alter their patterns of living as they grow older; they don't walk about as much and use motor cars. This man was still very much in touch with what was going on, he knew the local parks, the footpaths and bus routes.

'He will be within the average to low average range of intelligence,' I said. 'He will not have performed well academically and may have received special or additional tuition in some subjects at school.' This went back to his methodology and his ability to elude the police. I saw nothing to suggest he was mentally ill in the methodology of the attacks.

'If he is employed, the work will be undemanding intellectually and may well be manual. There is no cause to expect him to have solitary work or to be shunned by colleagues.'

Again, this related to what I knew of his intelligence. From the descriptions given by witnesses, he clearly didn't have the patient sophistication which would be a minimum requirement if he were to succeed in some sort of managerial or upwardly mobile task. Manual work was more likely.

I mentioned his relationships with work colleagues because I often meet with the expectation, 'Oh, he must be one of these weird loners.' Stereotypes and assumptions can be dangerous things and I wanted the police to keep their minds open. They were looking for a man who intellectually and emotionally might appear to be a poor fit in our world, but he wasn't going necessarily to stick out like a square peg in a round hole, and although there was no immediate evidence of mental illness, it wouldn't necessarily show even if it were present.

For this reason, if they came across a man who seemed quite comfortable around other people at work or in a social setting, it didn't mean he couldn't be the serial rapist. Similarly, I said the offender might see women during the course of his work, although I didn't expect him to have deep working relationships with them.

'He may enjoy the company of younger girls because they are less threatening and more easily impressed in superficial relationships,' I said, explaining how young men in their late teens and early twenties who have no obvious difficulties with women can sometimes fail to establish relationships. They need to feel important and admired and they find that younger girls can give them this admiration because they're often impressed by older men. This is why girls of thirteen to seventeen can often be found in the beds of men in their mid-twenties.

'There is clear evidence of sexual dysfunction, for example, erectile difficulties and premature ejaculation,' I said. 'I'd also expect an inability to sustain adequate heterosexual relationships on the grounds of poor communication and *possibly* alcohol abuse.

'He's a reckless risk-taker who seems relatively unconcerned about being apprehended or identified,' I said, but I knew this would probably change over time. Young offenders tend to be more reckless, unaware of the consequences of getting caught, but as they mature they grow wiser and more careful. Even though the day-time attack on Cathy had involved enormous risk, I felt this man would probably grow more cautious as time passed.

'Although he derives gratification from the effects that fear produces in his victims, he doesn't really meet the criteria for sadism,' I said. I knew this from the literature and my clinical work. This man revelled in making women do what he wanted, but he could have inflicted far greater pain and gained more extreme control if that had been his desire. Instead his violence stopped short of sadism.

At the same time, his anger or rage was considerable and the approach to the woman staff-member outside Eltham, if confirmed, indicated he might be taunting and challenging the police to catch him.

'He is likely to be known to the police covering the overall area bounded by the crimes, possibly for property offences which may include entering houses,' I said. This went back to the first rape, which I sensed the inquiry team was treating almost as an outlier, a rogue event that shouldn't be given the same weight or importance as the other attacks. I didn't see it this way. The offender had entered a strange house, cut a phone line and raped a woman while her children played downstairs. His movements and methodology suggested someone who had broken into strange houses before.

The local knowledge he showed wasn't shallow or shortlived. It strongly suggested clear connections with the areas by residence, education or employment. Although these were probably current, I said he may have moved away in the period between the first and second offences.

As with Rachel Nickell's killer, I expected that the rapist had enacted the attacks in fantasy well before he took them into the real world. This came back to my clinical work with offenders, drawing from them the histories of how they gained sexual gratification from just watching women through windows getting undressed or making love; and how this escalated into stalking women, stealing their underwear and then entering their houses.

'This man may well have a background of less serious sexual offending including indecent exposure and especially voyeurism,' I said. 'In this regard you may wish to pay attention to reports from couples in open wooded areas and especially to reports of voyeurism involving women in houses by day and night in the two to four months preceding the first offence. Thefts of underwear from clothes lines might also be indicative.'

So far, I'd delivered the profile without any feedback from the officers in the room. Normally, I reported back to the SIO and perhaps a few senior detectives. Now, having a much larger audience made it more difficult to judge whether the message was getting across. This became particularly acute when I started talking about how this man would be caught.

'In my view he will come to your attention finally in one of three ways,' I said and then listed them.

'One. By information provided by the public or area police officers. This is because he's going to stand out as a worry or a reckless minor nuisance who makes local people feel uncomfortable with his activities which will have either aggressive or sexual overtones.

'Two. By being caught during an offence.

'Three. By an elimination process based upon examination of the records. One way or another he's in your system. If you look at your files and, in particular, go and talk to the area police officers, he's there. You already know him.'

I ended by reminding them that they were hunting a very dangerous young man, who would continue to attack women. 'He will escalate his violence, depending upon the victim's behaviour, and this could lead to someone dying.

'I hope this has been helpful but I want to emphasize the probability factors that are involved rather than mislead you with the notion that I can somehow give you a photograph of this man.'

When I asked if there were any questions I looked at a sea of stony faces. Not all of my conclusions had been well-received, I decided, and no-one appeared interested in discussing the profile further. I went home and had my handwritten notes typed up and a copy posted to John Pearse. When I didn't hear from him again, it didn't surprise me. Having worked on dozens of cases – many of them still active – I was accustomed to not hearing the outcome. Unless the police wanted help in designing an interview strategy or further advice, there was no reason to call me. In the case of Operation Ecclestone, I'd done as asked and simply assumed that before too long the police would catch and charge the Green Chain rapist.

12

FROM A DISTANCE MARSH LANE POLICE STATION IN LIVERPOOL looked like a fortress in a wilderness of blighted factories, blocks of flats and row after row of neat, grey houses. The squat concrete and glass building, typical of sixties' architecture, was under assault on two sides by a mass of TV cameras, arc lights and vans with satellite dishes. Pizza cartons and plastic coffee cups filled the gutters – debris from the siege that was now in its fourth day.

It had taken three hours to drive the 150 miles from Leicester across country and up the M6 motorway on a grey, bleak morning devoid of warmth. Parking on a footpath near the station, I surveyed the scrum of journalists and cameramen and considered my options. The direct approach, I decided, and pushed through with my head down, hoping not to be recognized.

At the front counter a middle-aged sergeant with a frustrated face eyed me up and down as, nearby, journalists began to stir.

'Exactly what is your business?' he asked.

'Detective Superintendent Albert Kirby is expecting me. If you just tell him that Mr Britton has arrived.'

'Yes, but what is it about?'

'There are certain matters we have to discuss,' I offered.

'Listen, sir, you notice that lot,' he motioned to the reporters. 'Every one of them wants to discuss certain matters with the superintendent.'

I knew the sergeant was just doing his job – filtering visitors and assessing information – but I wasn't about to announce myself publicly. 'Look. Really. Just call him. He's expecting me.'

Only half-convinced, the officer disappeared to make a telephone call. A young woman appeared at my shoulder, with deep circles under her eyes and holding an almost empty plastic coffee cup.

'Are you anything to do with it?' she asked. I could see a large tape recorder slung over her shoulder.

'Excuse me?'

'Are you anything to do with Baby James?'

'Ah. No. I'm here about the catering.'

Until the phone call from Albert Kirby the previous evening, 16 February, 1993, I was only vaguely aware that a little boy had been murdered in Liverpool four days earlier. I rarely read newspapers and sometimes go days without being able to hear the radio or TV news. It's not a deliberate decision, I simply don't have the time.

The superintendent had chosen his words carefully. 'This little boy, Jamie Bulger, has been murdered. He was taken off by two boys – possibly teenagers. They might be completely innocent, of course, but neither of them has come forward. Whatever happened, Paul, I can't afford to jump to conclusions.'

'How can I help?'

'I need advice. We have to find whoever did this and do it quickly.' He paused. 'This is very sensitive. Jamie was injured in ways that are difficult to accept or understand. It's caused a lot of anger and bitterness in the local community and we've already had public order problems.'

I understood the shorthand.

'I can be there tomorrow.'

'Fine,' he said, sounding relieved.

We'd met once before, a year earlier at a Home Office seminar on psychological crime analysis that I had hosted in Leicester. Various senior policemen had been invited to put forward different cases for discussion. Kirby had impressed me. Tall and athletic, it was hard to imagine him being anything other than a policeman. He had a young face, wrinkled about the eyes, and a slow steady walk like a cricket umpire striding out to inspect the pitch.

The desk sergeant had returned – now all smiles.

'Sorry for the delay, sir. Someone is coming to collect you.'

The corridors were crowded and as we walked Kirby looked quickly at progress summaries that were handed to him. The tension of the previous few days was carefully controlled on his face. He had to lead the team and if he couldn't absorb the pressure, others couldn't do their jobs.

'We had a difficult night,' he muttered.

'What happened?'

'We picked up a youngster for questioning and a lynch mob wanted to burn his bloody house down. I had to take a dozen officers off house-to-house inquiries to guard the street. It's probably set us back twenty-four hours.'

I could see what was happening. The fate of Jamie Bulger had shocked the entire country but in Liverpool, arguably Britain's most emotional city, dismay had turned to anger and ugliness – the downside to community spirit. Initially the hostility had been undirected, but I knew from experience that it would eventually focus on the police as people demanded to know, 'Why haven't you caught these killers? What are you doing to protect us?'

Liverpool was once one of the most important trading ports in the world. However, its great moment as a commercial and industrial centre has long since passed and left behind ravaged acres of empty warehouses, abandoned factories and disused railway lines. The area of Walton where Jamie was found, had been swallowed as Liverpool sprawled outwards at the end of last century and the area is still typified by flat-fronted terraces and narrow, once cobbled streets. Unemployment is high and work often casual but there's a fierce sense of local pride and togetherness which manifests itself on the terraces at football matches and in the local pubs and bars.

Settling into an over-heated office not far from the incident room, Kirby motioned me to the largest chair and introduced two of his colleagues. One of them probably belonged in the office which was decorated with photographs and citations tracking a career from training college through to the senior ranks.

'Right, where do we begin?' the superintendent asked.

'At the beginning. What happened?'

It always impresses me that by the time the police are this far into an investigation, they have the most meticulous recall for fine details of times, events and sequences. They rarely have to refer to notes or charts; everything flows directly from memory.

I began taking notes. Jamie Bulger, aged two and a half, had disappeared from The Strand shopping precinct in Bootle on Friday 12 February, 1993. He was wearing a Noddy t-shirt, navy anorak with a mustard coloured lining, a blue woollen scarf, silver tracksuit bottoms, socks and white trainers.

Kirby handed me a photograph. Blond-haired Jamie had a face that I knew would elicit protective feelings from almost anyone in our culture. His relatively large forehead and big, widely spaced eyes were certain to pull at the heart-strings. He had slipped from his mother Denise Bulger's side while she was being served at A.R. Timms butchers at 3.38 p.m. An overhead security camera picked him up three minutes later on the upper floor with two older children nearby. Three minutes later, he was in the esplanade adjacent to Martin's newsagents, this time holding the hand of one of the older boys. At 3.43 p.m. they were seen leaving an exit leading to Stanley Road.

Kirby slid a cassette into the video recorder. The screen flickered and a grainy, time-coded image appeared. The camera angle was high and the focus uncertain but it was easy to pick out shoppers wandering through the arcade. Mothers pushed strollers, pensioners chatted outside the chemist and a lone gardener tended the greenery.

In the bottom right-hand corner of the screen, a toddler stood beside an older boy. A few yards ahead was another lad who turned and beckoned them onwards. It was tantalizing because the film wasn't sharp enough to pick out the faces or ages of the boys with Jamie, nor to give me any idea of the relationship between them. On the face of it, they could have been two untroubled youngsters taking a little brother for a walk.

Kirby rewound the video. 'About an hour before this was taken, two unidentified boys tried to entice another baby away from its mother at the shopping centre. We have a statement and descriptions. We also have a number of people who claim to have seen Jamie later that afternoon with two boys. We think we've established the route they took.

'Jamie was found on Sunday afternoon on the Edge Hill to Bootle railway line near the Cherry Lane embankment in Walton. A train had cut his body in half but he was dead well before then.'

'What were his injuries?'

Kirby slid an envelope across the desk. 'You're not going to like these.'

The photographs were in strip-form on several A4-size contact sheets, with a dozen images on each. I used a magnifying glass to study them closely. The first were general location shots of what appeared to almost be a disused railway line showing two sets of tracks. The sleepers were buried in broken stones and at one side of the tracks appeared to be the remnants of a bridge or platform. The other side showed a steep grass embankment. There were sufficient bushes and shrubs around to make it a relatively private place.

I noticed blood on broken bricks and there was a photograph of a single white trainer. Various other objects were taken in sequence as they were found including a tin of blue modelling paint found on the far side of the railway bridge. Then I saw half a child's body between the rails; the head and upper torso were lying face-down, clad in a blue anorak. A close-up revealed broken bricks around his head and blue paint in his left eye. Several yards further down the track was another bundle. At first it appeared to be almost an artist's model and it took me a moment to realize that it was Jamie's naked lower half.

The clothing which had been removed was scattered around the upper half of the body. His blue-striped white socks were slightly bloodstained, as were the grey tracksuit bottoms. More heavily stained were his underpants which were found hidden under a brick. His white scarf was found a distance from the body and several Tandy AA-sized batteries were scattered nearby. The sleepers and ballast around the scarf were bloodstained.

Kirby stood at the window staring at the brightening sky. He didn't want to see the photographs again. Like many of his team, he was a father who had lived in Merseyside most of his life and he shared the grief of his community.

According to the post-mortem report, Jamie's death had not been quick but it had been painful. There were twenty-two injuries to his head and another twenty to his body. His skull had been fractured by a series of blows with heavy blunt objects. At some point several of the batteries and the tin of modelling paint had come into contact with his body during the attack.

'There are several things I need to know, Paul,' said Kirby. 'Is it possible that injuries of this magnitude were inflicted by children? Or is it more likely that Jamie was taken by boys and then left with an adult, or abandoned and later found by an adult?'

He paused and found his next question.

'Secondly, I'd be grateful if you can tell us anything about the person or people who are responsible.'

Still glancing through the photographs, I felt profoundly sorry for anyone who had stumbled upon the scene and discovered

Jamie's body. The memory would stay with them forever.

'I'd like to see where it happened,' I said. 'And if it's OK with you, I want to retrace Jamie's last walk.'

The Strand shopping centre is a bland concrete building bounded by railway lines and flats. When it opened in 1968 it was called 'The New Strand' and was a model for the newly imported American concept of shopping malls. Although redeveloped in the late eighties, with attempts made to brighten the interiors with sculptures and ferns, it would never be truly attractive, particularly after what had happened five days earlier. From now on, it would always be the place were Jamie Bulger was taken; the last place he saw his mother.

A mound of flowers and cuddly toys marked the entrance and nearby was a poster bearing the legend 'Merseyside Police. Have you seen these boys?' It had four large colour photographs, one of Jamie in his Teenage Mutant Hero T-shirt with ice-cream plastered around his mouth. Other pictures, taken from the video, showed Jamie being led away and the enlarged faces of the teenage boys, still unrecognizable.

Outside the butcher's shop I began trying to relate the grainy video images to the real world of benches, potted ferns and children's rides. It would have been busy on Friday afternoon, with people shopping for the weekend. Of the 114 shops, the biggest three were Woolworths, T.J. Hughes and Marks & Spencer. There were also a number of discount stores – a sign of the economic times.

Shoplifting had proved to be a problem for traders and security had been tightened during the refurbishment in 1989. There were sixteen security cameras trained on the walkways and arcades, each recording a single image every two seconds. In addition, uniformed guards had been employed from a private security firm.

At A.R. Timms butchers, the brightly lit window was decorated with signs of daily specials. James had last been seen in the doorway eating a packet of Smarties while his mother fumbled through her purse to pay the butcher. Abducting him from such a place involved enormous risk – at any moment Denise could have turned and realized what was happening.

Walking through the main square, past Mothercare and towards Marks & Spencer, I reached the point where the cameras first picked up Jamie and the two boys. In all likelihood they left the complex through Marks & Spencer and then crossed Stanley Road towards the Leeds–Liverpool canal. Frogmen had searched it five days earlier after a witness reported seeing Jamie standing on the canal tow-path crying. She thought he was being minded by three or four older children further along the path.

Returning to Stanley Road, I turned down Park Street, past a Jehovah's Witnesses' hall and eventually emerged onto busy Merton Road. A half-mile further on, at a roundabout, my police chaperons took the left fork up Oxford Road past the offices of the AMEC Construction company. It was here on Monday morning that a caretaker, alerted by the publicity about Jamie, had reviewed the tapes from a surveillance camera trained on the car-park. As he searched through the footage from Friday afternoon, he saw the grainy image of two boys holding the hands of a toddler and swinging him between them as they walked. The time-code indicated it was 4.03 p.m.

Again the images were too poor to identify any of the subjects, but the brick wall pictured in the video gave some indication of how tall the boys were. For the first time it seemed possible that they were pre-adolescent.

Walking onwards we reached an odd landmark, a raised area like a flattened pyramid the size of several football fields.

'It used to be a covered reservoir,' explained a detective.

'Wasn't there a witness—' I didn't finish.

'Yes, a pensioner. She was out walking her dog. The two boys were pulling him up the slope and he had bumps and bruises on either side of his head and was crying. She asked them what was wrong and they said Jamie had fallen over and was lost. She offered to look after him but they said they were taking him to the local police station.'

Climbing the big stone steps onto the reservoir, I surveyed the grassy plateau which was strewn with broken glass and dog muck. Another witness had seen the boys sitting on the steps with Jamie in between them. Later she saw them standing on the far embankment, looking down over a row of houses.

Leaving the reservoir, we followed Breeze Hill Road towards the flyover and then turned down County Road with its back-to-back terraces, some well-kept and others with torn net curtains and grubby windows. At a florist shop a woman had seen Jamie at 4.30 p.m. She, too, had asked about the toddler who seemed tired and distressed. One of the boys said they'd found him by The Strand and were taking him to Walton Lane Police Station.

Having watched to make sure they safely crossed the road, the woman lost sight of the boys as they headed down County Road. A few minutes later, they doubled back and turned right into Church Road West and then into City Road where they crossed a railway bridge. Within a few yards, a footpath emerged onto the roadway. It ran alongside the railway line behind a row of terraced houses. I looked at my watch. It had taken forty minutes. Dragging a tired and frightened toddler, the boys had needed almost two hours.

The footpath was similar to many that exist in metropolitan wastelands; a trail that seemed to start nowhere and go nowhere; without signposts, neither clean nor dirty; but used very frequently. It was protected from the railway tracks by a miscellany of fencing, chain-link, stone and paling.

'That's where we found the missing hood from his anorak,' said a detective. 'In the branches of that tree.' He pointed through the chain-link fence.

'How did it get there?' I wondered out loud.

'We think it was thrown from here,' he said, indicating the path.

I weighed up the likelihood. Why strip Jamie on a public footpath and risk discovery? It didn't make sense. Children and adults have different mental maps of the same geographical areas. Adults think in terms of particular streets, but a child considers the shortcuts under fences and across fields.

'Not from here,' I whispered.

'Excuse me?'

'Remember the hole in the fence, further back?'

'It was too small,' argued the detective.

'Not for the boys. That's how they got Jamie down to the tracks. The hood was thrown from below.'

As we came to the end of the path, I looked up and saw Walton Hill Police Station. This is how close they came to being able to give Jamie up, if that had truly been their aim.

Yellow and black police tape marked the boundary of the crime scene and a mound of flowers was piled against a low stone wall. A dozen residents had gathered nearby; not sightseeing but simply knowing that they had to be there.

Forensic experts were still at work as I began walking across the broken ballast, following the railway line. A row of houses flanked one side of the embankment and the local cemetery lay opposite – a popular playground for the local children who used the railway line as a shortcut. Headstones were occasionally damaged and soft drink cans littered the grass pathways between the graves.

Looking up, I saw the police station. Ironically, the police canteen offered the perfect viewpoint, although until branches and bushes were cut down during the later search, it is likely that the line of sight was obscured.

Silently I began relating the surroundings to the crime-scene photographs. The railway line was grey and dirty from years of use but had obviously seen more productive days. The drabness and sadness of the place reminded me of the old newsreel footage of the final approaches to Auschwitz. Although the horrors of the Holocaust are incomparable to almost anything we can imagine, for Jamie it had been just as terrifying.

On either side of the tracks crumbling stone walls indicated an old platform or the foundations of a bridge. Later I learned that these were once part of a station known as Walton Lane Bridge and that during the Second World War, US servicemen arriving in Britain by sea had been transported down the line.

Detectives pointed out where the small tin of paint had been found and various pieces of clothing. I contemplated where Jamie had been undressed and how far he'd walked across the sharp, granite-like ballast. At the point where the final assault occurred, there was far more blood on the bricks and stones.

The lower half of the body had been found between the track and the embankment on the side nearest the police station. The upper half was five yards further down towards Edge Hill, lying between the same tracks. The train had obviously hit Jamie with an enormous impact – mercifully, he was dead by then – but I could see how the photographs had distorted the distance his body had been carried. Only by counting the sleepers, seven in all, did I realize exactly how far.

The light was beginning to fade as we drove back to the station. Passing various pedestrians, rugged up against the cold, I thought about the people who'd seen Jamie on his final walk. Although they bore no responsibility for what happened, I knew that for the rest of their lives they wouldn't escape the feeling of, 'If only!' Some would suffer sleepless nights and never be able to look at another child without thinking of that little boy, crying and frightened, being led to his death.

In the station office I spread the photographs, forensic reports, statements and maps across the desk. Ordinarily, I'd have taken them home and spent several nights going over the details, but this time the clock was ticking. The pressure for a result was enormous, there was intense national and international scrutiny of the investigation and growing anger in the community. Despite thousands of phone calls – sometimes 200 an hour – door-to-door inquiries, posters, press conferences and re-runs of video footage on television, the identity of Jamie's killer or killers remained unknown.

Taking a sip of coffee, I asked myself four questions – what actually happened? How was it done? Who is the victim? And what motivated the killer or killers?

Only when I had these answers could I tackle the most important query – who was responsible?

I leaned back, closed my eyes and pictured The Strand shopping centre on that busy Friday afternoon. There are two boys who should have been at school but are not. They're not casual acquaintances or youngsters who merely sit and share sandwiches in the playground; there's a bond between them, a feeling that they can explore things with each other and share secrets. It has qualities of a special friendship where they have expectations of one another and compete to win respect. All of these things can be drawn from the comfort with which they acquired Jamie and took him on his last journey.

At the same time, elsewhere in The Strand, Denise Bulger is going through a basic routine of her life – shopping for her husband Ray and her young son. It's an ordinary day and Jamie is a typically happy, playful toddler for whom the world is a playground and every new sight, sound and smell continues his process of learning and developing. Like most young children his curiosity and desire for exploration is enormous.

For Jamie the covered shopping centre has many of the characteristics of a large house. It's cold outside but the mall is more cosy and has been set up to be welcoming and to attract curiosity. The window displays, bright lights and greenery are pleasing to the eye and designed to make people feel comfortable.

Children of Jamie's age are very careful about straying too far from Mum or Dad unless they feel safe. Even when they extend their range of exploration, taking a few steps further, they look back to make a connection with a parent, usually line of sight. If they come across something which seems threatening, they will scuttle back but if everything seems OK they will go a little further, gaining in confidence.

Something catches Jamie's eye and he toddles off to have a look. He knows where his Mum is and feels safe. Once outside the shop, he is presented with a kaleidoscope of different sights and sounds, an almost infinite opportunity for imaginative play.

So we have two streams of existence – the two lads, pre-adolescent perhaps, and young Jamie Bulger and his mother. The day had started with them completely independent of each other but now each is moving inextricably to combine and be inseparable for ever.

What do I know of the boys? It's likely they came together early in the day and spent time speculating about what they were going to do. At some point this hardens into an undertaking, a mission. Although they won't have an absolutely clear picture of every detail of the plan, they'll have a general picture.

Perhaps it began with a chance remark such as, 'Why don't we take a kid . . .'

'What do ya' mean?'

'We could get one . . . take him away.'

'Yeah.'

Then they bolstered each other up.

'What if someone says something?'

'Nah, no-one's gonna see.'

'But what if someone does?'

'They'd just think we was messing about.'

Over a period of time this conversation develops into a clear, shared intention. For two boys to have reached this point, I knew that their backgrounds would be littered with disturbance and disruption, be it broken homes, delinquent siblings, violent or abusive parents, or simply a mother and father who have difficulty in building the emotional space into their lives to concentrate on nurturing. Time and again in clinical consulting rooms these factors emerge in the histories of emotionally disturbed children.

Two damaged boys came together in this case, perhaps because they could relate to each other. I would expect both to have been bullied and to be bullies in a family and a school setting. Equally, truancy is often flagged by problems at home for a child, as well as the inability to keep up with the academic and disciplinary requirements at school.

As they cruised through the shopping centre, the boys made a decision.

'Let's do it now.'

'There's one.'

'No, he's with his mum.'

'Why don't we try upstairs?'

'Yeah.'

They won't be able to carry out any detailed criminal analysis of the scene but they can sense when it feels wrong and bide their time. Then they see a child.

'Hello baby, do you want to play? Come and see what we've got. Come on.'

The toddler takes a few steps towards them.

Mercifully, at that moment, the mother turns and sees what's happening. She *sees*, but doesn't *recognize*. If a thirty-year-old man had been enticing her little boy away it would have been a different story, but here are a couple of lads who give her a cheeky smile.

'Just playing with him,' they say.

They've almost been caught but they don't panic. Nobody knows or expects they're planning a murder; they're just mucking about, that's all. They look at each other and smile because they know the mother doesn't have the slightest inkling of their designs.

Fear would have stopped many at this stage, but this is not a casual act for these boys; they have learned to deal with the adult world by challenging it and not accepting its values. Similarly, neither of them wants to let himself down in the eyes of the other.

Outside A.R. Timms butchers they come upon the perfect victim, Jamie Bulger.

He's alone and at precisely the age which makes him most manageable and controllable as well as being mobile.

If Jamie had been a few years older, the risk to his abductors would have been far greater. But at two and a half he doesn't have the vocal skills or the social insight to appeal to passers-by for help. Later, when people stopped and asked why he was crying, they talked to the abductors rather than the child; always about him, never directly to him. Similarly, with a more developed personality and vocabulary Jamie could have talked to the boys and they may have found themselves relating to a person rather than someone who was anonymous and impersonal. This could have made it far harder for them to kill him.

These boys regard Jamie as just somebody's kid but they also know they are breaking one of the most important taboos in our society. They might not be able to articulate it, because of their age, but they know the value that we place on children.

The actual approach is the most difficult moment of all. Their hearts are pumping and adrenalin surging. This they enjoy. It happens very quickly and without violence. Nobody notices because there were two worlds in the mall. In the adult world if a man takes a child or aggressively grabs a woman, people react, however Jamie's abduction took place in a different world. It didn't register with dozens of potential witnesses because, of course, boys don't snatch toddlers away from their mothers.

We don't know what they say to Jamie, perhaps very little. Maybe they simply hold out a hand and he reaches up and takes it because he's used to being treated with love and kindness. From that moment on, he's as good as dead because all that follows indicates that the boys were determined not to let him go.

As they take him through the shopping centre, neither shows any outward signs of anxiety or panic. The surge of excitement at having total control over the toddler and the ability to do whatever they liked to him outweighs any feelings of compassion or knowledge of wrong-doing. Their apprehension simply feeds into the enjoyment and they know, even if caught, they can argue that Jamie had simply followed them.

Outside, they carry the toddler across Stanley Road and down to the canal tow-path. They want to take him to a place where they can control him without interference but haven't got a detailed plan. All the while they're talking to each other.

At some point, possibly by the canal, Jamie is dropped or beaten and begins to bleed. Suddenly things are not right. The world has always been a 'caring' place for him but suddenly it's changed. These lads turn out to be a threat. Where's his mum, he can't find her. He whimpers and cries. Now he's becoming more difficult to control and the boys will use a combination of reasoning, cajoling and physical threats.

'Shut up or else!' says one.

'Yeah, shut up or else.'

One may push him and then the other will copy the violence.

Even though hurt and frightened, Jamie might still have followed the boys because they were the only people he recognized in the strange surroundings. If they'd hurt him too much or made him too frightened, he might simply have stopped and howled, knowing that it normally brought his mum. Or if the boys had wandered a little from him and a passer-by had moved closer, perhaps the distance might have separated Jamie from them and pushed him into the arms of someone else. But they weren't about to let that happen. They stayed close because Jamie was their prize and they wouldn't give him up.

This is one of the problems. Several witnesses saw Jamie tired and crying during the walk, but he seemed to be following the boys and not struggling. What does it tell them? It says that it's a typical scene – older lads who have been told to look after a young brother but think it's a drag and would rather be off on their own.

Each time they meet an adult, they easily satisfy their concerns by offering a plausible story such as asking directions to the nearest police station or talking to Jamie as if they knew him well. They're not in a hurry and seem relaxed, taking advantage of their intimate knowledge of the area. Perhaps they were waiting for darkness to fall or simply searching for the right location. Eventually, they make their way to a place they know well – a railway cutting away from the roads and constraints of the adult world. Jamie is now in their domain.

Once down the embankment, there's no longer any need to be gentle or cajoling with him. They take off his hood and throw it into the tree. Egging each other on, they begin to do the things they talk about. Rather than having a solitary offender who has some internal fantasy to which he or she responds, the attack on Jamie shows the power of two people combining.

They begin to torment him, taking off various items of clothing and causing pain. As Jamie gets more upset, they laugh and revel in their sense of control. They observe human discomfort and recognize the power they wield – raise a hand and see the child cringe, hit him and see the tears. You can even make the child behave positively towards you because he's hoping this will stop you doing it again.

Finally they reach a section of the tracks which is almost like a concealed arena – a little amphitheatre surrounded by shrubbery and undergrowth. This is their place and the adrenalin and excitement surge as they begin to systematically beat and injure Jamie. At some point a stone or brick lands. More are thrown and the toddler's distress increases. He then falls victim to a much more intense attack as the boys use exploratory violence, engaging in direct physical contact. There is no frenzy or loss of control, in fact the evidence shows great deliberation and a sense of exploration. For example, one of the boys holds Jamie's head while the other pours modelling paint into his eyes.

Finally, Jamie's agony and torment is over. He didn't die quickly. For the boys, there is an element of deflation but they feel no panic or remorse. If so, they would have run away. Instead, they carry Jamie's body and lay it across the railway track before trying to conceal it under bricks and ballast.

At six o'clock I telephoned my wife Marilyn and told her I wouldn't be home until late.

'Do you want me to keep your dinner?' she asked.

'No. I'll pick something up.'

'Are you OK?'

'Yes. Fine. Tired, I guess.'

After thirty years together, she knew me too well. She has watched the small changes in me, some of them temporary, others more enduring and she'd learned to cope with my defensive walls and pensive silences. Despite the horrors that I had to see, she knew that I couldn't turn my back when people ask for help, perhaps because she possessed an enormous capacity to empathize with people in crisis or distress.

'When will you be home?' she asked.

'When you see me.'

An hour later, I called Kirby and his colleagues back into the office. On a notepad, I had handwritten a fifteen-point psychological profile.

'It's a tragic but not a complex murder,' I said, straightening the page in front of me. 'To answer your first question, keep looking for the children. There is nothing in the post-mortem report that particularly suggests an adult predatory offender. There was no semen present on the body; the anal injury isn't consistent with penile or digital penetration. The blows to the body weren't sufficiently crushing to indicate the bricks and metal bar had been wielded by an adult. Equally, there's no history of predation by adults in or around the site and none of the caution, or the display, that I would expect to see characterizing an adult's work. The police station was too close.

'All the injuries are small injuries. The process which took James from the shopping centre to the scene of his death was a succession of small events. The murder scene is known to be a children's play area and the batteries and pot of Humbrol enamel paint are the tools of a child.

'Similarly, the attempt to *dispose* of Jamie by leaving his body on the railway track was a naive attempt at deception. An adult would have realized this and perhaps used other methods to hide the cause of death.'

Kirby sighed and nodded his head.

Moving to my next point, I told them I didn't believe that Jamie had died in a game that got out of control. Everything suggested calculation and intent.

'They meant to kill him?' asked Kirby, ruefully.

'What happened to Jamie wasn't a happenstance. Even though the final mechanics and the implements used in his death may not have been planned or chosen at the outset there was an intention to take a child and to ultimately kill him. We know that because Jamie wasn't the first child that they tried to acquire that day. We also know they took him by a long and convoluted route to the place where they finally killed him. During that journey, they overcame quite carefully, deliberately and systematically a number of hurdles along the way. They had numerous opportunities to walk away and give the child up at no risk to themselves but they were determined to hang on to him even if it meant lying. From start to finish there is a purposefulness to their journey.'

Kirby jotted notes into his operational record book. 'What can you tell us about them?'

'One or both of the boys will live very close to the scene of the murder, perhaps within line of sight, but certainly walking distance. People do things according to a mental mapping system built up by their knowledge of local surroundings. These boys knew where they were going. They knew the streets, footpaths and shortcuts – it was their own turf.

'You are also likely to find some domestic difficulty in their backgrounds, not necessarily broken families but the sort of disturbance that is associated with an unstable upbringing. This is a classic characteristic of children who exhibit antisocial and violent tendencies.'

Kirby asked, 'Will they have any previous form?'

'Not necessarily,' I warned. 'There's no reason to expect convictions or court appearances. They may have a history of untoward behaviour but it might not have brought them police attention.

'The same goes for any obvious sign of mental illness or other psychological pathology. It's easy to assume that these boys are grossly abnormal or mentally ill and would be known to the Mental Health Services or, at least, within the local community. But just think of how easily they dealt with each adult they met; they had the confidence and reasoning to dismiss their concerns easily and come up with plausible stories.

'This also indicates that they will be of at least normal intelligence and will be accomplished deceivers.

'Obviously neither of these boys was at school on Friday, which doesn't necessarily mean they will have a long history of truanting but I wouldn't be surprised, particularly if there's disruption in their home lives. Truancy is very common in these situations because the kids can't cope with the routine and the authority of the classroom.

'Both boys are likely to be isolated from their parents and to have embraced another, different set of values. There is a powerful delinquent street culture that attracts some children and these youngsters develop a system of relying on each other and sharing and enacting fantasies. The values they share with their peers are far more potent in regulating their lives than the values of their families.'

'Like a gang mentality,' suggested one of the officers.

'You could say that, although there doesn't need to be a gang, it's much more diffuse than that. There will be lots of young groups in the area which sometimes work together and sometimes compete. They may have different styles and rules, but there will be an overriding set of values that they all share which exclude, or even reject, the "straight" world of their families.'

'Will they tell anyone about the killing?' asked Kirby, hopefully.

'Certainly not their families. Their parents won't believe that their sons could have been involved in such a crime. Initially, the boys will take a keen interest in local publicity and attitudes. They will want to know what people think and whether it is being viewed as some heroic achievement or with horror.

'It will show on them. There'll be apprehension and evidence of excitement and anxiety, possibly of sleep disturbance. The sense of control and adrenalin rush that led to the killing of Jamie will disappear quickly. And when that adrenalin flushes away, they will begin to ask, "What on earth have I done?" Jamie didn't die silently, nor did he die cleanly. These boys will have vivid images of what actually happened and it won't be like the television – blood leaves marks; a child's screams cannot be turned down like a volume control.

'Equally, when they went their separate ways, they no longer had each other to fall back on. Now they will find that they can't quite shut it out and will suffer a trauma themselves. They will become frightened and worry about being found out. They will wonder if their partner will tell. Although they are a pair, they have now been catapulted into a league that they never contemplated and can't quite rely on each other.'

Kirby asked, 'I assume one of them will be the ringleader?'

'Perhaps,' I said, 'but that's not significant in the killing. Throughout the day there were numerous opportunities for either child to have left the other and gone home. None of these were taken.'

'And they definitely knew it was wrong?'

'Yes. They lied and deceived to protect themselves; they lay Jamie across the tracks to make it look as though a train had killed him. They knew exactly what they were doing.'

Outside, the ranks of journalists had thinned. Groups huddled in cars escaping the cold and occasionally wiping the fogged windows to keep the station entrance in view. I slipped outside, avoided eye contact and was relieved to see the car in one piece.

The journey home seemed to take a very long time. Although the heater was on I was cold. The sense of emptiness which I knew would come had arrived. It always does after I steep myself in reconstructing the terror of a victim and the exhilaration of an exploiter as they are joined in murder.

I stopped at a service station on the M6, just outside Stoke-on-Trent, and bought a coffee. The handful of others who had broken their journeys looked secure and relaxed as they quietly went about their lives. I envied them. My thoughts were with Denise Bulger and the horror that had entered her life when Jamie had slipped from her side and which now would never truly leave her.

It was very late and the village streets were deserted when I pulled into the driveway. A light was on downstairs, Marilyn had waited up for me. She had fallen asleep in a chair worrying about ice on the roads. I didn't mention many of the details of my day and she was kind enough not to ask. She, more so than I, had followed the daily reports on 'Baby James' as the papers referred to him. Like any mother she was shaken by the ease with which it had happened. She could remember times when our own two children were youngsters when, glancing away for just a second, she would turn back and not see them. For that brief moment, all mothers experience a sense of anxiety and fear which sends their pulses racing.

'Anything the matter?' she asked sleepily.

'Not a thing.'

'It was on the news again tonight. That poor mother . . . imagine how she must feel.'

I had leaned back into an easy chair.

'Are you coming to bed?' she asked.

'In a little while. I can still hear the road.'

I was still asleep when two teams of detectives assembled shortly after dawn at Marsh Lane Police Station and were briefed by Kirby. They had the names and addresses of two boys, Robert Thompson and Jon Venables, both aged ten and a half. Thompson lived less than 200 yards from the Cherry Lane railway embankment.

Following my advice, the police had refocussed their inquiries closer to the scene, and had come across a woman who thought she recognized Thompson from one of the video images. After discreet inquiries at the boys' school, it was discovered that neither had attended classes on the previous Friday.

After the furore created by the arrest of the twelve-year-old in Kirkdale, this latest operation was to be top secret and low-profile. Apart from avoiding mob violence, Kirby wanted to ensure that the calls from the public kept coming. Often when a suspect has been picked up, potential witnesses assume that their information is not necessary or important and vital clues can be lost.

He was also aware that *Crimewatch UK* was due to screen a reconstruction of James Bulger's last movements at 9 p.m. that night on BBC1. Video images from the security cameras at the shopping centre had been enhanced by Defence Ministry experts and were to be broadcast afresh to an audience that ran into millions.

At 7.30 a.m. detectives knocked on the doors of a house in Walton, and another in Norris Green. Detective Constable David Tanner, one of the arresting officers, said afterwards, 'When he [Jon Venables] came down those stairs in his pyjamas, I thought it had to be a mistake. He was just so small.'

The boys were taken to separate police stations while their homes were searched and clothing taken for forensic analysis.

Like millions of others, I watched *Crimewatch UK* that night, unaware that anyone had been arrested. A two-year-old boy who looked remarkably like Jamie posed as part of the murder hunt outside the butcher's shop in The Strand. His clothes were identical. Kirby, who had flown to London for the programme, made several references to the psychological profile.

Meanwhile, twenty-five special lines had been installed at Marsh Lane to answer calls from viewers. The deluge that followed produced about forty-three names and an important new witness.

It was not until early the following day that I learned of the arrests. I was at Warwickshire police headquarters, a rather grand-looking country house on the outskirts of the village of Leek Wootton, launching a long-term research project to identify and isolate the characteristics which make some police officers more successful interviewers than others. It was hoped that these interviewing skills could eventually be taught.

In a sense I was back where I started because thirty years earlier part of my police cadet training had been here and I remembered the cross-country races over open fields that had since made way for a golf course. Albert Kirby sounded more relaxed when he called. 'We have two boys in custody. Some of their clothing is stained with blue paint and possibly blood but it's all circumstantial at the moment.'

'Have they admitted anything?' I asked.

'No. That's what I wanted to talk to you about. They're only ten years old. They're so small it's hard to believe it could be them. You know the situation, we have to make sure that they know and fully understand what they are saying and, most importantly, if they were responsible for killing Jamie, whether they knew what they were doing. None of my officers have ever had to interview children this young. It's a whole new ball game and we can't afford to get it wrong.'

'You expected this,' I said and Kirby agreed. He wanted advice on what they could expect.

'OK, but I need every possible detail about their backgrounds and circumstances . . .'

Kirby said, 'Most of it's in your profile. They're both the same age, born twelve days apart in 1982. Robert Thompson lives two hundred yards from the murder scene and is one of seven kids in a single parent family. The father moved out several years ago and Robert apparently roams the streets with little or no parental control. Local intelligence records produced nothing on him, but he has an elder brother with some minor offences.

'Jon Venables has also had family problems and been monitored by social workers for the past three years. His parents are separated and there have been problems at school where he's complained of being bullied.

'The boys are friends and live close to each other. Both were missing from school last Friday and are regular truants. They've been held back a year because of slow progress.'

'Has anyone talked to them?'

'Only casual conversations, trying to build up a rapport.'

'How do they seem?'

'Frightened.'

'All right. I'll call you back.'

The clock was running. Thompson and Venables could only be held for a maximum of thirty-six hours from the time of their arrest. Meanwhile, their families had been moved to safe houses.

When I was a young lad growing up in Leamington Spa, we lived near a disused clay quarry which had all sorts of nooks and crannies to explore. Sometimes I'd play there after school or at weekends and one day I came across what appeared to be the skeletons of frogs. Moving closer, I saw that they were pinned to the ground by wooden skewers.

I didn't understand at first but later I watched as older boys, between nine and thirteen, actually caught the frogs, skewered them and watched them die. Or sometimes they would cripple a frog so it couldn't jump quickly and then take turns in throwing a pen knife at it. They seemed to get enormous enjoyment out of this, as if wielding such power and control gave them a thrill that they couldn't legitimately get by hurting someone else.

They knew it was wrong, just as it was wrong to shoplift, but in just the same way the sense of exhilaration kicked in and they carried on regardless. These same children would then go home and have their tea and be tucked into bed, perhaps not little angels but basically unexceptional. Catching and killing frogs was just something they did when they came together.

What happened to Jamie Bulger is just this, writ very large. Such a mundane, banal explanation shocks people because it means that his two killers are not so different from us. There is a pathway by which most of us could have ended up there.

This doesn't mean, however, that they were helpless in the face of some irresistible force. They chose to do what they did.

Sitting in an upstairs office at Warwickshire police headquarters, I began to plot an interview strategy for the young boys. But if the interrogators were going to discover what happened to Jamie, they first had to understand why it happened. What was it in two boys' lives that gave them the need to abduct an unknown baby, let alone kill one?

Many people have trouble accepting that a child is capable of serious crime and, as a result, want to believe that Jamie's death was somehow accidental or unintentional because the alternative is too dreadful to contemplate. We attribute to childhood a certain sort of innocence and purity of heart and we need to protect this image.

Yet I know from my clinical work that children are capable of doing dreadful things. When this happens, it would be easier if we went down the pathway that says they were somehow born evil. Primary psychopaths do exist. Very rarely born into the world are people who look like human beings, talk like human beings, but are something quite different; they have a defect; an inability to empathize, to share other people's emotions, to feel guilt or remorse or real anxiety.

On the basis of what I knew about Jamie's abductors, this simply wasn't an option, yet I also knew that their decision to kill didn't come out of nowhere – it evolved out of their relationships and upbringing. Children, like adults, have a very broad range of temperaments, abilities and inclinations. A goodly number of them would not gratuitously or sadistically hurt anyone or anything but there are some who get a kick out of bullying schoolmates or torturing animals and others who will go along and watch passively.

Even if you start off with the premise that all children are capable of being cruel, the question that arises is not what makes this so, but what it is that stops them. Again we come back to the morals and value systems that come down from their parents and the community. Moral understanding is something which develops slowly.

It seems an enormous leap to make between bullying at school or torturing animals and actually taking and killing another human being. Yet it is no greater than the step taken by, for example, a group of American soldiers who turn from pushing and shoving a group of Vietnamese civilians to suddenly massacring the entire village. This is the power of people combining.

For Jamie's killers, the idea could have come from a thousand different areas. They may have talked about doing something risky and stupid but not necessarily illegal, such as climbing a water tower or hanging from a balcony, and then started to dare each other. Or perhaps they began talking about someone involved in a fight at school.

'If someone did that to me, I'd kill 'em.'

'No you wouldn't.'

'Yes I would.'

'You haven't got the bottle.'

'I wouldn't bottle out of anything.'

'You'd be too scared.'

'Look whose talking.'

'Not me. I'm not scared of nothing.'

There are so many routes into this that have the most banal beginnings and, contrary to popular opinion, there doesn't have to be a graphic video or violent television programme laying out the plan.

But if you take a different pair of children – one of them perhaps from a more advantaged background, a little brighter and succeeding at school; a child who is valued as a person and comes to value other people – the conversation may take a different route.

'If someone did that to me, I'd kill 'em.'

'I hope you wouldn't.'

'They can't get away with it.'

'Yeah, but neither could you.'

It's a different reasoning process, a different person and a different result.

Although I'd gone over this in Liverpool with Albert, it would be vital to reinforce it for his interviewers.

Two hours later, I called him and was patched through on a speaker phone. 'I've got a dozen points – some of them are self-explanatory,' I said. 'To begin with, you have to understand that even though these boys may have killed, they will react like very ordinary, frightened children. This is what they are now; they are no longer in control.'

'I can believe it,' said Kirby.

'Initially they will deny any involvement – as I said in my profile, they are expert deceivers – but eventually they will probably begin to say that the other child was the instigator while they were passive or opposed to the assault.

'You also have to bear in mind that they will be emotionally traumatized by their actions. They will have tried to block it out but obviously any interview will put them back at the scene and take them through every dreadful detail. This will increase their trauma as they relive what happened.'

Kirby said, 'How can we avoid it?'

'Firstly, keep the sessions short with plenty of snack breaks and make them comfortable. Then take it very gently – one step at a time – allowing them to explain what happened. You can't treat them like adults or go over and over the same point, particularly if they're upset by it. Let the boys reveal their stories in their own way while you gradually help them unpack the memories but without suggesting things to them. Let them tell you something and then give them the chance to retreat to a subject that is relevant but isn't so sensitive or upsetting to them.

'Avoid showing hostility or criticism – even a negative tone of voice or facial expression. You must treat them like victims rather than perpetrators. They have to cope with what they have done and it would be very easy to traumatize them. Their psychological functioning isn't going to stand up to bang, bang, bang questions – it could push them into a deep psychological breakdown.

'Equally, you must consider the welfare of the interviewing teams who are also at risk of emotional trauma. None of them is going to forget this crime and their burden will become even greater if they become responsible for the emotional destruction of two children who may, or may not, be guilty. They will have to carry that knowledge with them for the rest of their lives.'

We went over the strategy several times until Kirby was satisfied that he understood each point.

I wasn't present at the interviews or asked to analyse the taped sessions. However, the conversations between the police and the two boys were made public when they were tried for murder at Preston Crown Court in November 1993.

'Bobby' Thompson slouched in a chair through most of the interviews, occasionally wetting his knuckles and drawing a finger around his mouth. He seemed bored with the delay. The interview room at Walton Lane police station is quite small with a single reinforced window and a tape recorder fixed to the wall.

Sergeant Phil Roberts and Constable Bob Jacobs, both detectives, sat close to Bobby, trying to establish an intimacy. If anyone in the room wanted a break, for whatever reason, the interview was halted and the tape switched off. Sometimes Bobby wanted drinks or crisps. Sometimes it was his mother, Anne, crying and distraught, who needed a break.

He spoke in a tiny, light voice, admitting he had been at The Strand on Friday afternoon but denying he took Jamie Bulger. He described how he and Jon had walked round the shops for most of the day, later leaving and going to the library before going home.

'Did you see Jamie?' asked Roberts.

'Yeah. In the morning. Me and Jon was going up the escalators. He was with his mum and wearing a blue coat.'

Forty minutes later, the interview ended having concentrated on establishing details of what the two boys had done during the day.

In the second interview, Roberts said, 'We believe that you left with baby James and with Jon.'

'Who says?' Bobby asked.

Roberts replied, 'We say, now.'

'No. I never left with him,' Bobby answered.

Roberts said, 'Well, tell me what happened, then.'

'It shows in the paper that Jon had hold of his hand,' Bobby replied.

This is the first admission that they had been with Jamie, but Bobby insists that they simply walked the baby round The Strand and then let him loose. He began to cry, without tears. 'I never touched him.'

At Lower Lane police station, Jon Venables was being interviewed by Detective Sergeant Mark Dale and Detective Constable George Scott. It had been Bobby's idea to 'sag' school, Jon said, and he described the day, playing on swings, messing about in lifts and visiting a local football ground. He made no mention of being at The Strand.

It wasn't until the third interview that Jon was told about Bobby's different version of events. He started to cry. 'We never got a kid, Mum . . . I never took him by the hand, I never even touched the baby . . .' He cried quietly, glancing up at his mother and father who sat at his side. Sue and Neil Venables encouraged Jon to be honest.

Meanwhile, the detectives challenged Bobby about being seen on the Breeze Hill reservoir with Jamie.

'I never took James on the hill. I never went on the hill. I never had no point.' He said the witness must be lying.

'Do you want to sort all this out tonight?' Ann Thompson asked him.

Bobby replied, 'Yeah.'

'Tell the truth.'

'I am.'

Finally Bobby admitted to being on the reservoir where Jamie was crying for his mum and had a graze on his head. He said they left him there. 'Why do I have to stay here? Jon's the one who took the baby.'

Both boys were interviewed three times on 19 February. The shortest session was only eleven minutes. Bobby, in particular, proved to be a skilful liar, who could steer the questioners away from any subject he didn't want to talk about. When pushed into a corner about whether he had stolen a tin of blue paint and batteries from The Strand, he finally admitted that 'Jon might have took them . . . It wasn't me . . . He might have stuck them in his pocket . . . I never. It weren't me . . .'

As I had expected, they pointed the finger of blame at each other.

In his second interrogation that day, Jon admitted for the first time to having taken Jamie from the shopping centre. 'I never killed him, Mum. Mum, we took him and we left him at the canal, that's all. I never killed him, Mum.'

To those watching, it was obvious that Jon was holding back. He wanted to tell the truth, but didn't want to hurt his mother and father. This was explained to Susan Venables, who then spent an hour with her son, reassuring him that she would love him no matter what happened. As she rocked Jon in her arms, he sobbed loudly and finally whispered, 'I did kill him.'

Over the next two hours, Jon slowly revealed what had happened. He was excited on that Friday morning because it was the last day before half term holidays and a teacher had said he could take some pet gerbils home for the week. He met Bobby at the school gates and they decided to sag off together. It was not the first time. Normally, they would hide their school satchels under a subway and set off for a day revolving around shoplifting – sweets, toys, tins of modelling paint, drinks, candles; anything really. Or sometimes they would simply mess around in shops, playing on computer games or sliding on the polished floors of The Strand.

They came across Jamie outside the butchers. According to Jon, Bobby said, 'Let's get this kid lost.'

'We walked through T.J. Hughes and he [Jamie] was following us. Robbie went, "Come on, mate." The baby followed us down the stairs. Robbie said, "Let's get him lost outside, so when he goes into the road he'll get knocked over."

'I said, "It's a very bad thing to do, isn't it?"'

Jon identified himself as the boy filmed holding Jamie's hand as they left the mall. Together they carried the toddler across Stanley

Road, Jon gripping his legs and Bobby holding his chest. According to Jon, when they reached the canal Bobby picked Jamie up and 'slammed him down and put a bump on his head'.

Describing the fatal attack, he said, 'We took him to the railway track and started throwing bricks at him . . .

'Robbie threw a brick into his face. Robbie said, "Pick up a brick and throw it." I just threw it to the floor. I just picked little stones up because I would not throw bricks at him. He did fall over. But he kept getting back up again and would not stay down. Robbie kept picking them up and throwing them. I was holding him back. I took some stones and I missed deliberately. I hit him about two times on the arm because I wanted to get the bricks at the side of him.

'Robbie hit him once with a bar and then we threw a few bricks at him. We ran away then. We got off the railway line the way we had come and went to the video shop . . .'

This is where Susan Venables had found the boys at 7.30 p.m. that night. Their hands and clothes were covered in mud and there were large splashes of light blue enamel paint on their jackets. Sue was furious and screamed at Bobby to keep away from her son. He ran home and told his mother that Mrs Venables had hit him. As proof, he showed a bleeding scratch he had sustained in the railway yard. Ann Thompson marched him to the police station to put in a complaint of assault. Similarly, Susan had taken Jon to the police and asked a constable to give him a warning about 'sagging'. Ironically, this put both boys in the Walton Lane police station within an hour of the killing.

It was not until the third day of questioning that Bobby finally admitted to having touched Jamie. For a brief moment his jaunty, devil-may-care manner dissipated and he said, 'I did touch the baby. I tried to get him off the track. I lifted him up by the belly. Then I put him back because I was going to get full of blood.' It was a clever explanation of the bloodstains that would link him to the crime.

'Jon sat on the wall throwing a brick in his face. Jon threw a brick on his belly. He fell on the floor, onto the railway. Jon then picked the metal bar up and hit him over the head . . . I never touched him except for getting him under the fence and seeing if he was breathing. So I've nothing to bother about. If I wanted to kill a baby I would kill my own, wouldn't I?'

There were few signs of contrition or remorse. Only Jon said, 'Tell his mum that I'm sorry.'

On Saturday 20 February, a short statement was released by Liverpool police:

> *Following tremendous public response, at 6.40 p.m. today two 10-year-old boys from the Walton area have been charged with the abduction and murder of James Bulger. The two boys have also been charged with the attempted abduction of another boy, aged two. They will be kept under police detention under section 59 of the Criminal Justice Act 1991 and appear before juvenile court on Monday.*

A deep melancholia rolled like a fog over the following days. Many people felt it – a national sadness that couldn't quite be explained but I knew it was associated with Jamie. A little part of everyone's childhood had died on that railway line.

People sometimes ask me how I cope with the sadness and stop myself bringing my work home and affecting my family. The truth is, it doesn't happen that way. Instead of bringing my work home, I leave a small part of myself behind at every crime scene and each time I wonder whether one day there won't be anything left of myself to bring home.

13

LIZZIE JAMES FIRST WROTE TO COLIN STAGG ON 19 JANUARY, 1993, saying that she was an old friend of Julie Pines who she described as being, 'a little old fashioned'. She mentioned having accidentally stumbled upon a letter that Stagg had written to Julie.

This letter has been on my mind and interests me greatly. I find myself thinking of you a lot, I would be very interested in getting to know you more and writing to you again.

I will tell you a little bit about myself. I am divorced (like Julie) and quite frankly have had my fill of shallow one way relationships, as I have had my fingers burnt too many times. I am 5'8", blonde, aged 30 and I have been called attractive in the past, my interests may sound boring, but I don't socialise much and prefer my own company, I read a lot and have often contemplated writing a book.

I have an odd taste in music, my favourite record being, 'Walk on the Wild Side' by Lou Reed. I am a bit cautious but not paranoid, I would appreciate it if you didn't let Julie know that I have written to you as our friendship has dwindled. I have taken an accommodation address in London so you can contact me there. I am in the process of moving flats and I don't want any letters going missing, I am in central London about twice a week. I hope you are not upset by this letter and I look forward to hearing from you soon.
Lizzie.
X
PS. My name is Lizzie James.

Stagg replied immediately and showed great caution, saying that he couldn't recall writing to someone called 'Julie'. He went on to say that he was interested in writing to Lizzie because he felt they were alike. He didn't socialize and led a quiet, comfortable life. His pastimes included walking regularly in the local parks, relaxing in front of the TV and listening to music. He also liked to do some nude sunbathing in the park during the summer but some small-minded people felt this was perverted.

Describing himself as being 'painfully lonely' sometimes, he said that he didn't like 'close-minded' people. Life was too short, he said, to let anyone else dictate how you should live.

Asking Lizzie to send him a photograph of herself, Stagg said he hoped she would write soon so they could get to know each other intimately.

Keith Pedder showed me the letter and I advised that Lizzie's reply should be warm in tone, like a typical lonely hearts letter. I set out the guidelines, saying what the letter ought to contain or reflect and it was up to the police to find the words and construct the sentences.

When Stagg's next letter arrived early in February, he remembered sending a letter to Julie and admitted it was rather explicit. He wanted to send Lizzie similar letters that revealed his fantasies about them being together. At the same time, he encouraged Lizzie to do the same and reveal her inner desires and fantasies.

Attached to the letter was a story that Stagg had written about having sex in his back garden. He described lying naked as Lizzie stripped off in front of him, wanting to make love in every possible way. Then he led her by the hand to the lawn and they lay on the damp grass as he slowly masturbated while stroking her hair. The thought that his neighbours might be watching excited him.

I didn't read the letter until I next saw Pedder on 15 February at Arnold Lodge when he looked very pleased with things.

'It's happened so quickly,' he said. 'His second letter and he's already writing fantasies.'

'An unexceptional fantasy,' I reminded him. 'It's a long way short of implication.'

Pedder said, 'But it doesn't eliminate him.'

'No.'

Stagg obviously remembered what he wrote to Julie Pines, so his first letter to Lizzie had been to test her reliability. And he'd quickly moved towards eliciting sexual fantasies from Lizzie without prompting. The only other points of interest seemed to be a preference for outdoor sex, an excitement at the thought of being seen and a slight indication of a dominant sexual attitude towards the female participant.

By this time, Lizzie and Stagg had exchanged valentines and another fantasy letter had arrived. He revealed a little more about himself, admitting to getting 'very randy' living on his own and masturbating while he read men's magazines. He hoped that Lizzie wasn't offended and that they would soon meet and have an exciting relationship.

The fantasy was very similar to the sort found in one of his pornographic magazines, but it reinforced the explicit sexual nature of his correspondence and what he wanted from the relationship with Lizzie.

Her return letter couldn't significantly raise the intensity of sexual expression, I advised, nor could she introduce sexual themes that were predicted of the offender. She couldn't shape him and he had to make the running.

Lizzie wrote back praising Stagg as a 'brilliant storyteller' but saying that he'd have to wait for a letter like that from her because she was a bit slow to start. She described living on the outskirts of Slough and planning to move out in a couple of weeks.

Meanwhile, the operation hit an unforeseen snag. A TV documentary on offender profiling was being planned, with the participation of David Canter, and the producers wanted to focus in particular on the Rachel Nickell inquiry. Canter had already told journalists that he believed he could help the investigators but had not been asked. The documentary was potentially disastrous for the covert operation because much of its usefulness depended on Colin Stagg believing that the investigation had gone quiet and was getting nowhere.

Pedder tried his best to have the programme shelved and when this failed he prevailed on me to co-operate, rather than let them just interview Canter who had no direct knowledge of the investigation. The idea was to hopefully deflect comment from the case and to talk in general terms about offender profiling.

Highly reluctantly, I agreed. The result was the biggest catch of red herrings and waffle I could possibly come up with. I felt sorry for anyone watching the show.

On 25 February, Pedder told me about the next letter. Again it was in two parts, the first designed to build the relationship and the second consisting of another fantasy, this one written under the heading, 'A Special Treat for my Beautiful Lizzie'.

He described how on a hot sunny day, they went walking over to a local park for a picnic. Coming across a small clearing with just a few trees to give some privacy, they chose a space under a fallen tree.

As he prepares the food and puts the wine in a nearby stream to cool, Lizzie strips down to a bikini and they sit side by side on a blanket. They begin fondling each other and undressing until Lizzie is lying naked on her back.

Stagg leads her to the fallen tree and bends her over the trunk so he can penetrate her from behind. She gives a stifled moan and he asks if she's all right. 'Yes, that's wonderful,' she says.

Stagg finished by promising to continue the fantasy in his next letter. For Pedder it was a revelation. He circled his office, clutching a photocopy and occasionally stopping to reread passages aloud.

'Look he's there – he's in the woods. It's just like it was – the fallen tree, the stream, he's talking about entering her from behind. He's recreating the scene.'

I tried to temper his enthusiasm. 'Yes, but that's all he's done. Nothing directly links him to the murder and from a psychological viewpoint, the fantasy is no different from what you might read in a men's magazine.'

It was easy to get carried away by the geographical features and the dominant male behaviour, but for the covert operation to have any real importance it had to move over time from being generally consistent with what I expected of the killer to being narrowly and specifically predictive of him.

'You shouldn't reply immediately,' I said.

'Why?'

'Give him time to reflect and withdraw from the relationship. It's up to him to determine the direction of the operation.'

'What if he doesn't go on with it?'

'Then he eliminates himself.'

It wasn't a case of wanting Colin Stagg to be guilty or minimizing details in his letters that were positive. I appraised each letter on its merits and indicated when I saw evidence in his fantasies of more female agency within sexual relationships – a factor that wasn't predictive of the killer.

When Lizzie did write again she didn't reject Stagg and she indicated a preference for truthfulness rather than fantasy. At the same time she had to indicate her openness to dominant male behaviour, without making any suggestion of extreme violence or any characteristics drawn from the murder of Rachel Nickell.

> *Your lovely fantasy letter was absorbing, I only hope these were your genuine thoughts and what you really think about us. I want it to be private and true, not the kind of usual story that everyone reads in magazines. My fantasies hold no bounds. My imagination runs riot. Sometimes this worries me and it would be nice if sometimes you have the same unusual dreams as me.*

Over the next fortnight, letters were exchanged regularly. Stagg wrote of his loneliness and his history of poor relationships with women. He couldn't believe how lucky he was to have a beautiful woman interested in him who had the same exciting outlook on sex. Normally the women he met looked at him as if they'd just wiped him off the bottom of their shoes.

Although his fantasies began to contain phrases such as 'screaming in ecstasy' and 'twitching violently inside you', I knew that too much could be read into such things. Yet the dominant male behaviour continued in the fantasies and I advised that Lizzie's next letter could respond in similar tone to his descriptions of control and humiliation. However, it was important that no defining example of these concepts be offered; Stagg had to be given total freedom to respond in his own way.

If this was done, I predicted he'd do one of three things.

1) withdraw from the relationship because the prospect of a sexual liaison based on such fantasies wouldn't interest him;

2) indicate his enjoyment of such things in a private relationship but this would be at a level no different to that of many consenting adults whose sex life is spiced up with symbolic exchanges of sexual control and submission, even sometimes involving restraints;

3) attempt to develop a relationship with Lizzie that increasingly focussed on physically and sexually violent fantasies that included her and would ultimately comprise the most serious kinds of sexual assault.

I knew that anybody who chose the last option, if he *had* been responsible for the murder of Rachel Nickell, would find the sexual excitement and expectation arising from these violent fantasies so great that, in due course, it would override his caution. Ultimately, he was likely to disclose his responsibility to someone he believed was a confidante, particularly if he felt that such a disclosure would be part of an even greater sexual gratification.

This is the motor that ran beneath the entire covert operation.

If Stagg chose either of the first two options, he would eliminate himself. Only if he chose the last option and indicated that his sexuality was consistent with that predicted of the murderer would the covert operation continue. However, it would not prove that he was guilty of murder.

Lizzie wrote:

> *You ask me to explain about how I feel when you write your special letters to me. Well, firstly, they excite me greatly but I can't help but think you are showing great restraint, you are showing control when you feel like bursting. I want you to burst, I want to feel you all powerful and overwhelming so that I am completely in your power, defenceless and humiliated. These thoughts are sending me into paradise already . . .*

The precise wording of the correspondence was outside my role; I advised on the tone and principles behind each outgoing missive and the ways in which each incoming missive could be interpreted or understood. I wouldn't have chosen the word 'humiliated' used in this letter because it hadn't appeared in any of Stagg's correspondence. Nevertheless, I felt it just stayed within the guidelines I had set down for the operation.

Stagg's next letter made it clear that he wasn't going to withdraw from the relationship. At the same time, his fantasy went way beyond 'control' and 'humiliation'. He introduced pain into the relationship.

After admitting that he was 'holding back', he described how he wanted to abuse Lizzie's body and call her names until she felt 'humiliated and dirty'. At the same time, he urged her not to regard him as a violent man. He would show her love as well as lust.

> *You need a damn good fucking by a real man and I'm the one to do it . . . I am the only man in this world who is going to give it to you. I am going to make sure you are screaming in agony when I abuse you. I am going to destroy your self esteem, you will never look anybody in the eyes again . . .*

The monitoring, caution and testing were obvious, as if he took a step forward and then came back again to make sure everything was all right. At the same time he had turned up the temperature and for the first time I noticed distinct elements of sadism in the letter.

He backtracked quickly when he next wrote, again revealing his loneliness and emptiness when seeing young romantic couples. He seemed concerned that Lizzie shouldn't recoil from the extreme content of his previous letter.

In reply, Lizzie didn't reject Stagg or show offence, but also didn't encourage him to develop more extreme themes. Instead, it was time for her to reveal details of her own history while pretending to be ultra-cautious. She had to indicate a dark secret in her past that she wouldn't talk about.

In his next letter, Stagg pleaded with Lizzie to tell him her secret and insisted that he couldn't be shocked by anything she had done in her life, even murder. There was no evidence of extreme sexual violence in the letter but he showed a willingness to pursue the relationship at all costs and regardless of society's rules and regulations.

Stagg's next fantasy was again set in open air parkland on a summer's day and featured verbal abuse and lack of consent as Lizzie was sexually penetrated by more than one man. Stagg also sent her a gift, an eyelet which he said would protect her from 'rotten, evil, closed-minded people' and would arouse her when worn.

Slowly Lizzie began to expand on her own particular history without introducing anything new. On 14 April, she wrote:

> *I have only ever met one man who could make me feel complete. These were due to the experiences we shared, these experiences have shaped me into the woman I am today . . . I believe I will only ever feel fulfilled again if I meet a man who has the same history as me. The things that happened when I was with this man were not what normal people would like, these involved upsetting and often hurting people and even though these things are bad and I feel guilty I can never forget how exhilarating they made me feel. I am keen to feel the same way but not by hurting others . . .*

Stagg wanted to move the relationship forward quickly and on 28 April they spoke to each other on the telephone for the first time. As expected, with the new level of contact came an increased degree of caution.

During the conversation Stagg referred to people in his neighbourhood spreading rumours about him.

'Oh why?' asked Lizzie.

'Well, I, I won't tell you on the phone, but I'll tell you in the next letter.'

'Oh yeah.'

'Mainly something that happened last year.'

'Oh yeah. Oh all right then.'

'Yeah.'

'People just can't keep themselves to themselves. I know what it's like, I mean it's . . .'

'Yeah.'

'It's even worse up north. You know what people are like up north, they just love to gossip about ya.'

'That's right, yeah. Well this is more than gossip you know.'

'Is it?'

'It's all about, you know, character assassination, you know.'
Stagg promises to write and explain what happened but, as advised, Lizzie shows little if any interest in the subject and concentrates on her own life and history.

'Do you think . . . would you prefer to do that?' she says.

'Yeah, it would be best I think, yeah,' he replied.

'All right then.'

'It's just that something terrible happened around here, you know.'

'Mmm.'

'You probably read about it in the news, like.'

'I don't really pay much attention to the papers, I haven't got a TV really.'

'I'm up . . . I mean . . . the thing is I was suspected of it.'

'Uh hum.'

'But I want to tell you like I told everybody you know I never done anything, you know.'

'Mmm.'
When asked what she thought of his letters, she answers him carefully, saying, 'They don't offend me, I don't mind in the slightest', thus avoiding saying that she likes them.

During their second call on the following day, Lizzie suggested they finally meet face to face and mentions the possibility of having a picnic in Hyde Park. In the same conversation, Stagg begins relating a fantasy that he had posted to her that day. It featured Lizzie being beaten and having her head yanked back with a belt as he enters her from behind and causes her pain.

I told Pedder that the violence described was more extreme than that found in the symbolic enactments of control and submission that sometimes arouse individuals or couples, and that this was a clear positive indication of the deviant sexuality predicted of Rachel's killer.

In the same letter, Stagg wrote of his past, describing how at the age of seventeen, he watched a pornographic movie and several days afterwards went nude sunbathing on his local common. Lying naked in the long grass he became aroused and began to masturbate. A man appeared from out of the bushes and asked to join him.

Stagg admitted to the homosexual encounter but insisted he wasn't gay. All forms of sex turned him on, he said, but right now he was only interested in women. He wanted to 'fuck the arse off' Lizzie and leave her helpless and in pain. He invited her to stay with him over the summer at Roehampton so they could take long walks on the common 'indulging in carnal lusts every five minutes'.

The covert operation had been running for more than three and a half months when Pedder asked me to a meeting at Norbury Police Station in London on 7 May. It was important, he said, without elaborating, and I understood what he meant when I arrived to find a room full of senior Scotland Yard officers, including the Deputy Assistant Commissioner and commander of the undercover squad SO10. The covert operation was under review and these men had the power to let it continue or to pull the plug immediately.

Pedder and Wickerson gave a presentation using slides, interviews, letters and transcripts from the operation. My role was small in terms of floor-holding and I simply answered occasional questions.

There was no question or uncertainty about the legality of the operation – that was taken for granted by everyone. Instead, the senior officers were more concerned with the practicalities and the operational issues such as viability, risk to the public of disengaging too early and money.

How much and how long were the questions that echoed loudest. Eventually, Pedder told me he had the green light to continue.

As promised, Stagg's next letter explained how he was arrested for Rachel's murder and stressed that he wasn't responsible. A number of single men had been pulled in for questioning, he said. His neighbours and other locals had told the police a load of rubbish and the police had believed them.

'I am not a murderer, as my belief is that all life from the smallest insect to plant, animal and man is sacred and unique . . .'

Stagg also mentioned being charged with indecent exposure, claiming it was the result of being victimized by neighbours who had seen his name in the newspapers. They'd also called him names in the street and children had thrown eggs at his kitchen window. He said the latest rumour doing the rounds was that he ran naked around his back garden masturbating at midnight.

At Lizzie's next telephone call on 13 May, it was already clear that the operation would move to the next phase of face to face contact. Up until now, she had revealed very little of her own history but now she promised that she was almost ready to reveal her dark secret to him. She began laying the foundations for her story about having been drawn into an occult group as a teenager and becoming involved in the sexual murders of a young woman and child. By opening up her heart to him, she hoped he would do the same in return.

Lizzie had said, 'You know I know you told me in one of the letters that you met this man in the park when you were seventeen and . . .'

Stagg replied, 'Yeah.'

'And I know what it must be like to sort of confess to something like that but . . .'

'Yeah.'

'. . . but don't worry about it, I don't think you're gay or anything like that I just think . . .'

'No, I know.'

'. . . you're just lonely, that's all it was.'

'Yeah, that's right, yeah.'

'So I wouldn't worry.'

'No, I don't. It happened such a long time ago anyway, you know.'

'Yeah, but I wouldn't worry about it and you know what you were saying about that woman, quite frankly, Colin, it wouldn't matter to me if you had murdered her. I'm not bothered, in fact in certain ways it would make it easier for me because I've got something to tell you. I'll tell you on Thursday that, you know, it just makes me realize that it's fate that has brought us together.'

'Yeah, I think so.'

'I don't want to talk about it now but I'll tell you on Thursday.'

'Right. You know I'm innocent of everything. I haven't done anything, you know.'

'Yeah, well, I don't want to talk about that but I've got something I want to say to you . . .'

They planned to meet on 20 May at 2.00 p.m. in Hyde Park for a picnic lunch. Stagg turned thirty years old that day and Lizzie had promised him a birthday treat. A day earlier, I sat down with Lizzie at the annexe at Arnold Lodge to prepare her. We'd always known that the operation could reach this point if the suspect hadn't eliminated himself.

Lizzie gave me an enthusiastic smile as she sat down, looking totally relaxed in jeans and a shirt. Her bright, bubbly personality could sometimes disguise her depth of experience and hard edge. It was hard to imagine that she had spent no small part of her working life using a combination of her womanly characteristics and charms to penetrate some very dangerous criminal organizations. She had risked her life and survived on her wits, looks and intelligence.

And each time an undercover operation ended, she had to be trained to repackage all of those things in a slightly different way and then go out and play another role. It was like the ultimate in method acting.

This time Lizzie had to be a damaged and deeply shaken young woman, nursing a dark secret and looking for a man who had shared similar experiences. She had to know how this woman would feel and act and talk – a far different prospect to playing gangsters' molls and vice girls. She had never done anything like this before and couldn't make assumptions, instead she had to soak up details and ideas like a sponge.

'He'll want to get close and touch you,' I told her, 'but you have to manage the physical distance and keep him away without rejecting him or showing disdain. If he sees or infers that you're not all that you seem, or interprets rejection he'll see you as another woman saying no to him. It won't be good for the operation or for you.'

'How do I manage the distance?' she asked.

'Fall back on your own distress. You're telling him about what happened to you as a teenager; about the ritual murders and the feelings they engendered. These are upsetting and uncomfortable and you can use this pain and hurt to hold him off.

'He's going to recognize a lame excuse – he's heard a lot of them from women. What you say has to be absolutely real.'

Hyde Park had been chosen carefully for the meeting. Lizzie would not only be wired, her every step would be shadowed by a team of undercover officers blending in with the lunchtime crowds. At no stage could anyone forget that she was meeting a murder suspect and, if unmasked, could be at serious risk.

I thought Lizzie should wear clothes that showed she was aware of her sexuality but was not promiscuous. Pedder had other ideas. He raised the issue of a knife-proof vest.

'I don't want one,' said Lizzie. 'It's going to affect what I wear and how I move.'

Pedder said, 'I'd prefer you had one.'

'And if he gets any hint of it, it'll compromise the operation.'

Lizzie resisted and settled on a floral dress that was pretty but not provocative.

Shortly before 2.00 p.m. on Thursday, after turning on the tape recorder strapped to her body, Lizzie dodged the puddles on the asphalt pathways and stood self-consciously beside a lamppost outside the Dell Cafe, waiting for her date to arrive.

Colin Stagg had been in Hyde Park for a long while already and now watched her from a distance. Having stepped up the contact to another level, he'd become cautious again. He recognized Lizzie immediately from her photograph and, as promised, she carried an M & S shopping bag.

He approached her from the south side of the lake, through the pouring rain.

'Lizzie.'

'You must be Colin.'

'Yeah.'

'It's like *Brief Encounter*, Colin.'

'I know, yeah.'

'You must be soaked, get under [her umbrella]. God, you're soaked. How are ya?'

'Oh, I got here a bit early actually.'

'Did ya?'

'Yeah, I was waiting round the back there.'

'Oh, I was here a bit early but not too early. Oh, it's such a shame we was gonna have a lovely picnic.'

'I know. Typical innit.'

'Oh, Happy Birthday.'

'Yeah. Thanks.'

The rain forced them indoors to the Dell Cafe, a self-service cafeteria, where they sat and talked generally about themselves. Lizzie told him the story of the ritual murders, explaining how deeply the experience had affected her. The impact had been so great that she felt she could never become truly intimate with a man again unless he possessed a similar background and could understand her feelings.

As I predicted, Stagg said he didn't have such a background but was desperately keen to be part of her life because they were so alike. He restated that he had nothing to do with the murder of Rachel Nickell.

The meeting lasted an hour and as they parted, Stagg took a brown envelope out of his jacket and handed it to Lizzie. As the cab pulled away, she looked at her watch and turned off the tape recorder at 3.05 p.m.

That afternoon, Pedder phoned me and couldn't hide his excitement. 'He's mentioned the knife,' he said eagerly, 'he's only gone and mentioned the fucking knife.'

'At the meeting?' I asked.

'No. No. In a letter. He wrote a letter to Lizzie and gave it to her.'

'What did it say?'

'Stand by your machine, I'll fax it to you.'

The letter was flagged with a warning that it had an air of danger about it. Stagg described taking Lizzie to a secluded spot that he knew on the common where they stripped off and lay on a towel in the hot sunshine.

They spy someone watching them from behind a tree and Stagg encourages Lizzie to put on a show for the peeping Tom. 'Suck me off,' he says, loud enough for the man to hear and Lizzie drops to her knees and obeys. Then he bends her over the tree trunk and penetrates her from behind, holding her down. Secretly motioning the stranger to come closer, Stagg withdraws his penis and offers Lizzie up to him. Then he grabs her hair, forces her head back and thrusts his penis into her mouth.

Suddenly the stranger suggests they do something dangerous and Lizzie agrees. He goes to his clothing and produces some rope and a knife. The two men grab Lizzie's arms and tie her spreadeagled on the ground face up.

> *The man sits astride you, his cock still dripping spunk onto your belly. He gently takes the blade of the knife and draws it down gently from your breasts to your cunt, not cutting you just teasing you. Then I place the blade under his cock, and squeeze a few drops of spunk onto the blade, then he places it to your mouth and makes you lick it clean, which you do, you are now so hot and red you are panting so excitedly. Then the man cuts himself on his arm, just enough to draw blood and he drips it onto your nipples. You massage it into your breasts making you rock your head backwards and sidewards as you go into a massive orgasm.*

The fantasy goes on to describe both men penetrating Lizzie and the knife teasing her nipples and being held against her cheek. The letter ends with Stagg saying that he hoped Lizzie found it satisfying and reassuring her that no harm would come to her.

Surprisingly, he claims the story is written along the line of what he feels Lizzie is 'into', yet at no stage had she ever mentioned knives, pain, verbal abuse, dripping blood, fallen trees, streams or woodland. And this letter couldn't have been influenced by anything that happened in Hyde Park because Stagg brought it with him, already written.

'It's just like you said. It's amazing,' said Pedder.

I pulled him up. 'Why is it amazing?'

'No offence, Paul, it's not that I didn't believe you. You just seem to know so much about Stagg.'

'No. Not at all. I know things about sexual deviancy.'

'OK, where does this fantasy put Stagg?'

'It's consistent with what I would expect to find in the masturbatory repertoire of the killer. It also has the various elements known to be relevant to the murder of Rachel Nickell . . .'

'Give me the bottom line.'

'You're looking at someone with a highly deviant sexuality that's present in a very small number of men in the general population.'

'How small?'

'Well, the chances of there being two such men on Wimbledon Common when Rachel was murdered are incredibly small.'

Colin Stagg had clearly shown himself to be a very lonely young man who was desperate to lose his virginity. To a degree, I knew that he'd say anything to get laid but this didn't explain why he chose to reveal such violent fantasies. There were endless other sexual liaisons and escapades he could have envisaged and written about, yet he chose this narrow specific pathway of his own accord.

Quite a large number of people in the general population have sex lives that include elements of symbolic coercion, bondage, or sadism. If this is all that Mr Stagg had revealed then he would have eliminated himself from the investigation. Instead, he went beyond this and showed his arousal at a tiny and specific strand of fantasy that featured extreme violence, rape and sexual pain. This had been predicted of the killer months before Stagg ever became a suspect.

Of course, I couldn't say that Colin Stagg killed Rachel Nickell and, equally, having the same rare deviancy wasn't proof of murder. The only evidence likely to satisfy a court was if the suspect disclosed details of the murder that only the killer could possibly know. Obviously, if Stagg wasn't the killer, he had nothing to fear because he had no guilty knowledge.

As June heralded the arrival of summer, the covert operation continued with the pace being carefully monitored. Meanwhile, I had several other cases to concern me.

The trial of Michael Sams had begun at Nottingham Crown Court where he'd pleaded guilty to the kidnap and false imprisonment of Stephanie Slater and blackmailing Shipways Estate Agents. However, he denied murdering Julie Dart or attempting to blackmail West Yorkshire police or British Rail.

Prosecution counsel Richard Wakerley said there was no doubt that Michael Sams had committed all of the offences and listed more than twenty conclusive links between the kidnapper of Stephanie Slater and the killer of Julie Dart.

'The game is up, Mr Sams,' he said, looking towards the dock.

I didn't follow the trial in the daily papers and was surprised to hear from Bob Taylor.

'Sams is due in the witness box either tomorrow or the next day,' he said. 'It's going to be crucial.'

The trial was perceived as going well for the prosecution but much depended upon how effectively Sams performed. 'You know him, Paul, I'd be grateful if you could observe him and give counsel your opinion on how Sams is functioning in the witness box.'

I met with Richard Wakerley and Taylor early the next morning, 1 July, and counsel asked me if I thought Sams could be brought to making an admission about killing Julie Dart. I shook my head.

'Only if he perceives that by doing so he will somehow enhance the Raffles-like image he has of himself; or if he decides he's definitely going to be convicted. The probability is very small.'

'Is he still playing the game?'

'Yes – a game in which he's invested everything. If he does confess, it won't be until after he's convicted.'

Although open to advice, I got the impression that Wakerley thought he could succeed where others had failed and tie Sams into knots under cross examination.

Taylor had to find me a seat in the crowded courtroom, somewhere I could see and hear Sams clearly. The public gallery was crowded and faced in the wrong direction. The press box was also full and I didn't fancy rubbing shoulders with Fleet Street's finest because there was always a danger of recognition.

Finally they found me a special chair next to the press box and no-one seemed to notice when I sat down and began scribbling notes. Michael Sams entered the witness box at 11.45 a.m. wearing a blue suit and gold-rimmed spectacles.

I jotted: 'Calm. Rehearsed story. Relaxed, leaning on box. He copes well with friendly questions. He has established a regimented construction which he is able to refer to as though it were memory. To do this he must hold the offence sequence to one side . . . Some notions are weak – developed post-arrest rather than part of the original scheme – so he's thinking on his feet.'

Sams admitted to planning the kidnap from as early as February 1991 when he built a box using four sheets of eight foot by four foot chip-board. This was later used to imprison Stephanie Slater but not, he said, Julie Dart.

Initially, he planned to kidnap an estate agent in Crewe, hoping to extort enough money to buy his wife Teena a house in Birmingham. He said that he made arrangements to view a house suitable for his plan and had disguised his appearance by putting two warts on the side of his nose. However, the plan was aborted because a builder in the house next door had started talking to him and he decided it wasn't safe to continue.

Two weeks later, he said he was watching TV with a friend in his workshop when the lunchtime news bulletin told of a body being found in Lincolnshire. His friend said to him, 'It was an accident. She ran away and I hit her.'

His friend encouraged him to write two letters to throw the police off the scent. 'He said he wanted something in somebody else's handwriting.' Sams said he agreed because of the parlous state of his marriage and at the time, 'I could not have cared less about anything.'

I was writing furiously and the chap sitting next to me in the press box assumed I was another journalist. During a lull in proceedings, he said, 'Don't I know you from somewhere? I'm so-and-so from BBC Radio, Birmingham.'

I'd been in and out of the incident room at Nechells Green station, that's where he'd probably seen me.

'Do you work around the Midlands?' he asked.

'I get about.'

I didn't want to be recognized or to be asked any questions. The incident stuck in my mind because when the trial was over, I had a call from the same radio reporter asking me to comment and when he heard the sound of my voice there was an 'Oh God' and a sigh down the line.

During Sams' evidence it was clear that he was still striving to present a positive image for the jury. I wrote, 'For Stephanie he's presenting himself as a kindly kidnapper, the negative being the callous brutal murderer of Julie Dart and the would-be killer of Stephanie Slater.'

I suggested to counsel that he explore the image Sams had of himself and the image of his friend. How did he account for nice people doing evil? How did he explain the totally unacceptable behaviour of others?

It was important, I said, to use a soft tone and incisive questions. Sams could cope with and gain resilience from hostile confrontation because it made him raise his defences.

Richard Wakerley was brilliant as he took Sams through each stage of his planning, letting the defendant revel in the richness of his strategy and how clever he'd been. He only claimed ownership of the good ideas and repudiated the mundane plotting or mistakes that were made.

Wakerley had woven a spell. 'Can we agree that it was the same man who killed Julie Dart and blackmailed British Rail?'

'Yes,' said Sams.

This was important.

Wakerley asked, 'Then how do we explain the connection between the fibres under the Sellotape in the letter to British Rail matching those of your blue trousers?'

Sams began to struggle. As each piece of forensic evidence confronted him – the bloodstains, carpet fibres, rope strands – his discomfort increased. It was clear that he had a high regard for such evidence and didn't know how to counter it. Similarly, when he had to think on his feet, without the opportunity to sit and plan, he was vulnerable.

Wakerley changed tack slightly and used my words, 'callous, brutal, killer and failure' with respect to Sams. Using the full vocal range, soft and hard, he picked up on the defendant's dwindling confidence.

Sams sobbed as he recalled the moment he snatched Stephanie Slater but the tears were for his wounded self-esteem and not for his terrified hostage. He never intended harming her, he said, provided she didn't remove the blindfold.

'And what would you have done if she had removed it?' Wakerley asked.

Sams sobbed and said he'd never hurt a woman. Wakerley then held up a board spiked with nails which Sams had designed to cripple Stephanie if she had tried to run. Sams squirmed. Wakerley softly and repeatedly used the phrase, 'killer of Julie Dart' and watched as each time the defendant recoiled in the witness box.

For me one of the most important confirming comments came when Sams said, 'I wouldn't be able to face it if I had killed Julie Dart.' Unwittingly he had admitted why he fought so hard against admitting he was a cold brutal killer.

Sams was asked whether he was still friends with the man he claimed had killed Julie.

'I haven't decided yet,' he said.

Then he suggested that he had assumed her death was accidental. Wakerley looked incredulous. 'An accident? This girl was beaten over the head and then strangled. How can that be called an accident?'

'Well that was my interpretation,' he said.

Wakerley then repeatedly asked him to name this friend.

Each time Sams declined, saying he might eventually do so once he had cleared his own name.

On 8 July, the jury retired to consider the verdicts and returned within two hours. Mr Justice Igor Judge sentenced Sams to four life terms and said, 'You are an extremely evil man. The jury has convicted you of murdering Julie Dart. This was murder in cold blood, deliberately strangling her to death while she was unconscious, a kidnapping gone wrong because she saw more than she should.'

Referring to Stephanie, he said, 'I have not the slightest doubt that she was in desperate and mortal danger for the first two or three days of her captivity. If it seemed necessary to you, she, like Julie Dart, would have been murdered in cold blood. Her survival was entirely due to her remarkable moral courage and the unostentatious display of qualities of character . . .'

Four days later at Full Sutton prison in Yorkshire, Michael Sams sent a message from his cell that he wanted to see West Yorkshire detectives. Bob Taylor made the journey, unsure if it was just another throw of the dice by the games player.

Sams sat at a table opposite him and admitted that there had never been any 'friend'. He had murdered Julie Dart in his workshop at 6.00 p.m. on 10 July, 1991. He was always going to kill her, he said, whereas Stephanie was always going to be allowed to go home.

14

LIZZIE JAMES HAD REVEALED HER MOST INTIMATE SECRETS TO Colin Stagg, admitting her part in the ritual murder of a woman and young child. Now she waited to see how he'd respond.

If the police suspicions were correct, I didn't expect him to openly confess to killing Rachel at this stage. I told Pedder that he'd probably invent a story about a murder if he thought it would get Lizzie into bed. Equally, it would act as a test. It wouldn't put him at real risk and if she went to the police, he'd know that he couldn't trust her.

Within days of their first meeting, Stagg revealed in a phone call how as a teenager he and a cousin had murdered a young girl and concealed her body in the New Forest in Hampshire on the south coast.

Pedder rang me and quipped that Stagg and I must be in league and 'taking the piss' out of the police.

We arranged a meeting at Arnold Lodge to talk about this development and to brief Lizzie on her next 'date' with Stagg planned for 4 June at Hyde Park.

'You have to minimize any apparent interest in the Nickell murder,' I told her, 'and to emphasize how vulnerable you feel at having revealed your own past. You've given him a secret that is very precious and fragile.'

'What about his story of killing the woman in the New Forest?'

I looked at Pedder who shook his head.

'We've checked it out. It's an invention.'

'All right, well, Lizzie, you have to treat it with scepticism. Don't accuse him of lying. Even if it were true, the incident he describes doesn't equate in scale with what happened to you. It doesn't mean he's automatically the man you want to give yourself to, or who could fulfil you.

'At the same time, you should ask him questions about the supposed murder. Ask him how he felt when it happened, make him see how you need to know if his experience really does parallel yours. Get him used to talking about the details.'

'Why?' asked Pedder, looking puzzled.

'Because that way he gets used to Lizzie's questions. If he eventually reveals himself to be Rachel's killer, he's not going to be surprised when Lizzie asks him lots of detailed questions, looking for the proof.'

As planned, Lizzie drew out details of the earlier 'murder' and stressed that she wanted complete honesty. She didn't want Colin to say things just to please her. She reiterated this in her letters and phone calls over the next three weeks.

From very early in their correspondence, Stagg had asked Lizzie to write her own fantasies back to him. So far, she had avoided this, letting him make the running, but now his demands grew stronger. She wasn't contributing to the relationship, according to Stagg, and there were suggestions that he doubted her bona fides.

At a meeting on 23 June, I advised Pedder that it would be appropriate for Lizzie to provide a fantasy but it had to be based entirely on elements that had already been introduced into the relationship by Stagg. Most importantly, Lizzie shouldn't escalate the depravity or physical and sexual violence already introduced. Her fantasy should reflect the language and descriptions employed by Stagg and, where possible, mirror an actual fantasy that he had already sent to her.

Having given the guidelines, I let Pedder and his team get on with drafting the words.

Lizzie eventually described walking with Stagg through woodland on a summer's day, hand in hand. They become excited and kiss.

> *Your hands are now pulling at my top. My breasts are now straining to be released. In your haste to release them my top rips. It excites me even more and I feel that special warm wetness between my legs. I claw at your t-shirt, pulling it up at the back. Let me rake your firm muscular back. I am filled with an animal passion, and begin to beg for you to fill me up.*
>
> *You tell me to shutup and wait, you have other things on your mind.*

The letter goes on to describe how their sex session is interrupted by a young woman with short blond hair who becomes aroused and accepts Stagg's invitation to join them. He then pulls a knife from the back of his jeans.

> *I get a shock. You are holding a knife. To see your hands on two powerful different swords really makes me pant. You must have noticed by the look of surprise . . .*
>
> *You walk over to us and speak to the girl, 'suck me'. She looks at me and then you and she doesn't need asking again. She is on her knees lapping you up. You hold the knife near her bright stiff nipples and gently circle one of them with it. A thin scratch appears in a crescent shape around her nipple. It slowly darkens and a small trail of blood begins to dribble down. She hardly notices, she is feasting on your cock . . .*

As advised, the fantasy was almost a mirror image of what had gone before. Stagg had introduced the woodland setting, the knife, the third party and dripping blood. He had also used the language.

Reassured of Lizzie's good faith and clearly aroused, Stagg quickly arranged another meeting in Hyde Park for 29 June. Sitting at the Dell Cafe, Lizzie read the contents of his latest letter and he grew embarrassed that someone might overhear.

He asked her to spend the weekend with him, suggesting they could go to places on Wimbledon Common. Lizzie pretended to finally make the connection.

'So that's the thing you were talking about, you said you'd been arrested for that thing on the common? It was that thing on Wimbledon Common, isn't it?'

'Yeah. It happened last year.'

'Oh, I didn't know that you were talking about it in your letters. I was thinking, what, I haven't heard anything about that.'

'Cos it was all in the papers weren't it?'

'Oh, I know, I remember now when, you know, it rings a bell. But, ah . . .'

'Yeah.'

'Oh, so you're not far from there?'

'No.'

'Oh, did you know her?'

'No, I've never seen her, you know. She was supposed to have been a regular over there but I've never seen her.'

'It's all very interesting, isn't it?'

'I saw someone who was, who was like her once. She was sunbathing over by the big pond over there.'

'Oh yeah.'

'There's like a big lake over there, you know, and ah that was a couple of years ago.'

'Yeah.'

'I told the police about it. That could have been her. But wasn't too sure, you know, cos she was tall, a bit thin, blonde, she had a little kid with her.'

'Oh that is interesting. Do you know who's done it? Have you got any ideas?'

'No, don't know.'

'Come on, you must know. If you were over there all the time.'

'So do a lot of people.'

'I'd like to meet him. I'd like to see what he's got to say, wouldn't you? He's home high and dry now, isn't he, I suppose. He's laughing.'

'Mmm.'

'What sort of things did they ask you?'

'What, the police?'

'Yeah.'

'Oh, a lot of things. It started off they were being nice to you, you know, asking me about my lifestyle and things like that and ah it got a bit nasty, you know, started asking me things like, you know, why did I murder her and that like, and I was saying, "I didn't murder her", you know, "I've never even seen her over there". I described the woman like I described to you and said that it could have been her but I'm not too sure, you know.

'And you know, to tell you the truth, they think I did it even now. I got pulled over by the police, ah, Bank Holiday Monday, May the thirty-first.'

'I wish you had done it – knowing you got away with it, I'd think that's brilliant. I wish you had. Screw 'em!'

'Thing was I was over there at the time it was happening.'

'Were ya?'

'Yeah. The thing was last year I was getting over that illness, you know I managed to put on a bit of weight and that . . .'

'Yeah. Did you see anything like that when you were there, if you were there at the time.'

'No, that's the thing, you know, cos like there's these like large hills . . .'

'Yeah.'

'And it happened on that side of the hill and I was over on this side of the hill, you know, it was very . . .'

'What, at the same time?'

'Yeah.'

'My God.'

'The thing was I had all these splitting headache and that, I couldn't take my dog too far otherwise we would have gone that way, you know.'

'Yeah.'

'I just wanted to get back home again and doze off.'

'God, you could have seen it couldn't you?'

'Yeah. I would see him doing it and running away . . .'

Later Lizzie asks him 'I wonder if you could have seen him, or seen him doing it?'

'That's right. Yeah.'

'Say, say he raped her and everything didn't he?'

'Yeah, he done everything, yeah.'

'Dirty sod.'

'He almost decapitated her as well.'

'Did he?'

'Yeah, he stabbed her 49 times they said.'

'Oh, my God.'

'Cos when I was being interviewed by the police they actually showed me a photograph.'

'Did you see her?'

'Yeah, you know, it was, you know, she was naked and that, you know, and ah, on the ground there was blood everywhere, you know, all over the grass and that.'

'God, you'd have had to be careful too not to give anything away.'

'Cos they thought like if they showed me the photograph, like, I'd suddenly snap and say, all right I did it, you know.'

'They didn't realize what a mind you've got. I think about things like that all the time, mister.'

'Yeah, 'cos I mean when they arrested me they searched my place and that because I've got three bedrooms and that, you know.'

'Oh yeah.'

'And in one of the main bedrooms I did paint it black and I had all these witchcraft motifs done in chalk all over the walls and that, you know, and as soon as they saw that, that was it, you know, I was the one who did it, you know, they were so convinced, you know.'

'When you saw the photographs of her, what did she look like?'

'Well the photograph they showed me she was laying down on the grass sort of, you know, when you're a baby and sort of curled up.'

'Oh yeah, yeah.'

'She was like, and ah, but the photograph was taken from her backside upwards and her head was sort of like round and ah there was blood all over the grass and that. She was completely naked and ah, from that viewpoint I could see her cunt and that, you know, and ah she was very wide open, you know, so he must have really forced her open, you know. At that time, he was obviously killing her at the time, and ah, I don't know the muscles or whatever, you know, in her body and that made her stay open, you know. The thing was, you know, as he's showing me the photograph I got a hard-on which . . .'

'Did ya? Oh God, I hope they didn't see it.'

'No, no, 'cos there was like a table there and that, you know. Cos they were taping it all as well, you know, like the police do and, ah, everything I was saying they were taking into, you know, seeing double meanings into 'em you know . . .'

At last Pedder and his team had the first evidence that they felt could possibly constitute guilty knowledge. Stagg had, indeed, been shown a photograph during his earlier interviews with police – a single image carefully chosen to show Rachel's body but also to ensure that little detail of her murder had been visible.

The photograph was a scene-establishing shot that showed Rachel naked and curled up on the grass, with her lower half nearest the camera. It didn't show her neck, hands, face or genitalia. Stagg had described injuries and other details that the police believed he couldn't possibly have gleaned from the image he was shown.

He described how Rachel had been almost decapitated, even though he couldn't have seen her neck. He said that she lay curled up like a baby and he could see her genitalia which were 'very wide open, you know, so he must have forced her open'.

This description graphically and precisely matched the condition of Rachel's anus yet from examination of the single photograph labelled KP27, Stagg couldn't have known such a detail unless it was a guess. He referred to her vagina rather than her anus, but sexually inexperienced men often confuse the two and merge them in their thoughts. Equally, he described Rachel as being 'very wide open', an interesting observation because not many people would realize that muscles don't contract after death which is why Rachel's anus was still dilated.

Stagg's account of becoming sexually aroused at seeing the picture was entirely consistent with the extremely rare and serious sexual deviation that he'd already shown.

Pedder's reaction was a mixture of elation and relief. From his point of view, he had wanted an operation in which the suspect either eliminated himself early, therefore saving time and money, or went on to confess. And although he never mentioned it, I sensed that the detective had staked a great deal on convincing his superiors to consider the operation. The decision, he assured me, had been taken at the highest level of the Metropolitan Police, which I took to mean the commissioner.

Now there was no question of the operation not continuing. Having made the breakthrough, Pedder still hoped that Stagg would disclose further knowledge to Lizzie or lead police to the murder weapon.

Yet within a week, his position was dramatically shaken by a national newspaper story. Splashed over the front page of the *Star* and two pages inside was an interview with Colin Stagg under the headline, I DIDN'T KILL RACHEL NICKELL. Inside, he claimed he was innocent and that the police were trying to pin the murder on him.

Wickerson, Pedder and Lizzie were driving north from London to see me when they stopped at a motorway service area for petrol. Pedder had glanced at the news-stand and seen the headline.

It was a disaster. Right from the outset, I had warned the investigators that external publicity would influence the disclosures of the suspect, if he was the murderer. Not only would exposure increase his caution regarding self-disclosure, he could also be the recipient of sexual interest from other women, which would obviously dilute the effectiveness of the covert operation.

Pedder looked fit to throttle someone. 'What the fuck can we do?'

'Minimize the damage.'

'I'm open to suggestions.'

I turned to Lizzie. 'You should get straight on the phone to him. Show him you're upset at the story. He's been careless. You've opened your heart to him and told him your darkest secrets and now he's put you in jeopardy by talking to the media. Get him to reassure you that everything is still OK between you.'

In their next few conversations Lizzie made her distress plain and Stagg tried his best to get back into her favour. He also wrote another letter apologizing for upsetting her and including another fantasy to 'cheer you up'.

He set the story on a warm summer's evening on the common where he sits on the grass beside a tree and relaxes. He notices someone walking towards him, a tall sexy blond woman (Lizzie), and they begin having sex against a tree.

Another man joins them and forces his penis into Lizzie's mouth. Meanwhile Stagg says he wants to experiment and retrieves a knife from his clothes.

> *I get between you legs and fuck you hard again. You are now impaled at both ends by two swollen cocks. As I fuck you I draw the knife around your neck. Drops of blood splatter the man's naked legs. You're now screaming in ecstasy. His cock springs from your mouth and you lap up the blood, at the same time he is wanking spunk into your hair and face.*

Stagg followed up the letter with a phone call saying that he wanted to act out the fantasy in real life as soon as possible. Here again was further evidence of serious sexual deviance and one which I regarded as being a more potent indication of actual sexual aggression than much of the material that had gone before.

On 20 July, Pedder and Lizzie sat down with me for one of the last times. Lizzie and Stagg were due to meet at Hyde Park again the next day and we had to discuss the strategy. Having re-established a rapport following the article, Lizzie had to now use a combination of positive attraction and appropriate reserve.

This was their fourth meeting and I knew that she'd find it harder to keep Stagg at a distance, particularly when his own sexual arousal would have increased.

Next morning, at 11.35 a.m., Lizzie secretly turned on the tape and sat down with Stagg at the Dell Cafe. Eventually she steered the conversation to Rachel Nickell and Stagg described his three days in police custody, when the police 'were just trying to break me down'. He said the main evidence against him came from several women who were walking on the common at the time.

As he told the story, he slipped his hands beneath the table and tried to run them up Lizzie's thighs. She shifted position and encouraged him to talk, but soon felt his hands again and had to move.

Lizzie admitted that the murderer fascinated her.

'I think about it. I try and imagine it and the thought of him is so exciting.'

Stagg said, 'I wish it was me who done it, you know, 'cos I mean I feel guilty about the thought of it too, you know. It does turn me on a lot, it did right from the beginning, you know.'

'But what bits turned you on? What was the bits that really, you know, turned you on? Seeing the dead body or imagining it, what was it?'

'Things that he did that he was actually having sex with her at the same time, force, forcing himself into her and that.'

'Is that what he did?'

'That's what he must have done. Yeah. But I mean he must. He probably went just crazy while he was, you know, while he was fucking her, you know, cos she was stabbed about forty-nine times, something like that . . .'

After leaving the cafe, they began walking through Hyde Park.

Lizzie said, 'Didn't they tell you where he'd stabbed her first?'

'No, no, all I know is that he stabbed her forty-nine times, you know, her head was decapitated.'

'Was it?'

'Yeah.'

'Why's that, what did he try and do?'

'Probably just trying to cut her head off.'

'You say she was just gaping wide open.'

'Yeah.'

'What, her genitals?'

'Yeah.'

'Yeah?'

'Yeah she was, that's the way it, 'cos, ah, the photograph was like, ah [he shifts position until he is lying on the ground on his left side with his knees pulled up, his head tilted back and his arms to the side, clasped his hands together as if in prayer]. She's like that and she was like that.'

'Lying, what lying on her side?'

'Yeah and her head was sort of over like that [he tilts his head right back], you know so it must have been sort of half off, but the photograph was taken from that end you know [he points to the direction of his backside].'

Again he had given detailed knowledge of Rachel's body which couldn't be explained by the single photograph he'd been shown. In particular, he showed how her hands were positioned, palm to palm, yet the image marked KP 27 didn't show her hands.

Stagg also repeated his account of being on the common at the time of the murder but specifically denied that he was the murderer.

The upper time limit for the operation that I had specified at the outset had now been reached and it was clear to me that the covert operation had run its course. At a conference between the CPS, the police and myself, it was agreed that Stagg was now unlikely to confess to Lizzie, even if he was the murderer. At the same time, in the light of the *Star* article, he would probably find that a number of women were willing to correspond with him.

Rather than taint the material already gathered, it was decided to end the covert operation and send Lizzie James into retirement. This had to be done carefully. With the police now increasingly believing that Stagg should be charged with murder, it was vital that Lizzie break off contact in such a way as to minimize the risk of him becoming angry and being propelled into harming someone else.

The last of the letters was sent on 10 August, 1993, and the following day I was in the incident room when Pedder told me that a decision had been made to arrest and charge Colin Stagg. Senior lawyers from the CPS had reviewed all the material and agreed there was enough to make a case.

Pedder and I discussed the interviews and both of us expected Stagg to immediately summon a solicitor and go 'no comment'. However, it was still important to put all of his non-answers on the record and Pedder asked me to listen to the early interrogations.

When Stagg was arrested on 17 August there was a tremendous sense of excitement in the Wimbledon Police Station. Many of the officers had invested more than twelve months of their lives into this one case and now felt that their efforts had been justified. At one point the deputy assistant commissioner arrived to add his congratulations. He strode through the door, resplendent in his braided uniform, and he turned to Pedder. 'We're not going to get egg on our faces over this, are we?' he asked.

'Trust me,' said Keith, unwilling to even contemplate failure.

* * *

Bruce Butler, the special case-work lawyer for the CPS, said that he'd need a statement from me to show the probity of the covert operation and to explain how it was designed to lead towards the implication or the elimination of the suspect. He explained to me the sensitivity and precedent-making nature of the case which meant the paperwork had to be perfect and every point covered.

Not being a lawyer, I wasn't aware of the difficulties being envisaged, in particular the likelihood of a defence motion that the evidence gathered during the covert operation was inadmissible because it amounted to entrapment or an interview not under caution. Right at the outset I'd been assured that this wasn't an issue.

'High-level policy discussions are involved,' Butler explained. 'This goes right to the top.'

'And who's at the top?' I asked.

'This case sits at the top of the attorney general's special case list. It's reviewed weekly.'

I remember asking Pedder what would happen if the evidence was ruled inadmissible?

'There's no chance of that,' he said. 'We have the very best advice. Trust me.'

I didn't ponder the question again, it wasn't my business or responsibility. The decision to undertake the covert operation and ultimately to charge Colin Stagg had been made by these people – it was their show.

Over the following weeks and months, I attended a number of meetings with CPS lawyers and Treasury Counsel acting for the Crown. Having been remanded in custody, Stagg would stay in a remand prison until the preliminary hearing before a magistrate in the New Year.

Any thoughts or dreams that I might have had about a quieter more normal life were rapidly punctured. Even when I took a few weeks' annual leave in October, ostensibly for my son's wedding, the time was hijacked by fresh cases. I was deeply involved in the murder inquiry into Nikki Allen, aged seven, who had been stabbed and battered on the Wear Garth estate in Sunderland. Elsewhere, I was looking into a number of rapes in Islington, North London, and also advising detectives from Cumbria about a series of indecent phone calls.

15

SOME CRIMES CAPTURE THE PUBLIC'S IMAGINATION AND OTHERS seem to get lost in the ebb and flow of other news events. Normally, it's quite easy to see why, for example if the victim is young and attractive and the crime is particularly public and chilling, however, this didn't explain why the deaths of Samantha Bissett and her four-year-old daughter Jazmine had received so little publicity in the final months of 1993.

It is something that the SIO Mickey Banks, a detective superintendent with the Metropolitan Police, asked me when we first met in southeast London a week after the murders. Publicity can be the life-blood of an inquiry, particularly when the crime is unusual and the suspect isn't obvious. Without meaning to sound callous, Banks complained, 'What more do the bastards [the media] want? Here you have a lovely mother and her child murdered in the most horrible way and they just won't take it. It should be all over the place.'

I understood his confusion. I very rarely use the word 'horrible' because it's uttered so often nowadays that it's become trite and impotent, but the deaths of Samantha and Jazmine were truly horrible and their killer had to be caught quickly.

Banks and Keith Pedder were friends and Pedder had mentioned my work on the Rachel Nickell case. It led to a call on Emma's birthday, 9 November, and an appointment to meet the next day. In spite of his directions, I still managed to get lost finding Thamesmead Police Station.

I'd never seen a station that looked more like a Portakabin extension or the high school from hell. It seemed to have been thrown together and surrounded by a tall chain-link fence. Now I knew why Banks had urged me to bring my car into the police compound, or risk losing it.

'Hello, Paul. You're late,' he said without sounding critical. 'Have trouble finding us? Decent trip? Glad you were able to get here. Where's your car? Cup of tea? Sugar? Milk?'

He continued chatting as we arrived at his office door which had a handwritten cardboard sign saying 'SIO' taped to the outside. Banks, in his mid-fifties with a craggy face and well-lined forehead, didn't stand on ceremony and immediately shrugged off his jacket, rolled up his sleeves and lit a cigarette. He struck me as an operational-style of detective without time for bureaucratic formalities or niceties; 'one of the boys' who gained respect from his team because he mixed with them, drank with them and worked harder than they did.

There seemed to be more cigarette smoke than air in the room but in deference to me he opened a window and only smoked one at a time.

He asked me, 'What do you want?'

'Whatever you can show me.'

'We've got a mum and a four-year-old daughter murdered in a bloody frenzy,' he said matter-of-factly. 'It's not something you see very often and I never want to see it again. Samantha Bissett and her daughter Jazmine lived in a flat in Plumstead. Their bodies were found last Thursday morning [4 November] by her boyfriend. We're not entirely sure of the chronology because he hasn't been eliminated as a suspect.'

Banks pulled out an album of crime-scene photographs and skipped over the establishing shots. 'I can tell you it was so bad that the photographer has been off work ever since. Sam was stabbed and mutilated. This is how we found her.'

The image was almost surreal. The naked body of a young woman lay on the floor with her entire torso sliced open and her rib cage pulled back so that her organs were displayed. So many thoughts raced through my mind and I felt a mixture of horror, sadness and disbelief. I'd seen dozens of scene of crime photographs before – every one of them is etched into my mind so that I'm unable to forget – but this was different. It was almost like a tableau, as if someone had butchered and opened her in a perverted display that they regarded as a piece of artistry.

Jack the Ripper would have been proud of this piece of work, I thought. I've seen the photographs of his victims and one in particular, the last attributed to him, Mary Jane Kelly, was left in a very similar way to Samantha Bissett. The major difference was that the man who stalked the prostitutes of Whitechapel a century earlier had opened them up crudely and quickly before escaping. Samantha's killer had taken his time and created his tableau joyfully.

This sense of theatrical display was heightened by the almost complete lack of blood around the body. It triggered my first question.

'Where is it? Where's the blood?' I asked.

'Most of the injuries were after death,' said Banks, turning to another photograph. A large pool of blood stained the carpet in the hall. 'We think he killed her near the front door, then he dragged her into the lounge. There doesn't seem to be any sign of a break-in and she had good locks; the flat wasn't ransacked and we haven't found any evidence that anything was stolen.'

Although he tried to describe what happened, Banks didn't have the words and simply flicked through the photographs showing how she had been found. He pointed out a bloody shoe-print found in the kitchen – the only room in the flat that bore signs of having been rifled and disturbed – and then turned to a general shot of the bedroom.

I had to look carefully before I noticed the head of a very young child emerging from the duvet of a bunk bed in the left-hand corner of the room. Lying on her front with her face turned towards the wall, she looked like she was sleeping and dreaming of all the things that children dream about.

Sadly, it wasn't the case. Jazmine had been stripped, sexually assaulted, redressed, put back into bed and smothered with a pillow. What sort of person would do this? What part of hell's pit did he crawl from?

These are the questions that Mickey Banks wanted answered, along with my opinion on what the killer might do next. He took me through the incident room, introducing me to some of his team and explaining various actions that had been initiated. Officers were going door to door in the surrounding streets, others were tracking down Samantha's friends, past boyfriends and her movements in the days leading up to her death.

She was last seen on Wednesday 3 November, picking up Jazmine from nursery school. She'd hurried to get there on foot and arrived just in time at 3.30 p.m. She and Jazmine then took a minicab for the mile and a half journey home to their ground-floor flat in Heathfield Terrace, Plumstead.

Richard Ellam had been her steady boyfriend since early 1991. He told police that he stayed at Samantha's flat on weekends and occasionally during the week but based himself at his father's house in nearby Sidcup in Kent. He last saw Samantha on Wednesday at 12.45 p.m. when he dropped in to the flat. They were both excited about taking Jazmine on a holiday to the Gambia on 11 November and talked about the trip. An hour later he left and walked to his job at a chemical pigments factory.

On Thursday, Ellam woke at 8.30 a.m. and went to the bank and chemist before taking a Number 51 bus to Samantha's flat. When no-one answered the door, he used his keys and entered, calling out 'Hello'. He noticed the dark stain on the carpet and thought something had been spilt. Walking into the lounge room, he discovered Samantha's partially covered body lying in front of the gas fire. Moving to the bedroom he thought Jazmine might be sleeping but realized that she couldn't be, she lay too still.

'We haven't ruled him out,' said Banks, stabbing out another cigarette.

'Is he the father?'

'No. That distinction belongs to a New Age traveller from Hampshire. He's been in touch and we're checking his alibi.'

The door-to-door inquiries had also thrown up several unknown vehicles and unknown males seen in the area in the weeks beforehand. Neighbours reported hearing a man and woman shouting in the flat between 10.30 p.m. and 11.00 p.m. on Wednesday. Two witnesses reported hearing a man and a woman arguing 'in the vicinity' of the flat.

Ellam had told police that a week before the murder, Samantha had told him about a man looking through the window when she went to bed at night. He ran off before she could get a good look at him.

Susan Dewar, whose home overlooked the ground-floor flat, recalled being woken by the sounds of a short scream at 3.00 a.m. on 4 November. She looked out of her window and saw the lights on in Samantha's flat. A fortnight earlier, she was ironing and saw a man staring in at her back door. She described him as being frightening and having piercing eyes.

At this stage it was virtually impossible to say which details were important to me and which were less so. I simply gathered them all so that I could eventually sort the wheat from the chaff. In the meantime, I wanted to visit the flat. We drove and parked the car in front of a small, low-rise development of council flats in a quiet cul-de-sac. A steep flight of concrete steps descended from the road along the side of the building to the front door of number 1a. Below this, the ground fell sharply away into the gardens of several houses and then rose again to form a grassy ridge upon which a half-dozen high-rise apartment blocks overlooked Samantha's flat and Heathfield Terrace.

A large door of wood and steel had been installed by the police. It took a strong shoulder to open it and as light spilled into the hall I saw the large bloodstain on the carpet between the doorways of the bedroom on the left and kitchen on the right. A nearby cupboard had blood splatters draining down the door, but the drips were quite thin and opaque as if they might have fallen from wet hands, I thought.

It was a small flat, quite cluttered and lacking storage space but even though things were stacked in corners and behind doors there was a neatness and purpose to it. Clothing still hung on the radiators and none appeared to have been knocked down in a struggle. Similarly, there was little evidence of searching or robbery.

Going from room to room, I made a rough sketch of the layout and made a note of which windows were locked and where things were found. Was anything disturbed on the window-sills? Is anything out of place, even something as seemingly insignificant as the plug hanging from a chain in the bathroom?

Entering the bedroom, I saw a child's bunk bed in the left-hand corner and beneath it, at right angles, was a full-size mattress with the duvet thrown back as if someone might have just got out of bed. This is where Samantha had slept. Jazmine's toys were everywhere, lining the window-sills, spilling out of the corners and cupboards and weighing down the shelves.

The drag marks in the hallway showed how Samantha's body had been moved by the ankles and put in front of the gas heater in the lounge room with a large cushion under her hips. A mattress in one corner of the room was possibly a spare bed. The large bamboo blind had been rolled down over the window and door to the balcony – something which Samantha never bothered to do, according to neighbours.

In the kitchen, clothing and linen had been taken from cupboards and lay scattered across the floor. This is where the footprint had been found along with traces of blood in the kitchen sink where the killer had possibly cleaned himself. The microwave door was open and there were cups on the bench. A knife was missing from its block and another faced the wrong way.

'How do you think he got in?' I asked.

Banks had seen the flat before and would sooner have been outside where he could smoke. 'The same way we did,' he said. 'I think he probably conned his way in the front door. Either that or it was someone she knew. There's no sign of forced entry, he attacked her in the hall, it makes sense.'

I walked outside, looking up at the balcony, judging the height. Then I turned and looked across at the grassy bank overlooking the rear of Heathfield Terrace and weighed up the potentials.

Banks lit a cigarette. 'Why don't you think she let him in?'

'Maybe she did. I just think this sort of man makes his own arrangements.'

Back at the station I began collecting copies of statements, photographs and the post-mortem reports. It quickly emerged that Banks had another reason for suspecting that Samantha had known her killer and perhaps been expecting him. A neighbour living upstairs had earlier reported her to social services because of men visiting at odd hours.

'We think she might have been on the game,' he said, riffling through a bundle of papers on his desk. 'Not big-time, on the fringes – and only just starting out.'

'What makes you say that?'

'Among her papers we found some letters and newspaper ads. The first few suggest she was lonely and looking for friends.' He handed me a photocopied page of classified ads from the *Greenwich and Eltham Mercury*. One ad had been circled: 'Single mother, 27, needs friends. I'm an honest, reliable, artistic ex-hippy who smokes roll-ups and doesn't eat meat.'

'That was in early 1993,' said Banks. 'The ads changed later in the year. She could have been short of money. Some of them were published and others were refused. We found the draft copies where she worked out the wording.'

He showed me a classified ad from the *London Weekly Advertiser*, dated 8–14 September:

'Up-market, tall, erotic blonde escort, 27, and aching to hear from you generous men. Just tell me what you want. All letters answered.'

Another in a contacts magazine read: 'Young sexy long-legged blonde requires a nice gentleman with spare cash to pay small child's school fees in return for regular, discreet, no strings, fun liaisons. Cannot accommodate. Very genuine.'

She had also written to a photographic and video magazine: 'Deliciously hot and sensual blonde female model, 26, available to amateur and professional photographers for well paid work. No time wasters.'

The ads appeared in a number of London free-sheets and newspapers and, according to friends, resulted in Samantha receiving several disturbing phone calls. Banks had a team of detectives checking telephone records and addresses in a bid to trace any of the men who contacted her. There was also evidence that Samantha occasionally answered advertisements she read in the personal columns from men seeking partners.

Certain things that I had seen at the flat now began to make sense, but before I could be sure, I needed to learn more about Samantha and her lifestyle. Banks filled in some of the details and promised to send me a statement from her mother, Margaret Morrison, who was under sedation suffering from shock.

Samantha, the daughter of an artist, had been born in Dundee in Scotland but spent much of her early life in London and nearby Hemel Hempstead in Hertfordshire. Her father had died of lung cancer when Samantha was fourteen years old and she and her mother moved back to Scotland. Well-spoken and well-educated, she showed her father's artistic flair and dreamed of going to art school. But she found life in Scotland rather restricting after London. Having an English accent didn't help and she struggled to make friends.

Leaving school disillusioned and unhappy, she rebelled against her conventional middle-class background and took to the road as a New Age traveller, spending time in various hippy communes and 'peace convoys'. She was a restless free spirit, almost like a sixties flower child who dabbled in various drugs, wore flowing clothes and let her hair grow long.

When Samantha became pregnant by a fellow traveller, she wrote to her mother giving his qualifications – well-educated, father a barrister, mother a teacher – as if to say that this was the father she desired for her child, but it was never on the cards that they were going to be a couple.

Jazmine was born in London and Margaret travelled down to help find Samantha somewhere to live. She settled down in the flat in Plumstead and the baby transformed her life. She devoted herself entirely to Jazmine, sparing no expense and spending her days taking her on outings and playing on a patch of lawn outside the flat. Apart from the abundance of toys, there were paintings and drawings by Jazmine on almost every door and wall.

Samantha's free-wheeling lifestyle had changed with motherhood, although she still wore flowing dresses, sunbathed topless in the back garden and walked around semi-dressed without drawing the blinds or locking the balcony door.

She talked to her mother on the telephone every Sunday and took Jazmine to Scotland for holidays. Mrs Morrison, who had remarried, had sent her £1,000 to pay for the holiday to the Gambia because she sensed that Samantha needed cheering up.

But why would a woman so committed to her child and who had a steady boyfriend and a history of free and open relationships be meeting people for money? And where was the evidence of it? The answer was to be found in Jazmine's room. Whereas the rest of the council flat was extremely modest and in need of paint and wallpaper, the bedroom looked like Santa's grotto filled with toys and games. According to her boyfriend, Samantha had been prepared to make any sacrifice for Jazmine, even going hungry to buy her toys.

She was concerned about her daughter's education and talked of moving to an area with better schools. Living on single mother benefits and cheques from her mother, she sometimes became depressed about her finances. Initially, she considered modelling and had a portfolio of portraits taken. She also answered ads in magazines from photographers looking for new talent. When these came to nothing, she tried the personal columns.

Here was a naive young woman, I thought, who probably didn't fully understand the rapaciousness of what she was exploring. She was the sort of person who might easily have been seduced or steered towards the seedier areas of photography without being streetwise enough to realize the dangers.

Equally, I felt that she hadn't seriously embraced prostitution. If so, the flat would have shown the trappings of the profits. Samantha was more than attractive enough to find men who would take care of her and Jazmine, but she lived in a modest flat, without a bedroom of her own. She had ordinary friends and inexpensive clothes; and her mother had provided the money for the Gambian holiday.

All of this told me that she couldn't really be classed as a prostitute because she didn't have the street wisdom or ruthlessness to capitalize on her looks to make money. I think she was an idealist who had rather glossy romantic aspirations of her future and imagined falling in love, marrying a successful man and giving Jazmine the best up-bringing possible.

There is not a single scene of crime which I have seen that I cannot remember in every haunting detail. They stay with me, as if engraved into my mind and I can't always control when they come back into full focus. Samantha and Jazmine were like that. Over the next week, their images flashed back to me no matter how hard I tried to shut them out.

At night when I sat in my study reviewing the details, I didn't mind the intrusions, but it was harder when they visited during a case conference at Arnold Lodge or a prison interview. A difficult crime can sometimes push away the rest of my life. There might be a birthday celebration at home and, amid the laughter and gaiety, the reality of a murder comes back to me and steals some of the joy away.

This work has changed me over the past fifteen years. Others around me can see the differences, although I'm not sure how much is to do with growing older and how much can be attributed to the nature of the material I deal with each day. If you look at me now, I am a relatively quiet person. I've always been reserved but I suspect that I was more outgoing and capable of striking up friendships a decade ago. Most people would say that I laughed more back then and mixed more easily.

Emma and Ian tease me about my unadventurous nature. We've lived in the same village for ten years and I know the name of the neighbours on one side but not the other. The local pub is less than a hundred yards away and I've been perhaps a dozen times, mostly dragged there by Ian. Emma used to joke that I'd get lost going to the local postbox.

I don't see myself as being unsociable or a loner. Unfortunately, the reality of my life is that I spend most of it in other people's depraved, dangerous or wounded minds so that when I get home and sit in a familiar armchair, I simply want to turn off for a while, draw my family close and try to forget.

I have no doubt that I draw tremendous strength from my faith. I know many people will think, how the hell can you believe in God when you've seen such dreadful things? I struggle to answer such a question, but faith doesn't have to be explained or defended.

There was a time when I had my doubts and, equally, if I had the chance to do it again, I'm not sure I would have chosen the same pathway and become a forensic psychologist; not if I'd realized the depth of the pain and disquiet. This may sound like self-pity, but it isn't meant to be. These are simply the kind of thoughts that occur to me at one o'clock in the morning, sitting at my desk, staring at the post-mortem pictures of a four-year-old girl.

At the same time, the pain is leavened with a cold anger that says, 'Do whatever it takes, but get whoever did this off the streets.' Somewhere in between these two feelings, I find my balance.

Questions kept forming as I looked at the lividity marks on Jazmine's body, indicating where the pull of gravity had caused the blood to settle in the lowest points of her body after death. She had obviously been found lying on her face but other lividity patterns indicated that for some time after death she was in a slightly different position. Why had she been moved?

Other things spoke to me. I noticed her underpants were stained with blood from the sexual assault in such a way as to mean they were replaced afterwards. Her panties were also stained with urine but the flow was wrong for it to have happened in precisely the position in which she had been found. In all likelihood she lost bladder control during the attack and the staining indicated she had probably been sitting up when it happened. Sadly, this clearly indicated that there had been a more complex interaction with the killer who hadn't simply assaulted her as she lay in bed and then smothered her with a pillow.

Following the photographic sequence down the hall and into the lounge, I saw Samantha with her arms stretched out above her head, with her buttocks supported by a large cushion. She wore a blood-stained bathrobe which had three knife-holes over the right shoulder, dark blue socks and a bra. Her upper body and face were covered with the robe and various pieces of linen and clothing taken from the kitchen.

One by one the various materials covering her had been removed and photographs taken. He had cut through her body wall and into the internal cavity from the base of her neck to her pubic bone with a series of jagged incisions and then across her torso before her chest cavity was peeled open with enough force to snap the ribcage.

Mickey Banks and his colleagues had talked about the knifeman being 'frenzied' and 'out of control' but that was wrong. There was no slashing or uncontrolled stabbing as in Rachel Nickell's murder. By comparison, this was a precise surgical or anatomical exploration. Stabbing was the least of what was done to her – she was almost filleted.

At some point a clear attempt had been made to dismember her legs, but the knife had probably by then become blunted and the killer didn't have the anatomical knowledge of how best to fully sever a joint.

Because Samantha had died and bled in the hall, there was little blood in the lounge. However, this meant that a single, isolated stain on the sofa stood out and puzzled me. Had he sat down to survey his handiwork, I wondered, leaving the stain, or did he rest Samantha against the sofa while he prepared the room? Another possibility occurred to me and I made a note to ask Mickey Banks whether Samantha's body had been reassembled at the mortuary.

The Home Office pathologist had found few defence injuries apart from small grazes on several fingers. He found that Samantha had died from multiple stab wounds, four of which passed through her heart, while her other injuries occurred after death. There were possibly two knives involved, both thin-bladed, very sharp, and about seven inches long.

The sequence of events eluded me at first and I began writing questions for Mickey Banks. Things like: can you confirm that the toys on the window-sill weren't disturbed? Is Jazmine's head at the right end of the bed? The duvet on Samantha's mattress has been thrown back – did she make it up every morning? Apart from the kitchen is there any other evidence of the killer walking blood through the flat? How freshly used are the coffee cups on the kitchen worktop? The phone book is open – is anything marked or highlighted? There are daubs of blue paint on the kitchen wall, could Jazmine reach that high? There are paint chips on the balcony handrail, how new are they, where do they come from? Could the marks on the brick wall beneath the balcony be shoe scuff marks?

I also jotted down questions that Banks couldn't be expected to answer, but I had to consider them. For example, why didn't Jazmine have a cuddly toy with her? Why was there no foot impression on the mattress below her bed? One of Jazmine's pictures is missing from the wall, who moved it? The door to the cassette player was open and a cassette box rested on the fire screen, did he play music to himself?

These might seem like insignificant details, but you can't take anything at face value when dealing with people who commit bizarre crimes. For example, just because there is a paint daub on a wall in the same flat as a child, it doesn't mean the two automatically go together.

In early December I went back to see Mickey Banks. We'd talked several times on the telephone and he'd been sending me new material. In particular, I wanted to ask about the post-mortem report. Through a cloud of smoke, I sat in his office explaining the psychopathology of different sorts of murderers. In this case I saw a deliberate, relaxed, almost euphoric mutilation of a young woman along with the almost incidental murder and rearrangement of a child.

'But I need more detail. I want to know where he started cutting her and what order he did things in. He savoured this, and to understand him I have to know exactly what he's done. For instance, did he take anything away?'

Banks asked, 'What do you mean?'

'The photographs don't show me if any part of her body has gone. If it has, then you're looking at a trophy-taker.'

Banks looked horrified. 'Surely if something were missing, the pathologist would have told us?'

'I don't know if they put her back together or simply assumed she was all there.'

I could see that Banks didn't relish asking the Home Office pathology unit to reassemble the body; he was looking for more justification.

'You remember the bloodstain on the sofa?' I asked. 'Did you ever wonder how it got there?'

Banks nodded.

I went on, 'The way I see it, there are three likely scenarios. He could have rested Samatha's body against the sofa at some point; or maybe he sat down to admire his handiwork. But I think he might have put something on the sofa – a part of her.'

I could see the detective's disgust. He didn't want to believe it, but said, 'I'll get them to check.'

A supplementary report was prepared on 14 December, nearly six weeks after the first post-mortem. The pathologist wrote, 'I reconstructed the incised wounds of the chest and abdomen and noted that a portion of the abdominal wall approx 12 cm by 10 cm was absent on the right side.'

Banks was annoyed and couldn't understand how this had been missed the first time.

However, it didn't surprise me because the idea of sexual mutilation and trophy-taking is uncommon and outside the experience of most murder investigators and pathologists; it doesn't even enter their thinking. Normally the most urgent priority is establishing the cause of death and, in this case, how many knives were used and their measurements.

However, the trophy-taking had confirmed my worst fears about the killer. The final pieces were in place and I could tell Mickey Banks about the man responsible and the most likely sequence of events.

'Is it a one-cup, or a two-cup story?' asked Banks, ordering some tea. An intelligent and softly spoken man, he had a very pragmatic and practical approach to his work. He wanted to be shown the whole picture and to understand more about his quarry. In some ways I felt sorry for him. Unlike other investigations I had been involved in, particularly those that were high profile like the murder of Rachel Nickell, Banks was operating in a virtual backwater in southeast London without the mainstream attention of his superiors in the Metropolitan Police.

Compare this to the Nickell investigation where senior command at New Scotland Yard took a great deal of interest from the very beginning. Intense media scrutiny seemed to set the agenda, along with influential community groups, although it was also suggested it might have something to do with the Metropolitan Police commissioner's wife being on Wimbledon Common at the time of the murder.

Banks listened as I explained to him the nature of sexual deviancy and its various manifestations. Again the seeds were likely to have been sown in this man's infancy and childhood.

'I would expect to find disturbance in his early life, particularly within his family,' I said. 'At some point he became a problem and quite likely the victim of other people's problems.'

'He grew up with a different set of values from most of us and these may have brought him to the attention of the police or social services. Any attempts to repair the psychological damage that may have been present at the time clearly failed.

'Within this childhood he was probably the victim as well as the inflictor of violence,' I said. In the process he learned how aggression could be used to solve problems and it became a substitute for talking. It's far easier to lash out and force someone to do what you want than to learn the social skills necessary to help them see things your way.

I've interviewed patients who suffer from violent tempers and they talk about a pressure building up inside their heads as if someone is squeezing their skull with a steel clamp. This tension builds up and up and finally explodes into violence. Immediately, the pressure goes away and for a short time there is a tremendous sense of relief as if the steel clamp has been loosened.

Samantha and Jazmine's killer is likely to have grown up feeling that he isn't valued and his hostile attitudes are based on the assumption that if people aren't well-disposed to him, it's far better to act first before they hurt him. This also manifests itself in his attitudes towards sex and his relationships with women.

As with Rachel Nickell's killer, an anger and sense of bitterness develops and can fuel fantasies of being able to punish, control and dominate women, making them do what he wants. If this process escalates, fantasies are taken into the real world and are acted upon. This pathway isn't necessarily a nice, neat linear climb from indecent exposure to minor sexual assaults to rape and then to murder. Offenders are opportunists as well as planners and will do whatever is available if that means raping one day and exposing themselves the next.

Understanding this meant appreciating the delicate interaction between opportunity, sexuality and the other factors in an offender's life because his day-to-day existence will have a layered richness just like everyone else. He's going to enjoy the cinema occasionally, eat at restaurants, catch a cold and prefer certain types of clothes and haircuts. The patterning of all of these things determines who he is and what he does.

'Yeah but not everyone enjoys slicing up a woman's body,' said Banks incredulously.

I explained that men respond to a broad range of sexual stimuli; one only has to look at the array of pornography produced to cater for them. People tend to assume that what they see in magazines on the top shelf of the local newsagent is what pornography is all about – pictures of naked women and risqué stories about adultery and over-sexed housewives.

Unfortunately, there are publications that pander to far narrower and more specific tastes. These include pornography that deals with sadism, violence, and rape, as well as the most dreadful child sex films that can range from showing the child as an apparently willing consenting lover who is groomed and seduced, to the extreme of showing the child clearly in agony as he or she is grossly sexually violated. For people who are excited by this last category, the child's agony is the important thing.

There are others who fantasize about the acquisition of women who are kept as slaves, tortured and humiliated, before ultimately being killed and then mutilated. Certain people's deviancy locks on to different aspects of this process. For some it is the whole scenario that excites them, for others it is the victim's death and for Samantha's killer it was the mutilation.

'In many ways this is the ultimate sexual offence,' I told Banks. 'It might not look sexual but if you consider Samantha's injuries, most of the cruel damage is in the vulval and vaginal area and he took his trophy from the lower region. The mutilation was part of a refined sexual fantasy that had matured over years. Her killer wanted complete control of a woman and he couldn't have achieved more intimate control than being able to do what he did to Samantha's body, not even if he'd tortured her or turned her into his sex slave.

'This man wasn't sadistic, otherwise he would have kept Samantha alive for longer and taken enjoyment from her suffering and fear, and from his control over her. Instead he killed her quickly and then focussed on his main source of pleasure, the interaction with her body.'

From the very beginning I'd been asked to consider whether the same man could have been responsible for the murder of Rachel Nickell on Wimbledon Common. Both victims were blond attractive mothers who were savagely murdered. A child had been present in each case and a knife or knives had been used.

In my view the presence of a child in both attacks was the single largest differentiating factor between them, rather than a link. In the first case Alex was entirely a matter of disinterest to the killer, while Jazmine had been an important object of sexual gratification for the killer. Equally, the Plumstead murders involved a much more refined scenario where the pleasure gained from the post-mortem injuries was greater than any joy taken from the actual killing. There was a sense of exploration and discovery whereas Rachel's murder had been frenzied and over within six minutes as the killer downloaded his anger and bitterness. It was a completely different scenario.

Banks said, 'You mentioned his fantasy having "matured". How old is he?'

'Twenty-five plus. This isn't his first crime or his first sexual crime; his sexuality grew into this very narrow and particular direction but he will still have vestiges of an earlier, less discriminate range of sexual pastimes.'

'Such as?'

'Voyeurism, indecent exposure, indecent assault, rape. He may have used prostitutes and have hurt or attempted to hurt them with a knife rather than sexually assaulted them. He may also use contact advertisements to arrange meetings with women.'

'I thought you favoured the balcony as his likely point of entry?'

'I still do, but it's not clear how he became aware of Samantha. He could have met her through the contact ads and then started to watch her or follow her. It can't be ruled out. If he does use contact ads, it's even more likely that he's had dealings with prostitutes in the past.'

Moving on to the next point, I said, 'There's no reason to expect him to be of other than normal intelligence. This is a man who is now confident in his ability and his motivation. The way he was able to gain access to the address and spend upwards of an hour in the flat leaving relatively few identifying traces behind indicates a man who is in control of himself and the situation. He's thinking all the time.'

My opinion of the killer's intelligence related to his cognitive functioning rather than his mental state or any possible personality disorder. People often make the mistake of assuming that someone must be mentally ill to have done such a thing. In fact the presence of mental illness alone neither implicates nor eliminates a person from an inquiry, except when it so limits their functioning as to make it impossible for them to actually carry out the act. Similarly, people assume that if a person is mentally ill then any crime he or she commits must be a consequence of this illness. Again this is not necessarily so. It's perfectly possible for a person to commit an offence that is not related to their mental illness. Equally we must remember that mental illness is not a constant state and a person can suffer only periodic problems. This is what often makes it so difficult to establish exactly what went on in someone's mind when they pulled the trigger or used the knife.

'He's a calculated risk-assessor and self-preservation is important,' I told Banks, referring again to how few traces were left behind in the flat. 'But he wasn't always this way. He's matured into this careful sexual murderer and in the early stages of his offending he may have been more careless.

'It's also clear that his sexual interests aren't restricted to adult women. They're quite broad.'

This is one of the things that the investigators had struggled to understand. If this man set out to murder and mutilate Samantha, why bother touching Jazmine? One reason, of course, is that Jazmine was in the way. But if this was his only concern he would simply have smothered her with a pillow. Instead he penetrated her which indicated a broader range to his sexual deviancy. It meant that the police search for possible links with other crimes had to consider offences involving children as well as adult women.

Continuing with the profile, I said, 'He's always going to be looking for new victims and will respond at short notice to high risk victims or when an opportunity presents itself. This might mean indecent exposure or a minor indecent assault or going out and raping while the dinner is cooking. However, periodically, he will have much stronger urges that relate to the fantasies that have driven Samantha's death. He will need to seek out new women victims and he will be driven in those times by strong levels of anger and lust, together with feelings of personal inadequacy. He's going to want a particular woman because she stands out in his mind but he knows that she's never going to say, "I like you, let's go to bed." He knows that he can't have her and it makes him angry. He will have an escalating sense of being insulted by her and by women in general.'

Banks asked, 'Is he likely to be married or to have a girlfriend?'

'I doubt it. I don't think this man will have the empathic ability to make a marriage work or to sustain a relationship. His sexual deviation has matured but not his personality and he clearly has some form of psychological dysfunction, although I don't know the shape of it. These things would prevent him sustaining a relationship.

'Having said that, there's no reason to expect that he has poor social skills and couldn't get by in the community without standing out. I think he's personally confident in what he does and what he wants but I doubt if he could cope with a woman who had her own sexual needs and who presented herself as an equal partner rather than in a submissive role.'

Banks asked, 'What about employment?'

'Given his intelligence and social skills I see no reason why he can't be holding down a job but it's going to be unexceptional work, most likely unskilled manual labour.'

I mentioned that pornography would feature in this man's life, particularly anything that focussed on the mutilation of women if he could get access to it. In the course of the investigation, if detectives came across intelligence regarding underground publications of this nature, they should look closely at the mailing lists.

'This man isn't seeking attention or notoriety. He doesn't care about making *News at Ten.* By this stage, his focus is on the pleasure he receives from post-mortem contact with a body rather than any sense of notoriety on a grand scale. He does, however, have a sense of display evident in how he left the bodies. But this was designed to impact on the people who found the scene and not for a wider audience.

'Because this man knows that he doesn't like the world and that the world doesn't appreciate him, he could be provoked into further killings by perceiving himself as being regarded as a monster or being despised by those referring to him.'

This was an important point for Mickey Banks to remember when making statements to the media. Because the killer was being driven to some extent by anger and a sense of personal inadequacy, if he saw himself being referred to in a way that confirmed all of the bad things he believed people felt about him, it would fuel the inadequacy and lack of self-esteem, making him angry again.

At the same time I knew he probably had a strong psychological defence against seeing himself in a negative light and would project blame outwards. I told Banks, 'This is not a man who goes home and beats his chest and tears his hair out, saying "Oh my God, what have I done? How can I stop?" He doesn't want to explain or negotiate or to make excuses. He can do what he likes to a victim because, "She's mine and she's mine on my terms." There's no remorse.

'He will have a previous history of aggressive offending against women and *may* have a history of animal mutilation.' The latter potentiality is supported by a growing amount of literature that has established a link between mutilation murderers and a childhood or teenage fascination with injuring animals. This goes back to a desire for power and control.

Having explained the psychological profile, I began plotting the most likely sequence of events. This man is a watcher, I thought. He's likely to stalk a victim if he becomes preoccupied with her, particularly a woman who becomes important to him, someone he wants to savour. Samantha is such a woman. It doesn't mean he won't respond to short notice or high risk victims like prostitutes or women who let him inside their houses, but the conditions would have to be right in terms of self-preservation and privacy.

This man has lots of psychologically familiar places from where he can watch women undress or make love. One of them is the grassy bank overlooking the rear of the houses and flats in Heathfield Terrace. The bank has an unfortunate combination of features; while it isn't used very often for pedestrian traffic, certainly at night, someone sitting there wouldn't necessarily attract attention. This made it perfect for watching a young attractive mother and daughter living in an accessible flat. Samantha never bothered closing the curtains or blinds. He could see right into her lounge and bedroom, absorbing the rhythms of her life into his fantasies.

Perhaps he'd seen her have sex with her boyfriend in front of the gas fire in the lounge with a cushion under her hips. Real life episodes such as this would be incorporated into his fantasies, increasing the clarity of the experience and also the pleasure.

He probably watched Samantha get ready for bed and turn off the light on Wednesday 3 November. Then he came over the balcony, using the handrail to pull himself up and scuffing his trainers on the moss and mud-splattered bricks nearest the ground. He knew about the balcony and the layout of the flat because he'd been watching. Otherwise he would have left more traces of himself as he fumbled in a strange place.

The sequence of what happened next has never been entirely clear and each of the possible scenarios has weaknesses. On one level, you might think what does it matter who he killed first? It matters because what he did, how he did it and when he did it determines why he did it – and everything comes back to the motivation.

I don't think any intruder could have assaulted Jazmine unless Samantha had been already dead or dying. Everything I had learned about Samantha cried out that she would have fought and died to save her daughter. Most likely, she heard a sound, pushed back the duvet, put on her bathrobe and went to investigate. He attacked her in the hall, stabbing her eight times in the neck and then leaving her for long enough for her blood to have drained away.

The fact that no blood traces were found in the bedroom suggested that the killer had cleaned his hands before he entered, perhaps using kitchen towels. The only blood on Jazmine was her own. Similarly, Jazmine is unlikely to have been woken by the attack on her mother and to have confronted the killer because he wouldn't have had time to wipe his hands. I think she was probably still asleep when he entered the room. After sexually assaulting and smothering her, the killer went back to the hall and dragged Samantha into the lounge, feet first, until she came to rest in front of the gas fire, lying face up. He pushed a large cushion beneath her hips, this raised her vulva towards him, emphasizing what he was working towards.

By now his excitement had built up and reached a controlled plateau. He began the mutilation, getting to know Samantha in a way that was so intimate and pleasurable for him that it transcended ordinary sex. Women had rejected him and he couldn't understand why, but now he was getting to know them in an intimate exploration as well as in punishment and revenge.

Imagine a person whose great mission in life is collecting paintings. There are two levels of need – one is the urge to locate and acquire the art, and then, afterwards at leisure there is the tremendous contentment at being able to look at it and say, 'It's mine.' This man was creating his own 'work of art' in a place that offered quiet pleasure and deep fulfilment.

Afterwards he rifled through cupboards and drawers in the kitchen, pulling out tablecloths, teatowels and unironed clothing. He wanted material to cover Samantha's body and, in so doing, to create a little tableau that someone else would find, like gift-wrapping a present. In this way, whoever came across the body would be unprepared and would never be able to rid themselves of the memory of his creation.

This depraved tableau continued in the bedroom. The lividity marks on Jazmine's body indicate that she had been moved some time after her death which means the killer must have returned to the room and rearranged the scene. It was almost as if he wanted someone to open the door, look into the room and think, how lovely, a child sleeping under a duvet and then have them discover the awful truth.

When it was all over the vivid images would remain in this man's mind. He would replay them over and over in his masturbatory fantasies in the same way as other men or women remember a particular love-making experience.

I said to Banks, 'When these recollections begin to dim – and they will – he's going to think to himself, "I could have done better." He'll look at his trophy and say, "Next time, I'll do this and that . . .". You have to remember, this is the most unique, pleasurable and exciting experience of this man's life and when the urge is strong enough, he's going to want to do it again.'

16

CHRISTMAS COULDN'T COME QUICKLY ENOUGH. FOR A FEW WEEKS I wanted to forget about work and slip into the comforting embrace of my family with nothing more serious to worry about than whether I had any spare bulbs for the tree lights. Marilyn could see I was tired. It had been a hectic year and she had begun to question whether I had trained so long and hard to go through the rest of my life surrounded by horror and depravity. I had started asking myself the same question.

This had never been an issue before. Having seen what predatory murderers and rapists do; and having treated the victims of violent crime, I couldn't ignore requests for my help. Similarly, in my clinical work, I felt that if I could prevent just one person from going on to commit such crimes and save people from ever becoming victims, then it had to be worthwhile. Yet none of these things could overcome the reality that the very nature of the work erodes you.

Because forensic psychology involves building up a rapport with offenders so that you can actually help them to change, one of the fundamental principles is an unconditional acceptance of them as potentially valuable people. You cannot look upon a person as some evil creature who, nevertheless, you have decided to help. Instead, you have to engage with them at a human level in order to help them to change.

One way to build such a rapport is by diverting your mind from the horror of what was done to the victim and to focus only on the clinical need of the patient in front of you. Unfortunately, my psychological profiling work meant that I had seen the terrible deeds first-hand and spent hours looking at the remains of dreadfully defiled young women and children. It's not easy to put aside these flesh and blood memories when you sit across a desk and look into the eyes of someone who has committed a similar crime or is excited by the prospect.

For this reason, it's not a case of one side of my work being any more or less disturbing than the other. The impact of looking at crime-scene photographs and walking through the crime scene is enormous, but it's equally disturbing when you sit and listen to someone recalling their darkest deeds or fantasies and you see how much joy and pleasure this gives them.

Some of these patients are able to conjure up and create events in their minds that are so extreme and sadistic that, mercifully, you hardly see anything like it in real life. Worryingly, not all of these people are securely detained. Unless they have actually committed an offence, they can be free to walk the streets and perhaps the only thing stopping them enacting their fantasies may be the clinical hold that I or a colleague have on them. I can't force them to come and see me, only encourage them, and then use all of my experience to hold them in check.

Other cases can involve making decisions that determine the future of people's lives. It might be a risk assessment on behalf of the Social Services Department, or a psychological report for the defence or for the Crown. Depending on my judgement, a court may well decide that someone is a danger to themselves or the community and should be detained. I think of cases such as a stalker who had threatened to kill two women. I had to decide if his threats were serious and whether he should be viewed as a criminal or a person who was psychologically disturbed and, if so, what was the actual degree of risk he posed to his victims.

Such decisions have enormous implications. If I get it wrong then someone may die, or a man may be sent to prison or a secure hospital and lose everything that he holds precious – his house, his job, his wife and his family.

Or perhaps I have to assess whether a father is safe to be left with his daughter. If I think he poses a danger and that the mother is unable to protect her, then the girl will probably be taken away into care or freed for adoption. Not only will the father never see her again but forever-after he will be labelled as an intractable sex offender. On the other hand, if his daughter stays and he doesn't respond to treatment then I know that she will be badly sexually abused and her life will be destroyed. I can't afford to be wrong.

All of this creates a burden and Marilyn had seen the subtle changes in me. It had been more than three years since we had taken a holiday; and every weekend and Bank Holiday seemed to be taken over with work. At the same time, a question had arisen about my eyesight.

When I turned forty in 1986, a routine eye check had revealed I was suffering from glaucoma, or more technically – intra-ocular hypertension. This is a blinding illness caused by pressure building up inside the eyes. Each eyeball is basically a ball of clear fluid with the amount of liquid carefully maintained. Too much and pressure builds up until it can cut off the blood supply in the tiny veins at the back of the eye and ultimately cause the nerve to die. Blindness is the result.

When my consultant first gave me this diagnosis, he told me that we'd become good friends. He was right. Over the years I've taken a merry-go-round of different medications to control my eye pressure, with none of the combinations really working for any longer than a few months.

Right from the beginning the consultant stressed to me that lifestyle made a difference. Long hours, irregular sleep, work pressure and financial worries could all have an impact on the condition. This is what Marilyn feared whenever she saw me looking tired and run-down. She wanted to know how much longer I would keep trying to do so many things at once.

At one stage I had twenty-seven active investigations where police had asked for my help. I simply couldn't get to them all, and so responded to the most urgent. As a result, I never reached some of the others, or by the time I did get to them my advice wasn't necessary or relevant. It didn't make any sense to have SIOs and investigations waiting on the convenience of my diary. There had to be a better way of doing things.

Although the Home Office had accepted all of my recommendations for the development of offender profiling in Britain, the wheels turned very slowly in Whitehall. In the meantime, I was receiving a growing number of requests to lecture and teach offender profiling. Some of these were very worthwhile, particularly those that fitted in well with the review recommendations. Surely this is the way forward, I thought.

'Are you going to spend the rest of your life going to crime scenes?' Marilyn asked me on Christmas night. She'd asked the question many times before. She wanted to know when our lives would settle down and we'd have weekends like other people and be able to take holidays.

These were perfectly reasonable expectations. Our children had married and left home and she reminded me of the conversations we'd had all those years ago, talking about the things we'd do when they'd gone.

'Things are going to change,' I said.

'When?'

'Maybe next year. We'll see what happens after the Rachel Nickell trial.'

We talked about what I might do and although I wasn't exactly clear I knew it might involve leaving the NHS. A clear direction was to offer consultancy and training services in risk management, hostage and kidnap negotiation and crime analysis. I also wanted to use my organizational and forensic expertise to advise individuals, corporations and the law enforcement agencies on specialist aspects of crime prevention. Rather than picking over the pieces of a crime scene, I knew that many crimes could be stopped from happening in the first place. From these vague plans, I felt sure I could fashion a more normal life.

On Boxing Day, Keith Pedder and I flew to Washington, with Marilyn coming along as my secretary. The aim of the journey was twofold. On the one hand we were looking for examples of where offender profiling had been used as evidence in American criminal trials. At the same time, we also wanted to subject the covert operation to independent scrutiny by our opposite numbers in the FBI.

The committal hearing for Colin Stagg was due to begin in February and the prosecution had decided to rely heavily not only on Lizzie James's evidence, but also on the probative value of my evidence concerning the extremely rare sexual deviation that I expected to find in the killer of Rachel Nickell.

Neither offender profiling nor psychological crime analysis had been used in evidence in a British courtroom before. There were, however, examples in America where FBI profilers had given evidence and the CPS wanted first-hand views on what obstacles they had faced and whether any of the cases were comparable.

Aside from answering these questions, Bruce Butler had also asked us to look at the differences between offender profiling techniques in each country. He wanted me to be sure that we were up to the moment with the American methodology and to be able to compare it with work done in Britain should the need arise.

Arriving in Washington, we were met by Judd Ray, an FBI agent who looked like a young Sammy Davis Jnr. I'd met Judd previously when he spent a six-month fellowship in the UK, at the Bramshill police training college. A fascinating man, he'd spent eleven years working for a New York Homicide division and had once been the victim of a contracted 'hit'. Three bullets were pumped into him and although he survived his marriage didn't; his wife couldn't live with the worry that it might happen again. During the Vietnam War he was a member of a deep penetration group working behind enemy lines and was the only one of the platoon to survive the conflict. These experiences showed in the man who had a stillness about him that was almost touchable.

The FBI training facility at Quantico, Virginia, has gained an almost mythical status since films like *The Silence of the Lambs* threw a spotlight onto offender profilers. The Behavioural Science Unit is based in 'The Bunker', a nuclear bomb shelter built for the White House staff. It has no windows or natural light and all life is accompanied by the low level hum of the air conditioners.

Over Christmas most of the staff were on vacation but some of the pioneers of offender profiling had agreed to give up their time to meet with us, including Roy Hazelwood who was on his last day with the Bureau before retiring. Initially he was only going to sit in for a few minutes but stayed for most of the day.

Sitting next to him Judd Ray introduced Greg Cooper, another senior agent, and Janna Monroe, a striking blonde who had the distinction of being the only female profiler at Quantico. Over the years a number of female agents had joined, but none of them had stayed except Janna. I think the nature of the work had proved to be too disturbing. Although I'd never seen *The Silence of the Lambs* I couldn't help but imagine her from a film-maker's point of view.

I felt this conference was of crucial importance. It would be the first time that my analysis of the murder and conception of the principles behind the covert operation were critically examined by an independent group of experts.

As Pedder began to describe the crime, Roy Hazelwood interrupted, 'Oh this is a disorganized killer.'

This is one of the categories the FBI uses to differentiate offenders

– 'disorganized' referring to crime scenes that show evidence of impulsive, violent acts with little evidence of forward planning or attempts to avoid discovery or detection.

I picked up on Roy's comment and went over how Rachel had been acquired and controlled, the manner in which her body had been displayed and how quickly and effectively her killer had disappeared from the scene, leaving few clues behind. 'These aren't the classic signs of what you refer to as a "disorganized" offender.'

'No, you're right,' said Roy, altering his view.

All of them were fascinated by the covert operation – never having seen anything like it before – and we spent the best part of a day going over the case. Subtly, a transition took place and instead of checking legal precedent, the meeting became a forum for swapping knowledge. I could tap into the enormous experience of these investigators and detectives, while they were fascinated by the psychological principles that underpinned my work.

The Americans have developed two separate strands of profiling. The first is computer based and is to a large extent a number-crunching exercise. The details of hundreds of previous crimes are carefully catalogued and categorized within the computer database and can then be compared with the features of any new crime. This can indicate whether the fresh offence is linked to any other cases in the database and help keep track of serial offenders.

The second strand deals with the development of individual profiles that are rooted more in the psychology of the criminal and his crime. FBI agents study particular cases and draw up profiles using their own personal experience as investigators, as well as the knowledge gained from attending lectures and courses run by psychologists and law enforcement professionals acknowledged to have a special expertise in this area.

In Britain some schools of offender and psychological profiling use the number-crunching approach developed by the FBI for linking crimes. Essentially, they rely upon an arithmetical series of results. For example, let's say, 80 per cent of serial sexual murderers are committed by men aged between twenty and twenty-five; and of these 50 per cent have previous convictions for minor sexual offences. These arithmetical abstractions – based on convictions in earlier cases – are then used to support conclusions about a wanted sex killer's most likely age, education, criminal history and locale, etc.

However, if this is *all* that an offender profile is based upon, then what about the twenty per cent of serial sexual murderers who don't fit into the criteria?

As a psychologist, I view each case as being unique. There is no theoretical reason why a crime must fit into neat clear boundaries, much less the criminal who committed it. Unless there is something else at the crime scene to support such findings, I think it can be very dangerous to make judgements based solely on conviction rates and past crimes that have no specific connection with what you are investigating.

The FBI approach to generating individual profiles is well tailored for a huge country with a high level of diverse and violent crime. However, it's proved difficult to transfer it to Europe without adaptation, as the Dutch discovered when they chose the FBI system of categorizing sexual crimes and then found that 90 per cent of their rapes, when profiled, fitted into just one FBI category. This clearly made offender differentiation – the point of the entire exercise – extremely difficult.

On the strength of that single meeting at Quantico, the visit to America had been a success. Clearly there was a great deal we could learn from each other and we ended up discussing how we might work together in the future, perhaps on an exchange basis.

For the next few days we stayed in visitors' quarters at the Academy, which were on a first-floor landing in the main reception building, overlooking an atrium featuring a huge wall of softly tinted glass. The complex felt vast and empty at that time of year and I think most of us were missing our families. One evening Marilyn and I left our room and heard the sound of a piano playing in the atrium below us. We walked across and looked over the railing. In one corner, under soft subdued lights, Pedder sat at a grand piano playing to the emptiness. We listened for a few moments to the wonderful sound of Christmas and I recognized a man who was homesick for his wife and missing his two young boys. It seemed too private a moment to intrude upon, so we returned to our rooms until the tempo changed and the theme tune from *The Sting* filled the whole atrium.

Over the months, Keith and I had become good friends. A big man, who looked and sounded like a detective, he had a dry, sardonic wit which sometimes made him sound world-weary. After a long and successful career, he'd committed a great deal of himself to the Nickell inquiry.

As we flew back to the UK, I felt contented that the FBI profilers had independently agreed with my conclusions about the case and Pedder believed we had ample evidence of the American legal experience with using offender profiling in a courtroom setting. However, it had never been used alone as proof of identity, but rather as a piece of evidence in the chain.

The prosecution team for the committal hearing consisted of Bill Boyce and Nigel Sweeney, two brilliant lawyers who quickly grasped the psychological principles that underpinned the covert operation.

Boyce was particularly interested in how the evidence about the disposition of Rachel's body should be considered. Stagg had portrayed her lying curled up with her hands together as if in prayer. Photographs showed that Rachel's hands were together but not palm to palm, instead they were crossed at the wrists.

'There's a sound explanation,' I said. 'When Alex was found by a passer-by, he was shaking Rachel and asking her to "wake up". If the killer had left her hands palm to palm, Rachel's hands would have naturally slipped apart as Alex shook her. That's why they were crossed at the wrist.'

Already the prosecution realized that Colin Stagg's defence would concentrate on attacking Lizzie James's evidence in a bid to have it discounted. Boyce asked me about the evidence relating to guilty knowledge.

'If that were excluded, Mr Britton, is your evidence sufficient basis to convict Mr Stagg? Now be careful before you answer because you have to see a man walking down the steps for the rest of his life. That's what hangs on the answer.'

'Of course it's not sufficient,' I said. 'I can't say that Colin Stagg killed Rachel Nickell. I can only say that the probability of there being two people on Wimbledon Common that morning who suffered from the same extreme and violence-orientated sexual deviation is incredibly small.'

'I'm pleased to hear you say that,' said Boyce, looking reassured.

The old-style committal hearing began on 17 February 1994, before the very experienced and highly respected stipendiary magistrate Terry English. He would have to decide if the Crown had established a prima facie case for murder against Colin Stagg and, if so, to commit the defendant for trial by jury.

Stagg had been on remand in Wandsworth prison and his appearance had changed markedly. He'd lost weight and let his short spiky hair grow out. He'd also lost the muscle bulk built up in his homemade gym.

Despite a media blackout on revealing details of the evidence, journalists gathered early at the courthouse to catch a glimpse of Stagg arriving. The case had become too important not to monitor every twist and turn. As Bill Boyce began his opening address the press seats were overflowing and the newly built courthouse at Wimbledon hosted its most important case to date.

The early witnesses for the Crown were people who had been on Wimbledon Common at the time of the murder and also neighbours and acquaintances of Mr Stagg. The prosecution argued that Stagg's alibi about being at home asleep on his sofa could be shredded. A neighbour Mrs Susan Gale remembered seeing him at about 8.50 a.m. when she returned home from the common after walking her two dogs. She spotted him near the A3 underpass, close to where Stagg later spoke to the policeman, and she remembered that he was wearing some sort of black 'bum bag' around his waist.

Jane Harriman, a solicitor's wife, had been walking on the common that morning with her four children and family dogs. She walked the same route as Rachel only a few minutes earlier. Near a small wood she noticed a man walking towards her who she described as being in his late twenties or early thirties, about five foot ten inches tall, with close-cropped dark brown hair, wearing a white t-shirt and dark trousers and clutching a dark-coloured sports bag. They passed each other going in opposite directions and the man appeared to turn his head sharply, hiding his features.

Mrs Harriman continued walking with her children until they reached Curling Pond where they sat for a while. On the far side of the pond she noticed a woman walking a dog into the trees and a few minutes later the man who had passed her earlier took the same path, almost as if following the woman.

Something about his behaviour concerned Mrs Harriman. After several minutes the man appeared again, retracing his route. Now he appeared to have a thin belt around his waist, over his t-shirt.

As she led her children back towards the Windmill car-park, Mrs Harriman probably passed within twenty-five yards of where Rachel Nickell already lay dead in the grass. She was able to provide police with a very clear description of the man she had seen by Curling Pond and had helped compile the artist's impression shown on *Crimewatch UK*.

After Stagg's first arrest, she had picked him out of ten men in an ID parade as being the man she had seen on the common that morning at ten minutes past ten. She had absolutely no doubt.

Another witness, Mrs Amanda Phelan, had also given a description of a man she saw washing his hands in a stream just after 10.30 a.m. She described him as acting suspiciously and thought he might have been wearing a cream or white sweater and blue jeans. Mrs Phelan did not pick out Stagg in an identity parade and neither did Pauline Fleming who told the court that she had seen a man walking near Curling Pond at about 9.30 a.m. carrying a dark bag in his right hand.

Various local traders including a butcher and a newsagent recalled seeing Stagg that day and described him as being quite excited as he talked about the discovery of a body on the common. Having known him for years, they described Colin as a loner who seemed more comfortable in the company of animals than people.

Cheryl Lewis, a friend and neighbour from Ibsley Gardens, recalled a conversation she had with Stagg after his first arrest. He had described being shown photographs of Rachel which made it look as if her head had been removed from her body and then placed back on her shoulders and that she was lying in a foetal position. He also admitted to having seen Rachel before on the common, sunbathing by a pond.

Then it was my turn. When I teach my psychology students court reporting skills, I try to help them understand that when they are cross-examined they need to have an idea of where the questioner is trying to take them. Every good barrister will at times seem to go round the houses and appear to have no clear logic to their questions. But they do have a plan and it's important to see it early so as not to be overwhelmed or to be led into agreeing with a suggested answer to a question that you know is not quite what you wanted to say.

Jim Sturman, for the defence, is a very fine lawyer and he set out his stall early. He aimed to discredit me and therefore, he hoped, the entire covert operation. If he couldn't cast doubt on my professional qualifications, he would attack offender profiling and, if necessary, the entire field of psychology and psychologists. Not surprisingly, it made for an interesting two days in the witness box.

The heart of my evidence concerned the integrity and purity of the covert operation, both in its design and execution, and also my finding that Colin Stagg's sexuality was indistinguishable from the sexual deviancy analysis I had drawn up for the unidentified killer of Rachel Nickell. This was such a rare kind of sexual deviance that the chances of two people sharing these characteristics and being in the same place at the same time, other than in a special hospital or prison, were extremely small. More importantly, his behaviour during the course of the covert operation had been *exactly* as predicted for this very unusual person.

Not surprisingly, Mr Sturman took a more cynical view of my findings, calling them 'speculative and unsupported' by anything other than my instincts.

He asked me whether Colin Stagg was mentally ill.

'I don't know, I've never examined him,' I replied.

Mr Sturman said that if I hadn't examined Mr Stagg, how could I draw any positive conclusions? Did he suffer from any abnormality within the terms of the Mental Health Act of 1974?

'I don't know.'

He was trying to draw me into giving clinical opinions that he knew I could only properly give if I had examined Stagg. I think he also hoped I might make the mistake of bolstering my statement with a little extra and go beyond what I could safely say.

'How many murders of young women in broad daylight with a young child have you analysed in your career, Mr Britton?'

'None,' I said. It was a fatuous question. I might just as easily have asked him how many people he had defended who were alleged to have stabbed a woman forty-nine times? My conclusions are based on my knowledge of human behaviour and experience of having worked with psychological dysfunction of different sorts.

The questioning was sharp and aggressive, but occasionally Mr Sturman tried a little too hard. During one exchange, he asked, 'Mr Britton, was this an "overkill" murder?'

(He clearly hoped that I'd never heard of the term, or would agree with him.)

'When you say "overkill", do you mean that in the sense used by the FBI?' I asked.

'Yes,' he said.

'That's where they say that when a certain number of stab wounds are inflicted, twenty I think, then the assailant must have known the victim?'

Sturman said, 'That is correct, when there are twenty or more stab wounds the victim knew their assailant.' (Rachel had been stabbed forty-nine times and Stagg was thought to be a stranger to her.)

I replied, 'The notion that when someone has twenty stab wounds then they knew their murderer, but if they only have nineteen then they didn't, is not a view that we think is particularly helpful here in the United Kingdom.'

Not surprisingly, Sturman dropped this line of questioning.

Taken over the covert operation in detail, I explained how it had been specifically designed to present the subject with a series of ladders that they would have to climb in a conceptual sense, rather than creating a slippery slope that a vulnerable person would inexorably slide down should they be pushed.

Sturman asked me if I thought Stagg would have said anything to Lizzie James in the hope of losing his virginity?

I told him that I saw nothing in either the correspondence or transcripts, or indeed anything else concerned with Mr Stagg, which indicated otherwise than that the fantasies were genuinely held.

How many people were likely to have responded to Lizzie James in the same way?

'I would say the proportion that would produce the fantasies, the detail, the intensity, the aggression and who could give precise knowledge of the disposition of the body of Rachel Nickell would be vanishingly [sic] small.'

The cut and thrust continued. Sturman wanted to know how I could make such judgements and I explained my clinical work and experience treating sexual dysfunctions. I agreed that within Stagg's correspondence there had been no fantasy that mentioned anal sex or killing anyone. Even so, the sexual frenzy was clearly evident and I believed that these activities could have led to the death of the participant. Similarly, Stagg had reported sexual excitement at the contemplation of just such an attack as that on Rachel Nickell.

When I finally stepped down from the witness box, I felt exhausted. The committal hearing continued with evidence from Dr Richard Shepherd, the Home Office pathologist, Lizzie James, who appeared behind a wooden screen because of the nature of her undercover work, and finally Keith Pedder.

The expected fireworks when Lizzie took the stand didn't occur. Jim Sturman had perhaps decided by then to keep his powder dry should the case be sent to trial. He questioned Pedder on what other lines of inquiry had been followed up, suggesting that Stagg had been targeted from an early stage and the police had stopped looking for other suspects. Pedder explained how all potential avenues had been followed up, including a visit to Italy to visit a gravedigger who had worked at nearby Putney Cemetery at the time of the murder.

In his summing up, Sturman launched a scathing attack on the entire operation, claiming that it preyed on Colin Stagg's sexual immaturity and desperation to lose his virginity. He was so frustrated and embarrassed by this he would have written anything to Lizzie if he thought it would get her into bed.

According to Sturman, Lizzie's letters were come-ons contrived to have Stagg invent wilder and wilder fantasies. She had portrayed herself as a woman who wanted to be dominated and humiliated and he had simply picked up on this and given her what she wanted. My evidence, he argued, was entirely speculative and unsupported by anything other than my own intuition. I had no medical qualifications and had 'guessed' at Stagg's sexual behaviour.

'We simply do not know what lunatic was loose on the common that day. Mr Britton is trying to prove possible guilt by giving an opinion. Not one single case can the prosecution quote in which a psychologist has pronounced guilt. You are being asked to create legal history.'

I hadn't pronounced 'guilt' on Colin Stagg. I had simply said that his behaviour patterns and fantasies were indistinguishable from those I predicted of the killer. Bill Boyce argued that I was a respected clinical and forensic psychologist with many years' experience. He said the jury should be given the opportunity to hear *all* of the evidence and then make up their minds if Colin Stagg was a murderer or a victim of his own fantasies.

After eleven days of evidence and submissions, Mr Terry English concluded that while the defence argument had attractions, these affected the weight to be attached to the evidence rather than its admissibility. He committed Colin Stagg for trial. Mr Sturman immediately made a new application for bail, arguing that the prosecution case had just limped through. Mr English rejected this suggestion and refused bail.

17

IT RAINED IN THE MORNING, HARD SHEETS THAT DRUMMED ON THE plastic jackets and hoods of those who were digging. At first the neighbours paid little attention, assuming that perhaps a pipe had burst or a drain was blocked. It was simply the men from the water board fixing a problem at 25 Cromwell Street, Gloucester.

For two days police officers in wellington boots and dark overalls slowly removed layer after layer of the sodden soil from the back garden. Shielded by fir trees and the red-brick wall of the neighbouring Seventh Day Adventist Church, they carved out the dark black clay, first with a mechanical digger and then by hand, working into the night as the arc lights threw disturbing shadows on the mounds of earth.

The first bone found was only three inches long and proved to be that of a small animal.

Three paragraphs in the *Daily Mail* on Saturday 26 February, 1994, finally revealed the reason for the search.

> *GARDEN SEARCHED FOR LOST DAUGHTER*
> *A couple were under arrest last night as police dug up their back garden in a search for their missing daughter.*
>
> *Heather West vanished about seven years ago when she was sixteen, but her parents Frederick West, 52, and Rosemary, 40, never reported her missing. They say she left home of her own volition.*
>
> *The couple were taken to Gloucester police station for questioning. The search at the semi-detached house in Cromwell Street, Gloucester, is expected to continue today.*

There is something quite incongruous about Gloucester; it's almost like a piece of England's industrial belt that has floated off like an iceberg from the Midlands and settled in the middle of beautiful rolling hills in the West Country. Strongly working class, with a large transient population, it has some of the hallmarks of a country town and others that are more suggestive of an industrial city struggling to recapture its past glory.

Cromwell Street is at the heart of bedsit land where Edwardian terraces, many converted into flats, line the narrow streets and from the windows and open doorways mothers watch their children playing on the footpaths.

Number 25 is a flat-faced, end-of-terrace house with a pebble-dash front and freshly painted green windows. Faded daisy patterns decorated the net curtains and a lucky horseshoe hung above the front door. At the neighbouring church, built from warm new brick, a notice began, 'Is there hope for our world?'

After three days of digging, the police had found nothing but pressed on, working mainly on their hands and knees, clawing at the earth. They were tired and back-sore by the time one of the trowels struck a hard object – a human skull embedded in the clay.

The man entrusted with heading the investigation, Detective Superintendent John Bennett, was quickly becoming an old friend. He met me at the front desk of Gloucester Police Station and immediately chided me for being late with my written report for the coroner's court on a case involving a man found with a knife sticking in his chest at Newton, near Stroud. Initially, police set up a major murder inquiry with a £10,000 reward, but having looked closely at aspects of the victim's life and personality, I advised Bennett that I didn't think it necessary to look for a killer – the wound had been self-inflicted.

'I'm glad you brought the report with you,' he said, on a later visit, 'because if you hadn't, I had given instructions to Terry here to put you in handcuffs and take you down to the cells until it came.' He grinned broadly and introduced me to Terry Moore, a detective chief inspector and Bennett's deputy.

The ageing lift clanked and shuddered up two floors and Moore saw the look on my face. 'Don't worry. Sometimes it gets you there and sometimes it doesn't.'

The SIO's office was adjacent to the incident room which had a familiar buzz of ringing phones and flicking keyboards. Yet here there was a totally different atmosphere to those I'd sensed before. In a typical murder investigation all of the energy is focussed on catching someone. It's almost as if there is an empty picture frame on the wall and everything is directed to filling in the missing face. In this case, there was already a picture – Frederick West was sitting downstairs in a spartan interview room, sipping cups of tea and eating chocolate biscuits.

'Well, Paul, it's good to see you again,' said Bennett leaning back in his chair. 'I'm sorry it has to be in these circumstances. You must have formed an awful view of Gloucestershire – every time you come down here there's been another terrible crime. Don't hold it against us.'

Half-closing his eyes, he began the briefing. 'In the rear garden of twenty-five Cromwell Street – a house not far from here – we have recovered the remains of three people. The property is owned by Mr Frederick West, aged fifty-two, and his wife Rosemary, aged forty. We believe that the bodies are those of young women and one of them is the couple's eldest daughter Heather Ann West who was last seen alive in May 1987.'

'We have a most unusual situation,' said Bennett, 'we have someone who comes across as a cheerful, charming and straightforward working man. Most people have a friendly word for him. He and his wife have lived at the address for more than twenty-two years. They are, by most accounts, outwardly friendly and good neighbours. At the same time, we have three bodies – none of them positively identified by the Home Office pathologist. Much of what I tell you is provisional but I can reveal that the bodies were not left in a way that we'd normally expect.'

'What do you mean?' I asked.

'They were dismembered and decapitated.'

An alarm bell sounded in my head.

Motioning to several thick files on his desk, Bennett began running through a brief history of the family, prompted occasionally by Moore. Frederick Walter Stephen West had been born on 29 September, 1941, the eldest son of a farm labourer and wagoner from Much Marcle, near Ledbury, on the Herefordshire–Gloucestershire border. There were seven children in the family, four boys and three girls.

Young Fred grew up in Much Marcle and after leaving school did various jobs including labouring and lorry-driving. On 7 November, 1962, he married Catherine 'Rena' Costello, an eighteen-year-old waitress who worked at a cafe in Ledbury. They had two daughters, Charmaine, born in 1963 and Anna-Marie, born a year later.

The family spent some time living in Rena's native Glasgow where West worked as an ice-cream vendor; and then returned to live at a caravan site in Bishop's Cleeve, Cheltenham, twelve miles from Gloucester.

The files suggested that the marriage had been quite turbulent and several times during the mid-sixties the children were placed in care and then taken out again several weeks later. In January 1969, Fred told friends that Rena had left him and run away with an engineer to Scotland.

That same year West took up with Rosemary Pauline Letts, a fifteen-year-old girl, who lived in Bishop's Cleeve. Her parents were concerned by the twelve-year age gap and contacted social services who agreed to take Rosemary into care, but once she had reached her sixteenth birthday the authorities were powerless to intervene.

Rosemary moved into the caravan with West and his two daughters and soon fell pregnant. She gave birth to Heather on 17 October, 1970, at Gloucester City maternity hospital. The couple married fifteen months later, having moved to a terraced house at 25 Midland Street, Gloucester, and soon afterwards transferred to 25 Cromwell Street. Mae June was born in June 1972 and Stephen arrived a year later. Five more children followed, three of them of mixed race.

Meanwhile, Fred worked at a variety of jobs as a builder and tradesman. He had a criminal record and had made eleven court appearances, mainly for petty theft, receiving stolen goods and motoring offences. In 1970 he was sentenced to three months in jail when the court lost patience with him.

So far nothing in the accounts had suggested a dangerous pathology. Yet it surprised me that the police seemed to have such a deep knowledge of a man who had only minor convictions.

'There are several embarrassing aspects to this inquiry,' said Bennett, clearing his throat.

'What do you mean?'

'Well, for one thing, Heather was only sixteen when she disappeared. Several people raised questions but Fred explained that she'd gone off with a friend. Essentially, that was the end of the matter.'

I knew there had to be more than this.

Bennett explained that the police had been interested in the family for some time. Their school-age children had been in care for more than a year after a series of allegations of indecent assault. Mr West was accused of having sexual intercourse with one or more of his daughters, while being encouraged and assisted by Rose.

'She'd supervise the penetration,' said Moore, 'telling him the girl was ready.'

Bennett said, 'Apparently, it was all part of furthering Fred's various genetic theories.'

'Genetic theories?'

'Don't ask me – I can't explain,' said Bennett, going on to describe how the couple had been due to stand trial twelve months earlier in connection with the allegations but at the eleventh hour, as the court was waiting, the principal witness backed out of giving evidence. 'We didn't have it nailed down tightly enough and the Crown had to withdraw.'

Over the subsequent months, the police stayed in touch with the children who had been taken into residential care and eventually were to hear stories about Heather being buried under the patio. They attempted to trace her whereabouts but failed.

As I jotted down the chronology, I noticed several time-lags between when information had been received and action taken. Is that what concerned Bennett? I wondered. Then again, police couldn't just dig up a garden on the say-so of a child. There had to be something more to cause Bennett, the most relaxed of men, to be so circumspect.

He slid a folder across the table which contained a bundle of statements and charge sheets. The first five pages were a statement provided by Caroline Owens, a local woman who at the age of seventeen had spent a short time working for the Wests as a nanny. With the agreement of her parents she had moved into 25 Cromwell Street to look after Anna, Heather and the new-born baby, Mae June.

Caroline began to feel uncomfortable in the house, particularly when her new employers began taking an unhealthy interest in her, making suggestive comments and talking about her genitals. Frederick West had claimed that he knew of operations that could increase a woman's sexual pleasure. Eventually, Caroline went for a drink with a former nanny who asked her whether Mrs West had tried to seduce her yet. Shocked, Caroline decided to resign.

Several months later, on 6 December, 1972, at 11.00 p.m., her boyfriend left her opposite a pub on the outskirts of Tewkesbury and she started to hitchhike home to Cinderford, twelve miles from Gloucester. A grey Ford Popular pulled up and she recognized Mr and Mrs West. They offered her a lift and, despite feeling uneasy, Caroline accepted because it was cold and late.

Rosemary lifted the front passenger seat so Caroline could climb into the back and then joined her and Fred drove off, through Gloucester and along the road to Cinderford. According to Caroline's statement, Fred asked her if she had sex with her boyfriend and what they did together. Then Rosemary began touching her breasts through her clothes and trying to put her hand between her legs. She began yelling but Rosemary laughed and taunted her, while Fred asked, 'What's she feel like?'

As Caroline continued fighting, he stopped the car, reached over the seat and punched her until she blacked out. When she regained consciousness, her hands had been tied behind her back and broad sticking plaster wrapped around her head until it covered her mouth, nose and ears, forming a kind of mask.

Caroline was driven back to Cromwell Street and carried inside to the front bedroom on the first floor. Fred made a cup of tea and then used a double-bladed knife to cut the tape from her face. The blade sliced her skin below her left ear and she lost large chunks of her hair when the mask was pulled away.

Her clothes were removed and she was told not to struggle or she'd be hurt. Gagged and blindfolded, she was made to lie on a low bed or mattress and her legs were forced apart. The couple began exploring her vagina and discussing the size of her vaginal lips and whether these would interfere with her sexual pleasure. Fred said he knew how to improve them surgically.

Rosemary took hold of Caroline's heels and raised her legs, spreading them apart. Fred then began striking her vulva with a two-inch-wide leather belt with a heavy buckle. Afterwards, the blindfold was removed and Rosemary, now naked, started kissing the teenager and having oral sex with her while Fred undressed and had intercourse with his wife from the rear. When Rosemary went to the bathroom, Fred told Caroline that he planned to keep her in the cellar so his friends could use her. When they'd finished she'd be killed and her body buried under the paving stones of Gloucester where there were hundreds of girls that the police would never find.

Having been left bound and gagged overnight while they slept, Caroline recalled how early in the morning someone had knocked on the door and she had tried to make a noise to attract attention. Rosemary forced a pillow over her face, smothering her until she no longer struggled. When the visitor left, Rosemary went upstairs to check on the children and Fred climbed onto Caroline and raped her for several minutes without ejaculating.

According to Caroline, he then pleaded with her not to tell his wife because she'd be angry at him. He said the abduction had been for Rosemary's pleasure because when she was pregnant her lesbian urges became stronger and she particularly wanted Caroline.

When Rosemary returned, she made Caroline take a bath and brought her back into the bedroom. They made her promise that if they let her go she would come back and live with them. Alternatively, they would find and kill her. When Caroline agreed, they told her to help dress the younger children and then she accompanied Rose to the local laundrette. It was here, surrounded by people, that Caroline slipped away.

Severely traumatized, she went to a friend's house instead of going straight to the police. She couldn't bring herself to tell her mother and stepfather at first, but eventually the police were called and photographs were taken of the rope burns on her wrists, weals on her legs and the cuts and bruises on her face.

Finishing the statement, I leafed through the folder searching for the outcome to the case. Bennett and Moore sat silently, as if waiting for my reaction. The alarm bells inside my head were almost deafening.

Mr and Mrs West had been arrested and interviewed but had denied everything. Eventually, they agreed to plead guilty to charges of indecent assault and actual bodily harm if Caroline dropped the rape charge. By doing so, she would avoid having to give evidence in open court about her ordeal.

Unbelievably, the case had ended as a relatively minor matter before Gloucester Magistrates on January 12, 1973. Fred and Rosemary pleaded guilty to the lesser charges and were each fined £25 on each count. Rosemary revealed she was pregnant and said of the attack, 'I don't know why I did it, it just happened.'

Bennett could see the look of disbelief on my face.

'Don't ask me to explain,' he said. 'I doubt if anyone can.'

*   *   *

On a floor below, Mr West was still being held for interview. A short man, with dark curly hair and rock and roll sideburns, he wore a blue cardigan, open-neck shirt, t-shirt and grey trousers. They were the same clothes he had been wearing when an unmarked police car drove him away from Cromwell Street the previous Friday morning. He was proving a difficult subject to interrogate and Bennett wanted me to advise the interview teams and discuss possible strategies to unlock the truth.

When first arrested he had insisted that the police would find nothing in their search. When it was made clear to him that officers were digging up the patio – and it was obvious his lie would be exposed – he finally admitted, 'No, she's [Heather] not under the patio, she's in the garden.' Shortly afterwards he was taken back to the house where he pointed out the locations of two more bodies in the garden.

Their deaths, he said, were accidental and unfortunate. He had argued with Heather who was behaving unreasonably so in a fatherly way he tried to disabuse her and suddenly found that she'd died on him. Because Rosemary would be upset about this, he took Heather to the upstairs bathroom and dismembered her. He kept the pieces in the cellar and later buried her in the garden.

The other deaths were equally unfortunate. Shirley Robinson, an eighteen-year-old lodger at the house, had been pregnant with Fred's child and was causing problems. When he tried to disabuse her, he found himself with another dead woman on his hands. The third girl was apparently a friend of Shirley's who came looking for her and he didn't really have a choice but to kill her.

Moore said, 'Yeah, he's one unlucky son of a bitch, is our Fred. Women just kept dying on him left, right and centre so he figures he'll cut up the bodies and bury them rather than tell anyone.'

Glancing through the interview transcripts, I saw that Moore had pretty much summed it up. West continually tried to minimize his responsibility. That didn't surprise me; it's quite common for killers to diminish their role rather than completely acknowledge their crimes.

As far as the police were concerned the case seemed relatively straightforward. Three young women had been killed by Mr West who maintained that he had acted alone. His wife was on bail because they felt that Rosemary, at the very least, was an accomplice or was covering up for her husband. It wasn't a question of there being more victims – the focus of the investigation was on Fred and the girls in the garden.

Later I met with Detective Constable Hazel Savage and Detective Sergeant Phil Onions who were conducting the interviews. Bennett and Moore made the introductions and we pulled several chairs around a formica-topped table in a large and deserted police canteen. Only two of a dozen fluorescent strip-lights were on, casting gloomy pools in the darkness.

Hazel Savage was in her late forties with short dark hair and glasses with heavy plastic frames. She had an intensity about her and I recognized a woman who had probably devoted her entire working life to the police and spent most of it as a constable.

As Bennett had explained to me on the way down, Hazel more than any other person was responsible for the digging. She had been involved in building the case against the Wests for abusing their children and had stayed in touch with the family afterwards. It was she who started asking questions about what had happened to Heather and began looking for the teenager, checking databases, talking to her friends and becoming close to her brothers and sisters. When one of them suggested that Heather was buried in the garden, Hazel stepped up her search and eventually convinced her superiors to get a search warrant.

As we sat and went over the details, I was struck by Hazel's intimate knowledge of the family. It was far beyond what I would normally expect of a police officer and was more in the province of a social worker who had spent weeks or months of contact. It was obvious why the files held so much information about the family.

At every opportunity, as we talked, Hazel would interrupt and comment not just on facts but with opinions on how the different children felt about what had happened and to what extent they were frightened of their parents. This was unusual coming from a police officer and it was obvious that she was deeply, deeply involved. Yet I sensed a vulnerability in her. The precise shape of it wasn't clear but her colossal personal investment in the case, while not necessarily unhealthy, could create problems.

'What more can you tell me about Mr and Mrs West?' I asked, looking for the fine nuances and subtle shadings that would reveal more about them.

'He's a queer 'un,' said Moore.

'What do you mean?'

'He's more than happy for Rose to have sex with other men.'

Hazel said, 'They have a bedroom on the top floor which is done out like a sort of bridal suite – there's a four-poster bed specially carved. This is where Rose took her men friends. Whoever Fred brought home.'

'Brought home?'

Bennett said, 'It's a form of quasi-prostitution.'

Hazel explained, 'Fred would pick up men in local pubs and bring them home. There's a room on the first floor that looks like the reception area of a brothel. It's all done out in red velvet, with a hand-carved bar. Fred brings the chap in, pours him a drink, they get chatting and then Rose would take him upstairs to the four-poster bed.'

Moore said, 'Fred listened to it all from the next room. We found video and listening equipment and some homemade pornographic tapes.'

'There's more,' said Hazel, glancing at John Bennett. 'Rose made the men use condoms. She used to save the sperm and then she and Fred would inject it into their daughters, trying to impregnate them.'

'The genetic theories again,' commented Bennett, raising an eyebrow.

They went on to describe how 25 Cromwell Street had become a boarding house during the 1970s when the upper two floors were converted into cheap bedsits and West would advertise the rooms in local newspapers and at the social security office. Dozens of teenagers and young people were believed to have passed through the address.

At the same time, Rosemary West also began advertising her services, using the name 'Mandy Mouse' in sex contact magazines.

Understandably, considering the deaths on the one hand and the history of the sexual assaults on the other, the police thought they were describing separate events and aspects of the Wests' behaviour, but I didn't see them as disconnected. I could see a continuous thread of profound depravity and sexual deviation; and no matter how terrible the current position appeared to be, I knew the reality would be far worse.

The three women in the garden may have died for the sake of convenience – because they got in the way or caused problems – but it takes an unusual kind of person to dismember a body; to cut through the flesh and sinew and bend back the joints until they break and separate.

We had a man who seemed to be relaxed, even blasé when acknowledging that this is what happened. A man with a clear history of sexual aggression in partnership with his wife, including allegations in 1972 of abduction, rape, sadism, restraint, sexual torture, physical abuse and threats of killing. Twenty years later, we had evidence of gross sexual deviancy where their own children were systematically abused. In between, three women had died and been dismembered.

I felt a cold emptiness deep in my stomach. It happens every time I encounter a history with such features, because I know that there will be bad news for families and more work for the police.

'What are we dealing with?' asked Bennett. The faces around the table were concentrated on mine.

'You are looking at evidence of predatory and sadistic sexual psychopathy,' I said. 'I've seen it before and dealt with it clinically but this case has a particularly dreadful feature. We have a combined depravity – a husband and wife whose energy bounces off each other, each legitimizing the actions of the other. They are both involved and are equal partners. They didn't just kill for the sake of taking a life, their victims were playthings who were tortured and abused.'

I went on to explain the continual process which had a marker in 1972 with the attack on Caroline Owens and then, two decades later, the more refined sexual depravity with their children. There could not have been a silence in between, that's not the way these things work. Mr West didn't just wake up one morning and find he was a sexual psychopath. It starts early in life and it doesn't end until either it burns out towards the end of the fourth or fifth decade of life – if it burns out at all – or until they get caught.

'So what exactly are you saying?' asked Bennett.

'I'm saying that you are dealing with prolific murderers – what people now call serial killers. You have found only three of their victims.'

As the knowledge sank in, Bennett was the first to speak.

'Let me be quite clear about this. There are missing girls all over the country; families who haven't seen their children in years. If this gets out then every one of those families is going to be wondering . . .'

I was painfully aware of the consequences. Wounds would be opened that could literally never be closed for the families involved.

If it is confirmed that their daughter is a victim, the uncertainty is ended, but then they simply step from one level of torment to another and begin speculating about what might have happened. Only in this case, I knew that they could never imagine the dreadful reality.

'But where are they?' asked Moore. 'Where are these other victims?'

'Everywhere he's lived. Everywhere he's worked,' I said. 'Sometimes sexual psychopathic murderers get comfortable with disposing of bodies in a particular way – some leave them in ditches, some put them in rivers, some bury them. Mr and Mrs West looked after them – they kept them close.'

'So that's why he used the back garden?'

'Not exactly,' I said. 'He used the garden because the house is full. You should take it apart, every square inch, the floors, the walls, the roof. There'll be more bodies, I'm sure of it.'

As they asked more questions, I tried to give them a suitable explanation but knew it wouldn't be complete until I knew more about Mr and Mrs West and how they interacted. I talked about how their sexuality had developed in a way that blended powerful sexual desire with aggression and the need to dominate. 'They derive pleasure from the pain and terror they instil in their victims and this is more important than any intercourse or sexual union, which may never actually occur. It's not necessary,' I said.

Bennett asked, 'They were tortured?'

'Almost certainly.'

Expelling a deep breath, he half closed his eyelids and leaned back. 'How can you be sure?'

'You're dealing with people for whom the limits and features of what you and I would regard as ordinary sex have long ago dissolved. Enough is never enough. Even the act of dismembering the bodies is going to give these people pleasure.'

Moore said, 'The press are going to have a bloody field day with this.'

Bennett replied, 'No, they're not. The lid stays on.'

The immediate task was to construct an interview strategy that would encourage Frederick West to talk freely and to hopefully reveal how these things came to happen. I asked the interview team how he had reacted so far – was he fighting them, or refusing to talk, or only conceding things when he knew the truth would come out? Did he boast of his exploits and see himself as someone unique who they hadn't seen before?

'Actually, he's quite friendly,' said Hazel. 'He wants to be liked. If he thinks things are going well, he seems to enjoy himself.'

Phil Onions added, 'He's pretty well impervious to the physical side of it – not deeply troubled by hearing the gruesome details. He won't talk about them.'

'He doesn't make admissions,' interrupted Hazel, 'although he's got this thing about not lying to us – not directly anyway. It's like when we asked him about Heather being under the patio and he denied it over and over again. Then when he realized we were going to keep digging till we found her, he sort of said, "Oh well, in that case, she's not under the patio, she's in the garden." He didn't want to be caught lying.'

This is one of the characteristics I expected.

'You have to understand that Mr West is a man who has no desire to get it off his chest,' I said. 'He has managed to deal with the police and hold them off for years and years. He's going to come across as a pleasant, almost avuncular figure, a little lost and bewildered. He seems to talk easily, enjoying the audience. He wants to be approved of and will never say, "I am a depraved sadistic sexual murderer and nothing pleases me more than taking women and torturing them."

'Mr West is not an intelligent man but neither is he stupid. He has killed for years and years and been involved in the legal process before. He knows precisely what he's done but he also knows that the people interviewing him don't and never will.'

My advice to the interviewers was to let him talk. Once he started, even though he was controlled and would steer them away from certain areas, he would keep talking and this would reveal details that could be used to construct later interviews.

I advised them to focus on open questions which invite Mr West to wax lyrical. They should avoid any show of repugnance or shock and be totally non-judgemental. 'You can show disbelief but not in a disparaging way. He has to understand and know in his own mind that you're interested in him and want to understand.'

I knew it would be a long process. There were layers that had to be peeled back that, hopefully, would eventually reveal not only what happened at 25 Cromwell Street, but elsewhere and also what had occurred over the years in Fred West's life that had led him along this path.

It was after 10.00 p.m. when I left Gloucester Police Station armed with my own notes and the other materials available. I knew there was still a great deal to learn about Mr and Mrs West but one thing was painfully clear. Britain had stumbled onto a new pair of serial killers and the biggest question wasn't why, or where – but how many?

18

IN SOUTHEAST LONDON MICKEY BANKS WAS PRESSING FOR A national TV appeal to bring the Plumstead murders into the spotlight and produce a possible breakthrough. He had a very difficult investigation on his hands because of Samantha Bissett's large number of friends and acquaintances – many of them with rather non-conventional lifestyles who were difficult to track down.

Even though Banks and his team were now convinced that they were looking for a stranger killer and a serial sex offender, they couldn't simply look at the psychological profile and disregard the traditional pathways such as searching for jilted lovers, former boyfriends or family feuds. All of the usual avenues of investigation and conventional motivations for the murder had to be covered to guard against any future suggestion by a defence team that police targeted a particular suspect or type of suspect and failed to follow up other important leads.

Most of Samantha's newer friends she had met through the local nursery and church groups, but she had also kept in touch with people from her past who tended to be more transient – living in squats, bedsits and caravans. Equally hard to find were the men who met her through contact magazines. Many of these services involved the advertiser having a prerecorded message and people being invited to ring in and leave their details. The numbers changed regularly and nobody kept copies of the tapes. Even so, detectives managed to take statements from more than 100 people who fell into this category and, in doing so, had to eliminate a thousand others.

Samantha had been establishing contacts that might have been leading her towards prostitution which meant that any one of these men could be a possible suspect. Because of her easygoing lifestyle and the legacy of her past, I knew that many men would perhaps view her sexually as being easily available.

Banks had talked to *Crimewatch UK* about doing a possible reconstruction but the initial response from the BBC had been lukewarm. Apparently, the producers felt there wasn't enough detailed information to produce an accurate picture of events. This is the down-side to such a successful show. I'm sure that in its early days *Crimewatch UK* was probably grateful for any cases that the police put forward, but now it could pick and choose which crimes to cover.

In this case, the benefits of a good reconstruction couldn't be ignored, particularly in raising public and media awareness in south-east London. This is where the killer would live – somewhere local to the crime. Putting pressure on the producers, Mickey Banks showed them my psychological profile which finally sparked their interest. They decided to do a full reconstruction but only if I agreed to appear on the programme.

'I'm not comfortable with that sort of thing,' I said.

Banks replied, 'If you say no, they won't go ahead.'

'I think they have this notion of me appealing directly to the murderer, but I can't see it producing anything. We've got no way of knowing whether he'll even be watching. To be honest, I think the probability of it leading to detection is low.'

Banks asked, 'How low?'

'Well, you're looking at not more than ten, maybe fifteen per cent.'

'Well, that's fifteen per cent better than we have at the moment. As far as I'm concerned, I'll do anything to catch this bastard. Obviously, I can't make you do it, but I'm asking you, very seriously, to say yes.'

How could I say no?

In the past I had helped draft scripts for *Crimewatch*, including one for the Julie Dart inquiry team, but had deliberately managed to avoid appearing. I have nothing against the programme – it does a very worthy job and the reconstructions don't glamorize crime or offer criminals a "How To" guide – I simply don't feel comfortable as a talking head.

The producers wanted me to give a breakdown of my psychological profile on air, but I successfully argued that Mickey Banks, as the SIO, should be the person who released the information. Certain details weren't to be mentioned, particularly anything that suggested that Samantha may have been working or living on the fringes of prostitution. This might reduce the public's sympathy and compassion for her and deter people from calling the incident room or studio phones. At the same time, we had to be careful not to misdirect the public and miss important elements that could help us catch the killer.

I was also aware of provoking him into further offences by portraying him as some kind of monster. It was important not to show rage, disgust or to make any judgemental remarks. Not only could this feed his perception that the world didn't appreciate him but it could also prevent people calling with vital information. Those close to the killer, who perhaps worked with him or shared a house, weren't going to regard him as a monster. Portray him as one and they'd convince themselves the police must be looking for someone else.

On Thursday 8 February, 1994, the programme went out showing Samantha and Jazmine's last movements using look-alike actresses. There was also a home-video of mother and daughter at the seaside.

A local cab driver who had dropped them home from nursery on the week of the murders told how Samantha expressed concern when she saw a yellow van parked outside the flats in Heathfield Terrace. Other witnesses also remembered the van and described two men with a dog. Police believe they were linked to Samantha, although she hadn't mentioned them to anyone.

Two people seen on the night of the murder still had to be ruled out. One was a man seen crossing the road and heading towards Samantha's flat at about 10.15 p.m. and the other, whose presence had only recently come to light, had been seen at about 7.30 p.m. hanging around the area. He had also been there the previous Wednesday night.

Mickey Banks gave descriptions of the men and asked, 'Did you know Samantha or did you respond to one of her ads? Do you know who the men in the van are? Do you recognize the artist's impression of the boyfriend from the summer? Did you see either of the two men seen on the night of the murder?'

For the first time he revealed publicly that Jazmine had been sexually assaulted. 'I am appealing to people who feel they might know the person responsible to help us with this murder inquiry. Once they realize what has happened to this poor young child, a defenceless young child, four years of age, then I am hoping they will contact us.'

Nick Ross, the presenter, then gave details of the psychological profile and asked me how well I knew the man responsible.

I told him, 'I think we know quite well what was going through his mind at the time of the offences. But I would like him to tell me how he got started on the pathway that led him eventually to kill Samantha. I would also like him to tell me why it was necessary to harm the child as well.'

Crimewatch UK is structured in two parts with the reconstructions earlier in the evening and a follow-up several hours later to update viewers on the calls received. During the break I wrote a few sentences on a scrap of paper aimed directly at the killer. The cameras rolled and Mickey Banks made a second appeal for people to come forward and directed the camera to me.

'I don't know his name. I don't know his address. But I do understand some aspects of the way that he feels. I understand the contentment and excitement that he got from the way he left both Samantha and Jazmine. Sometimes he may recognize that what he has done just can't go on and I would like him to telephone me and tell me about it.'

As I expected, he didn't call but the appeal did bring more people forward who had answered Samantha's lonely hearts ads. Each new lead had to be checked out and alibis verified. As had been hoped, the press began picking up on the story and Banks fed them more details of the profile.

On 23 February, he told the *London Evening Standard*, 'We are looking for someone who could be anyone's neighbour. He is probably personally quite confident and may have a job. From what we have been told, he doesn't seem concerned with seeking attention or notoriety, but is nevertheless interested in the effect he has on other people. He has no sense of remorse for what he has done and probably has a previous history of aggression to women. If he is in a relationship it is unlikely to be successful. He will have problems relating to women with dominant personalities.'

A veteran of many murder inquiries, Banks admitted that this case had been hard to stomach. 'What sickens me personally is that the little girl was sexually assaulted. Because of the nature of the injuries, we don't know if Samantha was also sexually assaulted although we are still carrying out tests.'

After *Crimewatch UK* I didn't hear from the inquiry team for three months during which time I happily returned to my NHS caseload. Equally, I was still occupied by the on-going search for bodies in

Cromwell Street and preparations for the Nickell trial.

'We think we've got him,' said Mickey Banks and I could imagine him punching the air in triumph.

'Are you sure?'

'His prints are in the flat – we thought we'd eliminated them but came up with a match. Robert Clive Napper, aged twenty-eight, he works at a local plastics factory and has grown up in the area. He's got some form.'

'What sort of form?' I asked.

'That's what I want to talk to you about. We've also linked him to a series of rapes and there's some stuff I want to show you before we pull him in.'

The next evening, I found myself back in the smoky, frontier-style Thamesmead police station. The paperwork seemed to have increased and bags of files and statements were stacked beside every desk in the incident room. Apparently the photocopier had surrendered earlier in the day.

As the office door closed behind him, Banks lit up a cigarette and got straight down to business.

'You nailed him perfectly. He matches the profile, right down to the history. We also think he's responsible for a series of rapes. The Ecclestone rapes, you know them, don't you?'

I didn't answer. My attention had been left behind as I tried to comprehend what he had said.

'The Green Chain rapes? How sure are you?' I finally asked.

'We'll be bloody positive when we do the DNA tests.'

I now had a far greater need to discover everything that I could about Robert Napper. If he was the Green Chain rapist, I wanted to find out why it had taken so long to apprehend him. He'd been raping with little regard to his self-preservation more than twelve months before Samantha and Jazmine were murdered.

Napper had been identified by a number of sets of finger and palm prints originally thought to belong to Samantha that had been found at the murder scene. There had been confusion over the classification because the first set of fingerprints taken from Samantha's body had been of poor quality and, unusually, her prints were quite similar in their characteristics to Napper.

This meant that prints found on the bedroom doorframe, the handrail of the balcony and on the cornerpost of Jazmine's bed were initially thought to belong to Samantha. Only later when a further set of elimination prints were taken from the victim, was it confirmed that these marks belonged instead to Robert Napper.

'He hasn't surfaced as a friend or an acquaintance of Sam,' said Banks. 'And the prints on the balcony indicate someone climbing into the flat.'

Even as he talked I began recalling the similarities between the profile I had drawn up for Operation Ecclestone and the one I had done for the Plumstead murders. Details fell into place. Samantha's flat was almost on the southern edge of Winns Common and to the north, across the parkland, was the house where the first rape had taken place. Both Samantha and Jenny were known to sunbathe in their back gardens and Samantha walked about semi-dressed without drawing her blinds. Both left doors unlocked and lived in places where someone could observe them without attracting undue attention.

The detectives had done their homework on Napper. Banks had on his desk every known fact and piece of intelligence about the suspect. This is what he wanted me to see. Being able to place Napper at the flat in Heathfield Terrace didn't prove that he'd killed Samantha and Jazmine. He might claim to be a friend and say that he'd dropped by to visit in the days before the murder.

Napper lived in a rented room at a Victorian house in Plumstead High Street and worked at Glyndon Plastics in Thamesmead. He had grown up in the area and attended Abbey Wood Comprehensive School, before leaving with qualifications in seven subjects and doing a City and Guilds diploma catering course.

Since then, he'd been rarely out of work, albeit of a fairly menial nature, and at the time of the earlier rapes had been a warehouseman in the publications and forms store for the Ministry of Defence. He kept good time and did the job reasonably well according to workmates but kept himself to himself.

He first came to the notice of the police in August 1986 for carrying a loaded gun in a public place. He was given a conditional discharge and asked to pay £10 costs.

The next date struck me as familiar – 29 October, 1992 – the same day that my psychological profile had been typed up for the Ecclestone rape inquiry. Napper had been arrested in Plumstead after going to a printer and asking for fifty sheets of Metropolitan Police (Greenwich) notepaper to be copied and printed. The printer called the police who were waiting when Napper arrived to pick up his order.

A search of his address uncovered a .22 pistol, 244 rounds of ammunition, two knives, a crossbow and six crossbow bolts.

Napper pleaded guilty to possessing a firearm and ammunition without a certificate and was given two eight-week custodial sentences to run concurrently. The court file contained several references to his disturbed mental state and a psychiatric report requested before sentencing concluded that Napper was 'without doubt both an immediate threat to himself and the public'. This was twelve months before the murders of Samantha and Jazmine Bissett.

Banks said, 'We've still got photocopies from that inquiry – they pulled some really interesting stuff out of his room – diaries, letters, maps.'

I looked directly at him, trying to read his thoughts. Is this how Napper had been linked to the rapes? I wondered.

Banks said, 'I'd like you to look at them, Paul, to see if they tell you anything more about our suspect. You can have copies to take home but I need some idea now.'

The photocopies consisted of pocket diaries, hand-drawn maps, notes written on old envelopes and newspaper borders and, most importantly, a London A to Z street guide. As I began studying Napper's papers, much of his writing seemed obscure but there were clear signs that dark thoughts dominated his thinking.

Curious words and phrases appeared on his hand-drawn maps, including a reference to 'cling film on the legs', which suggested a method of restraining someone. He also named particular streets and gave map references which correlated to the A to Z. Within his pocket diaries, he mentioned different women but there was no suggestion that any of them were long-term girlfriends or friends. One reference had an address and afterwards the words, 'sodden filthy bitch'.

I could also see signs of paranoid thinking. Interspersed between day-to-day notes about dental appointments and tax returns, Napper referred to arguments he had with people and his fears that his food was being doctored. He believed that people talked behind his back and that things never went his way.

However, by far the most intriguing and disturbing documents were the street maps. Particular pages of the London A to Z had been marked up with thick black dots indicating certain locations and others flagged by dashes that looked like compass points. Most of the marks were concentrated in the Plumstead, Woolwich, Bexley Heath, Eltham and Ecclestone areas of southeast London.

'This is what links him to the rapes,' I said, looking at Banks for confirmation.

'Some of the markings correspond but not all of them,' he said. 'There seem to be far more dots than there were rapes.'

He explained that the A to Z had contained a membership card for a fitness centre in Eltham. It belonged to a young attractive blonde who lived in Grange Hill Road, Eltham, at the time. Napper had somehow got hold of her card and had placed it in the A to Z at the appropriate page with Grange Hill Road circled.

'We've talked to her and she's never heard of Napper,' said Banks.

'Then she's a very lucky lady.'

Among Napper's papers were personal hand-drawn maps that were far more intimate creations, zeroing in on particular parks or streets and including tiny details such as the locations of storm water grates, foxholes, drainage channels, sandpits and old Second World War bomb shelters. Certain pathways and walking trails were shown in relation to woodland areas and access gates.

'He's not just pinpointing rape sites,' I said. 'Some of the marks are probably surveillance locations where he knows women can be found and he can watch without being seen. Others are likely to be hides where he keeps his souvenirs and tools.'

'Tell me about these "hides"?'

'You have to think to yourself, "Where is his special place?" and then look at his sketches and the references to the depths of holes and drains. He knows these areas intimately and could very easily hide his knives and any trophies or souvenirs.'

Banks leaned closer. 'How often is he likely to go there?'

'I don't know but it's not something he'll neglect.'

'Is it worth us surveilling him? If we watched him, could he lead us to his hide?'

'Quite possibly.'

Banks knew it was a difficult strategy. For Napper to be left out there meant watching him and never losing him because if he was the killer of Samantha and Jazmine he posed a grave and immediate danger. At the same time, the detectives had to make a case and wanted more than just fingerprints. A murder weapon or souvenir such as the missing piece of Samantha's abdomen would remove any doubt.

As the surveillance operation got underway, I returned home with copies of Napper's papers and details of his life and times.

An important characteristic of the British police is that once they have a particular suspect in sight, then they relentlessly pursue every possible avenue of information.

Napper's name had come up on the intelligence files at Plumstead Police Station because he'd come to their attention twice since his arrest in October 1992. Most notably in July 1993, four months before the Plumstead murders, when Napper had been seen in the back garden of a house in Rutherglen Road, Plumstead, at 9.30 p.m. A husband and wife reported seeing a man on their side wall, peering into the house next door, where a pretty blonde twenty-four-year-old was in the habit of walking around semi-clothed with the curtains open.

While his wife phoned the police, the husband followed the intruder and identified Robert Napper to the police. Napper readily gave his name and address. When asked about his activities, he shrugged and said he'd been 'going for a walk'.

The witness had said that Napper appeared to drop something as he jumped down from the rear wall, but nothing was found in a search.

One of the officers wrote in his notes: 'Subject strange, abnormal, should be considered as a possible rapist, indecency type suspect.'

Equally important was the location. The properties in Rutherglen Road looked over a field towards Bostall Woods, part of the Green Chain Walk.

All of this should have immediately flagged Napper as a strong potential suspect in the serial rapes. Apart from being known to the local police, he fitted many of the other criteria in the psychological profile, including the likelihood that he had engaged in property offences and his strong knowledge of the local area.

My profile had described the suspect coming to the attention of police in one of three ways.

1) By information provided by the public or area police officers.

2) By being caught during an offence; or

3) By an elimination process based upon examination of the records.

He was always going to be in the system, it was just a case of looking for him.

My initial response was great anger and sadness. At the same time, I didn't know what difficulties the Ecclestone rape team had faced and what influenced the decisions that were taken. I simply knew that a mother and daughter had been murdered twelve months later and it now seemed likely that the killer had been the Green Chain rapist.

The surveillance operation continued for ten days, during which Napper maintained a regular pattern of leaving home at 7.30 a.m., walking to the plastics factory where he worked a twelve-hour shift and then returning home. Over the weekend he journeyed into the West End and was seen entering several shops which sold soft pornography and also looking at knives in the windows of outdoor survival stores.

On his way home, he ignored a train to Plumstead and instead travelled to Sidcup and began walking through the back streets in the pouring rain before catching a bus home to Plumstead. This walk seemed to have no point or significance but probably included some of his favoured locations for looking at women in houses.

With no sign of Napper revealing his 'hides', Banks made the decision to arrest him on Friday 27 May, prior to the Bank Holiday weekend. He asked for help in designing an interview strategy and wanted to know if I'd come to London for the early interrogations.

On Friday morning, officers gathered outside 135 Plumstead High Road, a large Victorian house divided into bedsits. At 9.40 a.m. they moved in and arrested Napper for the murders of Samantha and Jazmine Bissett in Heathfield Terrace, Plumstead, and also for a series of serious sexual assaults.

As he was led outside and put into a police van, Napper said, 'I heard of the murders in the paper, I don't know Samantha Bissett. I have never been to where you said.' This was jotted down by the arresting officer in his notebook.

After SOCO had been through the ground-floor bedsit, I was asked to look inside in case it provided any extra insight which could assist in the interview strategy. Small, clean and well-ordered, the room had a wardrobe, two chairs, a table but no bed. This surprised the landlord who had let the room with an iron-framed bed. Napper's possessions consisted of clothing, suitcases, footwear, a TV, music system and, most significantly, a padlocked red metal toolbox.

When opened, a card was found Sellotaped inside the lid with the message: 'Lonesome? Bored? Like Excitement? Want to be noticed? Want to meet strange new people? Then just leave your security container open.'

When the card was removed, a footprint was found on the back made by an Adidas Phantom basketball boot. Very few pairs had been sold in the UK and it matched the bloody shoe mark found in Samantha's kitchen.

In the top tray of the toolbox was another London A to Z street guide. When examined, this contained more markings and idiosyncratic notations, including an ink dot beside Number 1a Heathfield Terrace. The lower tray contained photocopied pages from a martial arts book, handwritten notes and drawings. The martial arts book gave descriptions of how to control and disable an opponent. In particular, I noticed an illustration of the neck showing how the various human muscles work and interact. Another showed the internal anatomy of the torso and, in many ways, reflected how Samantha had been found with her ribcage pulled open and her internal organs on display.

Among his notes, Napper had drawn rather grandiose diagrams of seemingly unrelated words linked by arrows or scattered on a page. He also had a list of words and their definitions taken from a dictionary and a significant number of them related to death, control, predation and distorted relationships.

His references to women were disparaging, suggesting they offered 'instant sunshine' but only wanted to exploit him. At one point he uses the phrase, 'Mengele's way', an apparent reference to the Nazi doctor who practised surgical and psychological experiments on living and dead victims.

Having seen the correspondence and maps taken from his house in October 1992 when he was previously charged and convicted, it was interesting to compare them with the later material. All of it reinforced my belief that Napper had hiding places where he kept his more precious belongings. I couldn't see anything to indicate someone out of control, on the contrary I saw a man who taught himself to monitor, plan and not to rush.

Appearing calm and unruffled, Napper had been taken to Bexley Heath Police Station where the first of the interviews would take place. Mickey Banks seemed to be lighting one cigarette from the other and was in his element, but he knew that only part of the job was done. I warned him not to expect Napper to be driven by any anxiety to make an easy admission.

'I know it's easy to think he's mad but today this man is fully in charge of his faculties,' I said. 'He's intelligent enough to recognize certain lines of questioning in advance and will try to avoid incriminating himself. To begin with, you may find he co-operates when asked general, harmless questions but as soon as you confront him with the harder evidence, he is likely to go "no comment".'

Recognizing that a previous psychiatric examination had highlighted Napper's risk, I had already advised that an 'appropriate adult' should be present during the interviews.

Napper's statement to the arresting officer about not knowing Samantha or having been to her flat now became very important. If he confirmed this at interview it would nail down a provable lie because his fingerprints had been found at the scene. Yet it had to be done in such a way that it didn't flag the crucial importance of the statement to the investigation and, at the same time, didn't trick or entrap him in a way that might be considered unfair.

The interviewers had to be warm as well as authoritative in their interactive style because Napper would scan for, and be distanced by, cues of a negative disposition, I told Banks. They had to establish his account of his day-to-day life including his work schedule, his spare time and his social life. This could then lead on to his history with women.

'Eventually, begin to focus on his sexuality and invite him to explain what may have happened in his past that first started his aggressive behaviour, who is to blame? Give him a psychological face-saving opportunity to lay the blame on someone else such as his parents, or his early life or whoever seduced him.

'Then ask him what it was about Samantha that drew his attention to her? What was it that she did, or she said, or she was, that gave him no choice but to kill her and cut her.

'There's no need to mention Jazmine at this stage – come back to her later.'

I suggested they move on to the weapons and ask Napper how he came to collect his knives and what he found attractive about them. If he introduced the supernatural, or demons or other psychotic phenomena, they weren't to resist or show disbelief but to continue collecting the information and carry on. Eventually they could confront him with the fingerprint sequence found at the flat and ask him what happened afterwards.

The first interview began at 4.01 p.m. and I watched on a live video monitor in an adjoining room. Napper, six foot two inches tall with receding brown hair, sat easily in a chair and seemed perfectly intelligent and self-assured during the preliminaries, politely giving his name and address.

When asked to confirm the all-important arrest notes of Acting Detective Sergeant Alan Jackman, Napper agreed and signed them. A provable lie had been established. Afterwards, he asked to speak to his solicitor in private and then began to 'no comment' police questions.

The next day, he was interviewed about the Green Chain rapes and again showed a calm assurance as he deflected questions over a number of hours. His maps and the marks on the London A to Z were 'just doodles' and references to his training runs and mileage points, he said. As the questions focussed more directly on his alleged crimes he slammed shut and stuck mainly to no replies.

On Sunday, 29 May, he was charged with the murders of Samantha and Jazmine Bissett and remanded in custody.

Detectives continued questioning him about the rapes and a live identification parade was held at Southwark Police Station on Monday 4 July. The victims Leanne and Cathy picked Napper out unreservedly, Susan thought it looked like him and only Jenny couldn't pick him out. Her attacker had been wearing a mask. Interestingly, the teacher walking her dogs who had been assaulted in Elmstead Wood by a man she described as being intellectually sub-normal, failed to pick Napper out. This simply strengthened my belief that she'd been attacked by a different man.

With positive identifications and strong DNA evidence, the police charged Napper with the rape attacks. Meanwhile, the search continued for every detail about his lifestyle and regular movements. Statements were taken from his family, work colleagues, former landlords and casual acquaintances which helped to build up a picture of Napper. Most of them described a strange, quiet individual. He paid his rent on time, went for long walks at night and meticulously cleaned his muddy shoes on his return.

The oldest of four children, Napper's early life had been exposed to a combination of matrimonial violence, the divorce of his parents and various stints in foster homes. Raised by his mother, Pauline, on the Abbey Wood Estate not far from Plumstead, he soon attracted attention for truanting and shoplifting.

Increasingly disturbed, he was counselled at the Maudsley Hospital in Camberwell and continued treatment for six years. His problems were exacerbated at the age of twelve, when a cousin introduced an older man into the family who took the boys camping. Robert was sexually abused and the man was later imprisoned.

By the time Napper reached adolescence, he had become introverted and spoke to others only when necessary. Obsessively tidy, he spent much of his time alone in his room, emerging only to bully his younger brother and to spy on his sister dressing.

After leaving school and finishing the catering course, he took on a variety of jobs and didn't leave home until the age of twenty-one, when he moved into a bedsit in Plumstead. His mother recalled an incident in early September, 1989, when Napper went missing for several days and attempted to commit suicide by taking an overdose. Later he explained that some men were after him because he'd raped a woman on Plumstead Common.

Pauline claimed that she checked with the police but no trace could be found of any rape recorded on that night. It's worth noting that the first indoor rape was four weeks before the suicide attempt and that Jenny's house backed on to Winns Common. The Winns Common area was often called Plumstead Common by locals.

Further research and identification parades also filled in the three year 'silence' between the attacks on Jenny and Susan. A string of women pointed Napper out as being the man who indecently assaulted them, or exposed his penis, or peered in at their windows, or followed them home or ducked behind bushes when they approached. These incidents dated from as early as 1988 and ran through each subsequent year.

Prior to the trial of Robert Napper, the inquiry teams suggested that I might give a statement about my role and the similarities between the psychological profiles I had given for the Ecclestone rapes and the Plumstead murders. Ultimately, it wasn't necessary for me to give evidence, although in due course I did learn what had happened during the rape investigation.

It emerged that Napper had, in fact, been interviewed by detectives as a suspect for the rapes. Acting on information from a neighbour two detective constables stopped him on his way to work on 28 August, 1992. At six feet two inches tall, Napper was considerably taller than the five feet seven inches to five feet nine inches suspect that the police had chosen to seek. In addition to this, he had no convictions for sexual offences and had also volunteered to take a DNA test – something the police felt was inconsistent with the behaviour of a guilty man. As a result, he was eliminated from the inquiry.

The reference to his height is quite important. Two weeks after I provided the Ecclestone psychological profile, *Crimewatch UK* featured a reconstruction of one of the rapes and it prompted almost 1,000 calls from the public, eclipsing all previous appeals. With such a vast number of leads to follow and suspects to trace and eliminate, the inquiry team decided to establish 'elimination codes' that would help officers to concentrate their efforts.

In Operation Ecclestone this code contained obvious elimination parameters such as a suspect having the wrong DNA, or being in prison at the time of the attacks. However, it also relied heavily on descriptions given by victims and witnesses. It set the offender's age at between nineteen and thirty years old and his height at a minimum of five feet five inches and a maximum of six feet. This is despite the fact that the last rape victim had described her attacker as well over six foot.

On the basis of this code, Robert Napper could be immediately ruled out as a possible suspect if his name came up in the course of inquiries. Therefore, he wouldn't be invited to Eltham police station at a convenient date to supply a sample of blood, a photograph and a palm print.

As I studied the elimination code it became clear that the psychological profile hadn't been used when the parameters were established. This was unfortunate because often the main value of a profile can be to narrow the number of potential suspects and allow police to focus their attention on the most likely individuals.

Ultimately, Operation Ecclestone investigated and eliminated nearly 900 suspects for the rapes up to March 1993 when the decision was made to close the operation down because of the absence of further attacks. At this time, another 390 investigatory actions had been raised by the inquiry but still remained incomplete.

How could it have happened? I thought. I know it's easy in hindsight to make judgements and I'm the first to appreciate the pressures placed on the police when investigating violent crime, but there seemed to be so many warning signs and clues that were misread or ignored. Samantha and Jazmine Bissett should not have been murdered.

A part of me will always believe that I could have done more. I should have been more pushy and bloody minded when I delivered my profile to the rape inquiry. I know that some of my conclusions were not well received and I should have said, 'Listen, this is where you'll find him. Examine your records, talk to local police.' I should have told them to get out and keep looking or, 'I'll bang on your door until you do.'

Robert Clive Napper professed his innocence until his Old Bailey trial in October when several days were taken up with legal argument as to whether he was mentally able to stand trial. Five psychiatrists had reached the conclusion that he was suffering from schizophrenia or similar mental illness but that Napper was desperately trying to conceal his madness within himself.

On 9 October, 1995, only minutes before a jury was to decide whether he was fit to stand trial, the defendant decided to plead not guilty to the murder of Stephanie and Jazmine but guilty to their manslaughter on grounds of diminished responsibility. He also admitted a rape and two attempted rapes in 1992.

Accepting the pleas, Mr Justice Hooper said Napper had been responsible for offences of 'grotesque magnitude' and posed a 'grave and immediate risk to the public'. He ordered him to be detained 'without limit of time'.

Sadly, the sentencing came too late for Mrs Maggie Morrison, Samantha's mother, who died three days earlier at her home south of Aberdeen. According to her husband Jack Morrison, a retired builder, she had never recovered from the 'purgatory' of having lost both her daughter and her granddaughter in such a way.

Mr Morrison praised the police but said the system had failed. 'The police have been excellent throughout the whole investigation but a man like Napper should never have been on the streets with the freedom to kill.'

19

EIGHT DAYS AFTER THE SEARCH BEGAN, SEVEN BODIES HAD BEEN uncovered at 25 Cromwell Street which had now been labelled the 'House of Horror'. After dinner each evening, I shut the study door and went over the interview transcripts of Frederick and Rosemary West looking for anything that I might have missed. What else could I tell John Bennett?

He called me on 7 March with something new on his mind. Despite extensive enquiries the police hadn't managed to trace West's first wife Rena Costello or their eldest daughter Charmaine. No-one had seen or heard from Rena since 1969 when she was known to have been living with West in a caravan near Kempley, about fifteen miles from Gloucester.

Charmaine and her sister Anne Marie had stayed with their father and moved into 25 Midland Road in 1971. This is where Charmaine, then aged eight, had last been seen.

'What does Mr West have to say?' I asked.

'He says Rena came back for Charmaine and took her away.'

'I think they are dead,' I said, sadly.

'Yes,' Bennett replied.

We both knew there was only one way to be sure. The police would have to go back to every place West had worked and every place he'd lived and start looking. The logistics and cost of such an exercise were virtually incalculable. Where would it end? How many houses would be torn up? How many workplaces? What about the poor people living at those addresses now?

Over the next two days, two more bodies were found at Cromwell

Street – the first concealed under the bathroom floor of the extension and the second in the cellar. There were now nine known victims and police were confident they knew the identities of five of them. It had been a massive task checking missing persons reports from as far away as Holland and Germany.

A week later Bennett called again, keen for me to go back to Gloucester. The pathology reports had been delivered and he wanted to update me on the latest interrogations of Mr West.

'I can probably make it on Thursday.'

'That's fine,' he said, pausing as if about to add something.

'Anything in particular I should know?'

'Well . . . ah . . . certain bones are missing from the skeletons.'

'Missing or unrecovered?'

'Missing. We've been bloody thorough,' he said, somewhat touchily. 'Mainly kneecaps and neck bones, but also a shoulder-blade and parts of the sternum.'

There are several explanations, I told him. The bones could have been taken as trophies, or removed during the process of constraint and torture. 'There's one other possibility but I don't really want to talk about it now. Let's leave it till Thursday.'

Bennett had his shirt sleeves rolled up above his elbows and wore the look of a man who had spent all night working in the office. Around him, the walls of his office were papered with computer print-outs and wheel diagrams. Hundreds of missing person files were being checked and cross-checked, matched against the known movements of Frederick and Rosemary West. Diagrams numbered the bodies, the locations and what order they were found in.

Bennett, an old-fashioned detective who was born in Stroud and educated at the local grammar school, had got to grips with modern technology more quickly than many younger policemen. For this inquiry, he had his own software specialist in the incident room and he explained to me, in typically sanguine style, how he managed to get what he required.

'I told him that I had a dream,' he began, raising an eyelid to make sure he had my full attention. 'I dreamed that we could take all the dates and locations of missing people and match them up with all the different information we have for Mr West. That could be very useful. Can you do that?'

The software expert had shuffled nervously opposite him and said,

'Well, there isn't really a programme that can do that. It's never actually been done like that before.'

Bennett smiled and issued the gentle instruction, 'Well, you go away and you see what you can do and then we'll talk about it.'

A few days later the specialist had come back to him. 'I've done it,' he said proudly.

'That's good,' Bennett told him. 'That's exactly what I want.'

Then the SIO paused for a few moments, before saying, 'I had a dream' – there was a twinkling in his eyes – 'the computer has done this for me, but I would want it to show me even more . . .'

He then asked for the databases being compiled on each victim, whether known or still to be identified, to be interfaced with the database holding the computer-generated graphics of 25 Cromwell Street and the sequence in which the bodies had been discovered.

By integrating and displaying as much information as possible in this way, Bennett knew it would assist him in keeping sight of the big picture in what was a massive investigation. It would also help him anticipate the obstructions West might raise and the challenges that would surely come from the defence team in any future trial.

'We can't do that,' the specialist had said apologetically. 'There is a system that does one thing and another for the second, but they belong to different companies and have been developed along different lines.'

'You find a way of bolting them together then,' Bennett had said.

'But we're not allowed to – there are copyrights on the software.'

'Oh, you just get the companies together and sort it out.'

The computer specialist had looked rather dubious.

'Listen,' said Bennett, his voice harder. 'This is relevant to my murder inquiry. If Mars Bars become relevant to this inquiry then I shall have them in that machine outside. You just go and do it.' He did. Although neither of them realized it at the time, the result of their working relationship was the development of a new computing tool which would be enormously helpful to investigators in the solving of future serious crimes.

Opening a file, Bennett ran through the details of those victims who had been identified. Four of the women, including Lucy Partington, the twenty-one-year-old university student, had disappeared from bus stops or the vicinity, and a fifth had apparently been hitchhiking.

Carol Cooper, fifteen, was last seen by a bus conductor on 10 November, 1973, at 9.30 p.m. getting off a bus near her grandmother's home in Worcester after going to the cinema with her boyfriend. Juanita Mott, seventeen, of Newent, disappeared on 11 April, 1975 after telling her family she was going to take a bus to Gloucester, ten miles away. Shirley Hubbard, fifteen, was last sighted in November 1974 at a bus stop after leaving Debenhams store in Worcester to return home. Therese Siegenthaler, a twenty-one-year-old sociology student from Trub, Switzerland, was working as a nanny in London in 1974 when she wrote to her brother saying she was to spend the Easter holiday in Ireland. She planned to hitchhike to the docks at Holyhead, Wales, and then catch a ferry.

Finally Bennett turned to the pathology report and handed me a copy. As I'd feared, it revealed that six of the burial pits contained evidence that the victims had been bound and gagged in various ways including having brown parcel tape looped around their heads to form a crude mask. In one of these 'masks' a narrow plastic tube was inserted into the front curling upwards into the nostril.

Looking at the photograph I felt a profound sadness. It was clear to me that the pipe had been used to keep the victim alive and to open up the possibilities of what they could do to her. Unable to see or to cry out, she would be totally under their control.

Bennett turned the page and referred to the missing bones. 'There's something else quite odd,' he said. 'Some of the larger bones have marks on them. The pathologist says they don't make sense in terms of dismembering the bodies.'

'They make sense to me,' I said, looking up from the photographs. 'When you carve meat you often leave marks on the bone.'

Bennett's face fell.

I said, 'That's why I didn't want to talk over the phone. I suspected that cannibalism might be part of the ritual. It would explain the missing bones.'

'No,' he said, looking horrified.

Each new piece of information reaffirmed my original analysis of what had happened, but if I was to expand upon it and really walk through the minds of Fred and Rosemary West it was important to visit the place that meant most to them – the 'House of Horror'.

Terry Moore suggested we walk from the station. We strolled side by side in the bright sunshine through the quieter streets and quadrangles, beneath trees that were just beginning to bud. As we approached the back of the house I noticed a large television van with a saucer dish pointing to the sky. Two men were standing nearby and one of them looked up, his eyes lingering on my face as if I looked familiar to him. Feeling uncomfortable, I kept walking, not wanting to be recognized.

We turned left off the road onto a very short track that ran along the back of several houses. In the garden overlooking the rear of Number 25, I noticed a scaffolding and timber plank 'grandstand' that Moore explained had been put together by an enterprising neighbour so the various cameramen and photographers could get pictures of the excavation.

More than 300 tonnes of soil had been removed from the garden and it looked like a First World War battlefield. Now refilled, the muddy rectangle was criss-crossed by duck boards and well-screened by fir trees along one side and the red-brick wall of the Seventh Day Adventist church along the other.

'This is where Heather was found,' said Moore, motioning to a spot at his feet. 'Another body was found here and the third victim over there.'

Inside the single-storey extension that Mr West had built in the early seventies, it was like a demolition site. The police had removed floor-coverings, skirting boards, furniture, fixtures and fittings. When a house becomes a scene of crime and the scientists go to work, it ceases to be a home any more. So many details that make it cosy and intimate are lost. Even the things that do remain – the shaving gear in the bathroom, a photo album, a closet full of clothes – leave one with a very melancholy feeling.

Passing through a bedroom at the back of the house, we entered a kitchen area, a broad room with a concrete floor.

'What do you think?' asked Moore.

'I think Fred is a lousy builder. It's a bodge from one corner to the other. How on earth did he make a living?'

Moore smiled.

Worktops and the sink remained and I could imagine where the family had sat down to dinner as saucepans bubbled on the stove and food filled their plates – just as in any ordinary house. But I also knew that this is where Mr West had described putting down sheets and dismembering the bodies.

Off the kitchen, at the very back of the house, was a small bathroom. This is where the body of Lynda Gough had been found buried under the bath. She went missing in April 1973, two weeks short of her twentieth birthday, while working as a seamstress at the Co-operative Store in Barton Street, Gloucester.

Stepping over rubble and broken plaster, I walked into a more general living area which had been cleared of furniture. There was a large, neatly cut hole in the floorboards and the lower wall; with a hinged trapdoor resting open. Gingerly climbing down slippery steps and ducking my head, I emerged into a half-cellar, not wholly sunk beneath ground level.

About seven feet high, twelve feet wide and twenty feet long, it looked as though someone had put together a low cost version of Madame Tussauds' Chamber of Horrors without the wax models. Silver-grey fingerprint dust covered almost every surface and children's wallpaper curled and hung in torn shreds.

The cellar had apparently first been used as a storage area and then been converted to a bedroom for the children. There were no windows and the room was now lit by strong inspection lamps hanging from hooks or clipped to pillars. Duck boards crossed the floor which was little more than a series of deep holes and mounds of hard, wet, black mud – so dark it seemed to soak up the light. Each of the five holes had contained the remains of a separate young woman.

Beneath the wallpaper were the innocent scribblings of children, cartoon characters and games of noughts and crosses. Yet there were also more sinister drawings that hadn't been explained. Skulls had been painted or stencilled at various points and, as I studied them, they seemed to provide quite neat sighting lines across the locations of each burial pit. Perhaps it was important for Mr and Mrs West to keep track of their 'treasures' and these were the markers to remind them.

Then I noticed a hook in the ceiling which served no obvious purpose but it could easily have carried the weight of a person – someone suspended and restrained. The cellar itself was an ideal venue for imprisoning someone; no-one could see or hear and the degree of control attainable would be almost total.

Climbing out of the cellar, I turned through a doorway into the older part of the house. A narrow flight of stairs rose to the first floor. Halfway up, I turned and saw something that I knew was enormously significant. On the rear of the door was a colour poster – larger than lifesize – of a woman wearing a see-through negligee and posing provocatively with her arm draped up the doorframe. Like Rosemary West, she had long dark hair and a full figure.

Her facial expression and pose were saying, 'There are great delights here,' beckoning onlookers into her world. This was the dividing line. Every time the Wests passed through this door, they knew what lay on the other side. It represented complete fulfilment and their other life.

'This is Rosemary's reception room,' said Moore as we reached the first floor.

The photographs didn't do it justice. Like something from an ageing bordello, the armchairs and settee were done out in velvets and a large mural of the sea and palm trees covered one wall. Opposite was the carved-wood bar replete with spirits, ashtrays, ice-buckets and cocktail shakers. A sign suspended above it said, 'BLACK MAGIC'.

Moore said, 'Quite something, isn't it.'

I wandered around the room, looking at several display cabinets with glass shelves and wooden drawers.

'Is it OK to touch?' I asked.

'Yeah. We've been through it.'

The cabinets displayed various paraphernalia, ordinary cheap ornaments that you might have collected on holidays or bought at a church market. Several glass containers sat on a shelf containing ordinary bric-a-brac – loose change, cigarette lighters, hair clips and a number of wrist watches.

'Do you know where these came from?' I asked.

Moore replied, 'Why? Is it important?'

'Not any more, not in this case.'

I knew that Mr and Mrs West had savoured what they did to their victims. They would have taken keepsakes; souvenirs they could reflect on later. It wasn't significant any more in this particular case, but if the killers or victims had been unknown, such bric-a-brac would have become gold.

Opening a drawer, I came across a bundle of family papers – a typical collection of old bills, brochures, school reports and photographs. Every family has them and they can sometimes help reveal the fine details of who people are and how they live.

An ordinary family photograph album shows the heart of the family and how it develops. You will see the people who are significant; their relationships, changing friends and growing children. You will see the clothes they wear, the way the rooms were decorated and the numbers on the birthday cake. Who is standing close to whom?

Who seems to be more distant? How is the picture composed? Who is the photographer focussing on? How is the subject responding? What is their relationship? All of it tells you a little more.

In the Wests' album, it was what I didn't see that meant something. Many customary photographs were missing. There were long gaps and nothing to show a family bound together by love and harmony. The reason was because Frederick and Rosemary West lived for something entirely different. They chronicled their pastimes in home-made pornographic videos rather than family albums.

On the same floor, directly opposite, was a small, plain, drab bathroom. This is where Mr West claimed he had dismembered Heather's body, but it was immediately obvious that the room was too small to enable him to do the things he had said he'd done.

A final flight of stairs led me to a landing shielded by a curtain suspended from a rod. Walking into the larger of two bedrooms, I was surprised by the size of an elaborately carved four-poster bed with erotic motifs on the pillars and cross-beams.

'This is where Rose brought the men,' said Moore.

I didn't reply and instead wandered through the room, glancing through the dirty window down to the street.

Across the landing, the smaller bedroom had an ordinary double bed and the slightly ruffled appearance of having been searched. There was a cavity in the wall behind the bedhead and several wires spilled out and snaked downwards, leading nowhere. These were for the listening devices and video camera which monitored events in the next room.

Whatever had happened here was far more intricate than ordinary prostitution. People had been invited into the house, given drinks and polite conversation and then taken upstairs for sex. It wasn't a business arrangement for Mrs West – it was at the centre of her reason for living.

There is a term known as 'peak experience' which describes periods in a person's life when everything comes together and they are living and operating at their maximum potential. Everything is honed; their senses tell them more, life is richer and problems are tackled enthusiastically and effectively. It's what a coach has achieved when an athlete peaks at precisely the right time for the big event.

For Fred and Rosemary West, I would expect 'peak experience' to be when they were engaging in their sexual and sadistic pastimes. Everything else faded away when compared to the enormous buzz that it gave them. The whole house was a playground for their fantasies made real.

Walking into the sunlight was like emerging from a black, black sewer.

Terry Moore and I strolled in silence along Cromwell Street, until I stopped and looked back. It was a street indistinguishable from any other street and if you were to rise above it, you would see street after street all the same. The only thing that separated it from all the others is what the police had discovered inside Number 25.

Afternoon shoppers chatted in the shade of awnings and glanced at window displays. Children chased each other, laughing as they were caught and dashing away again. Gradually, I felt as if I'd been distanced from these happy carefree lives. When you experience death and bereavement vicariously every day of your working life, you can never escape from it. Each time I immerse myself, it erodes my capacity to enjoy. Colours are still bright, the sun is still warm and people still smile, but somehow I step into a domain which prevents me from fully appreciating these things.

As if replaying a tape in my head, I began going over the details and painting in the subtle colours and nuances of Mr and Mrs West. How was it that this outwardly friendly and affable couple had become predatory and sadistic sexual psychopaths? What was it within their lives that gave them the need and the energy to abduct, torture, rape and kill a string of young women?

In many ways Rosemary and Frederick West are no different from the rest of us. The very same developmental processes which moulded you and me made them what they became; it was only the content of those processes which varied. I know this because I've assessed and treated people who have the same motivations and pathology. Perhaps not people whose body count is as high, but sexual psychopaths just the same.

For Frederick it began early – in childhood when the vast majority of us are given the moral guidance and strictures that bind us to society and teach us what is right and wrong. In his case it didn't happen. I can't know why – it wasn't my task to find out – but it doesn't necessarily mean that his parents were negligent. Lots of children have raw deals or grow up in difficult circumstances, and they don't turn out to be sadistic murderers. They catch up because there are wider influences such as school, or important friendships which socialize them and make them frightened of doing things they know are wrong.

When Mr West was growing up and discovering his sexuality, his attention became focussed only on his own needs and wishes. He didn't really learn to see other people as separate, unique individuals who had the same rights, needs and wishes as he did. He could use the right words, but had no internal grip on the concept.

It's like a person who is born totally colour blind. They can get through the world, they see edges quite well and know what a traffic light is; you can even sit and talk to them about the grass being green and roses being red and they can say it back to you but they have no concept of what green and red really are.

Feelings for Frederick, as far as they existed, were 'my feelings'. He could never really grasp the notion that other people had feelings and theirs were just as important as his. This problem didn't permeate through every facet of his life – otherwise he wouldn't have survived at all; he couldn't have held down a job, or paid for things at the till. He would simply have walked out or taken them off the shelf. Some kinds of psychopath do that.

Frederick's problem manifested itself in his relationships with women. He had none of the honesty, integrity or regard that we expect when we meet, woo and have intimate contact with a partner. For him, women were sexual objects to be exploited in whichever way he chose.

He grew through his late childhood and adolescence with a very strong sexual appetite. He needed partners frequently and would expect women to be available to him almost constantly. However, his desire was much higher than his ordinary social capacity was likely to help him to fulfil. He didn't have the skills to have his way with the sophisticated women he was attracted to. Nor was he able to get women to do consensually all of the things he would have liked. Some would have gone as far as having sex but then drawn back when he wanted to experiment and go further.

In particular, he had a growing need for dominance and coercion – not out of bitterness or resentment towards women, as is so often the case with sexual aggressors, but as a means of personal enrichment and pure pleasure. Careful research suggests that this attitude may well have had its roots in his first sexual experiences.

Most men and women fantasize about sex and masturbate. The content of the fantasies will often be influenced and sometimes shaped by their early sexual experiences – in the family, or with friends at school or from seeing pornographic material.

Many more people than we realize are introduced to sexual activity in a family setting – be it with parents, a sibling, an uncle, or a cousin. Sadly, they are often seduced or coerced into some form of sexual degradation. I have seen case after case where a patient has revealed to me that his first sexual experience occurred in childhood when a man, either in his family or close to it, began touching him sexually and in due course sodomized him. Others have described how their sisters or cousins were routinely used for sex by men in the family and how they also were drawn into using them sexually. This can go on for years and years, so that it distorts the way they view sex and relationships.

Much the same holds true within a school or peer-group setting, although the constraints are more widely evident. Young couples experimenting with sex know that the risks from overstepping the boundaries are greater because a partner is more likely to complain if things are done which make them unhappy.

All too frequently, children are exposed to pornography and, in particular, pictures and literature with a coercive element. They may find that they become sexually aroused by seeing images of women being bound or hurt and they begin to associate coercion and dominance with pleasure.

Any or all of these factors will be in Fred West's background but he's not alone in having experienced them; they occur in many people's lives but for the vast majority of them, the wider social experiences of extended family, important friendships, school and their contact with the world are sufficient to compensate for these developmental deficits and to resocialize the growing child. In this way, they come to fear the consequences of serious wrongdoing.

However, in a very small number of cases this doesn't happen and we are left with a young man who isn't bound to society or its rules. He feels neither the warmth of genuine emotional empathy nor the repugnance of causing pain. At the same time he has a strong sexual need and a widening gap between the sexual contact he manages to find and his growing urge to control and dominate his partners.

Over time, he becomes more forceful in pushing his demands on women. He won't describe this as coercion or regard it as rape because he has no feelings other than his own. It doesn't matter what the woman thinks or says. 'I want it now and she'll go along with it,' he thinks. Soon, however, this isn't enough and he needs even more control.

In most relationships men and women place demands on each other such as fidelity and not being taken for granted. Mr West isn't able to take this responsibility and is annoyed when someone expects it of him.

At some point he kills a woman, perhaps because she makes too many demands and becomes an irritation. Maybe she's pregnant and asks him, 'What are we going to do?'

'What do you mean "we"?' he says.

'Well, you got me pregnant.'

'Listen, we had sex together. I liked it and it didn't do you any harm, so what's the problem?'

But it is a problem, so he kills her because there is no reason why he shouldn't as far as he's concerned. It's no different to putting a stray dog down. By the same token, he knows that he'll be sent to prison if caught, so he buries the body and makes up a story to cover her disappearance.

This is how Mr West eventually explained all his murders to the police and, from everything I knew about him, killing for convenience was very likely to be his early motivation. However, given what was done to the later victims in Cromwell Street, it's clear that a watershed was reached during one of these convenience killings . . . he became excited.

As he took hold of her, perhaps putting his hands around her throat, he saw her face distort and the terrible fear in her eyes. And as he squeezed her windpipe, he realized that he had an erection and his arousal became greater and greater as the woman struggled and died. It's not simply the act of killing that excites him, but her response to being killed. It is the terrified look on her face, knowing that there is absolutely nothing she can do; she is completely at his mercy.

Although he won't necessarily have a rich detailed fantasy of what happened, Frederick knows that it felt sexually wonderful – so good that he wants to do it again. Even the disposal of the body is pleasurable because he can do what he likes to it. He can have sex with the passive corpse – not necessarily because it is different or particularly pleasurable but because it further demonstrates his power. The same is true of dismembering the body and concealing it. This was a new experience for him and later, when he masturbates, the image will come up again and again in his mind.

Meanwhile, he carries on with his life – working, drinking with his mates, offering his help when they need a hand to build a patio, or paint their house. He doesn't feel remorse – the word means nothing to him. No-one suspects or confronts him because he has a very loose social network of friends and acquaintances who drift in and out of his life. He lives in a caravan and has the space to operate in without attracting unwanted questions. For this reason, no-one raises the alarm when his first wife Rena Costello goes missing in 1969. Why should they? After all, Fred is a nice chap.

Eventually, he takes up with a young girl, Rosemary Letts, fifteen, who has already experienced the world of sex. Her personality is not as fully formed as his, although within two years she, too, is a fully fledged sexual sadist.

There are two possible pathways to this. The first is that sexually she is effectively a blank canvas and when she fell under his control he simply painted the picture of the person he wanted her to be. The other possibility is that she already had a sadistic streak that would have been manifest in her own early life perhaps through cruelty to animals and to those around her.

Many of the factors that set Frederick on the path to becoming a sadistic sexual murderer will also have been present in Rosemary's childhood. She, too, had grown up without adopting or acknowledging the moral strictures which make sadism repugnant and inhuman to most of us. In all likelihood, she hadn't experienced the feelings of warmth and reward that come from mutually consenting and caring sexual intimacy and this left her pliable.

The precise reason doesn't alter what then happens. She is drawn to Fred and in the early stages is probably quite passive – a turn-on for a man who more than anything else wants to control. She is open to whatever he puts before her and doesn't find herself responding with repugnance. To begin with, they possibly act out scenes of domination and humiliation, not for real but like many ordinary couples who might dress up in provocative clothes and play sexual games.

Then, in just the same way that a man might introduce his girlfriend or wife to his hobby – for example, ballroom dancing – Fred acquaints Rose with his pastime. He opens the door to sadism and discovers that they enjoy the same 'music' and 'dance steps', only in this case the 'music' they hear is the screaming and pleading of dying young girls.

The key to all that follows is that Rose responds with delight and sexual excitement. She discovers that her own sadistic potential can be unleashed and revelled in by Fred. For her, this form of sexual expression makes up for all of the emptiness in her early life.

Under his tuition, Rosemary learns quickly and becomes as good a 'dancer' as he is and probably better. She can hear far more subtle rhythms and beats in the 'music' and begins to produce new ideas and new steps. What was once quite crude becomes refined and they both begin to devote more and more of their life towards their deviant dancing until it becomes the centre of their being.

By the time Caroline Owens is abducted in 1972, it is Rosemary who seems to be choreographing the torture and abuse as well as being directly involved. She is the first to start kissing Caroline in the back seat of the car without any direction or urging from her new husband.

Frederick has found a soulmate – someone who shares all his needs, hopes and fantasies – and it becomes the most important relationship in his life.

Rosemary's sexuality grows, flowers and becomes rapacious. Although quite capable of an orgasmic relationship with her husband, it's not enough, she wants new foods and flavours. She takes a succession of partners, perhaps both men and women, but even with another lover in her arms, her husband is part of the act because the sex enriches them both. He procures, introduces and approves her lovers; listening and watching what goes on.

They begin to turn their home into a playground – it's not a torture chamber or a dungeon, for them it's a theme park separated from the rest of the world where it's safe for them to experiment. By now, neither is passive, both have a gnawing need to control, dominate and inflict pain. This is how they measure their reason for being.

They practise and develop a methodology, discussing how to capture people and confine them. And then one day they pick up a young girl. Exactly how she is lured into Mr West's car may never be known. However, the case history gives some clues.

Mr West knows where to find potential victims and has an image of what he's looking for. She has to be young, perhaps with long hair, or full breasts, or wearing certain types of clothes. Or maybe she has a look about her that he can't easily explain but when he sees her, his hormones begin racing and Mrs West's sexual ambiguity attracts her to the girl.

If she appears passive they will know that this person will be so terrified they can play on her fear and reach notes that they've never heard before. Or if she is proud and resistant, they will revel in the knowledge that they can reduce her to a pleading, compliant bundle and, then literally, to a pile of flesh and bones.

How does he get her into the car? When Rosemary is with him, it's easy. The young woman sees a woman in the car and relaxes; after all, sexual assailants don't come with their wives, do they?

'Look my wife is ill, can you help?'

'She's having a baby and we're lost.'

'It's dangerous walking at night, can we give you a lift?'

The number of ploys are endless. All that has to happen is that she comes within arm's reach. Mr West is strong and brutal; he can easily drag her into the car and quickly tape her head and hands.

Or perhaps he uses the long confidence trick, chatting to the girl after she accepts a lift. The casual conversation adds to his pleasure because he gets to know a little bit of her history.

Then, in a blitz attack, her head is taped and hands are bound. She is taken to Cromwell Street and abused during the journey because the temptation is too difficult to resist.

The anticipation is joyous. Mr and Mrs West have managed to capture someone, which in itself gives them an enormous sexual buzz. The thrill is so intense that in the early murders the torture and abuse could well have been over quite quickly. They rushed the killing and for days afterwards savoured the pleasure.

As time goes by they extend the process and get as much as they can from each victim. They learn that you don't have to kill someone straightaway – you can delay it, teasing it out and heightening the pleasure. Each time, their methodology is refined and improved upon.

We know from the abduction of Caroline Owens that they talked of surgical intervention and operating on her genitalia. Although horrifying to contemplate, I would expect they did, indeed, begin 'operating' on victims, explaining what they were doing and talking to each other as it took place.

We know that six of the victims were found with evidence of having been gagged or having had their heads completely taped. One of these 'masks' was found with a narrow plastic tube inserted into the front and bent upwards to enter the nostril. Not only did it keep the victim alive but it gave the Wests a way of introducing things into her body. We also know that their victims were found naked, dismembered and with evidence of bindings within the burial pits. Given the other evidence, they were most likely suspended, beaten, physically mutilated and used sexually by both husband and wife.

At some point in the process, skin was probably bitten and blood began to flow. Flesh was cut away possibly before and after death. A meal can be a very special event. People dress up, have a glass of wine, sit at a neatly set table and eat a nicely prepared dinner. It's a shared experience. Of course, I can't be absolutely certain that cannibalism took place, but the unusual scraping marks on the long leg bones make it a very strong probability.

This is supported by what we know about sexual psychopaths and their crimes. Some stop when they reach a particular plateau of sexual pleasure that is gained from a particular set of stimuli. With Mr and Mrs West there is no evidence of this – only a constantly escalating and growing need. When people have a continual desire for new excitement and to reach new heights, they introduce fresh elements into their repertoire. In a case where you have a couple who embark on a pathway of degradation, humiliation, sadism, control and murder, it is but a small step to go on to something like cannibalism.

Mr and Mrs West buried their 'treasures' close – in the cellar and the garden. Just as someone takes great care in selecting and hanging pictures in a room, they took similar care with placement of the bodies. The masturbatory return is important to them; it is reassuring to be able to go down to the cellar and lie on a child's bed, knowing what lies eight feet below.

What people find most difficult to understand is that this couple were able to live in the ordinary world as good neighbours, who may have had their idiosyncrasies but in the main seemed to be like anyone else; yet at the same time – in parallel – they existed in a dimension that very few people could conceive of as being real at all. What happened to these young women is probably beyond the ability of most horror writers to imagine let alone describe.

This is what prevents people from understanding. They can't readily grasp the intense pleasure, joy and exhilaration that Frederick and Rosemary gained from the terror and dying of their victims. For a sadistic sexual psychopath enough is never enough. The urge for discovery and expansion goes on and on and doesn't stop.

It showed in their dealings with their own children. Here were home-grown human beings they had complete control over; valuable assets which could be realized. And while Mr and Mrs West were cautious during their abductions, they became increasingly reckless in what they did with their children. Other people like teachers and social workers were bound to become involved eventually.

Back at the station, I spent more than an hour explaining my conclusions to John Bennett and Terry Moore. Afterwards, in a quiet corner of the Police Social Club I met for an update with the interview team. Beer was on offer but I opted for lemon and lime because of the long drive home.

West had come to acknowledge more about the crimes – accepting that the bodies were bound – but refused to admit suspending or torturing victims. In the same way he was still desperately resistant to the notion of implicating his wife.

'How can that be?' asked Bennett. 'If he's this psychopath, why isn't he saying, no it's not me it's her? That's what she's doing – she's been saying, "If anything happened, it's Fred's doing." Why is he protecting her?'

'You have to understand the nature of their relationship. His bond is enormously powerful. Look at it this way: many men look at pornographic magazines and find themselves indulging in the fantasy of meeting a sexually uninhibited woman; someone who is not only willing but will egg them on and introduce them to activities that their dear wife at home would never engage in.

'Mr West didn't have to wish. He had this already. He had a partner who could reinforce, extend, develop and amplify his fantasies almost beyond the imagination of the ordinary person – not just once, but again and again and again. His wife wasn't just passive, she shared in the thinking and feeling, taking their sexual games to new heights. This makes her an unimaginably valuable asset to him and he would never do anything to harm such an asset. He will never give her up.'

Moore asked, 'What about Rose? Is she likely to talk?'

'I doubt it. From what I've seen, she's more intelligent than he is and more psychologically robust. Everything you've told me about her suggests she's a woman who thinks that if she holds her nerve she'll get through. She doesn't have the same need for reinforcement and approval as Mr West. It doesn't mean that she's more wicked; it simply means she can go for longer without external praise.'

Hazel asked, 'Does she know Fred won't give her away?'

'Absolutely. I think she knows Fred much better than he knows her. They have plumbed the depths of human depravity together and she knows what she represents to him. She knows that he'll never give her up.'

Moore said, 'So she'll just try to hold on?'

'I think the only chance of getting her to make any admissions is if Fred West can be helped to acknowledge her participation. If he starts disclosing details about Rose being involved, then she may begin to talk. She won't confess. She'll blame him and claim that she was the unwilling, passive, intimidated participant. I doubt if she will ever acknowledge any responsibility – certainly not before being convicted.'

This is one reason why I had fewer concerns about her safety when Bennett asked me whether either suspect was likely to harm themselves. I told him that Rosemary was likely to stick it out to the end, confident that she could beat the charges. Mr West, however, was a different story. While he remained in police custody and enjoyed being centre stage of the interviewing process, he'd be fine, I said, particularly if he thought that Rosemary was still committed to him. But once the interviews were over and he was moved to a remand prison, he would begin to feel increasingly isolated; this would be magnified if he believed that his wife was repudiating him, not in neutral terms but in language that portrayed him as an inhuman monster.

Knowing his personality and his approach to interviewing, particularly the completely implausible but recklessly impassioned way he insisted that Rosemary played no part in the murders – I knew how important she was to him. I explained that when he learned that she was rejecting him and he realized that there would be no contact between them again in their entire lives, I knew the risk of self-harm would increase dramatically.

Although Rosemary West had maintained her innocence, I had no doubt of her full involvement. On the purely logistical side, nine bodies had been cut up in her house – probably in the kitchen area – stored for a period of time and then buried in the garden. Each of the holes in the house was up to eight feet deep and dug by hand in heavy black clay. Where was she while all this was happening? She had to know about it – anything else strains the bounds of credibility.

More importantly, there was the firm evidence that she shared the same sexually deviant psychopathy as her husband. She had an enormous sex drive, sleeping with dozens of men and enjoying the knowledge that her husband was listening. She decided when her daughters were ready to be initiated into sex and supervised the penetration. And when Caroline Owens was abducted, it was Mrs West who seemed to be in charge – choreographing the torture and abuse.

On 20 April, Rosemary was arrested and charged with twice raping a 13-year-old girl and also an assault involving an eight-year-old boy. Eventually she would be jointly charged with nine murders, including that of Charmaine West, whose body was found in a former coal bunker at 25 Midland Road on 4 May.

Three weeks earlier the remains of Charmaine's mother, Rena Costello, had been uncovered in a cornfield near to where the family had been living in a caravan in 1969. Ground penetrating radar had been used in the search.

On my last visit to Gloucester on 18 May I learned of the interviews with Rosemary. As predicted, she gave little away, acknowledging her many lovers but refusing to admit any responsibility for what had taken place in her home. She was able to describe how an ordinary loving mother should behave and claimed this is what she had always been.

When told of the allegations by Anne Marie, her stepdaughter, that she had been raped by her father and sexually abused by her stepmother from the age of eight, Rosemary denied all knowledge and said that Fred might have been involved. Pressed further, she claimed, 'I only did what I was made to do. Fred organized it all. Fred may have made Anne Marie do it, I didn't.'

Then she began to say, 'no comment' and repeated this answer through hours of interviews. Even so, the interviewers continued questioning her, never browbeating or eroding her will, simply stating their concerns and carefully setting out the case against her.

Meanwhile, Frederick had begun to accept and acknowledge more of what he had done. He was able to describe how he picked up girls in his van and brought them back to the house. But he claimed that sex had been at their request and occasionally they wanted it rough and unfortunately the girls had died. Rosemary had no idea.

Early in June a twelfth body, that of Anna McFall, aged twenty-two, was found on the edge of a massive dig at Fingerpost Field,

Kempley, near where West's first wife had been found. Anna, from Coatbridge, Lanarkshire, had worked briefly as the Wests' nanny after arriving in Gloucester in 1967. A post-mortem showed that she was eight months pregnant when she died.

Finally, almost four months after it began, the digging was over.

20

WHEN THE LAWNMOWER ENGINE FELL SILENT I COULD HEAR Marilyn calling me to the telephone. From the look on her face I could tell that another Sunday afternoon had been hijacked.

Within twenty minutes, showered and changed, I was on my way to Nottingham. A new-born baby had been abducted from the Queen's Medical Centre (QMC) two days earlier, Friday 1 July, and the hunt had become a national story.

Detective Superintendent Harry Shepherd, the officer in charge, hadn't been able to disguise the urgency in his voice. He was operating in real time, knowing that one wrong decision could lead to the death of a child.

On the fifty mile drive north to Nottingham I felt slightly uncomfortable because I knew so little about the abduction. I hadn't seen the Sunday papers that morning, which carried the story on the front pages. The parents must be devastated, I thought, and my mind drifted back to when Emma and Ian were born. Both were delivered at home – not so unusual back then before the health service began encouraging women to have their babies in hospital so that complications could be better managed.

We nearly lost Emma. She was born looking like a marble doll showing no signs of life. The midwife, who hadn't wanted to come out on such a foggy night, put her to one side assuming there was no hope. Marilyn, ill after a complicated labour, sensed something was wrong. I was filled with a deep fear that I was going to lose both my wife and daughter.

The midwife was preparing to remove the baby, when the GP

arrived and told her to hold on. He ensured Marilyn was safe and then started working on Emma who had apparently been born in shock with the umbilical cord wrapped tightly around her neck. It took a long time as he blew air into her tiny lungs and massaged her chest until finally she breathed and her colour began to change as she came to life.

We invest so much of ourselves into our children; we are wired that way and it makes the sense of loss enormous if something goes wrong. Marilyn didn't sleep for the first forty-eight hours because she was so afraid that Emma was going to die. I hooked up a bicycle lamp for lighting and she lay by the edge of the cot in our room.

Over the years I've had to assess and treat many mothers, and sometimes fathers, who have lost children at birth or shortly afterwards and I know that the consequences can be life-altering. The tragedy can have been decades earlier but the impact is still with them; some are still grieving, others have never been able to grieve openly.

At West Bridgford police station the incident room had been set up on the top floor. Like most of them, it had a makeshift feel as if put together with bits and bobs in a rush. Computer cables snaked across the floor and desks had been pulled together. But most of all I saw paper, piles and piles of paper, and it was clear that it didn't matter how many people there were, the paper was coming in faster than they could process it.

By comparison, Harry Shepherd's office looked positively spotless. He is a very gentle, quite heavy-set man – which makes him look shorter than he really is – with a well-trimmed beard mottled with grey. He's also very softly spoken, sharing one of my idiosyncrasies, which means we sometimes have trouble hearing each other. It does, however, help draw people closer, as they lean forward to catch what's being said.

'At ten o'clock last Friday morning, Mrs Karen Humphries, a local community midwife, gave birth to a baby daughter at the Queen's Medical Centre. Her husband Roger was present and stayed with mother and baby when they were transferred down to a small side-room on ward B27 . . .'

Shepherd gave a very detailed account, explaining how Roger had left the hospital at 11.30 a.m. and gone to pick up the couple's three-year-old son Charlie who was eager to see his new baby sister. They returned three hours later and joined Karen in the side-room. The baby, to be called Abbie, lay in a cot at the side of the bed in a cream-coloured hospital nightie and a pink shawl.

Shortly after 3.00 p.m., Karen got out of bed and walked along the corridor to phone her mother. A few seconds later a woman entered the room dressed in what appeared to be a nurse's uniform. She told Roger that the baby needed a routine hearing test and asked him when Karen was coming back. Then she left, saying that she'd come back in fifteen minutes.

When Karen returned to the room, she went straight to the bathroom before Roger could mention the test. As she disappeared from view, the door opened again and the same *nurse* said, 'Is it all right if I do that hearing test now? It will only take a couple of minutes.' She lifted Abbie out of the cot and calmly walked away.

Karen reappeared and was immediately suspicious. Being a midwife, she knew that new-born babies don't require hearing tests. She walked along the corridor to the nurses' station and it soon became clear that Abbie hadn't been taken by a member of staff.

Shepherd unfolded a plan of the hospital and pointed out the maternity ward and the various corridors and stairwells that led to the main hospital entrance about 270 yards away. I'd visited the QMC before for clinical meetings and knew the general layout.

'The abductor must have entered the ward through these double doors and passed the nurses' station to reach the side wards,' he said and then pointed to a nearby lavatory. 'We found a discarded blue uniform here.

'She didn't waste time. Within five minutes they were searching the hospital room by room and security guards were outside stopping buses and talking to pedestrians.'

A middle-aged couple leaving the hospital, Jim and Julie Morris, had been passed by a woman in the underpass leading from the main entrance to Derby Road at about 3.00 p.m. She had been walking quickly and carrying a baby in an odd way, very low on her stomach.

Mr Morris told police, 'She was five yards away and I saw a little pink leg sticking out from a blanket and an identity bracelet. The woman seemed nervous but I didn't think anything was wrong until she made to get into a red car, possibly a Ford Fiesta, but it was a ruse. She carried on walking very fast.'

The Morrises were worried and returned to the hospital to report the incident. By then staff were already looking outside the hospital but didn't realize the abductor had changed her clothes. She was now wearing a green top, half-length dark grey leggings and a pair of black plastic sunglasses.

Roger Humphries described the woman as white, in her early thirties, five feet two inches to five feet four inches tall with long flowing dark hair – possibly a wig. She had a pale complexion and local accent. He remembered seeing her earlier when he returned to the hospital with Charlie at about 2.30 p.m. As they walked along the main corridor outside ward B27, the *nurse* was about sixty feet in front of him, walking in the same direction. Although he only saw her for a few seconds, he remembered her because of her distinctive hair. He also noticed she had full or fat calves and thought she was wearing tights but couldn't remember the colour, although not black.

Shepherd slid two grainy black-and-white photographs across the table. The hospital had twenty-nine security videos and the police had closely studied the footage before isolating two images. The first frame, taken a few minutes after 3.00 p.m., showed the back view of a plump, dark-haired woman dressed in a nurse's uniform walking along a corridor towards the main doors of the hospital entrance. The second image, taken by the same camera twenty minutes later, appeared to show the same woman, now dressed in civilian clothes and possibly carrying something in front of her.

'She was probably doing a dry-run . . .' said Shepherd, indicating the first picture, '. . . surveying her escape route.'

Possibly, I thought, but I had my doubts. This woman already knew the hospital. It was entirely possible that she'd been there in the days beforehand, surveying the possibilities. 'It's more likely she was building up her confidence,' I said. 'Or the moment wasn't right, so she kept walking because she knows that if she's static someone is more likely to notice her and ask her questions.'

Other things made me less happy. Why did she visit the room twice? I wondered. Surely it made more sense to take the baby when she first talked to Roger about the hearing test. She couldn't have known that Karen was a midwife, otherwise she wouldn't have waited. Karen would have known that Abbie didn't need a test.

Equally, it was unlikely that she was a former member of staff because someone would have recognized her, and the blue dress she wore *looked* like a nurse's uniform but wasn't.

Shepherd had stopped talking. The real time sense of urgency was even stronger than I had recognized on the phone. He and his team were working on what I call the edge of oblivion. If they got it wrong, they could lose a child but at the same time they had to move forward at a very rapid pace. Everything inside says to you, 'Slow down, don't make mistakes,' but you can't because a baby is missing, the world is watching and the clock is running. It takes an enormous mental effort to be acting in real time, yet sitting above it and monitoring everything you do so that you don't make a tragic mistake.

In the silence that followed the briefing, I began trying to see the shape of the abductor's mind and to consider all the possible motives, even the most malign. I began relating her behaviour to that of other troubled women whom I'd treated in my clinical work, as well as the wider psychological knowledge-base on child abductions.

The main source of information for Abbie's abduction had been Roger Humphries. Not surprisingly, he'd been deeply traumatized by what had happened and this was reflected in his police statement. There were numerous detailed questions about the abduction sequence and the woman which I needed to have answered if I was to give the police a precise understanding of her.

What were the woman's exact words to Roger? Where did she stand and how did she walk? Did she stay in the doorway or step inside the room? Did she make direct eye contact or smile? Did she use her right hand or left hand to scoop up Abbie? Why did he think she wore a wig? How well was it fitted?

The answers to these questions and many more could tell me something about the abductor's carefulness, confidence and motivation. Without them, it was like trying to find someone through a fog when the breeze is constantly making it swirl and thicken, only occasionally giving you glimpses.

The only person who could fill in the missing pieces was Roger Humphries and I suggested to Shepherd that a cognitive interview taking Roger back over the events might extract more detail. The detective agreed and arranged it for Tuesday morning, 5 July.

Until I had enough information to identify and rank in order the likely reasons for the abduction, I couldn't draw up a psychological profile.

In the meantime, we turned our attention to the pressing question of how best to use the enormous media interest in the abduction. Shepherd knew the media was a powerful tool capable of helping or hindering his investigation. Through newspapers, radio and television he could communicate with the abductor and those around her, but he had to find the right strategy to keep her calm and protect Abbie.

It meant getting the media to co-operate, not always an easy thing to do. Since the abduction, reporters had been screaming for access to the security camera footage taken of the bogus nurse. Unfortunately, the issue was straining relations between crime correspondents and the police. Shepherd wanted my opinion on the issue.

For the rest of that evening and much of the next day I worked on a communications strategy. On Monday, back at West Bridgford, I sat downstairs with Shepherd in a custody suite and outlined my proposal.

I said the woman holding Abbie was unlikely to harm her as long as she wasn't panicked. 'But the longer she has the baby, the closer they are going to bond. That's why the next forty-eight hours are vital. You have got to appeal directly to her and show her the enormity of the anguish being suffered by Roger and Karen – especially Karen. She's got to see them as real people and not cardboard cut-outs.'

Shepherd asked, 'Why forty-eight hours?'

'If you haven't reached her by then, one of two things has happened – either she's heard the appeal and isn't willing to respond, or she's cut herself off and isn't listening. At the same time, she's bonding more strongly with the baby and will be beginning to regard Abbie as *hers*. This diminishes her appreciation of Roger and Karen as real people and reduces the likelihood of her giving Abbie up voluntarily.'

'What happens after forty-eight hours?'

'You change the focus. Instead of appealing personally to the abductor, you talk to those around her; friends, family and neighbours. You give them reasons why it could be someone close to them who has become so misguided as to lose sight of what is right and wrong. You have to convince them that the best way they can help her is to get in touch with you. Of course, this audience has already been listening to the earlier, direct appeals to the *nurse* and this should help convince them to come forward, knowing that they are helping rather than just turning someone in.'

The central tenet of any appeal had to convey the clear understanding that the police did not see the woman as a criminal who they were going to catch and punish. Something dreadful must have happened in her life to lead her to take such an extreme step and deny Roger and Karen *their* child. The police understood and wanted to offer compassion and support.

There would be no demand to, 'Give yourself up!' – that needed too big a step from the abductor. Instead she would repeatedly hear the gentle urging for her to let Karen know that Abbie was safe. If she could take this small step then we would have established contact and could gradually help her to come in.

These principles weren't just pulled out of the air. I based them on my understanding of the relationship between human emotion and behaviour, confirmed by years of experience with hostage negotiation in clinical and crime-related situations. This was a logical area of study when I began working at Arnold Lodge, because occasionally patients would take hostages.

If Abbie's kidnapper had been perched on a narrow window-ledge high above the street, the tactics would have been very similar although in some ways it would have been far easier. If she'd been sitting on a window-ledge, she could be identified and her background uncovered, pinpointing what had driven her this far. This information could be used when I talked to her. Instead I was attempting to negotiate via policemen and the news media with an unknown woman who may or may not have been listening.

There was another problem, however. Although the media were invaluable, reporters invariably want to pump up the emotion, finding different angles every day and tracking down various relatives of Karen and Roger to make appeals. This made the message seem less simple and personal when it was most important that a single person be associated with the appeal – someone who could build up a rapport and speak to the abductor almost on a one to one basis.

'It can't be some harsh, sensationalist, unemotional or uncaring face,' I told Shepherd. 'It will scare her off.'

'Why not you?' he suggested.

'No. That would be completely wrong. I was thinking more of you.'

Shepherd had already fronted daily news conferences and made earlier appeals. He had the perfect mix of sensitivity with a soft voice and friendly face. He could look directly into the camera, forgetting how many millions of people were watching, and talk directly to this woman. He could offer empathy and understanding, playing down the crime and punishment aspects, and appealing to her to contact Karen to let her know that Abbie was OK.

'And if she does get in touch, we need a trained police negotiator to take the call; someone who's been well-briefed about this woman's state of mind.' I knew that such a person could help her and also give police valuable extra time to trace the call.

Unfortunately, it was a fact of life that some of the responses would come from hoaxers. These had to be filtered out by testing their offence-related knowledge – asking the caller to give details of how Abbie had been taken and other information that only the true abductor could know.

Finally, we came to the vexed question of the security video from the hospital. The grainy black-and-white images showed the partial rear view of a woman who was possibly wearing a wig. The media were demanding access to the pictures but I recommended that the photographs be held back.

The public weren't going to recognize her, but she would obviously recognize herself and then could easily believe that others could identify her. This might well cause her to panic and abandon Abbie where she wouldn't be found until it was too late.

As we ended the meeting and I left for home, I was confident that with the right approach and by hitting the right psychological buttons we could shape the abductor's emotional responses. In the meantime, I still needed to find out more about the *nurse* and that meant interviewing Roger Humphries.

The next morning, I found myself stepping out of strong sunlight into the reception room of a suburban house dappled with shadow. The high ceilings made it seem airy and cool, a blessed relief on another hot day.

Roger and Karen had been staying with friends at this secret address, avoiding the media spotlight. They had made a tearful plea at a news conference on Saturday afternoon at the hospital in which Karen had said, 'I have got a little boy at home who wants to know where his new baby has gone. If anybody knows any information can they just let us know.'

Roger shook my hand and I recognized a person in post-traumatic shock. His movements were lethargic and slow, or occasionally quite agitated. Although able to focus, he was easily distracted and his face didn't work as it normally did.

A quiet, well-mannered man, he had been married to Karen for nine years and they lived in a small detached house on a new estate in Nottingham's Sherwood district. He worked as a supervisor at a local painter and decorators and told me how he'd painted the porch the previous day – 'the first time I've used a brush in six years'. It was his way of relieving the tension.

I explained to him the nature of cognitive interviewing and how it could help people recall more about what they've been through and enhance the information gleaned by the police by 40 to 50 per cent. Although it was painful, I had to take him back to Friday afternoon. He sat down in a comfortable chair, leaned back and closed his eyes.

Starting at the birth of Abbie, he described his happiness at having a girl and how they took a few photographs before moving to the other ward. He went to pick up Charlie at about 2.00 p.m. and they came into the QMC through the back entrance, using a staircase to reach B-floor.

He knew his way around because his company had done some painting and decorating work at the hospital. Beside him, Charlie tugged at his hand, very excited.

'Tell me about the corridor?' I asked.

'It has a padded rail; it's well-lit and has a nice atmosphere.'

'Who is in the corridor?'

'Just people coming and going.'

'Can you see the woman?'

'Yes.'

'Where is she?'

'She's thirty or forty feet in front of me, walking in the same direction. I can't see her face.'

'How is she walking?'

'She looks as if her arms are folded . . . she has a funny walk, I suppose, almost bent, you know. Stooped with her body forward, looking down but ahead.'

'Does she pass anyone?'

'No . . . I don't think so . . . wait on . . . Yes, she did, there are two women sitting on a seat – she must have walked right past them.'

'Who are they?'

'A mother in her fifties and her daughter. I remember now, I had a card and wanted to borrow a pen. As the woman turned left towards the nurses' station, I asked the mother and daughter if I could borrow their pen.'

(This was important as it gave the police two more possible witnesses who might have seen and could possibly describe the abductor.)

'OK, the woman is walking in front of you, what is she wearing?'

'A blue uniform.'

'What sort of blue?'

'Royal deep blue.'

'How long is it?'

'Ah, I think it's slightly above knee length. I can see her calves and they're out of proportion.'

'What's the style?'

'The sleeves are short; there's a belt pulling it together at the waist, at the front.'

'What colour is the belt?'

'I'm not sure. I can't remember. I'd remember if it was white.'

'What about her shoes?'

'They're black.'

'Is she wearing stockings?'

'Yes, but not black. I think they're flesh coloured maybe.'

This painstaking and difficult process slowly yielded results. Roger had only seen the woman in the corridor for a short period, yet he was able to give new information about her clothes, how she tied her hair, her skin complexion and how she walked with quick short steps, like someone with a purpose.

I took him through the double doors, past the nurses' station and on to 'side-room one' where Karen and Abbie had been waiting. The door into the room has a viewing screen. At each point, I ask Roger what he could see, hear and smell. He described people feeding babies, visitors arriving and staff carrying out their work.

Karen began fussing with Charlie and introducing him to his new baby sister, who was asleep in a cot beside the bed. A few minutes later, she left the room in her nightdress and walked along the corridor to telephone her mother.

Ten to fifteen seconds later the nurse came in, knocking on and opening the door in one action. The walk to the phone took less than ten seconds so Karen should have passed her in the corridor. Charlie was lying on his mother's bed with the baby at his side. Roger was looking down at his hands, assembling a child's model 911 Porsche – a present from the baby to Charlie. He half turned to see her.

She asked, 'Is it all right to take the baby for a hearing test or do you want me to wait for the mother to come back?' (So she must have seen Karen walk out.)

Roger replied, 'She's making a phone call.'

'I'll pop back in fifteen minutes.'

By taking Roger through it in great detail, he recalled how the woman seemed to hover in the doorway, partially inside the room, holding the door open with her right hand. He described her hair . . . it didn't seem natural, he couldn't see her forehead, she might have worn glasses . . .

Confident and relaxed, she smiled at him with full, alert and positive eyes.

'I want you to look at her hands,' I asked. 'Can you see any jewellery? Is she wearing a watch? Does she have a name badge? What about a belt buckle?'

Roger shook his head.

'OK, now look at her face. What do you see? Is she above you, below you, or at the same height as you? How much of her face do you see? Is a part of the door in the way? Tell me more about her hair.'

Slowly a new picture began to emerge, strengthening some details from Roger's initial statement but casting doubt on others. It wasn't an easy interview and he shed tears as he described the moment Abbie was taken.

Karen came back into the room and went straight to the toilet. The *nurse* seemed to follow her, entering while the door was still open. She must have expected Karen to be in the room. Roger half assumed she'd spoken to Karen because they seemed to come in together. He and Charlie were playing with the Porsche 911.

'Is it all right if I do this hearing test?' she said. 'I'll only be a few minutes. I'm just down the corridor.' This time her tone was firm and instructional rather than apologetic. Somewhere outside, she'd taken a deep breath and steeled herself, saying 'This is it.'

She scooped up Abbie as she spoke and then calmly left the room. Karen emerged from the bathroom about ten seconds later, but by then the nurse had left the ward. It took several more minutes to establish that she wasn't a member of staff and by then she was outside the hospital.

The interview had taken nearly three hours and Roger's answers had grown more confident as he began to detach the emotion from the memory. Three important benefits had emerged. The physical description of the offender had been enhanced, the chronology of events was more accurate and I knew far more about the woman's demeanour – the slightly tentative quality when she first came to the room and then how she pumped herself up before trying again.

Karen came into the living room and sat leaning against Roger. She was totally raw. Here was a person who had gone from being confident, ebullient and joyous, for whom all life had come together in that wonderful moment when a baby is born, and then in a few seconds it was all taken away from her. The trauma had closed her down. Her ability to plan, make decisions and conduct herself had gone and I could see a woman who wanted two things – to have her baby back and to curl up in a regressed ball and melt into a puddle of human sludge.

Roger was different; he kept thinking about the 'if onlys' – if only he'd asked for identification; if only he'd said no, etc. Now he felt that he had to try to do something; even if it meant getting in a car and driving round the streets looking for Abbie. It might not make any sense but at least it was something.

I explained to both of them that they weren't cut off from the outside world and still had a vital role to play in the investigation. The chances of Abbie being physically hurt were reasonably low and usually such cases have ended with the child being found safe and well.

Seeing Karen's pain, I set in chain the possibility that should there ever come a time when this was all over, that they needed or wanted to talk to someone about what had happened, they only had to call me.

While I'd been interviewing Roger Humphries, a major news conference was underway at West Bridgford police station. Harry Shepherd revealed the communications strategy to waiting journalists. In an off-the-record briefing, he said the next forty-eight hours were vital and that the media had an important role to play in recovering Abbie Humphries.

Journalists are often dubious about such rhetoric. Some assume they are being denied information or access due to a conspiracy. In this case they wanted the photographs from the security cameras; and also 'talent' to interview each day. They respected Harry and trusted him when he promised them greater access and certain concessions once the forty-eight hours had elapsed. One of these was that I be made available for interviews. Unfortunately, this was agreed without asking me. I would have preferred to have been left out of any publicity.

The gathered journalists accepted the terms and as the cameras rolled, Harry Shepherd delivered the carefully phrased appeal. With so little time to rehearse, I made sure he used words he was comfortable with so that it sounded as genuine as possible.

'Abbie is being missed by her family and I know that all of the people sympathize and support her through this time. I'm sure that everyone would join me in saying that whoever took Abbie from the hospital has our sympathies also. It must have been difficult to take such a lonely step. I want to appeal directly to you, the woman who is now holding Abbie. You have needs of your own and problems that have led you to take her. I realize that you love Abbie, but she is Karen's child, not yours.

'Karen is suffering such anguish, that of all people you will understand, not knowing if her baby is safe and being unable to hold her. Please, please telephone and let Karen know if Abbie is well. You more than most other people will know how important your telephone call will be.'

He added, 'We do understand and are ready to give you all the help, understanding and support appropriate to your needs. Our only consideration at this time is to restore all the important people closely associated with these difficult events back to some degree of happiness.'

'One of the most important people I have in mind is the woman who was driven to take Abbie from her mother.'

Back at West Bridgford, I sat upstairs and drew up a psychological profile of the abductor. The interview with Roger Humphries had confirmed the accuracy of the media strategy launched earlier that morning. Equally, the enhanced physical description of the woman had reaffirmed the earlier decision not to release the video stills or artists' impressions. They would definitely have misled potential witnesses and informants.

After reviewing the information, I drew up a sixteen-point psychological profile.

I wrote, 'The woman is aged from twenty to her early thirties. She is comfortable in a hospital setting and familiar with the QMC.' This was clear from how she managed to conduct herself over a long period of time without attracting attention or being deterred. She didn't appear lost, nervous or frightened.

'She has good intelligence, with an education at least to secondary level.' I knew this because of the planning. She needed intelligence to conceive the plan, acquire the dress and wig, and to deal with unexpected events. As soon as she opened the door she couldn't know what Roger was going to say. She had to be able to look at him, smile, read his verbal and non-verbal behaviour – all of this required a quick mind.

'She is likely to be married or in a similar relationship, but not a stable one because of her desire to secure it (the relationship) by taking a baby.'

'She is confident and easy in deceit.' Not as obvious as it sounds because there are so many physical signs of a person being nervous, they blush, stammer, perspire, or fidget, this woman gave none of these clues.

'She is a careful planner but not exhaustively so,' – good at the outline, perhaps, but not the meticulous detail. I could see her limitations. When she walked out of the hospital, she seemed unsure of what to do next. She hesitated and appeared hurried, looking downwards and drawing attention to herself. Why? Because she hadn't planned this far ahead. Real scholars have the ability to think things through the whole way, relentlessly looking at every possible scenario. Most people, however, get frustrated or impatient and plan as much as they have to and then improvise. This woman hadn't thought about how she was going to get the baby home. She hadn't brought any clothes or blankets for Abbie. The hospital had become a labyrinth and she had to get out. Suddenly onlookers began to notice her and see her anxiety. Here was the evidence that she was prone to panic under pressure.

'She is a risk-taker.' Through each step of the abduction the chance of discovery increased but she carried on – changing her clothes, walking the corridor, penetrating the heart of the hospital. At any time a member of staff could have asked, 'Excuse me, can I help you?'

Once inside the bedroom, Roger could have sensed something was wrong when she picked up Abbie; or a proper nurse could have walked into the room, exposing her lie and cutting off her escape route. The abductor might have considered all of these things but she certainly recognized the risk.

She had acted alone and would have prepared a home for the baby, with a credible rationale such as faking a pregnancy to cover Abbie's arrival. This had to be convincing because she wasn't going to make a fool of herself.

Clinically, I'd examined a number of women who were capable of abducting a child; some who had trouble with relationships, others who were delusional. I was also familiar with the somewhat limited clinical literature on infant abductions. Since 1971, 171 children had been abducted in Britain and all bar one had been recovered safe and well. It was a reassuring, although very thin, numerical database.

I delivered the psychological profile to Harry Shepherd. We were both tired, but there was still work to do.

'You have three major possibilities for her motivation and five others which are less likely,' I said. 'Of the major three, you are firstly looking at the possibility that the abductor could be a woman who is grossly psychologically disturbed. This will include some sort of delusional system where she sees Abbie as her baby, being reclaimed, and no-one else's.

'Secondly, you may be dealing with a woman who is trying to protect or sustain a failing relationship and she thinks that a baby will influence things. Either she wants to make someone think they're the father of her child; or she wants to hold together a marriage or relationship. This could include women who are told they cannot have children.

'Thirdly, you may be dealing with a person who is psychologically isolated and unable to build up relationships with adults but who feels confident with children. She wants to be loved and needs a baby who will love her unconditionally.'

I stressed again that these were the most likely motivations, but also listed the others: it could be a personal matter. The woman may be obsessed with Roger and has taken the child because it should have been hers and not Karen's. Or it could be personal against Karen and police should look at women she has come in contact with as a midwife. It may be aimed at the QMC rather than the parents. A disgruntled member of staff or a patient who feels they lost their child as a result of some perceived mistake might want to punish the hospital. Abbie might have been stolen to order in a commercial transaction; or abducted for some ritual or religious purpose.

Based on what Shepherd had told me, I excluded these last five possibilities. Karen and Roger were originally meant to be in a different ward and had been moved at very short notice to the side-room. The abductor couldn't have known this, which meant she wasn't aiming to punish the Humphries specifically, she simply wanted a baby . . . any baby.

Nor did I believe it was an attack on the QMC. There are far easier ways to punish a hospital and these don't involve hurting innocent parents. Mercifully, the likelihood of Abbie being stolen to order or for ritual purposes was so remote that it could be down-graded although not dismissed entirely.

One rationale stood out from the others – I was sure that Abbie had been taken to weld a marriage or relationship together. If I was right about the motivation, then the entire strategy to recover Abbie had to flow from it.

One of Shepherd's first questions to me had been, 'Is she going to harm the baby?'

I told him, 'Not ordinarily, but the risk will increase significantly if she panics or feels fearful of being punished if she is caught. If she thinks she might be trapped in a difficult situation, she might run off and abandon Abbie who isn't going to survive more than a few hours on her own.'

Shepherd said, 'Which is why I want to make sure we don't do or say anything that is going to lead to a child being hurt.'

For the next two days, Harry Shepherd was to be the caring, avuncular face of British policing . . . at least that was the plan. Yet within hours of the press conference, the strategy was threatened from an unlikely quarter.

Central TV, the regional station, has a monthly programme called *Crimestalker*, fronted by the former deputy chief constable of Manchester, John Stalker. Like *Crimewatch UK* it is a mixture of offence reconstructions, stolen property reports and a showcase for various photofits and video footage. Both shows appeal directly to the public to help in solving crimes, and I had appeared on each of them at various times.

From my experience, John Stalker was a man of considerable intelligence, crime-fighting expertise and personal integrity, although I regarded *Crimestalker* as having the more sensationalist style.

One of the regular segments was called 'Brief from the Chief' and had the Chief Constable of Nottinghamshire Dan Crompton giving a rather chatty update on particular investigations or on developments in policing.

Harry Shepherd found me downstairs at West Bridgford on Tuesday evening and took me to one side.

'You're not going to believe this. I don't know how to tell you.'

Oh, my God, I thought, they've found Abbie dead.

Shepherd said, 'The Chief Constable is going to make his own appeal on *Crimestalker* tomorrow night. He's also going to release the photofits and hospital video footage.'

'Has the strategy changed?' I asked incredulously.

'No, it's nothing to do with me. It's out of my hands.'

I could see Shepherd was bitterly unhappy; he wasn't a man who could conceal his distress or frustration. I suspected that some people thought he was a bit of a pushover but they were wrong. Rather, he was one of those people who expected that folks were going to be decent and do the right thing, despite years of experience as a policeman that told him this didn't always happen.

For a few moments we stood in complete silence and I found myself thinking, what on earth is going on? I didn't have an executive role and didn't make operational or policy decisions, but my concern was for Abbie, for her parents and for her abductor. What were these other people thinking about?

'Will you talk with them?' asked Shepherd.

'With whom?'

'Headquarters – help them understand what they're doing.'

'Yes, but I'm an outsider. Are they going to listen to me?'

I felt sorry for him. He was head of a difficult investigation with enormous external pressures. He had decided on a particular strategy, coaxed the media on-side and knew exactly where the investigation was going. Now all this was in doubt and all he could do was try to limit the damage.

A meeting was convened at West Bridgford and officers from the 'management corridor' arrived for what I assumed would be a meeting to explain the strategy and put paid to any talk of separate television appeals on *Crimestalker*.

About seven of us sat in a quiet corner off the incident room, shrugging off jackets in the heat. The detective chief superintendent from headquarters was in his shirt sleeves behind a desk. He explained what they planned to do. The chief constable would make an appeal on *Crimestalker* and they would release the relevant photographs.

'You know what my views are,' said Shepherd who was sitting beside me.

'I appreciate that, but this is a major case which is receiving attention from media all over the world. We have to respond to it.'

Shepherd replied, 'With respect, sir, we are responding to it. We have a very detailed, carefully planned strategy and we want to maintain it.'

I explained my negative feelings as strongly as possible, pointing out that the driving focus of the existing strategy was to build up a personal relationship between DS Shepherd and the abductor. We wanted to de-emphasize the sensationalist coverage of the crime whereas using *Crimestalker* would have precisely the opposite effect. It would also, I argued, waste resources, be traumatic for the parents and deflect real callers.

The chief superintendent listened but made it clear that it was non-negotiable. The chief constable had a scheduled slot on *Crimestalker* and it was inconceivable that he could appear on the show and not make reference to the biggest case in the county and the country.

'OK, well couldn't he just introduce the subject and then hand over to Harry to do the appeal?'

'No.'

'Why not?'

'You can't have a senior officer taking what is clearly a subsidiary role to a lesser ranked officer.'

Oh, come on, I thought, there has to be some way of making this work.

The chief superintendent wouldn't budge. As far as he was concerned the chief constable would go on TV, make the appeal, release the pictures and the resultant public response would resolve the case.

And everyone will live happily ever after, I thought.

It isn't my business what the police choose to do and not to do. I can't say, 'You're being stupid or bloody-minded.' But I'd never experienced this before. Normally, I dealt with a senior investigating officer who managed the inquiry and made the decisions. It was his case, he called the shots and if something went wrong, his head was on the block. Now I could see how internal politics could threaten this autonomy. It made me angry because I considered that people were forgetting that a child's life was on the line, and I was completely helpless to stop it.

Having failed to halt the broadcast, I urged them to rethink the decision to release the video stills and photofits. It was, I said, a serious threat to their own self-interest. The massed media had been made aware of the strategy and, probably for the first time that I could remember, had wholeheartedly taken up their role with the understanding that should the various photofits and video images need to be released, everyone would get them at the same time.

'If you give Central TV an exclusive first airing of those pictures, by next morning you'll have the entire massed ranks of the media saying that you stitched them up; that you lied to them. They'll massacre you and, given the circumstances, I wouldn't blame them.'

This message finally got through to him. You don't make enemies of the media groups, not when they have been public spirited enough to put the interests of the child and parents before their own.

I had the impression that Chief Constable Crompton probably had absolutely no idea that such decisions were being made. Given his commitments, he probably arrived at the Central TV studio each month without knowing exactly what he'd be talking about. Those decisions would have been made by those beneath him in the management corridor.

To make the best of an unsatisfactory outcome, I agreed to draft a script for his appeal, concentrating on all the important factors that had been identified.

I was in London on Wednesday night when *Crimestalker* went on air. I didn't get home until 1.30 a.m. and was on the road to Nottingham six hours later. When I arrived at West Bridgford I learned of the previous evening's events.

Chief Constable Crompton had gone ahead with the appeal but my script had been dropped and another redrafted by senior police and staff of the programme. Following this, a mystery caller, 'Gary', had phoned the hotline number several times and said that his wife was holding Abbie. He spoke for ten minutes to presenter John Stalker and assured him that Abbie was being well looked after. 'Gary' rang off before police could get enough details to trace him and Mr Crompton appealed for him to get back in touch.

For many it appeared to be a breakthrough but Harry Shepherd couldn't hide his disquiet. There had been no trained negotiator to deal with the call and no offence-related knowledge had been required of the caller. To make matters worse, John Stalker had appeared on breakfast TV confidently declaring that his 'policeman's instincts' told him that the caller was genuine.

Being an experienced policeman, Stalker no doubt assumed that the call had been through the formal filters that weed out hoaxers and that his job was to hang on to 'Gary' for as long as possible and elicit more details.

However, from my point of view, none of the formal filters had been in place and none of the technical questions had been asked – no proof of life had been sought nor analysis of the mental functioning of the caller. As I quizzed Shepherd, he could only shrug and admit it had nothing to do with him; the programme was outside the parameters of the investigation.

His mood grew even blacker in mid-afternoon, when he learned that a uniformed police officer had made a special live appeal to 'Gary's wife', who 'Gary' had said normally watched TV between 2.00 and 3.00 p.m. Approval had been given by senior police at headquarters.

For Shepherd it was like having a second investigation being carried out without his knowledge and input.

Even so, he decided to continue with the original strategy and launch stage two. This was based upon the likelihood that the abductor had cut herself off from the outside world and not listened to the earlier appeals. As a result, as she became more secure in her new domestic environment and the baby became more identified with her, neighbours and onlookers would become less suspicious. For this reason, stage two of the appeal was explicitly aimed at those close to the abductor – friends, family, acquaintances and neighbours who might have suspicions and could hopefully be encouraged to come forward, particularly if they felt that their friend or family member wasn't being seen as a callous criminal by the police.

At this point, the video pictures could be released because the risk of Abbie settling into the abductor's life outweighed the risk to Abbie from possibly startling or panicking the woman. I had also suggested that it would now be appropriate if further faces could be drafted into the appeal – such as Karen's sister – who would both give variation and confirm the parents' anguish.

On Thursday afternoon, the much awaited video images were released, along with three photofits drawn up from descriptions given by Roger Humphries, Jim and Julie Morris and staff at the QMC. By the following morning every national newspaper carried the pictures and the incident room took more than 400 calls in twelve hours, stretching staff to the limit.

Although Harry Shepherd was still the main face of the investigation, I had grudgingly agreed to give several interviews at the request of the police and couldn't now avoid it. I didn't want to build up my role at the expense of the police and insisted that I was simply a resource they could use. After answering general questions at a news conference, I gave a handful of one-on-one interviews explaining the likely mind-set of the abductor.

Someone asked me what I thought she would be doing now.

'On the one hand, she will be trying to develop a completely exclusive relationship with Abbie, blocking everything else out until she has nothing in her world except her and her child,' I said. 'At the same time, she'll be trying to integrate the baby into her existing family life. She wants Abbie to be her daughter; she wants a child to love her; and she wants both of them to forget there is anyone else – in other words Karen and Roger.

'Someone close to her must realize that this isn't true or at least have suspicions. They are the people we want to come forward.'

That afternoon I was back behind the steel-mesh fence at Arnold Lodge, catching up on my NHS work and reviewing an interview with a young girl from a clinical case. Now it was up to the media to reach out to those people who had genuine information about Abbie Humphries.

There are many sad ironies in the work I do and the Abbie Humphries case was no exception. Less than half a mile from the incident room at West Bridgford was a home for mothers who have difficulties looking after their children. One of my patients was there, a woman with a very young baby, who had to show that she was capable of looking after the infant or risk having the baby taken into care. My task was to assess her and I found myself pondering how on the one hand there were Mr and Mrs Humphries – many people's ideal parents – who had their new-born child snatched away from them. Yet not far away lived a girl with a baby and my decision would influence whether it should be taken away from her.

That same week I also spent a day in prison examining a man who had been charged with grievous bodily harm after his child had been scalded in a bath. The police alleged that this was done deliberately, but there was some contention about who had really been responsible because of the man's vulnerability to suggestion.

On Friday 8 July, a week after Abbie's abduction, the police were back in force at the QMC, reinterviewing staff, quizzing visitors and stopping pedestrians, buses and motorists outside, hoping someone might remember a vital detail. The sheer number of calls being generated indicated that the campaign was reaching every corner of the country, although I still felt sure the actual abductor would probably live within a few miles of the hospital.

On Sunday afternoon Shepherd called, apologizing for interrupting another weekend. A woman had phoned the incident room, claiming to be holding Abbie.

'What makes you think it's genuine?' I asked.

'We're still not sure but she can't be ignored, she's distraught and keeps hanging up.'

I drove to West Bridgford and arrived to find that they had no trained police negotiator available in the early stages, but one was apparently en route. The woman had called again, giving vague details but hanging up before the call could be traced. I quizzed the officer who had talked to her, looking for the details that would separate this call from the many hoaxes received among the 3,000 messages from the public in the previous week. Proof of life and knowledge of the crime hadn't been established but it was clear that the woman sounded emotionally unstable and, if she did have Abbie, nothing should be done to panic her.

When the negotiator arrived, I briefed him on what I knew about the emotional functioning of the caller, suggesting how to keep her on the line and extract information from her without tipping her over the edge.

Then we waited for her to call again. This time the police came up with a name and address – a young woman known to social services who had two children, neither of them babies.

'I heard a baby,' insisted the officer.

'Are you sure?' asked Shepherd. 'You have to be sure. It can't be the television, or the radio. You're sure it was a baby?'

He nodded.

It was 11.00 p.m. and Shepherd and I found ourselves at the local social services office, trying to get hold of the files on the woman so we could learn more about her. Although she wasn't threatening to harm the child, she clearly showed histrionic responses and rapid mood swings. We weren't dealing with someone in charge of her emotions and it was likely the police would have to go in very, very fast.

A response team was quickly briefed and at 2.00 a.m. we drove out of Nottingham and gathered in a small village police station a few miles away. The response team was armed with riot shields, vests and battering rams. After a final briefing we drove off following several police transit vans, through darkened streets and lanes lined with sleeping bungalows and houses.

We pulled up about a mile from the house, well out of sight, and while several officers went ahead to recce the situation I waited with the response teams. In the hot night air, the two-way radios crackled loudly and heavy boots shuffled in the gravel. Soon lights came on and people wandered out of their houses to find out what was happening.

'Everything's fine. Please go back inside,' the officers said. 'Nothing to worry about.'

The message to move ahead came through and we began walking, taking what seemed to be a circuitous route through quiet streets. Although we tried to spread out and look inconspicuous, it was hard to hide what looked like an army coming down the street with heavy boots, helmets and shields.

We reached the house – a small, two-storey terrace, two-up-two-down with an extension at the back for the kitchen. The plan was to telephone and have the woman come to the phone while the police waited outside, ready to enter. She'd be told someone was about to knock on her door and she was to stay completely calm. If she panicked, the response team would enter by force.

I heard the telephone ring and after a nerve-racking few moments the front door opened. The police went through the house fast, going through every cupboard, box, drawer, bench and panel. The officer had heard a baby crying – where was it? Had it been smothered or hidden? Had we lost control of its fate?

The woman, in her late twenties, was deeply shocked and denied having made the calls. Not surprisingly, her own children, aged four and eight, were distressed and crying as heavy boots echoed from room to room. When the search found nothing I began to relax a little. Having eye-balled her and heard her answers, it was clearly a hoax, although the police did find newspaper clippings related to the abduction hidden under the carpet.

Regardless of whether she had taken Abbie, her emotional state clearly showed that she needed counselling and care. Her children were looked after by a social worker, while the mother was taken to Oxclose Lane police station.

Although Abbie hadn't been recovered, I didn't attach any blame to the officer who had taken the calls. He'd been so intensely locked into the inquiry and determined to find Abbie that he had convinced himself that he'd heard a baby crying in the background. It was an index of the extreme strain that such responsibility puts on a negotiator or courier during that time when the whole focus of an investigation falls onto his or her shoulders.

Unfortunately, later that same day, the mystery caller 'Gary' was also exposed as a hoaxer. Amid angry scenes, the thirty-six-year-old unemployed divorcée from Gloucester appeared in court the next day (Tuesday 12 July) charged with grievous bodily harm to Karen and Roger Humphries.

Meanwhile, the inquiry team pressed onwards but risked being buried under a mountain of paper. With reports coming in from as far afield as Ireland and London, it was important that good information wasn't lost in the wash. In my view every child of the appropriate age encountered during the search had to be checked and cross-referenced with doctors, health visitors or midwives. Questions had to be asked about where the baby was born; when it was born; who was your doctor?

Although there were rumbles from the media, Harry Shepherd didn't let any outside pressures distract him from the strategy. His task wasn't made any easier when his superiors at headquarters granted Central TV permission to make a 'fly on the wall' documentary about the hunt for Abbie. It was a policy decision, I was told, and the inquiry team had no option but to co-operate. I was asked by the media relations officer and then Central TV if I'd take part but declined. I didn't want to be interviewed. However, the documentary team had free run of the investigation and occasionally I would look up to find them filming me through doors or in the corridors.

Twelve days after the abduction, questions were beginning to arise about whether something could have been missed. Perhaps someone had reported their suspicions and it had been wrongly prioritized among the thousands of reported sightings of Abbie.

I had time to think about this while convalescing in bed on Friday 15 July, laid low by the vagaries of whatever disc, vertebra or strained muscle damage had turned my back into a stiff plank and my slightest movement into torture. I was similarly disposed on Saturday morning when an early news bulletin announced that Abbie Humphries had been found safe and well in the early hours of the morning at a house in Nottingham.

Three people had been arrested including twenty-two-year-old

Julie Kelley, a former dental nurse who admitted to abducting the baby from the QMC two weeks earlier. She shared a house with her boyfriend Leigh Gilbert, twenty-three, a motor mechanic, and his mother Susan. The story that emerged during interviews was that Kelley had taken Abbie in order to cement her deteriorating relationship with her boyfriend. The previous August, Gilbert had threatened to break it off after meeting someone else, but Kelley then told him that she was pregnant.

She kept up the charade in the months that followed, allowing him to decorate a nursery for the baby and letting his family buy a pram, cot and presents. The deception was so well thought out that she pretended to have morning sickness and food cravings. She walked around heavily padded and persuaded Gilbert to take her to prenatal appointments at the QMC, making him wait in reception while she pretended to see the doctor.

In March, craving more of his attention, she told him that tests had shown the 'baby' might have Down's syndrome and this led to the couple visiting a school for severely handicapped children.

Ironically, Kelley became genuinely pregnant in May yet didn't abandon her elaborate deception. By the beginning of July, her pregnancy had stretched to ten months and she was under pressure to produce the child that all those around her had been awaiting. Using her former dental nurse's uniform, she disguised herself with a wig and snatched Abbie from the maternity ward. Then she returned home to the red-brick house in Brendon Drive, Wollaton, less than a mile from the hospital. She rang Leigh Gilbert at work and told him that she'd given birth at home. Amid the excitement and family celebrations, nobody questioned her account of events.

Similarly, most of the neighbours knew of her pregnancy and weren't surprised to see the line of fluffy toys appear on the window-sill or the baby clothes on the washing line. Yet one or two had concerns, particularly because Kelley had earlier told them she was having a *boy*. A home birth was also unusual and there were no sightings of midwives or health care visitors who closely monitor new-born babies.

When Julie Kelley eventually stood trial, she was described as suffering from a personality disorder in which she became overwhelmingly dependent on relationships. She believed a pregnancy and a baby would solve all her personal problems.

Consultant psychoanalyst Dr Lawrence Bell, who examined her, said he felt that she had developed an obsessive relationship with Mr Gilbert, her first real boyfriend who she had met when she was seventeen. 'She felt unable to stop the escalator and get off. She was unable to tell them what had happened. She could not bring herself to tell them the truth.'

From my point of view, the campaign to recover Abbie had been extremely successful. She was reclaimed without resistance, with no question of hostage-taking or anyone being harmed. Abbie had been well cared for and within hours was back in the arms of Karen and Roger who were both enormously grateful for the efforts of the police.

However, in the days that followed, the inquiry team faced growing criticism. It emerged that the incident room had received five tip-offs suggesting that Abbie was in the house at Brendon Drive. The first was an anonymous call, little more than four days after the kidnapping which gave only the street name. The second caller, Mrs Glenis Smith, a neighbour of the Gilberts, voiced her suspicions and two days later police visited the house and found a family celebrating the birth with presents and cards.

Shepherd told journalists, 'They were looking for a child to rescue. What they found was a child who appeared to be in a correct and caring home.'

Two more anonymous tip-offs came from a chemist worried that a woman wanting cream to treat a baby's navel might be holding Abbie. Later, the neighbour Glenis Smith discussed her fears with a friend who passed on the information to a midwife who checked the records and found no trace of a home birth at fourteen Brendon Drive. When this tip-off came, detectives were already preparing to raid the house.

These five calls (three of them anonymous) were among 4,700 received over fifteen days in the wake of the media strategy and illustrate precisely the lessons that must be learned for the future. I don't blame the officers who visited the house four days after the kidnapping – they couldn't be expected to recognize Abbie, only Roger and Karen could have done that. But what happened to their report? Were salient details lost in the mountain of paperwork?

When a successful media campaign generates so much diverse information, you need a system of accurately classifying and prioritizing it, giving it shape and order. Without this, a lot of time can be wasted chasing less likely tip-offs instead of concentrating initially on those that fit the pattern of the profile. Making these decisions isn't easy. It means not letting the urgent, compelling, emotional thoughts about a young baby, possibly in peril, block out these information management requirements. By all means, understand the pain and the risks involved, but stand back and look at the search in almost a mathematical way.

Harry Shepherd and his team didn't deserve the criticism. Shepherd had worked twenty-two hours a day on what he called his most emotional investigation in twenty-eight years of service. 'But you can't let emotion get in the way of the job you are doing,' he told a news conference. 'There was never any despair. Worry, yes, but not despair. I was never one hundred per cent sure we'd get Abbie back – but I always felt we would.'

21

THREE WEEKS AFTER THE COMMITTAL HEARING AT WIMBLEDON Magistrates Court, an entirely different prosecution 200 miles away in Leeds would dramatically alter the complexion of the Rachel Nickell trial. A mobile grocer, Keith Hall, was acquitted of murdering his wife Patricia when a judge ruled that the evidence of an undercover policewoman who had befriended him was inadmissible.

Hall's wife had disappeared in the spring of 1992 after what the neighbours described as a fierce row. He claimed that she had simply walked out on him, taking the family Ford Sierra Estate which was later found abandoned. The driver's seat was positioned close to the wheel, as for her, rather than him, but a milkman had recalled seeing a man in the car.

Unable to find any trace of her, police believed that Patricia Hall had been murdered but could find nothing to directly implicate her husband. On legal advice he refused to answer questions and watched quizzically as police unsuccessfully dug up the garden at the family semi in Pudsey, on the outskirts of Leeds. They also excavated a newly laid concrete roundabout near the house.

Eventually, in October 1992, the inquiry team had a call from a local woman, Eliza, who had placed a lonely hearts advertisement in the *Wharfe Valley Times* and been astonished to receive a response from Keith Hall. She recognized his name, having read about the case, and knew that his wife had only been dead for six months. On police advice, she wrote back to Hall to see where it would lead.

As the correspondence continued, the police replaced 'Eliza' with an undercover policewoman from the West Yorkshire Regional

Crime Squad. The relationship progressed over the next four months from letters to phone calls that contained long meaningful conversations about life, love and ambition. Finally, they met in the car-park of the George and Dragon pub where every word and hesitant cough was picked up by a microphone worn by 'Liz'.

They were to meet five more times over the next five months, mostly for a quiet drink at the same hotel. Unexpectedly, Hall fell in love with Liz and bought her a wedding ring. When he asked her to move in with him, Liz declared it was impossible because his missing wife might come back to him at any time.

The following evening, 26 February, 1993, as they sat in the hotel car-park, Hall told her there was no chance that Patricia could come back because he'd murdered her and burned her body in an incinerator.

He was arrested and charged with murder and stood trial at Leeds Crown Court on Thursday 12 March, 1994. After days of legal argument, the judge, Mr Justice Waterhouse, ruled that the evidence of the undercover officer – including Hall's tape-recorded confession – was inadmissible. Keith Hall was found 'not guilty' without any of the evidence being put before a jury. He walked from the court a free man.

That afternoon, I was driving back to Leicester from an outpatients' clinic when I heard about the case on a radio news bulletin. I remember being shocked. An operation that bore all the hallmarks of what had happened in the Nickell investigation had been rejected by a court. Did it mark the end of the Colin Stagg prosecution, I wondered. Had the Crown lawyers got it wrong?

I called Pedder as soon as I reached a telephone.

'You've heard,' he said.

'Yes. Does it mean our case is over?'

'No, of course it doesn't.' He went on to explain that the prosecution team had already looked carefully at the Hall case and believed that the covert operation in the Rachel inquiry had been designed and run along very different lines and could not be considered in the same light. It had been 'whiter than white' with no hint of entrapment.

Pedder said, 'You know yourself, Paul, that our operation wasn't intended to manipulate a man into making a confession. It was intended to allow him to either eliminate himself entirely, or to further implicate himself entirely by his own choices.'

'Yes, I know.'

'Which is why you don't worry. It's being looked at by lawyers at the top of the legal tree.'

He was right. These were decisions for experienced lawyers to make and I accepted their judgement without question. However, as the trial grew closer it became clear to me that there wasn't quite the same optimism and confidence as previously. Until then, we'd been racing towards justice but now the probabilities had been reassessed.

The Crown had a new leading counsel, John Nutting QC, and we gathered for a final case conference in his chambers on Friday 2 September. The trial was due to begin on Monday at the Central Criminal Court, the Old Bailey. Seated around a long table covered in green baize were Pedder, Mick Wickerson, Bruce Butler, John Nutting, junior counsel, myself and several others.

Nutting went over the preliminaries and explained that the defence were likely to launch a pre-emptive strike to have the Lizzie James material declared inadmissible and the case thrown out. He advised me that I may be required to be in court on Monday.

He asked me for an opinion, 'If the evidence of Lizzie James is not admitted do you think that your evidence would be sufficient to base a conviction upon?'

'Of course not,' I said.

'I'm glad you said that, because that's exactly what my view is.'

He began to ask me questions about the statements that I'd given, pressing me harder and harder on the detail and interpretation. I began to feel embarrassed at what felt like a cross-examination in front of the others. Then I realized that Nutting was testing me. He was assessing for himself how I'd bear up if faced by a very hard defending counsel in court.

As the meeting ended, the road ahead was clear – if the undercover evidence wasn't admitted then the Crown would fold its tents and go home, dropping the case against Colin Stagg. As I left the meeting I said to Nutting, 'I get the impression that you're somewhat pessimistic about the case.'

'Well, let's just say I'm not optimistic,' he said wryly.

'I don't want to put you on the spot, but do you have a view on the likelihood of the Crown being successful?'

There was a long pause. 'I think it's very finely balanced,' he said.

For the next week I waited, with my diary rearranged so I could leave for London at short notice. Meanwhile, the legal heavyweights slugged it out, arguing before Mr Justice Ognall whether the case against Colin Stagg should proceed.

Eventually I learned that the judge didn't need to hear from me and would rule on Lizzie James's evidence 'from paper'. The defence team, led by William Clegg QC and backed by Jim Sturman, submitted an outline of their objections to the judge and, as expected, used the Keith Hall case in Leeds as a legal precedent.

Before hearing the arguments about admissibility, the judge had to familiarize himself with the 700 pages of correspondence, telephone conversations and tape-recorded meetings between Colin Stagg and Lizzie James. Having done so, he invited Mr Clegg to make a submission.

The defence counsel claimed that the defendant had been the victim of a sophisticated 'sting' operation aimed at taking advantage of a lonely, vulnerable young man desperate to lose his virginity. It had been designed to entrap him into making a confession, yet Mr Stagg had always denied his involvement in the murder of Rachel Nickell.

Dipping in and out of Lizzie's evidence to illustrate his points, Mr Clegg claimed that Lizzie James had shaped the relationship, holding out the offer of sex and that Mr Stagg's replies were nothing more than you would expect from a painfully shy and sexually inexperienced young man. My evidence, he argued, should also be thrown out because it went hand in glove with the covert operation.

John Nutting countered that the possibility of sex had indeed been implicit in the relationship but Lizzie hadn't told Stagg what to write in his fantasies – the ideas were all his own. He had been the first to mention the woodland setting, the trees, the stream, the knife, the extreme violence, the rape and the inflicting of pain.

He submitted that Stagg's detailed description to Lizzie of how Rachel had been lying could not possibly have been derived from the only photograph shown to him by police during the investigation. In particular, how he had illustrated the position of her hands being palm to palm. Nutting submitted that such a detail could only have been known by the assailant and that this amounted to a confession.

Mr Clegg totally disagreed and pointed out that Rachel's hands were crossed at the wrist and not palm to palm – hardly a minor discrepancy.

On 14 September Mr Justice Ognall delivered an eighty-minute judgment that tore the heart out of the case against Colin Stagg and shocked many observers with its extreme criticism of the police. Describing the covert operation as misconceived and doomed to failure, he said, 'I would be the first to acknowledge the very great pressures on the police in their pursuit of this grave inquiry but I am afraid this behaviour betrays not merely an excessive zeal but a substantial attempt to incriminate a suspect by positive and deceptive conduct of the grossest kind.'

He accepted that Colin Stagg had made the first mention of a knife in his correspondence with Lizzie and that he had spoken of being sexually excited on learning of the circumstances of Rachel Nickell's murder. However, he said, any attempt to edit and separate the material collected through the undercover operation was 'bound to fail'.

'The prosecution sought to persuade me that the object of the exercise was to afford the accused an opportunity either to eliminate himself from the inquiry or implicate himself in the murder. I am bound to say that I regard that description of the operation as highly disingenuous.'

Referring to Stagg's description of Rachel's body, the judge said that this was the only part of an otherwise undisputed record that could not be verified by anything other than Lizzie James's memory. It had not been videoed during the Hyde Park meeting and only Lizzie had seen Stagg lie on the ground and demonstrate how Rachel had been lying.

The fact that Rachel's hands were crossed at the wrist and not palm to palm, was not a minor difference but a major discrepancy. 'I am not satisfied having heard submissions on both sides that this one very small piece of evidence does amount to, or is properly capable of, being viewed as incriminating material of the character of a confession . . .

'I would add that even were I to be persuaded that this material could fairly and properly warrant the status of a confession I regard it as so flimsy in its nature as to demand the conclusion that its potential prejudice clearly exceeds any probative value. The best the prosecution could do here would be to persuade me that overall the material obtained in the undercover operation was not unfairly obtained. They have failed to do so.'

He ruled that the letters, telephone calls and taped conversations were inadmissible and the Crown immediately withdrew its case. After more than twelve months in custody, Colin Stagg was officially declared not guilty and walked from the Old Bailey a free man surrounded by television cameras and photographers.

At the mother and baby unit at West Bridgeford, in Nottingham, I had an urgent call from Diane. 'The phones have gone mad. It's chaos here,' she said.

I rang Pedder and he told me of the judgement. He sounded empty inside. As he quoted the judge's words, I tried to comprehend the ramifications. Right from the beginning, the undercover operation had been scrutinized and overseen by the most senior officers commanding the Metropolitan Police. They were advised by senior Treasury counsel and the operation sat at the top of the attorney general's list of most sensitive cases. None of these people had ever cast any doubt over its legality, at least not in my presence.

'He mentioned your evidence,' said Pedder.

'But he didn't even hear legal arguments about my evidence,' I said, surprised.

'I know.'

'What did he say?'

'He said the Crown would have had an "even higher mountain to climb" to persuade him to accept it. And that the notion of a psychological profile being admissible as proof of identity in any circumstances was "redolent with considerable danger".'

This angered me more than anything else. I had never suggested that a psychological profile or sexual deviancy analysis were proof of guilt – quite the opposite. Colin Stagg chose to reveal his sexuality. Even though this matched exactly the analysis I drew up of the unidentified killer, it did not make Stagg the murderer. Only when he disclosed real-world information about the actual crime did he implicate himself in the eyes of the police. It also upset me that Mr Justice Ognall had decided to comment on my evidence without hearing arguments or hearing from me.

'What happens now?' I asked Pedder. 'My phone is ringing off the hook at the office and apparently I've got journalists on the way.'

There was a hesitancy in his voice. 'Please don't make any comment. There's the possibility of further legal proceedings. The Met [Metropolitan Police] and the CPS are getting together to make a concerted response.'

Throughout the afternoon and evening, I fielded dozens of calls from the media, referring them back to the Metropolitan Police.

Some of them took this rather badly. A television producer on one late-night news programme presented me with the ultimatum, 'Either you come on our programme tonight or we're going to hang you out to dry.' They did exactly as promised, portraying me as some sort of distasteful mastermind of an operation designed to frame an innocent man.

When I arrived home, I walked into the lounge and found Marilyn and the family watching the programme. How surreal it was to look at a group of people sitting in a TV studio in London all talking about me. Behind them, a huge photograph of me had been projected onto the wall. The basic thrust of the debate was to lay the blame for the undercover operation, the arrest of Colin Stagg and the collapse of the trial securely at my feet.

A storm had broken around my head and the daily headlines made harsh reading. RACHEL CASE COLLAPSES. FANTASY JUSTICE. WHO'S IN THE DOCK NOW?

I arrived at work just before 9.30 a.m. and the phones were already jammed. The switchboard at Arnold Lodge became gridlocked with no-one able to get through. Journalists were arriving at reception asking to see me and waiting outside the perimeter gates for my appearance.

Meanwhile, I waited for the media statement from the Metropolitan Police and the CPS which would set the record straight. I was being depicted as having 'persuaded' the police to launch the covert operation and then having convinced 'sceptical CPS lawyers' that they should charge Colin Stagg with murder. Of course, this is absurd and I expected that at any minute the Metropolitan Police commissioner would come out and say, 'Hang on now, you've got the wrong end of the stick, Paul Britton did no such thing.'

I contemplated putting out my own press release, even jotting down a point by point rebuttal of the claims being made in the media, but chose not to issue it because I'd given my word to Keith Pedder that I wouldn't make any comment. Eventually the commissioner and the director of public prosecutions did make a statement but it did nothing to remove the hounds from my door. I wasn't consulted beforehand or invited to the media conference, even though I appeared to be the person copping most of the flak.

Of course, I realize now that different levels in the police service had different agendas. The detectives who worked on the ground, Keith Pedder, John Bassett and Mick Wickerson, concentrated on the job at hand but at a more senior level the policy-makers and managers were concerned for the image of the police service and if someone else seemed to bear the brunt of the criticism, then, pragmatically, that was easier to deal with.

When the trial collapsed having cost the taxpayer a considerable amount of money, the media went looking for someone to blame. The judge's comments allowed them to look for a target and they were confronted with three possibilities – the monolithic Metropolitan Police force, the faceless Crown Prosecution Service and me, Paul Britton. I had a face and a name and was by far the easiest target to hit. When I refused to comment, I think it angered the media beyond measure.

The others seemed quite relieved when they saw how much heat and vitriol came my way. I'm sure they thought, Well, that's not right, but I'm ever so glad it's not me.

This was driven home to me a year or so later, when I was back at New Scotland Yard, having been asked to design another covert operation, this time to investigate the sabotaging of health care equipment. I said to a senior policeman from the covert operations team, 'I've been here before, you know. And the last time we were all at this stage, everyone said how well things were going and what a good job was being done. Come the trial when things went badly, I was the only one standing there. No-one else was around.'

The policeman laughed, 'Yes, you got a fucking raw deal there. But you're a big lad, you've got broad shoulders, you can look after yourself.'

I'm not an apologist for a legal system that keeps a murder suspect in prison for more than a year awaiting trial. The police and the lawyers thought they had a case against Colin Stagg and a stipendiary magistrate agreed.

In any investigation some material will be admissible as evidence, other material will be inadmissible and some will require a judge to decide which is which. The stipendiary magistrate examined the evidence and sent a man to trial and then Mr Justice Ognall decided that the evidence gathered by Lizzie James should not be put before a jury. The Crown withdrew and, quite properly, Colin Stagg was released.

The people I felt most sorry for were Andre Hanscombe, young Alex and Rachel's parents, Andrew and Monica Nickell. Mr and Mrs

Nickell had sat through the entire proceedings and, that night on the television news, I watched Mr Nickell make a very dignified and heartfelt statement from the steps of the Old Bailey.

'We have been here for the last week because in August 1993 Colin Stagg was charged after a long undercover operation organized by the police under the direction of an eminent psychologist. The police undertook this operation because they thought it was the only way to prove or disprove their suspicions that Colin Stagg was the murderer.

'There was no physical evidence, only strong circumstantial evidence. What were the police to do? Were they to let a man they suspected and believed was guilty of a hideous murder to roam free? What choice did they have? They have to keep the peace and protect society.'

22

ON THURSDAY MORNING, AS THE STORM BROKE OVER MY HEAD, ONE caller managed to get through to Arnold Lodge who made no reference to the day's headlines. Detective Chief Superintendent Colin Port, the head of Warwickshire CID, had a murder to solve.

Three days earlier a building society manageress from Nuneaton had been found dead beside a busy local road. Her office had been burgled and when detectives arrived at her home they found her husband bound and gagged in the lounge.

'It's thrown up some interesting questions,' said Port, without elaborating. 'If you're available I'll get the SIO Tony Bayliss to call you.'

'Have you seen the morning papers?' I asked.

'Why?'

'Apparently I'm receiving some criticism as a consequence of the Rachel Nickell trial.'

He laughed. 'Yes, I'm aware of that.'

'If that made you feel uncomfortable or nervous, I wouldn't be upset if you wanted to ask someone else to help.'

'Absolutely not. I'm asking you.'

When I hung up, I felt relieved. One of the ways I tend to deal with problems is to carry on doing what I always do. It helped to keep my eye on the ball.

That afternoon I drove to Nuneaton, a small market town just south of the A5, between Coventry and Leicester. The town centre is quite compact and encircled by a busy ring road. Right in the middle is the police station which looks like a vast shoebox resting on its side.

As I pulled into the adjacent car-park, I saw a van with blacked out rear windows moving away. Suddenly it stopped and reversed. I'd been recognized by a TV crew, but managed to duck inside before being challenged.

Detective Inspector Tony Bayliss had a broad Midlands accent that sounded informal and chatty, yet a sharp mind lay behind his genial exterior. A family man, Bayliss had a reputation for being old-fashioned and had spent a number of years at Leamington Spa, where I grew up.

'What some people will do to get their name in the paper,' he joked, referring to the Nickell case.

'And all I want is a quiet life,' I said.

He took me upstairs to a suite of rooms on the second floor – the largest of them being used as the incident room. Clearly, a lot of thought had gone into the layout. Numerous computer terminals were set up in logical relationships with each other, depending upon the task of each operator. The paper flow generated by the investigation was already significant but being well controlled by the office manager. Equally, the police and civilian staff had an easy confidence, despite being obviously tired.

What flagged the set-up as being different from many others that I'd seen was that Bayliss had put a dedicated Intelligence cell immediately next to the incident room. The officers involved had two special functions, to consolidate and evaluate information received, transforming it into useable 'intelligence', and to assist in the consideration of how it could be used.

Another room had been set aside for confidential management policy meetings and this is where we settled into chairs. Glancing up at the door, Bayliss motioned to his deputy Gino Varriale to join us. 'I'll run through the chronology and then we'll look at the details,' he said. 'It seems to bear all the hallmarks of a thoroughly planned abduction and robbery that went tragically wrong.'

At 8.35 a.m. on Monday, the body of a well-groomed middle-aged woman had been found beside a lay-by on the A444 Weddington Lane, two and a half miles from Nuneaton. Police immediately launched a murder inquiry and began checking missing persons' files.

Just over an hour later, staff arriving for work at the Woolwich Building Society in Nuneaton reported a suspected bank raid. The safe had been opened and there were papers strewn across the floor.

Nearby, a discarded sandal matched the one found lying near the woman's body in Weddington Lane. The two scenes were now connected and the police had a name – Carol Wardell, the assistant manageress at the Woolwich.

Police went to her home in Bonneville Close, Meriden, twelve miles from Nuneaton and found the curtains drawn, milk on the doorstep, but no signs of forced entry. Just before 2.00 p.m. two officers approached the front door and heard muffled cries. They found Gordon Wardell lying on the floor of the lounge wearing only his underpants. He was gagged with a strip of cloth around his head and tied to a refuse sack holder with his legs over the horizontal bar and his wrists bound with a plastic ratchet-type tie.

Clearly distressed and showing signs of having been beaten, he was taken to hospital and treated for trauma and superficial injuries. Mr Wardell continually asked after his wife until his father broke the news that Carol had been killed. A tear ran down Gordon's cheek.

'We waited twenty-four hours before we could interview him,' said Bayliss. 'He says the gang jumped him when he arrived home from posting a letter on Sunday night. They drugged him and held a knife to his wife's throat. Next thing he remembers is waking up next morning.'

Gino said, 'In the meantime someone used Carol's personal access code to break into the Woolwich.'

'How much is missing?' I asked.

'About £14,000 worth if you include the cheques.'

Bayliss added, 'It's not much money for the planning and risk. A professional gang would have been after much more . . .' Thinking aloud, he continued, 'And why would professionals kill Carol? It just draws the heat. One of them must have spoken out of turn or let her see his face.'

'Or it could have been unintended, an accident,' I suggested.

'What about the security code?' said Gino. 'A computer at the Woolwich recorded Carol's access code being punched in at 5.22 a.m. on the morning of the robbery. But each key-holder has a "duress code" with a single digit different from their normal entry number. It's designed for this sort of abduction. Carol could have punched it in and secretly let us know without triggering the alarms. We would have been there within minutes.'

'I wouldn't read too much into that,' warned Bayliss. 'In my experience people behave very differently in real life to the way they think they will.'

I agreed. 'Just because you have a duress code doesn't mean that when the time comes you'll have the courage and presence of mind to use it. She would have been terrified: her husband was at home being held hostage; perhaps she thought she couldn't take the risk.'

Bayliss had already discussed my role in the inquiry. He wanted me to provide an independent crime analysis, which meant evaluating all the facts, reports and observations without reference to any particular theory the police might have. If, independently, I came to the same conclusions, it would reaffirm that the inquiry was heading in the right direction. If not, then they would have to consider other possibilities.

Already, there were aspects of the case that concerned me. It was like looking at a jigsaw puzzle that had been carefully put together and the picture that emerged was of an abduction and robbery that had gone wrong. Yet I couldn't help feeling that the pieces had been shoe-horned in too tightly.

Bayliss could see my disquiet. 'You don't think it looks right?'

'No.'

'Well, it's interesting that you should say that.'

He explained that he'd given me the straightforward scene of crime facts and statements, withholding some of his own concerns so as not to prejudice my opinion.

'There's something in Mr Wardell's past, isn't there?'

Bayliss nodded.

'He attacked a woman twenty-four years ago in front of her two young sons. Almost killed her. He served four years in prison for grievous bodily.'

'Who was she?'

Gino relpied, 'His geology teacher's wife.'

Instantly, I grew uneasy. Teenage boys don't usually launch unprovoked attacks on women they have never met unless they have some form of personality disorder or sexual pathology, or they are mentally ill.

'You'll have the original statements,' said Bayliss. Gino made a note.

But from my point of view this wasn't enough – so often formal statements don't contain the fine details that can indicate motivation and state of mind.

'Can the victim be re-interviewed?' I asked.

Bayliss raised an eyebrow. 'It's been twenty-four years.'

'I know that, but I need to know what he said, what he did, how he looked . . . all the nuances.'

A glance at Gino and a nod confirmed that this would be done.

I wasn't suggesting that Gordon Wardell was anything other than a bereaved husband who had gone through a terrible ordeal. He hadn't made any attempt to hide the previous conviction, telling the police at the hospital. He also answered questions at a news conference and said how much he regretted the incident being brought up again. 'I feel it is almost another injustice to my wife,' he said.

The bearded forty-one-year-old had appeared in a wheelchair wearing tinted glasses and said that Carol had meant everything to him and he couldn't imagine life without her. He appealed for anyone with information that might help identify his wife's killers to contact the police.

Bayliss handed me a statement.

Wardell had been interviewed for two days and eventually signed a lengthy statement. He described himself as a warehouse manager for a motor components distribution company, Veng UK, based in Hinckley, Leicestershire. He'd joined the company in June 1994 with prospects of early promotion and elevation to the board of directors.

On Sunday, he and Carol had spent a fairly ordinary day together, pottering around the house and watching television. After dinner Carol had put on a video and watched a movie, *Delta Force*, which ran out just before the end because she hadn't recorded it all.

Then she asked Gordon to post a letter for her. It was addressed to a Mr Taylor from Exhall and he imagined it was something to do with her work. Assuming it was important, he ignored the local box which didn't get collected until 7.30 a.m. next morning and drove instead to the post office in Bishop Street, Coventry, six miles away, which had a large sorting office and would deliver the letter first thing on Monday. Bishop Street, he said, had a video camera on the wall covering the postbox.

Afterwards, he drove towards home and stopped off at the Brookland Pub for a drink. He remembered Paul the barman telling jokes in the lounge and motorcycle racing being on the TV.

After two pints, Gordon drove home, arriving at about 10.00 p.m.

'As I shut the front door I got a whiff of cigarette smoke. This was strange as my wife and I don't smoke. I saw the lounge door was partially open. I could see a light from the kitchen. The lounge was in darkness. I pushed the door open and took one step in at which point I was grabbed by the arms from both sides. I could see there were two hands holding my arms on each side and then a cloth was put over my mouth and nose.

'I remember saying, "What the bloody hell."

'I could smell something on the cloth that smelled acrid and dried my throat. My arms were pushed up behind me and then the wall light directly behind me switched on. The dimmer light had been turned down.

'As the light came on I saw a man wearing a clown's mask and dark blue boilersuit holding Carol by the chin with his right hand. Her head was held under his right arm in a sort of headlock. In his left hand was a knife with the blade held to her throat. I saw that she was gagged with something and looked petrified . . .'

'This man said, "Keep quiet, do as you are told, get down on your knees." He had a soft Irish accent but it was a bit muffled because of the mask. I was struggling, trying to free myself . . . I was pushed down onto my knees. As this happened, I felt a blow in my stomach. I don't know who did it. I was starting to go woozy. They forced my head forward, I felt something being put on the back of my legs hard. The last thing I remember was looking down at the person's shoes to my right who was holding me. These shoes were black in colour, the lace-up-type with thick black rubber soles. They were highly polished. I remember he was wearing black trousers . . .'

Gordon estimated that from the moment he stepped into the lounge, to the point he lost consciousness, three or four minutes had elapsed. He woke the next morning tied to the refuse sack holder. He heard the answering machine pick up several calls and the postman arrive at about 8.00 a.m. Distraught and in great pain, he struggled to free himself until the police found him at 2.00 p.m.

Mr Wardell's long and complex statement recounted a dreadful story yet aspects of it perplexed me. People generally imagine that at times of great stress we have the most astonishing extended recall for detail but the reality is very different. It's actually very difficult to help people remember, yet Gordon recalled small details about shoes and light switches.

Similarly, he said that three or four minutes had elapsed from the moment the attack started until he lost consciousness. This is really quite a long time, yet the sequence of events he related probably took no more than thirty seconds. What happened to the missing minutes?

Maybe I expected too much. After all, Mr Wardell had lost a wife and had been deeply traumatized by a brutal attack; wasn't it reasonable for there to be anomalies in his statement?

The SIO had his own questions. The letter posted on Sunday night had informed 'Mr Taylor of Exhall' that his cash-point card was ready for collection. 'Surely it could have waited until the next day,' said Bayliss. 'So why go out on a Sunday night and drive all the way to Coventry?' Even more intriguing was the strange coincidence that the only envelope that had obviously been opened at the building society had also been addressed to Mr Taylor of Exhall.

We mulled it over in silence, looking for explanations. Something had happened which was far more complex than originally described, although I couldn't yet give it a shape or colour.

'I need to know more about the state of their marriage,' I said, making notes. 'And also more about his work. Find out what he's been doing for the last twenty years. How long had they been married?'

Bayliss said, 'Twelve years.'

'With no children?'

'Apparently they tried but when Carol couldn't fall pregnant she began concentrating on her career.'

'That sort of issue doesn't go away very easily,' I pondered.

It had grown quite late and would soon be dark. Checking my diary, I arranged to come back in daylight to visit the crime scenes. Then I collected copies of statements and photographs.

'Sky News are waiting downstairs,' Bayliss said.

'Well, I can't tell them anything. I don't know enough, myself, yet.'

'No, they'll want to talk to you about the Nickell case.'

I sighed.

'I'll send someone down with you,' offered the SIO.

'That's all right.'

'No, someone can help carry your bags.'

As I pushed through the swing doors, a camera appeared in front of me.

A voice said, 'Mr Britton, what are you able to bring to this case?'

'You will have to ask Mr Bayliss,' I said.

'How do you feel about the verdict in the Rachel Nickell trial?'

'I'm awfully sorry, but you'll have to direct that question to the Metropolitan Police Commissioner.'

'Oh, come on, Mr Britton, you can speak for yourself, you must have some feelings on it.'

I kept walking and the cameraman continued filming as I got in the car and drove away.

There was no escaping the fallout. The weekend newspapers carried long wrap-ups of the Nickell case, stirring the controversy even further. Commentators began asking whether offender profiling had been dealt a crippling blow. My sense of disbelief and outrage hadn't diminished but for Marilyn I think it was worse. She couldn't believe how wrong the stories could be and how isolated I had become. Why hadn't the police set the record straight?

'How can they do it?' she asked, almost in tears. 'And after all you've done. When I think of all the hours you've spent helping the police – all the weekends you've had to work and the holidays we've never had. You've never asked for a penny and this is what happens. Those, those, those . . .' she couldn't think of what to call them and finally said, 'It's just not fair.'

I tried to help her understand. 'Has there ever been a case in which I have been involved that has been reported accurately?'

'No,' she said.

'Then why should we expect it to be any different now?'

She shrugged. 'There's no reason.'

Ironically, when my closely guarded anonymity had first been blown during the Stephanie Slater kidnapping, the stories about me were quite positive. However, I knew then that eventually someone would bite me. Australians call it the 'Tall Poppy Syndrome' where anyone who is perceived as having grown too tall is hacked down.

Marilyn would have been quite happy if I walked away and never again looked at another crime scene or drew up another psychological profile. For quite a while we'd been making plans for the future that didn't involve giving my spare time to the police. I'd actually decided that the trial was going to be the last time I offered advice to the police in murder cases.

This had all been turned on its head. If I stopped now, people would draw the wrong conclusions and think that I'd gone away with my tail between my legs. If the Nickell verdict was going be seen as a setback for offender profiling then I would carry on to help people understand that this shouldn't be so. There were too many positives to allow the outcome of a single case to damage an important investigatory tool.

I explained this to Marilyn and said that our 'normal' life would have to wait. Although disappointed, she understood. I think she suspected as much when I agreed to help on the Wardell case.

I'd already spent several days immersed in the statements and pictures of the abduction, the robbery and the murder scene. The overall impression these created was of a crime that was hopelessly inept when viewed as the work of a professional team. At the same time, it was so complex and so demanding as a solo undertaking. I told myself that I'd know a lot more after visiting the scenes.

Bayliss and I left through the back entrance of the police station, avoiding any journalists. We first looked quickly at the Woolwich branch less than 100 yards from the station. A pyramid of flowers rested against the front window and occasionally pedestrians would pause and glance down, paying their respects. Carol Wardell had been a popular figure.

Afterwards, we took picturesque B-roads through Warwickshire, past pick-your-own farms and orchards before reaching Meriden, a small village twelve miles from Nuneaton. Early autumn is my favourite time of year but there was nothing enjoyable about the drive.

Bonneville Close is part of a relatively new estate with rows of similar looking houses lining quiet streets. The Wardells lived in a two-storey red-brick cottage with pretty leaded-pane windows and a neat garden. A ceramic butterfly perched on a wooden beam near the front door.

Stepping out of the car, I noticed how fully we were on display; not much was going to escape the attention of neighbours. A burglar alarm box on the front wall and security lights indicated that the occupants had been extremely security conscious. Friends had told police how Carol feared that someone might follow her home and snatch the building society keys. She had even mentioned the possibility of not being a key-holder.

This added to the mystery of how the gang got into the house. Carol wouldn't have opened the door to a stranger, yet there were no signs of forced entry or evidence of glass being taken out of the windows.

Police duck boards formed stepping stones across the floor of the garage as we entered through a rear door. It looked very orderly and tidy. Everything had its place – the tools, glues, sealants, string, sandpaper, flex and pieces of rope – with no obvious evidence of rummaging or disturbance.

It was the same through the rest of the house. The kitchen benches were spotless, with no sign of someone even pouring themselves a glass of water. On the dining room table a fruit bowl sat undisturbed. Every cupboard door was closed and all utensils neatly stored.

Entering the lounge, I saw where the settee had been pushed against a far wall and faced the wrong direction. One armchair had been picked up and put upside down on top of the other.

Certain things didn't make sense. Wardell described being jumped by two men – one on each side of him – as he entered the lounge, yet there was no room for someone to stand behind the door. And why had the furniture been rearranged in such a way?

The metal-framed refuse sack holder still lay in the centre of the floor and nearby a yellow plastic ratchet-type tie. It was an unusual way to bind someone, I thought. Elsewhere in the room, a hearth rug had been tossed aside and the contents of Carol's handbag spilled out on the carpet. Gordon's clothes and shoes lay on the floor nearby. Yet the scene looked ever-so-slightly wrong. The handbag hadn't been rifled vigorously, instead the contents seem to have been almost spread out. Similarly, Gordon's clothes looked as if someone had carefully placed them before getting into the shower rather than flung them aside as they bound an unconscious man. His shoes and Carol's slippers lay in pairs.

The small knick-knacks and bric-a-brac of their lives still sat neatly on the mantelpiece and window-sill. Flowers stood in vases and a jardinière with a delicate stand had been moved four feet into a congested part of the room, but had not been smashed or even chipped. Absolutely nothing had been shattered, soiled or stained in the violence.

My task was to look at the house in terms of the account given. A violent, brutal gang of four men had overwhelmed a woman; beaten, drugged and stripped her husband before tying him to a metal frame they found in his garage. This gang had been in the house all night but hadn't been tempted to have a glass of water, piece of fruit or to open the drinks cabinet.

Where was the evidence of violence and struggle? I asked myself. The hallway bore no signs of someone overpowering a woman and the lounge looked rearranged rather than rifled – as though someone had been cautious about not making a mess. Meanwhile, Gordon Wardell had spent nearly sixteen hours lying on the floor yet there was no evidence of him having lost bladder control.

At the top of the stairs, on the landing, was a sanitary towel box. It jarred because Carol Wardell had obviously been so tidy. Where did it come from? Who put it there? Perhaps it meant nothing but in trying to make sense of what happened, every detail counts.

The questions began coming quickly. Why would robbers take nothing from the house? They didn't even bother to search it. Why use a bin frame dragged from the garage? And why strip Mr Wardell?

Upstairs in the second bedroom, I saw a computer and small printer. A job application lay beside it, with a curriculum vitae. The police had no reason to be particularly interested in these items but a 'cv' could tell me a great deal more about a person than simply their work experience. It made it possible to match what people say about themselves against what is actually known about them. You then begin to get some idea of how much deception they use and perhaps how grandiosely they view themselves.

Glancing at the first page, under the sub-heading 'Personal Profile', Wardell had described himself as a 'first class leader with excellent communication skills. Highly motivated energetic character with a hands-on management style, creative and visionary, versatile achiever, disciplined, strategic, analytical approach with a proven track record in warehousing and distribution.'

After listing his previous employers, he had written the sub-heading 'Professional Qualifications' and underneath – *'Member of Institute of Logistics'*. When Bayliss saw my reaction he immediately asked me what I'd found.

'This is the key,' I said, showing him the words. 'If Mr Wardell did kill his wife then this is how he made it work. It's in his background.'

'What do you mean?'

'We've looked at what's happened and at Mr Wardell's story and we agree that it doesn't square up,' I said.

Bayliss nodded and I continued, 'At the same time, it looks too big for one person – too many miles have to be covered and obstacles overcome. But really it's been a logistics problem – getting from point A to point B to point C and back again in a particular time frame and solving certain physical and technical problems along the way. It's like a project management exercise, being able to conceptualize and plan a series of simple actions that will achieve a complex goal when they're linked up.'

Bayliss soaked up the information, trying to relate what I was saying to the forward progress of the investigation.

On the drive back to Nuneaton, I began reflecting upon the vast array of facts, reports and observations from neighbours, friends and workmates of Carol and Gordon. Having sifted through all of these, I knew that a lot of them made little sense in the context of Carol's death but every piece had deserved equal weight at the beginning. Now I had to allocate each piece into categories, deciding which bits were reliable and could be corroborated; and how they related to the various accounts.

Bayliss had invited me to join the crime advisory team which meant having an on-going involvement and formal responsibility in the shaping of the inquiry. Outsiders rarely get this close to the beating heart of an investigation and I regarded it as a significant compliment. In many ways I had an advantage. Unlike officers who may already have invested hundreds of hours in an inquiry and were faced with pressures of time, money and media scrutiny, I could step back and look at the big picture.

One of the easiest traps that detectives can sometimes fall into is developing a notion or hypothesis about what happened and then trying to find facts that fit it. Incoming information is treated differently in their minds, depending on whether it fits or not, and the problem is magnified when you have dozens and dozens of officers all working with a common purpose and all with a high investment in time and effort. If a piece of information suddenly emerges that doesn't fit, there is a tendency to devalue it. They find reasons to discount the source or convince themselves the lead isn't trustworthy.

Another difficulty that can affect a large investigation occurs when individual detectives feel that their own inquiries are of greatest importance because this is where their own investment lies. I remember during the Stephanie Slater abduction, I was at the incident room in Nechells Green where various detectives had been tasked to follow up different possibilities, such as checking prison release files, local intelligence and other estate agents. At least three of them came to me separately, convinced that the answer to the abduction lay in the work that they were doing.

Tony Bayliss knew how easy it would be to focus exclusively on

Gordon Wardell because of his previous conviction and the anomalies in his statement. Yet I agreed that there should be a deliberate policy of not focussing just on him. Every line of enquiry had to be kept alive, otherwise potentially vital information might be missed. Just because Mr Wardell had a violent offence in his history, it didn't make him a killer and nor did it protect him against bad luck. Offenders get robbed, mugged and run over by buses just like the rest of us.

Carol Wardell had been born and bred in Coventry and worked her way through the ranks of the Woolwich Building Society from cashier to assistant manageress of the Nuneaton branch. An ex-Sunday school teacher, she was considered quite timid and nervous, not assertive in physical situations and very security conscious, especially at home.

She had met Gordon at a local ten pin bowling league when he was twenty-five and she was twenty-three and they married four years later at the Holy Trinity church in the heart of Coventry on 17 April, 1982. They were regarded as a quiet, loving couple who entertained regularly at home.

According to Gordon, Carol was his only intimate girlfriend and there had never been any infidelity or physical violence in the marriage. He said that Carol knew about his previous conviction and that he still used his prison number (522537) as a combination on his briefcase so he wouldn't forget what he'd done.

On the Monday before Carol's death, he had gone to work and complained of feeling sick and having diarrhoea before going home to bed. The following day he was still unwell and spent the day wrapped up at home while Carol went to work in her grey Peugeot 106. On Wednesday he got up at about midday and went for a job interview on an industrial estate in Coventry. He said he was unhappy at Veng UK because of the company's attitude 'to their legal responsibility and safety of workers'.

He had another job interview on Thursday, leaving home at 10.00 a.m. and driving to Keighley in Yorkshire, a distance of 140 miles. He left a note which read: 'To Carol, popping out, back at 6 o'clock.' This was odd. Why would a man seek a new job in a different part of the country and not tell his wife about it?

Carol had last been seen alive by a work colleague June O'Connell and her husband who dined with the Wardells on Saturday night. There were no obvious signs of friction between Carol and Gordon and as the O'Connells left, they saw their hosts arm in arm at the front door waving them goodbye.

Studying the crime-scene photographs, I kept tripping over more inconsistencies in Mr Wardell's account. On the one hand he described elements of a carefully prepared crime, the masks, gloves, boilersuits and staccato commands, yet despite all this planning, police were asked to believe that the gang didn't bring their own equipment to tie him up. Instead they had to find something and chose to look in the garage. They came across the yellow plastic ties that Gordon used in the garden. It was an unusual way to bind someone, I thought.

A photograph of the garage showed one or two of the ties just visible in one of the plastic shelving bins attached to the wall. Yet there were so many other more obvious things in the garage to bind someone with – material that was closer at hand and more effective. Not only had the gang ignored these things, they found the ties without causing any disturbance or signs of searching.

Similarly, I would have expected a semi-professional gang to tie someone up more effectively, with his hands behind his back, not in front, and a gag that wouldn't allow him to utter a sound. Instead they wrapped a simple cloth around his head and brought the refuse sack holder from the garage. It was a nonsense. He could have been tied up to the table or the chairs; or his wrists and feet could have been bound together.

All of which begged the question – could Mr Wardell have staged the attack and used the ratchet-ties as DIY fasteners?

I came to the crime-scene photographs of Carol's body. She'd been found lying face-up on the grass, wearing casual weekend clothes, with a sling-back blue sandal near her left foot. The strap was done up, just as it had been on the sandal found at the Woolwich. To lose one sandal in a struggle seemed possible, but to lose both in different locations began to stretch the imagination. There were no scuff marks or drag marks on the road or grass verge near Carol's body. Equally, the sandal had no marks to indicate it had been dragged off her foot or along the ground. Post-mortem lividity suggested that Carol hadn't been wearing the sandal for any length of time after death.

I noted a question for the pathologist, 'Can you put the sandals back on her feet at the same buckle setting as when they were found? Are they a good fit? Do they come off easily?'

I remembered something Wardell had said in his statement. He described how Carol normally wore her slippers around the house and kept a pair upstairs in the bedroom and downstairs beside her chair in the lounge. Surely on a Sunday evening, at home in front of the TV, she'd be wearing them? Why would a gang of brutal robbers have let her change into her sandals before taking her out to rob her own building society?

Finally, I studied the third 'scene of crime' – the Woolwich branch – and quickly realized that the raiders must have had a good knowledge of the security system. They had to get inside, blackout a security camera, move a desk to reach the video recorder that held the tape and then open the office safe – all probably done in darkness. Such knowledge was far too complex to have been interrogated from Carol. Either she had to be there or the gang already had an intimate knowledge.

On Monday 19 September, a week after the murder, police stopped cars and passers-by at three locations, trying to piece together Carol Wardell's final hours. From 4.30 a.m. road blocks were set up at the lay-by, in Nuneaton town centre and also near her home. Later that morning, I was back at the incident room. Some joker had cut a large photograph of me from the Sunday papers and pinned it to the wall. The colours had been two-toned to make me look more Machiavellian.

The crime advisory team consisted of Bayliss, Gino Varriale, myself and the manager of the Intelligence cell. Occasionally, we were joined by the assistant chief constable (Crime).

Gino, I soon realized, was the sort of officer central to the inquiry because he made sure things happened. As the SIO, Bayliss was responsible for the strategy and gave the orders but it was Gino who ensured that they were carried out.

As we began to review the case, every possible interpretation was examined. Little had been found to support Mr Wardell's account apart from two pieces of information that hadn't been corroborated. A neighbour, Sarah Harper, had reported that in the fortnight before Carol's death, she'd seen a white transit-type van being driven along the road leading to Bonneville Close. Twice she saw it parked in the road and thought there were possibly two men inside. Another witness told of seeing a metallic silver or misty-green Austin Montego near the Woolwich early on Monday morning with several men inside.

These pieces of information could be vital or mean nothing at all. I had to ask myself, How far does it lead before the information falls down?

'Gordon hasn't been entirely honest about his perfect marriage,' said Bayliss.

He had my full attention.

'He's been getting some on the side.'

'An affair?'

'Seeing prostitutes. We've got statements from two of them and the names of two more.'

Christine, a mother of three, had been seeing Wardell regularly for six or seven years after they met in the Hillfields red light area of Coventry. Paying up to £50 a time, Wardell liked to be driven to the open countryside, tied up with rope from the boot of his car and then to have his penis handled extremely roughly.

She'd last seen him three months earlier when Wardell had been driving a small Peugeot with soft toys in the back (possibly Carol's car). He only had £15 on him which she accepted 'out of kindness' and then masturbated him and talked dirty for about five minutes.

Another prostitute, Jenny, had described being taken to Wardell's house 'somewhere towards Nuneaton' during the day. Gordon had referred to his wife as 'Her' and said she was at work.

As police continued to delve into Wardell's past, it emerged that seven years earlier a friend of Carol's had told her that she had seen Gordon going into a pub of low repute in Coventry. Carol wouldn't believe her and later challenged Gordon who denied it. The issue appeared to be forgotten.

Bayliss had managed to get the details of the teenage attack that had led to Wardell's imprisonment. 'Her name was Brenda Jane Hayes – the wife of Wardell's geology teacher at Woodlands School in Coventry,' he said.

'When was it?'

'June 1970. He was seventeen.'

I began reading. Wardell had telephoned Mrs Hayes at home during a weekend and introduced himself as one of her husband's pupils. Brenda was surprised that a schoolboy had their home phone number which had only been connected the week before. Her husband Peter was away on a school field trip to Derbyshire and she was looking after their two young sons.

Wardell told her that he'd found a plant that Mr Hayes wanted and asked Brenda to collect it because he was on his bike and couldn't manage it without help. She agreed and met the teenager on a country lane not far from where the family lived. Leaving her sons, aged five and four, in the back seat of the car she took a trowel and seed tray from the boot and followed Wardell a little way off the road, through into a small wooded area. Motioning her ahead of him, he then grabbed her from behind and put a sheath knife to her throat.

'What do you want?' she pleaded.

He said he was Paul Newman and wanted her money. Then he asked her to lie down on the ground so he could tie her hands. She refused so he tied them while she was standing. Brenda said that she had money at home, hoping Wardell would take her there. He led her to the car, stopping once and trying to force her to her knees. When she refused he yanked her arms up and kneed her in the back.

He forced Brenda into the passenger seat and drove off, ignoring the boys on the back seat. She pleaded with Wardell to let them go, promising to tell no-one, but he pulled into a gateway further along the road and hit her in the face. Then he sprayed de-icer in her eyes and put his hands up her skirt, tearing her panties. The eldest boy tried to protect his mother but Wardell swung a blow at him.

They set off again in the car and stopped in another gateway. This time Wardell got out of the driver's seat and took up a position at the passenger doorway. He punctured the back tyre with his knife and then forced Brenda to move into the driver's seat before stabbing her once in the throat and twice in the back of the neck.

As he stood back from the blood, she slammed the passenger door. He attacked it but Brenda managed to drive off and find a passing motorist. An ambulance was on the scene within six minutes but Brenda needed nine pints of blood in a transfusion and was extremely lucky to survive.

The entire incident had lasted forty-five minutes. Afterwards, Wardell fled on his bicycle and was arrested when the eldest son gave a detailed description. He was initially charged with attempted murder but this was eventually changed to grievous bodily harm. A Warwick court heard that the attack was wholly motivated by sex with a strong degree of fantasy. Wardell was said to have been gripped by a 'Paul Newman infatuation'.

The alarm bells were ringing. Clearly, Gordon Wardell had once had a very serious problem and if it hadn't been treated there was no reason to expect it had gone away. Although the precise nature of the sexual fantasy that underpinned the attack on Brenda Hayes wasn't clear to me (I didn't know what he wanted from her or if he brought the knife to control rather than stab), but it clearly showed a willingness to use potentially lethal physical violence and a fair degree of planning. He had to get Mrs Hayes' phone number, make the call, entice her into the woods and bring a knife and rope with him.

That was twenty-four years ago, yet Wardell's predilection for prostitutes and his uncommon sexual preferences showed that his sexually deviant interests were still in place and being covertly maintained. However, Wardell had put his marriage forward as being almost sacred and had talked of his profound distress at not having children. In similar vein, he portrayed himself as a successful business manager yet his career consisted primarily of temporary contracts and redundancies. For all his apparent promise, things never quite came to fruition for him. He blamed poor economic conditions for this, but I saw a man who exaggerated his own worth and abilities.

Certainly, his bosses at Veng UK were beginning to recognize this and described him as incompetent and disengaged from the actual work task. They were due to have a meeting to discuss his lack of progress in specific projects but Wardell chose that day to be sick. Quite clearly he ducked it and chose instead to spend the rest of the week at home and going to job interviews.

This use of deception had also emerged during discreet interviews with medical staff and others who had seen Mr Wardell after the murder. Paramedics who treated him at the house told detectives that he displayed none of the symptoms of trauma which would normally have been associated with such an ordeal such as increased blood pressure and pulse rate. At the hospital he had a normal appetite and was quiet and unemotional.

Others spoke of him being cold and unresponsive unless discussing his own injuries. At the same time, the physical pain he expressed seemed to be greater than his actual injuries and he continued to need sticks to walk although doctors could find no reason why he should.

When told of Carol's murder, Wardell had asked whether she'd been badly hurt or interfered with sexually but hadn't asked any questions since then about the progress of the inquiry.

There were various ways of understanding this behaviour. Under stress some people disassociate and become self-absorbed, but it doesn't mean they're killers.

'What else can you tell me about his demeanour?' I asked.

'He's very careful,' said Gino. 'In safe areas of conversation he talks quickly and confidently but when he's answering other questions he pauses and takes his time. When he was having his injuries photographed, one of the sergeants casually asked him, "Where were her sandals?"

'Wardell says, "They were in the back bedroom," then pauses and says quickly, "What sandals do you mean?"' Gino raised his eyebrows. 'Makes you wonder, doesn't it? How could he have known about the sandals – he was unconscious all night.'

'What does he say about the previous attack?' I asked.

'He blames exam stress and a domineering mother,' said Bayliss, unable to hide his disbelief.

'Is he talking to anyone in particular?'

'His mother and father were at the hospital every day,' said Gino. 'She got a bit hostile about him being questioned, said he was too frail. His dad seems more laid-back.'

As they talked, the picture that emerged of Gordon was of an egocentric and narcissistic man who expressed no anger at what had happened to himself or his wife. He gave details of his injuries to anyone around but made no reference to his marriage or to Carol. He wondered if he still had a job and was uncertain of how his colleagues would regard him now that his past had become known.

As if acknowledging that his behaviour might be considered strange, Wardell referred to 'blocking things out', using concepts and terms that he would have heard decades earlier when he was treated at Grendon Underwood during his prison sentence.

I told Bayliss that I expected Gordon to have good face-to-face skills and to be able to withstand some interpersonal pressure. He was obviously accustomed to managing his image and would be reluctant to admit any negative personal characteristics. He was proud of his logistical training and also claimed to have communication and audio-visual experience, which indicated practice in visually rehearsing desired scenes and story lines. At the same time, he was confident, intelligent, good at DIY and someone who claimed to channel his stress by training and jogging.

No-one was surprised when I produced another list of questions that needed considering.

Did Mr Wardell have his own blue boilersuit for DIY work?

Were the clothes on the floor of the lounge the ones he actually wore or were these a feint to deflect forensic examination from the actual clothes?

Why are his glasses so comprehensively broken, yet he has no facial bruises or injuries at all?

If a gang had abducted Carol, why had no-one been left to guard Mr Wardell in case he escaped and raised the alarm? If no-one stayed behind, how did they convince Carol that Gordon's life was in danger unless she co-operated?

Where does the anaesthesia enter into it? How long would it render someone unconscious?

Having reviewed all the new information, we looked at the direction of the inquiry. Local intelligence officers were shaking the trees, trying to find any underworld link to the robbery. We all agreed that the £50,000 reward was likely to flush out details if they existed. At the same time, neighbours were being re-interviewed, along with friends and workmates.

'I think it's time to put Wardell under surveillance,' said Bayliss. 'What do you think?'

'I think it merits it. You should also ask him a little more about his marriage.'

'No, from now on we are regarding him as a suspect,' said Bayliss. 'We can't ask those sorts of questions without cautioning him. We'll see if the observation brings anything up.'

The next morning, eight days after the murder, Gordon Wardell was followed as he drove to Birmingham for an appointment with his wife's bosses. He was due to discuss Carol's pension and insurance entitlements at the regional office of the Woolwich.

Arriving early, he went for a walk through the Pallisades shopping centre, moving freely and looking at various window displays. Then he returned to his car, collected a walking-stick and transformed into a hobbling downcast figure as he approached the Woolwich office. All of this was captured in an eight-minute video, some of it recorded by the city's closed circuit TV system.

At the meeting with a regional manager, Wardell was told that his mortgage would be paid along with any other debts. He also stood to gain an annual pension and a lump sum of more than £56,000. Looking surprised, he denied any knowledge of his wife having a 'death in service' pension, although police later found that he had signed some of the documents setting it up.

Meanwhile, anaesthetists were casting serious doubts over his story of having been knocked unconscious for more than eight hours by some sort of chemical soaked into a cloth and held over his mouth and nose. Experts had been consulted and none of them knew of any chemical or drug administered in such a way which would render someone unconscious for more than a few minutes. It simply wasn't possible.

Even if the drug had been injected, the amounts needed would have been substantial and been likely to cause side effects such as memory loss. Wardell had no injection marks and could remember precise details about what happened.

I was back in Nuneaton on Thursday by which time detectives had followed up 340 lines of inquiry and taken over 1,000 calls from the public. Several new strands had emerged including the sighting of a man by the Woolwich cash machine at about 5.20 a.m. on the morning of the murder and a car parked nearby with a light on and radio playing. These were being followed up.

Yet by far the most interesting development was the discovery that four days before the murder a woman claiming to be 'Carol at Nuneaton' had called the customer service department of the Woolwich head office in London. David Smith, who normally dealt with customer complaints, answered the call between 1.00 and 3.00 p.m. It came through the internal branch telephone system and the woman initially asked for Charles Crouch who had been Smith's predecessor. The company's internal phone directory still listed Crouch on that number.

The woman said, 'It's Carol at Nuneaton. I want some advice about a man standing outside the branch.' She said he was acting suspiciously and was concerned about the public relations aspects of calling the police and creating a scene.

Where did this piece of information fit into the puzzle?

David Smith had advised 'Carol' to contact the police but no record could be found of her making this call. Peculiarly, it was also the wrong procedure for this sort of inquiry and Carol Wardell was known to be a stickler for procedure. More importantly, her office didn't face the street so she couldn't have seen a man outside and no member of staff reported anyone acting suspiciously. Yet whoever made the call showed extremely good local knowledge because they said they knew the name of the previous office on the site three years earlier.

After locating a recording of Carol Wardell's voice from a training video, the police played it to David Smith who said that the caller was definitely not her. But why would somebody pretend otherwise? Whoever made the call had a good local knowledge and access to an internal Woolwich phone directory. Gordon Wardell had both of these and if he *was* planning a murder, such a call to head office might muddy the waters.

But who was the woman? The possibility that Wardell might have an accomplice had already occurred to Bayliss, who had yet to find anyone who could remember seeing him at the Brookland Pub on that Sunday night. It would explain how Gordon could recall exactly what he'd seen on the satellite TV in the bar.

Interviews with staff at Veng UK had also thrown up new information with various possible interpretations. Colleagues recounted conversations where Gordon had spoken of Carol's fear about being robbed because she took the building society keys home. Michael Russell, the transport distribution manager, said that two or three weeks before the murder, Gordon had told him how the spare wheel of Carol's Peugeot 106 had been stolen. Gordon said he reported the theft and then had to verify the police telephone call because he was afraid it might be someone trying to discover his address.

Was this evidence of a professional gang tracing Carol's movements or another example of her husband muddying the waters to conceal what was to come? Someone had pinned a sign on the wall of the incident room which put all of these unanswered questions into context. It read, 'It is one thing to have an opinion, it's another thing to have the facts which support it.'

A fortnight after the murder, a major step was taken towards establishing this. In an unusual reconstruction an officer of the same height and build as Mr Wardell was asked to strip and try to replicate exactly how he had been found bound and gagged. The result was remarkable. In less than a minute the officer had tied himself to the rubbish sack holder. He then managed to move throughout the entire ground floor of the Wardell house and to shout loud enough through the gag to be heard on the far side of the street. In addition, he released himself unaided within a matter of minutes.

Other pieces rapidly fell into place. Forensic officer, Graham Smith, described 18 Bonneville Close as 'the cleanest house he'd examined in twenty years'. He reported absolutely no trace that a gang had been there, not even a glove mark or a vestige of cigarette ash, yet according to Wardell his attackers wore gloves and he could smell cigarette smoke.

Police surgeons now confirmed that the bruising to Wardell's upper arms was inconsistent with being grabbed from behind and that the bruising to his chest could have been self-inflicted by a hard punch. Medical experts also raised doubts about whether it was physically possible to be tied up for sixteen hours and not urinate.

By the beginning of October, Bayliss and his team were waiting for two last vital pieces of evidence before they decided whether to pull Wardell in for questioning. Home Office pathologists had re-examined Carol's body, trying to establish a more precise time of death.

When the findings arrived, it became clear that here was the glue that could hold together so much of the circumstantial evidence gathered against Gordon Wardell. The post-mortem examination had found a moderately large meal in Carol's stomach, consistent with what she was said to have eaten for Sunday lunch. Looking at the degree of digestion, it was determined that she had died within three hours of the meal, which would have meant she was dead on Sunday afternoon and not early on Monday morning.

'We got the bastard,' said Bayliss, looking jubilant. 'Let's see him try to explain this one.'

'You have to be careful,' I warned.

'What do you mean?'

'Put the question to me. Pretend I'm Wardell.'

He paused. 'Ah, well, Mr Wardell, the pathology report shows that your wife's lunch was still in her stomach on Monday morning which tells me that you're lying. She died on Sunday afternoon.'

'Oh, that's perfectly understandable. We had leftovers for supper,' I replied.

'But in your statement you say you had ham and salad for supper.'

'Yes, I did, but Carol had leftovers.'

'Why didn't you mention it before?'

'Well, it didn't seem important.'

The enthusiasm drained from the SIO's face. I could give him two or three entirely different but plausible answers to account for the post-mortem finding. The new information was crucial but if they asked Wardell directly about the stomach contents he would realize what lay behind the question and cover himself.

* * *

There are many motives for murder in marriage and it wasn't clear what underpinned this crime although I didn't put greed high among the likely grounds – Carol's pension and the £14,000 from the robbery didn't warrant such planning and risk-taking.

Gordon Wardell had created an illusion about his success and abilities. He portrayed himself as a creative and visionary manager destined for great things. The reality, however, was a man unable to cope occupationally, who feigned illness, invented schemes and changed jobs to avoid discovery and to bolster his own self-image.

Carol had been excited when he joined Veng UK. A directorship was on offer if he proved himself, but how long could he maintain the facade? How did he acknowledge it himself, let alone tell his wife?

At home Gordon had presented himself as the witty achiever but he knew that he couldn't sustain this indefinitely. For years Carol had been willing to see him through rose-coloured glasses, but now she heard whispers of him seeing prostitutes. Coupled with this, he wasn't sleeping with her, didn't want children and refused to take fertility tests, despite her misery at being childless. I suspect there were also money difficulties.

When you have a person who creates illusions to protect their public image and constantly fears discovery, they can become so absorbed in their own plight that they will happily sacrifice someone else in order to relieve the pressure and to have the problem taken away forever.

As a bereaved husband, Mr Wardell knew that the world would sympathize with him; his problems at work would disappear and his secret life with prostitutes would be safe. Murdering Carol wasn't a huge leap – he'd already shown a willingness to use extreme physical violence.

What triggered it on that Sunday? Perhaps Carol confronted him about the prostitutes, or accused him of being a sham and failing at his job? Possibly, the day had been selected sometime earlier as the episode with the 'stolen' wheel suggests. Whatever the catalyst, he decided that 'today is the day'. He sat opposite her all morning, telling himself that provided he didn't lose his bottle she'd be dead by that afternoon. From what I knew of the man, he was probably very sweet and pleasant to Carol, rather than unloading the last of his venom.

I didn't know where she was killed or how messy it had been, although with chloroform I assumed there was minimal disruption. I still wondered about the sanitary towel box on the landing – it was so out of place and out of character. Could anger over something as simple as running out of towels have led to bitter words about sex or pregnancy? I doubted if this detail would ever be accounted for.

Wardell would have tidied up afterwards and have felt quite exposed while Carol's body was in the house – what if someone knocked on the door asking for his wife, or telephoned?

She had probably been wrapped in something and kept in the garage during the evening because there was no evidence of loss of bladder or bowel control in the house. Finding a letter among her possessions, Gordon then set out to establish his alibi by going to the postbox in Coventry. He knew this particular box had a video camera but couldn't have known that it wasn't working that night.

Ultimately, we don't know whether he visited the pub on his way home. No other customers recalled seeing him and there was no record of him buying his favoured beer on the till roll. Yet he remembered what jokes the barman told and what was on the TV. Also unconfirmed are the claims of a strawberry-blonde prostitute called Tina who said that she was entertaining Mr Wardell at her fifteenth-floor tower block apartment that night. She remembered showing him her child's model collection.

When he returned to the house, Gordon had to get his wife outside and put her into his car. Carol was quite a large woman and lifting and moving a dead body is extremely difficult. I know this because I once had the misfortune of colliding with a full-grown red deer which I then had to move off the road. It was like lifting a huge bag of heavy jelly and each time I grabbed one end the other would slide.

Although a strong man, I suspect that Gordon used something as a cradle or sling to make it easier for him to move Carol. Getting her from the house into his car was an enormously risky time and his anxiety would have continued to rise on the twelve mile drive to Nuneaton in the early hours. Feeling exposed, he drove carefully. He knew Carol's security code because he'd accompanied her to the office on occasional Saturday mornings when she needed someone to lift furniture and boxes. He also knew about the security camera and concealed video recorder. Even so, it took time because he probably worked in the dark. He had to open the safe and organize the room as he imagined it would look after a robbery.

Afterwards, Gordon had to rid himself of the cheques, the keys, his gloves and clothing. I think he probably did this before dumping

Carol's body because he knew that once she lay on the grass verge, the stakes would rise dramatically because she could have been discovered at any time. His hiding place had to be somewhere discreet that he could reach easily and wasn't going to make his clothes or his car dirty. It had to be reasonably close to the safest route to the lay-by.

He worked quickly because every moment away from the house increased the risk of being seen by someone and endangered his story of being tied up at home. He also had the added danger of his neighbours waking early and glancing out their windows to see him arrive home. This, again, is where his logistics background came into play and he made probability judgements of what was the greater or lesser risk. He knew what things he could leave to chance and those he dare not.

Back at the house I suspect that the lounge had already been rearranged, awaiting his arrival. Wardell took off his clothes, which may have already been wetted to conceal the presence of a covering garment. Then he faked his injuries using his fists and tools from the garage, before tying himself around the metal sack holder.

The advisory team gathered at Nuneaton Police Station to discuss the timetable for Mr Wardell's arrest and interviews. No-one expected any easy admissions and the interview strategy had to explore his account of events in such fine detail as to pin down any provable lies. If the evidence was woven around him in precisely the right way he might slip up and incriminate himself.

Bayliss said that with no compelling reason to arrest the suspect immediately, the police had a rare opportunity to prepare themselves for the interviews, even to the point of choosing the best people and rehearsing them.

'Will you do it?' he asked.

'Yes, if you want,' I said, although I warned him it could be bloody. The interviewing officers had to be prepared for Wardell to suddenly adopt 'no comment' tactics, if his solicitor advised it. If this happened the team had to be able to carry on asking questions and putting issues to him without getting angry or frustrated.

Six possible interviewers were chosen, one of them a woman, and we gathered on a weekday morning in a room at Nuneaton station that became very hot and uncomfortable as the day wore on. Initially, I asked each of them how they would go about conducting an interview with Gordon Wardell. Their general outlines were quite good but then I stopped them, suddenly. 'Ask me the question.'

There was silence.

'What do you mean?'

'I've heard your outlines, but none of the specific questions. Ask me your precise questions.'

Quickly, it became clear that they didn't have the fine details of their plan – the building blocks of their interviews. I explained to the officers that they needed to have their questions prepared and have others ready for every possible answer that he might give. Equally, they had to be equipped to deal with how Wardell said things.

A week later I returned to the station and was placed under 'arrest' before being escorted to an interview suite – the same room that Gordon Wardell would soon see. For the next few hours I had to step into his shoes and see how the interview teams fared.

Sitting at a table I waited . . . and waited for the first pair to arrive.

Finally Tony Bayliss put his head around the door. 'Paul, I don't know how to say this.'

'What?'

'They won't come.'

'What do you mean?'

'They think it's unfair. They're worried that this is some sort of exam, you know; that they're being assessed and that if they don't cope it's going to hurt their careers.'

'That's ridiculous,' I said quizzically.

'Ah, I'm really quite embarrassed. I don't know what the bloody hell they're playing at. I'll talk to them again.'

It wasn't my place to comment, but I was surprised; these were experienced detectives. Yet I sometimes forget how much pressure interview teams are under. They were preparing to interview a very dangerous and devious man who would only be charged with murder if they could succeed in winning a chess game on an invisible board. The focus of the entire, high-profile and expensive investigation came down to their skill in that small room.

After what I imagined were robust discussions, the first pair arrived and the role play began. Various pairs were tried through the morning and two officers proved to be particularly good. I threw in lots of curve balls in a bid to disrupt them and at one point exploded in anger, almost sending one of them toppling out of his chair.

'What Wardell sees helps him,' I explained. 'If you aren't holding it together he'll know. He can read the way you sit, speak and look at each other. This man is not going to admit anything. He's extremely dangerous and devious. You have to set his story in stone and make a case from the provable lies.'

The most important example of this involved fixing Wardell's account of Carol's last meal. Traces of Sunday lunch had been found in her stomach and the post-mortem concluded that she had probably died within three hours of eating it. No trace had been found of the ham and salad that Wardell claimed his wife had eaten at 7.00 p.m.

The interviewers had to cement his account of the meals and guard against the possibility of him retracting or altering his recollections. They weren't dealing with a stupid man and he was likely to pick up on direct questions about Sunday lunch. So instead they had to embed the questions in a mountain of other inquiries about what happened that day.

'Tell him you want to understand his daily routines because the robbers had to have known his and his wife's movements on the day. Ask him about waking up, who got out of bed first, did he shower, what did they have for breakfast, who cleared the table, who scraped the plates, who washed up? And then go through the entire morning in the same detail so that when you ask about lunch it's entirely consistent with what's gone before. Without realizing its significance, he's going to give you that crucial record of events.'

The second important strand was to allow Wardell a rationale for blaming someone else, for instance to let him say that Carol had died accidentally and afterwards he had covered up for her parents' sake. Or perhaps he'd been a victim of blackmail or coercion by raiders who had promised that his wife would be OK if he co-operated and it devastated him when the truth emerged.

The interviewers had to also emphasize the lack of gross violence – Carol wasn't defiled or degraded – and allow Wardell to be respected for the cleverness of his plan and the calm way he responded. This would appeal to his illusions of grandeur and self-importance.

To my knowledge, training in this depth had never been done before during an operation, but I knew that success could only be measured by what happened when the real suspect heard the questions.

At 7.30 a.m. on Thursday 20 October, Gordon Wardell was arrested at his home. For three days he was interrogated before appearing at Nuneaton Magistrates Court on Monday morning charged with murdering his wife and robbing the Woolwich Building Society.

That afternoon, Tony Bayliss called and invited me for a drink in the police social club. The interviews had gone well, he said. Wardell had given more and more detail that helped prove he was lying. Later, as I shared a beer with the detectives, I could understand their sense of satisfaction. Not only had they discovered the truth beneath layers of falsehood and deceit, they felt they had the evidence to prove it.

But from my point of view, the case couldn't stop there. Wardell was an extremely dangerous man with a history of sexual deviancy and violence in his youth. Similarly, I could see many of the same elements of preparation and planning present in Carol's murder as in the earlier offence. What had happened in the intervening years? Had his dealings with prostitutes given Wardell a vent for his deviant fantasies, or were there other incidents of sexual violence in his past that had gone unreported or undetected?

There was only one way to be sure. The police had to go back and look at Wardell's life, point by point, tracing his movements and whereabouts to see if there were any links to unsolved murders and sex crimes. We still have much more to learn about Gordon Wardell.

23

ON NEW YEAR'S DAY IAN TURNED ON THE TELEVISION AND I immediately recognized the face of Frederick West. The file photograph made him look younger than his fifty-two years. He was smiling, tilting his head slightly and showing off his rock and roll sideburns.

The news reader announced: 'The Gloucester builder Frederick West was found hanged in his maximum security prison cell this afternoon, a month before he was due to be committed for trial accused of murdering twelve young women. 'Staff at Winson Green prison in Birmingham tried to revive him but he was pronounced dead at 1.22 p.m.'

The Control Room at Arnold Lodge phoned me. 'Have you heard the news? A journalist has been calling trying to get hold of you.'

'I'll ring him back, but tell anyone else I'm not available,' I said, unwilling to get involved.

My mind was with the families of the victims and the Wests' own children – the forgotten victims of Cromwell Street. How would they accept the news? I also recalled my conversation with John Bennett months earlier when he'd asked me whether Fred and Rosemary were likely to harm themselves.

Sadly, my fears about Mr West's sense of isolation and abandonment had proved correct. Once the interviews were over and he realized that his beloved wife and soulmate had repudiated him, he opted for suicide. Letters that he wrote in prison to his children revealed his state of mind. He was angry at Rosemary for not standing by him and accused her of turning people against him.

Committing suicide was never going to be a problem. Life was unimportant to him. He'd murdered enough people to know that you die easily or you die hard; and he'd seen how quickly the transition could be made from being in pain and torment to being dead. However, despite his criticisms of Rosemary, nothing could diminish his love for her and I think Frederick recognized his own weaknesses and felt that at some point in the future he might stumble and unwittingly point the finger of blame at his soulmate. Once dead he could never accuse or implicate Rosemary in what had happened.

Rosemary, who was also being held on remand, said very little about the suicide. Her lawyer, however, went onto the offensive claiming that the charges against his client should be dropped because of lack of evidence and the saturation media coverage which, he said, made it impossible for Mrs West to get a fair trial.

'Why have a go at a rather naive and manipulated, short-sighted young woman who happened to be involved with an older man who had a dark side to him which he was able to keep screened from all who met him?' He described the Wests as having had an 'alternative lifestyle' and said that the 'horrendous and exceptional and unbelievable things that he [Frederick] is supposed to have done were a mystery and completely unknown to Mrs West'.

Ten months later on 6 October, 1995, a jury was sworn in at Winchester Crown Court and asked to decide whether this had indeed been the case. Rosemary West stood charged with ten counts of murder including the deaths of her daughter Heather and stepdaughter Charmaine.

Amongst the evidence presented in the eight week trial were several letters written by Rosemary to Frederick while he was in prison in 1971. In the first letter, dated 4 May, she wrote, 'Darling, about Charm. I think she likes to be handled rough. But darling, why do I have to be the one to do it? I would keep her for her sake if it wasn't for the rest of the children. You can see Charm coming out in Anna [another stepdaughter] now.'

Another letter dated 22 May, began with the words, 'from now until forever'.

'To my dearest lover, darling I am sorry I upset you in my previous letters. I didn't mean it, no joking. I know you love me, darling. But it seems queer that anyone should think so much of me . . .

'We have got a lot of things to do in the next couple of years. We will do it just loving each other. Better not write too much in case I put my big foot in it, ha, ha!'

Shirley Ann Giles, a next-door neighbour at the time, gave evidence that her daughter had once come home distressed after having seen Charmaine standing on a chair or a stool with her hands tied behind her back while Rosemary held a wooden spoon as though she was going to hit her. Later evidence from Mrs Giles was used by the prosecution to argue that Charmaine had most likely been killed by Rosemary while Frederick was serving his ten-month prison sentence.

Another neighbour Mrs Elizabeth Agius described how Mr West had boasted about his journeys from Gloucester to London searching for teenage virgins. In the presence of Rosemary he had said they preferred runaways and said it was easier to pick them up when Rosemary was in the car as the young girls thought it was safe.

In some of the most harrowing testimony, Rosemary's stepdaughter Anne Marie Davis described how she had been raped by her father and sexually assaulted by her stepmother from the age of eight. She learned to hide the injuries she received from frequent beatings and was absent from school more than sixty times in her penultimate years. From the age of thirteen she was made to sleep with Rosemary's male clients while her father watched and occasionally rewarded her with a box of chocolates.

When Rosemary West entered the witness box on 31 October, she described her troubled childhood during which she claimed to have been raped twice before she was fifteen, first when she was picked up by a stranger in a car and later when she was dragged from a bus stop. Interestingly, both offences were unreported and mirrored the abductions of several Cromwell Street victims years later. Either these attacks were a dreadful coincidence, or I suspect Rosemary simply used her later activities as a blueprint to help invent rape stories in an attempt to win sympathy from the jury.

Sobbing occasionally, she portrayed herself as the affection-craving victim of her violent and bullying husband and said that they had come to lead separate lives. She denied being Fred's 'willing assistant' and maintained that she knew nothing of the murders.

Under cross-examination from Brian Leveson QC, Rosemary said that she had only a vague recollection of the assault on Caroline Owens in 1972. Finally she admitted, 'Yes, there was an incident . . . it was a mistake in my life and obviously now I tremendously regret it . . . I was charged with indecent assault, not attempted murder. I am on trial here for murder not for abuse.'

Leveson said, 'Let me make it abundantly clear, this was the start of your career of sexually abusing girls, wasn't it?'

West replied, 'No, sir.'

Leveson asked, 'Girls that you picked up in some way or another?'

West replied, 'No, sir, it didn't happen like that.'

In his summing up, defending counsel Richard Ferguson QC laid the blame for the Cromwell Street killings firmly at the feet of Frederick West, insisting that there was no direct evidence to link Rosemary. 'He was a man devoid of compassion, consumed with sexual lust, a sadistic killer and someone who you may think was the very epitome of evil.' He said that Mr West had killed before he met his wife and did not need her 'knowledge, consent or participation to continue killing'. Although Rosemary had been shown to be a 'cruel sexual assailant' and a liar, he said: 'That does not prove she is guilty of any of these murders . . .'

'This is not like the trial of O.J. Simpson. There are no bloody footprints, no gloves, no DNA evidence. You are not being asked by us to acquit in the teeth of evidence – you are being asked by us to acquit because there is no evidence.'

Shortly before 1.00 p.m. on 22 November, the jury ended thirteen hours of deliberations by announcing guilty verdicts on all the charges. Mr Justice Mantell turned to Mrs West and said, 'On each of the ten counts of murder you have been unanimously convicted by the jury. The sentence is one of life imprisonment and if attention is paid to what I think, you will never be released. Take her down.'

Many in the gallery, crammed with relatives of her victims, roared in approval while others gave polite and decorous applause.

In the days that followed a great deal was to be said and written about the possibility of there being more victims and also whether the warning signs should have been recognized sooner. The police and welfare agencies defended decisions taken over the previous thirty years and argued that only with hindsight could they have known that they had serial killers in their midst.

The most common question that I was asked was how could so many people have gone missing over such a long period of time and no-one have discovered a link with the Wests? Although some of the victims were drifters and runaways, most had loving parents and friends, jobs and workmates – surely, someone must have known, or at least suspected.

However, it shouldn't surprise us that the Wests killed for a quarter of a century before being caught. We live in a culture now where people come and go all the time. Wives walk out on husbands, teenagers run away from home, hitchhikers fail to arrive, the list goes on. Their fate is unknown to their friends and families. Often the police are informed, private detectives are hired and publicity campaigns fill newspapers.

Some of these people simply go their separate ways or seek to make a fresh start unfettered by their past, but others are victims of violent crime. Yet without a body, or bloodstains or the proverbial 'smoking gun', the police may have little reason to suspect that someone has actually been murdered. They are simply 'missing'.

Five of Mr and Mrs West's known victims had no publicly known connection with the couple, they were brazenly abducted off the street or picked up while hitchhiking. Three were drifters or runaways who stayed briefly at the house. Even the disappearances of Mr West's own children, Heather and Charmaine, were explained to the satisfaction of those who enquired. One had run away from home and the other had gone off with her natural mother.

With the clarity of hindsight and the carefully structured presentation of the prosecution case, it all seems so obvious. Yes, there were warning signs which might have been heeded, but even today when police are far more sophisticated in dealing with crime, prosecutions still fail or flounder. One reason is that the crime and the criminal are sometimes beyond the comprehension of those investigating.

In the West case, how could it be otherwise? The police's long experience had prepared them for investigating killings spawned by basic lust, or revenge, or angry impulse. Now they were dealing with a man and a woman whose depravity was so shocking it was difficult to grasp the magnitude let alone the implications.

Frederick and Rosemary didn't have 'MONSTER' written across their foreheads; they were a likeable, affable couple who seemed close to their children. It's easy now, knowing their crimes, to look at photographs and immediately 'recognize' them as being evil.

I'm not surprised they killed and got away with it for so long. I say this because I know – not just suspect – that there are a dozen more people just like them still out there; serial killers who may never be discovered and whose secrets will stay buried beneath the garden, or the cellar, or beside some remote forest track.

I also know that the file on Frederick and Rosemary West can never be closed because there are more victims to be found. Of course, it's impossible to say exactly how many, although it could easily be as many more again. After all, this couple are known to have killed for twenty-five years, growing in confidence and refinement as they went along. Between April 1973 to April 1975 six girls were tortured and murdered. Then there was a gap of three years before Shirley Robinson disappeared and another year to Alison Chambers in 1979 and eight years to Heather West in 1987.

Given all that is known about the Wests and people like them there cannot have been a 'silence' during these periods or, indeed, since 1987. Consider, Mr West's first known victim was Anna McFall, the family's nanny, who disappeared in 1967 when he was twenty-six years old. As I've explained, his dangerous psychopathy would have manifested itself when he was young, perhaps in his late teens. There could well have been earlier killings which had as much to do with simple expedience as his desire to dominate women completely.

This realization saddens me because I know that hundreds of families with missing daughters will fear the worst. Others, who live in houses where Frederick West is known to have worked or lived, will suddenly be thinking, 'He built our patio . . . I wonder . . . ?'

So what can or should be done about it? I think a strong case can be made for the search to continue and to some extent it has, although I'm aware of the enormous financial and emotional cost. There were only two people who could have told us where further remains are buried and one, Frederick West, can speak no more. His wife has the knowledge but not the motivation. She will feel pity for herself but absolutely no remorse for the victims or their families – it's not in her nature.

Therefore, the only alternative is to go back to everywhere the couple have ever been – following their histories point by point – and, where necessary, to begin digging again.

As Rosemary West entranced the nation with her witness box performance, fifty miles away in Oxford, the fate of Gordon Wardell was being decided by a jury. He had almost been forgotten in the scramble to publicize the House of Horror.

Charged with murdering his wife as well as trespassing and stealing £14,130.92 from the Woolwich Building Society, Wardell had been in custody since October 1994 and continued to maintain his innocence. Prosecutor Richard Wakerley QC told the jury that he did not have to prove why Wardell killed his wife. 'In the process of marriage there may be many motives. There may have been a heated argument, all sorts of reasons. The prosecution do not, and do not have to, set out to prove a motive. We set out to prove his story is false.'

On 7 December, Wardell entered the witness box and choked back tears as he told of the last time he had seen Carol alive. He maintained his story of being attacked and tied up and said that when he heard of Carol's death, 'I felt as if my whole world had come to an end.'

A string of prosecution witnesses gave evidence to show how Mr Wardell could have faked his injuries but the defence produced its own experts who said the injuries he suffered were entirely consistent with being beaten and bound in the way he described. A consultant anaesthetist said it might also have been possible for him to have been injected with a drug to keep him unconscious for perhaps seven hours although this would have required the attackers to have some medical knowledge. Similarly, the only explanation for Mr Wardell not having urinated for sixteen hours was an extremely rare condition known as myoglobinuria which affects victims of earthquakes and car crashes.

At the end of a six-week trial involving 128 witnesses, the jury deliberated for nine and a half hours before finding Wardell guilty of killing his wife. Mr Justice Cresswell praised detectives for their efforts and told Wardell, 'You are an extremely dangerous, evil and devious man. You killed your wife in a brutal manner then cynically attempted to escape detection, going to elaborate lengths to make it appear that your crime was the work of a gang of raiders. This murder was an outrage to your wife, her family and to everyone who knew her.'

24

AS ONE CASE ENDED ANOTHER TOOK ITS PLACE. THE NEGATIVE publicity surrounding the Rachel Nickell case had died down quickly and the media had moved on to newer pastures. My anger hadn't diminished, however, and I had become more aware of the role I played in police investigations. I could be asked to help and my advice could be accepted and acted upon, but ultimately I was on my own.

At the same time, ever since I could remember I had deliberately stressed that my psychological skills and experience, although mine, were resources that the police could call upon. But the Green Chain rapes had shocked me and made me realize that I should be more direct and assertive, less willing to simply give my expertise and then walk away. Since then I'd become more insistent on things being done and on having details checked and rechecked.

In the process, I realized that sometimes the line between being a consultant psychologist and a consultant detective had become blurred. For example, many of the questions I asked in the Wardell case such as whether his wife's sandals could be fitted back on her feet, had little psychological value but important investigatory implications. By asking such questions I didn't mean to suggest that the detectives had been neglectful or unaware. I simply knew that an uncritical analysis of the information could cause enormous problems. If one detail is overlooked or misinterpreted then it can change the entire direction of the inquiry.

If the Wardell case had centred on the inconsistencies in the story of one man and how these fitted together, the murder of fifteen-year-old Naomi Smith was characterized by the sheer number of potential suspects. For me it began when Detective Superintendent Tony Bayliss telephoned me at home on Sunday afternoon, 17 September, 1995. Naomi had been found three days earlier with her throat cut and injuries to her genitalia. Her body was discovered beneath a children's slide little more than 100 yards from her home at Ansley Common, a former mining village on the outskirts of Nuneaton.

An incident room had been set up at Bedworth Police Station and Bayliss gave me travel directions. Following these to the letter, I found myself turning left into a pedestrian precinct at Bedworth, driving round bollards and bemused late Monday afternoon shoppers. As I found the station, I noticed a woman arriving at the same time carrying a briefcase. We were standing in the foyer, carefully avoiding eye contact, both of us fearing the other was probably a journalist. Ultimately we finished up in the same room; she was a scientist who had come to discuss DNA samples.

Bayliss began the briefing and certain details were added later by Gino Varriale and Detective Sergeant Jez Grew. On Thursday at approximately 9.45 p.m. Naomi Smith had left her parents' neat red-brick semi-detached house on the Bretts Hall Estate to post a letter for her mother Catherine. The postbox was by a bus stop on a busy main road less than 200 yards from her home.

Her journey would have taken less than two minutes past the houses of neighbours watching TV and beneath the street lights on Ansley Common Road.

'A twelve-year-old girl who lives across the road saw Naomi post the letter,' said Bayliss. 'She said Naomi began walking home, stopped, turned and walked back past the postbox. She paused at the entrance to an unlit alleyway – the locals call it a *jitty* – which runs behind houses and leads to the recreation ground where her body was found. According to the witness, Naomi stopped for a second or two and then walked down the jitty into the darkness. The girl's a solid witness.'

Gino said, 'We also have a motorist who says he saw Naomi standing by the postbox at about 9.35 p.m. He was waiting for traffic at an intersection and as he pulled away he noticed a teenage girl standing half on the road and half on the path, looking in his direction.'

'As if she might be waiting for someone,' explained Bayliss.

'Did she have plans to go out that night?'

Bayliss replied, 'Not according to her parents.'

'What about engineering a reason to get out of the house?'

'No. Her mum asked her to post the letter.'

In daylight the jitty could be viewed as another route home for Naomi from the postbox, but most of her friends insisted that she wouldn't use it at night. It led to the recreation ground, known locally as 'The Rec', which consisted mainly of open space, with swings, a slide and other brightly coloured playground fixtures fitted tightly into the corner nearest to the entrance.

Naomi's spreadeagled body had been found at 11.30 p.m., lying on a square of Astroturf in a children's sitting area that was covered by a sloping wooden roof and a playground slide. She was discovered by her father Brian Smith and her best friend Emma Jones who had gone looking for her.

Bayliss began flicking through crime-scene photographs to illustrate various points.

'We can't be sure of exactly how she was found. She was moved by her father into the recovery position and covered with a blanket. The ambulance team also touched her. From what we can ascertain, she was lying on her back with her legs open and knees drawn up.'

Naomi had been wearing jeans and a dark blue polo-neck jumper with an old white Aran-style sweater. Over this she had her favourite bomber-style jacket with the words 'Chicago Fire Department' emblazoned in flames of yellow on the front and their logo on the back, over the legend, 'BACKDRAFT'.

The photographs showed her semi-naked with her jeans and pants removed from her left leg but caught around her right ankle. Her unlaced left shoe lay close by, along with a slightly soiled sanitary towel and an empty cigarette packet. Her right shoe was still on and I noticed the double-knotting of the laces.

There was little in the way of bloodstaining, most of it confined to her neck area and down one side of her face. Her throat had been slashed rather than stabbed, according to the pathologist, and at some point she had clearly been rolled slightly and repositioned.

The assault on her vagina had been particularly savage. Something very large had been pushed inside her causing extensive damage. She'd been on her back at the time and the pattern of blood on her buttocks indicated that at some point her hips had probably been raised and then splashed down into a patch of blood. At the same time, the relative lack of bleeding from her genitals suggested that she was dead or dying when the vaginal assault occurred.

At some point her left breast had been bitten. I made a note to explore the sequence. I needed to know in what order the separate elements of the attack had happened; this would tell me more about the reason for the attack, and that in turn would tell me more about the killer or killers. I also had to be sure of exactly how Naomi's body had been positioned when discovered. How much could I rely on the recollections of her distraught father and her best friend?

'What can you tell me about Naomi?' I asked, focussing attention on one of the core questions that I needed to answer – who was the victim? The media had been portraying Naomi as a sweet, gentle, much-loved teenager and the most-publicized photograph of her in her school uniform seemed to affirm all of these things. Similarly, her teachers described her as 'a nice girl, although not particularly academic'.

According to Brian Smith, Naomi had been born in 1980 while he was still married to his first wife Jennifer. He'd been having an affair with Catherine who lived in Coventry with her three sons. Soon afterwards, his wife learned of the affair and Brian moved in with Catherine. He described Naomi as a normal teenage girl, who was quite shy and lacked confidence. She was self-conscious about a dead nerve on the left side of her face which made her face look a little lopsided. Apparently, it had led to teasing at school and playground jokes which upset Naomi and several times she had come home from school crying. Despite this, Mr Smith said Naomi was not unpopular and always had a lot of schoolfriends.

She enjoyed music and dancing and loved animals, keeping rabbits and a pet bird. Until recently the family had two dogs, Tammy and Sandy, which Naomi often would take for walks in the fields beyond The Rec. She was a below average student who struggled at most subjects, according to her father, who blamed this on the family being moved around so much.

Naomi's best friend Emma Jones had told police a slightly different story, describing Naomi as being far more streetwise and outgoing with a strong personality. Different perceptions of a person are not unusual. It comes back to the complexity of life and of each individual personality. The phenomenon I grapple with every day is that, in the main, people are not entirely what they seem to be. Naomi wasn't the two-dimensional figure described in the newspapers. Her life had been far richer and more complex than this. She had an image of herself that she wanted the rest of the world to see and, like all fifteen-year-olds, she would have secrets that she kept from her parents.

'Was she sexually promiscuous?' I asked, aware of how blunt it sounded, given her youth.

'There's a question mark here,' said Bayliss. 'She had two condoms in the back pocket of her jeans and ten in her bedroom.'

'What do her parents say?'

'They say she was a virgin. Dad says she was waiting for the right boy. They figured they couldn't stop her having sex, so he gave her a dozen condoms to be safe. He gave Emma a dozen at the same time because she and Naomi both talked about boys.'

I could see this worried Bayliss a little. He had a sixteen-year-old daughter of his own and I don't think he liked the idea that a friend's father might decide to give her condoms.

'He says Naomi might have had one or two boyfriends that he didn't know about, but they can't have been serious or she would have told him.' Bayliss didn't sound fully convinced.

'What does Emma say?'

'Much the same. The latest boyfriend is a Richard Mason who works at a local supermarket stacking shelves. He's been alibied out for Thursday night.'

Significantly, Mason had told police that he and Naomi met quite often at The Rec after Naomi got home from school. The two of them had been dating for a month but had recently split up and were talking about a reconciliation. The fact that he was eight years older than Naomi didn't seem to concern her parents or appear to be unusual for the area.

Naomi's parents had also been asked about drug-use and revealed that a few months earlier, her mother had found a rolled up cigarette in the bedroom which they feared might be cannabis. They contacted the police and a local officer came to the house and gave the family advice and a stern lecture to Naomi.

'She promised that she'd only tried cannabis and said she'd not really liked it,' said Mr Smith. 'She promised not to do it again.'

The Bretts Hall Estate had been built where Nuneaton runs out and the Warwickshire countryside takes over. George Eliot may have been born near here and set her masterpiece, *Middlemarch*, in the surrounding landscape, but the world she described couldn't be further removed from the realities of Ansley Common. This was the lower end of a working class area with more than its fair share of unemployment, domestic violence and boredom. Someone in the incident room described it as being full of 'perverts, hooligans and morons'.

Of course, such comments do no justice to the overwhelming number of decent, respectable residents of the area but unfortunately it only takes a few people to characterize a place and alter the crime statistics. I look for baselines and I was learning of a community that had a high number of sex offences, particularly acquaintance-based rapes and flashings. It also had a core criminal element that commuted out to steal and then returned home.

Equally, The Rec was a normal playground during the day but after dark became an arena for local youths, some of whom tried to cure their boredom with strong lager, glue-sniffing or soft drugs. Most of them were aged between fifteen and twenty-five, with outsiders who visited at the older end of the scale.

One of the cultural and social phenomena that can characterize such areas is the likelihood of greater promiscuity and irresponsible behaviour, particularly amongst the young adults and teenagers. This is because they are exposed to a different value structure and develop different social norms from the older residents. With little money, few jobs and nothing to look forward to, a culture with gang-like elements can develop. The young can begin to see authority structures such as the police and social services as the enemy on the outside.

Three months before the murder, two rival gangs had been reported fighting on The Rec with baseball bats, knives, knuckle-dusters and crowbars. Detectives had also compiled a lengthy list of all reports of violence, indecency and attempted abduction relating to the Bretts Hall Estate and Ansley Common.

Another feature often seen in these settings is the high prevalence of relationships between young teenage girls and older men. Girls of fourteen, fifteen and sixteen years old, who have reached this time of their lives without much good or fulfilling having happened to them, physically develop and notice how older boys in their twenties begin to show an interest in them.

Boys of their own age are a bit slower, shyer and less worldly whereas young adult men have money, cars and experience. Unfortunately, the older girls will have chosen the best candidates and have left behind the more unsuccessful young men. Younger girls are the only people they can impress with their macho charm.

Teenaged girls understand desire when they see it and the fact that they can make a man of nineteen or twenty interested in them is rather an exciting early sensation of power. However, they don't understand the dangers or realize that they are playing with fire.

Bayliss had a team of fifty officers who had interviewed more than 300 people so far and taken over fifty statements. Teams were going from door to door in Ansley Common, while others were tracing vehicles, confirming alibis and checking intelligence. Jez Grew was in charge of the latter and had already been liaising with CATCHEM, the national computer database indexing all murdered, abducted or missing children since 1960.

Based in Derbyshire, CATCHEM had been championed through some hard years by Detective Chief Superintendent Duncan Bailey, who saw it achieve international recognition before he retired in 1994. It played a significant role in the conviction of Robert Black for the murders of three young girls, Susan Maxwell, eleven, Caroline Hogg, five, and Sarah Harper, ten, as well as the kidnapping of a fourth girl.

As we sat and pondered, various scenarios were put forward with different degrees of confidence. On the one hand, the horrific nature of the assault led some to suggest looking for escaped mental patients and sexual offenders with a known history of violence. On the other hand, although Naomi had been portrayed as a relatively immature fifteen-year-old, witness statements suggested she may have gone out expecting or at least hoping to meet someone. She was seen looking up and down the road beside the postbox and then very purposefully walking into the dark entrance of the jitty. Who was she waiting for? Was she hoping that someone she knew might pass along?

Bayliss was looking for a psychological profile and any advice I could give on what had happened. I gave him a shopping list of what I needed, including important statements and a detailed map of the area, showing The Rec and the surrounding streets and houses.

Coincidentally, my visit to the Bedworth Police Station had corresponded with the arrival of various specialists who had been asked to help the inquiry. These included the woman scientist I had seen earlier from the scientific laboratory in Birmingham, as well as the pathologist and an odontologist who had been studying the bite-mark to Naomi's breast.

Bayliss chaired the meeting in a small conference room and asked me to sit in. I was more than happy because it gave me the rare opportunity to ask questions directly to the other forensic experts rather than relaying them through the SIO. Without doubt the most welcome news was the possibility that the scientists might be able to build a DNA profile of the killer from saliva found in the bite-mark.

After the various progress reports had been delivered, I asked the pathologist a question, 'Why is there such a narrow concentration of blood at the scene?'

'Most of it appears to have been absorbed through the Astroturf and the underlay,' he said.

'Was she lying on her back when her throat was cut?'

'Yes.'

'Any evidence of hand pressure on her neck?'

'It's impossible to say, the slashes will have destroyed any bruising development.'

This still left the question of whether she could have been partially strangled first, I thought.

'Can you tell me about the wounds to the neck?'

'There were at least two cuts, both linear lines.'

'Could they be stab wounds?'

'Yes but the size of the knife blade would be very small. They're more likely slashes.'

The suggestion had been made that a bottle had been used for the vaginal assault, something quite broad and with a heavy base. I needed to know how much force would have been necessary to drive such a weapon into Naomi.

There was a long pause and I sensed that the pathologist didn't understand the importance of my questions. Finally he said that a considerable thrust had been used.

'Why isn't there much blood on her lower half?' I asked.

'Not much was circulating at the time of the vaginal assault.'

'Which suggests that her throat had already been cut?'

'Yes.'

'Would the vaginal attack have been sufficient in itself to kill her?'

'Probably.'

'Were the throat and vaginal wounds all inflicted from the front?'

'In my view, yes.'

'So where in the sequence is her breast bitten? Was she alive at that point?'

Finally losing patience, he said, 'Exactly what is it you really want to know?'

I apologized and tried to explain why these things were vital. If the neck and vaginal assault had occurred at the same time it definitely indicated more than one attacker. Similarly, the force used suggested great anger towards Naomi, or at least great excitement.

The odontologist explained how the bite-marks to Naomi's breast included both the upper and lower arches of teeth. These appeared too far apart which indicated that the breast had been compressed when bitten.

'And she was lying on the ground when it happened?' I asked.

He nodded and explained how the skin, being elastic, was not the most yielding of moulds for bite-marks because it moved and distorted. It *was* possible to say that the bite had taken considerable pressure, with no suction and that Naomi had been alive at the time.

'Where was the biter in relation to Naomi?' I asked, wanting him to show me.

The odontologist thought about this and decided that the attacker had been on Naomi's left side, ninety degrees to her body as she lay on the ground.

I had a problem with this. This wasn't a love bite and Naomi wouldn't have just acquiesced. She would have experienced considerable pain. A person kneeling on her left, parallel to her and biting her left breast raised the probability of someone else being present holding her down. How many people were involved?

The odontologist – an expert on teeth and gums – offered to go back and check his findings and subsequently altered his advice, saying that the upper and lower arches were the other way around. This meant that a lone man could have been lying on top of Naomi, with her consent, or pinning her down to the ground by force, and then rotated her breast slightly before biting her.

Even so, I wasn't willing to exclude more than one man being involved.

As the meeting finished, Bayliss turned to me. 'You'll want to see the scene.'

'Yes.'

'Would anyone else like to come?' he asked.

There were several who accepted the offer.

The Smith family had moved to the Bretts Hall Estate eighteen months earlier and were well-known in the area. Naomi had two older brothers Andrew and Clayton and one half-brother, David. The curtains were pulled tight at the neat semi-detached house and a piece of paper had been pinned to the front door.

Retracing Naomi's footsteps in the growing darkness, Bayliss and I reached the post box and he reaffirmed the witness statements.

'The twelve-year-old lived in the house opposite,' he said. 'She was standing upstairs at the bay window.'

'There is no bay window.'

Bayliss stopped virtually in mid-stride.

'The only bay window is down there,' I said, pointing to a house more than 100 yards away.

'That can't be right.'

'Let's find out,' I suggested.

The house number corresponded with the girl's statement which meant that somehow her account had been misreported to the SIO. Bayliss suggested we see if the girl was home so I could evaluate her reliability as a witness. In a neat front lounge, he chatted with the girl's father before we took her upstairs to her parents' bedroom from where she'd seen Naomi walking alone on Thursday night.

In her statement, she had said, 'I could easily make out Naomi from my position, I had a good unrestricted view of her, there was no traffic on the road. I could not see anyone else around . . .'

After posting the letter, 'Naomi walked past the bus stop and then up to the big street light and then stopped. Then she turned around and walked back up the pavement in the direction of the post box. By now her walking pace had become much faster, not running but hurried . . . then saw her look down the jitty. Naomi only stopped for a second or two and then continued at her same hurried pace along the jitty and out of sight.'

As the girl pointed out the post box to me it was immediately clear that she couldn't have seen anybody's face, it was too far away.

'Oh, I recognized her jacket,' she explained.

I had no problem with her identification of Naomi, but the distance called into question the way she described Naomi walking purposefully down the jitty. She couldn't possibly be sure of this.

Bayliss and I walked back up the street, stopping to have a few words with a local shopkeeper before turning down the jitty towards The Rec. It was virtually an unmade pathway that provided rear access to the houses and a shortcut to the reserve. After walking a few dozen yards in complete darkness, a passive infrared light suddenly lit up in a starburst of light and night became day. Nobody had mentioned this before. If Naomi had walked down here, the light would have come on. Bayliss made a note to have it checked.

The Rec was so dark it was hard to judge any distances and I contemplated what Naomi would have seen. Whoever was with her had to know the area well enough to navigate without light. In all likelihood they knew about the seat and the Astroturf under the slide. Throughout Friday, police searchers had combed the entire recreation ground, hampered by driving rain. No trace of the knife or the weapon that penetrated Naomi had been found.

Walking back towards Naomi's house, we were suddenly blinded by another passive infrared light on the corner house of the estate, nearest to The Rec car-park. It looked new and Bayliss decided to ask the householder if the light had been installed since the murder as a security measure.

A lady answered with a toddler clinging to her leg and a baby crawling around her ankles. She confirmed that the light had been newly installed and then said, 'Did you find those three lads?'

Bayliss asked, 'What three lads?'

'The ones I heard running past here on Thursday night.'

'What did you hear?'

'I know what I heard. I was in bed and I woke up. Three men were running down there.'

'What time was this?'

'At eleven o'clock. I looked at the clock.'

'And you're sure they were men?'

'I heard them talking and shouting to each other as they ran.'

'Why do you say three of them?'

'I think it was three. It was definitely more than one.'

Bayliss shook his head. 'Why haven't you given a statement?'

She looked uncomfortable. 'Well, nobody's asked me.'

The SIO was fit to explode. House-to-house teams had been right through the area and the mobile incident room had been set up in a caravan directly opposite her address. Apparently officers had been going in and out of her house to get water for their kettle, but nobody had thought to ask her.

As we left the house I knew that heads were going to be knocked together back at the incident room. Bayliss was far too hard-nosed and professional to let such an oversight go without explanation. He wanted a statement from the woman on his desk by morning.

It was particularly important because police were already searching for three or possibly four youths seen loitering on the green opposite Naomi's council house between 10.00 and 11.00 p.m. on the Thursday. Bayliss had several times used media conferences to ask them to come forward.

He had also issued the description of a lone man seen running out of the jitty onto the pavement straight across Ansley Common Road. A cyclist had to swerve and mounted the pavement to avoid hitting him. He described him as being a white male, aged between twenty and twenty-five, six foot tall, with an athletic build and short blond hair that looked bleached and spiky on top.

On the Saturday after the murder, Bayliss also took the unusual step of revealing the extent of Naomi's injuries in the hope that it would convince anyone who might be shielding the killer to give him up.

'I think someone probably does know and may even be harbouring him,' he said. 'I want that person to think about what has been done – we have an innocent fifteen-year-old girl killed in horrific circumstances. Even though you may have mixed loyalties, I want you to put those behind you and come forward to tell us who is responsible.'

At the same time, Naomi's half-brother David Freeman tearfully told journalists, 'Someone must know who this evil person is. She was a beautiful young girl. She was just becoming a young lady. She never harmed anybody.'

The appeals were backed up by a £10,000 reward offered by an unnamed winner of the National Lottery.

Over the next few days I went over the statements of Naomi's parents and friends, as well as re-examining the crime-scene photographs. Bayliss had asked for a psychological profile and case analysis but I couldn't be sure about either until I sorted out the discrepancies in the various accounts. The wheat had to be sorted from the chaff and there seemed to be a lot of the latter.

The inquiry appeared to be taking very seriously details that suggested Naomi had gone out to meet someone. But how reliable was this conclusion? If the evidence wasn't convincing, it was best to concentrate on those facts that were more certain.

Within the statements of Brian and Catherine Smith I found the complete explanation of what Naomi was observed to do on Thursday night after posting the letter.

Brian Smith, a forty-five-year-old taxi driver who went to work very early each morning, described how Naomi had asked him on Thursday evening if he could call at Emma's house and wake her up on Friday morning for school. He suggested that Emma should stay the night at their house and told Naomi to nip up to the house to ask her if she wanted to stay. As Naomi was about to leave, Catherine asked her to post a letter on the way. She took the letter, went downstairs and he heard the front door bang.

Catherine Smith, aged forty-seven, gave a slightly different account.

'She [Naomi] asked me if we could pick up Emma on Friday morning and take her to school as Emma's father had to go to work early and he couldn't take her. I asked Naomi to walk to the postbox in Ansley Common and post a letter I had prepared for a Freeman's catalogue and while she was there to look further up Ansley Common to where Emma's sister Becky lived with her mother and see if Emma's father's car was still there. The object of this was that Naomi could then ask Emma's father if Emma could stay overnight at our house . . .'

A great deal of intellectual and investigatory effort had been wasted on the question of why Naomi had been looking up and down the road, yet the answer lay in the statements. Naomi had been looking to see if she could see Emma's father's car – not because she was waiting for someone.

At the same time, aspects of her parents' recollections posed questions, in particular Mr Smith's account of how he found Naomi's body. He described how she left to post the letter and he settled down to sleep. An hour later, Catherine woke him and said that she hadn't heard Naomi come home. He looked at the clock and it was 10.50 p.m. He got up, put on his dressing-gown and went downstairs. The lounge and kitchen lights were still on and he found the front door ajar and the lock on the catch.

Naomi had left the door open – hardly the action of a person who was going out to meet someone. Instead, it suggested that she expected to return in just a few minutes.

Mr and Mrs Smith decided that Naomi had probably got chatting with Emma and they decided to wait a few more minutes. At 11.15 p.m. when she still hadn't come home, Catherine telephoned Emma's mother and a family friend Alison Chapman to ask if either of them had seen Naomi. Afterwards, she and Alison went looking in the car, insisting that Brian try to get some sleep because he had to be up so early.

When they returned half an hour later without Naomi – having picked up Emma on the way – Brian immediately got dressed.

'Emma then said she would go to The Rec, the play area at the back of the house, to see if Naomi was there. She walked out. I said that I would follow her up in my car as it was unlit and very dark on The Rec and she needed the headlights to see.

'Outside the air was very dark and damp. Emma walked along the driveway situated some twenty yards to the left of our house which leads to The Rec and a small play area which has some swings and slides . . . I got into my car and drove after her up the driveway as far as I could go up to the fence which borders the play area. As I got to the top Emma was running back towards me screaming and shouting. She was shouting my name and telling me to come quick. As I stopped the car I could see a white shape lying underneath the slide on the playground. I jumped straight out of the car leaving the engine running and the headlights shining directly on the slide.

'I ran over the grass to the slide and saw Naomi lying on the floor. I immediately recognized her as she was lying on her back with her face towards me. As I ran to Naomi, Emma ran away from me, back down the driveway in the general direction of our house, screaming.

'Naomi was lying flat on her back, her head was the furthest away from me . . . it was turned to the right and facing me, both her arms were lying flat on the floor either side of her body next to her sides. Her legs were apart with her feet both flat on the ground, both her knees were up in the air. Her white jumper was pulled up slightly and a small part of her belly button was showing. Her jeans were pulled down around her ankles, I think that both legs were still in her jeans. I am not sure about her shoes but I think she had them on . . .'

Mr Smith went on to describe how he closed Naomi's legs and went running back to the house for a blanket to cover her – a father's attempt to save his daughter's dignity. Unfortunately, this made it difficult to be absolutely sure of how Naomi had been left by the killer or killers. For example, the crime-scene photographs showed her white jumper covering her breasts. Had she pulled it down after being bitten; or had the killer rearranged her clothes; or, more likely, had Brian Smith tried to spare his daughter further indignities?

Other things puzzled me. Why had Emma Jones suggested looking for Naomi at The Rec? And why had she run on ahead into the darkness instead of waiting for Mr Smith?

Her statement offered only some of the answers. She and Naomi were best friends and had spent the afternoon at a practice session of the Nuneaton Marching Brass Band where Naomi was learning to play percussion instruments. They were both excited about a band competition in London on the following Saturday. Emma's father had driven them home.

Emma had been in bed at 11.00 p.m. when Mrs Smith arrived looking for Naomi. She got dressed and went with them to look. As they drove, Emma directed Mrs Smith to an alleyway and walked part way along it, calling Naomi's name. Apparently it led to the house of a young man who had been Naomi's boyfriend and who she still had a crush on. When no-one answered, Emma turned back.

She said it was Alison who had suggested they search The Rec but didn't explain why she went ahead.

'Initially, I walked along by the fence towards the park, it was pitch-black and I was quite frightened. I shouted Naomi's name several times, saying, 'If you're here, tell me.' I got no response so carried on walking.

'Without Brian's car lights I was able to see something white which was under the slide of the children's play area. At first I thought it was just a carrier bag or blanket then Brian's car lights shone over towards the slide. Instantly, I recognized Naomi who was lying face up under the slide, her face was turned to one side. I thought that she'd had a blackout which I know that she has occasionally. Brian's car had stopped and his headlights lit up the park. I ran to Naomi and saw she was half naked. The clothes she had worn earlier were moved, dark blue jeans down to her ankles, long white jumper which was still in place. I could see a cut on her neck. I ran towards Brian and started screaming . . .'

Later in the statement Emma said: 'Naomi was my best friend and she would have told me if she was going to meet anyone that night. She walks the dogs over The Rec at night but she wouldn't go there on her own.'

The more I learned about Naomi's pastimes, the more complex her life became. Equally, so many different people attached to the case seemed to have secrets and aspects of their lives that were characterized by duplicity and deceit.

Even the descriptions of people seen in the area of Ansley Common had to be treated with care. None of them had come forward and been identified. Similarly, very little corroboration had been found. All of which raised the possibility that falsified details may be in the system. Every investigation has 'noise' of this type and it becomes even more important to filter out the pieces of the puzzle that don't belong and hone in on those aspects that have real value.

Bearing all this in mind, I began to reconstruct the collision of Naomi and her killer, retracing their footsteps on that rainy night until they came together. They didn't plan to meet. Naomi only expected to be gone for a few minutes. She posted the letter and then looked along the road towards Emma's sister's house to check for the car.

What she couldn't have realized is that someone is watching her from the jitty, someone she knows. That's why she turns back when he calls instead of simply walking home. If it had been a stranger calling from the dark she would most likely have run.

He sees what all the other witnesses see – Naomi looking up and down the road – and it allows him to ask, 'What are you doing, Naomi? Who are you looking for? Are you looking for me?'

With no reason to be afraid of him, she walks down the jitty. There are so many things he could have said to her.

'Hey, are ya comin' down The Rec?'

'Have ya got a fag?'

'Whatcha doing on the weekend?'

Naomi has to make a judgement. She's left the front door ajar and her parents expect her back. The jitty comes back towards her house anyway. Perhaps she decides to have a quick chat, just long enough to make plans and then she'll go home.

But what of her killer? Why was he out on Thursday night and what was he looking for?

Although he may have watched Naomi arrive home from band practice and waited in the hope that she came out, I thought it unlikely. He was a local lad in his teens to mid-twenties; someone steeped in the local value system. He'd gone out cruising, maybe hoping to meet someone but not necessarily looking for a victim. He took a knife with him but not the bottle, that's more likely to be something collected along the way that he wouldn't perceive as a weapon.

His track record is one of lack of awareness and unsophisticated relationships with girls. Although he has high sex needs, he lacks the refinement and wherewithal to acquire partners. At the same time, he has a masturbatory life with a range that is probably quite broad in terms of his fantasies. They are likely to include him seducing women and women seducing him; as well as elements of coercion. Local venues will also feature in his masturbatory fantasies and he may have followed local girls and previously interfered with them and aggressively touched them. This could have reached the point of attempting rape.

This man recognizes Naomi at the postbox. He sees her looking up and down the road, attracting attention to herself. Perhaps he knows that she has older boyfriends and assumes that she must be having sex with them. If she'll do it for them, then why not for me? he thinks.

Neither of them expected to meet like this but as they walk down the jitty, he already has the expectation or the excitement of sexual arousal. The lack of defence injuries or signs of struggle suggest that Naomi went freely to The Rec, unaware that she was going to her death. If so, it indicated that she might have been far more involved in the local value system which included underage girls having sex than anyone had imagined. She was willing to go with him to a place they both knew; a place where they could negotiate in the pitch-black. The wooden frame of the slide provided shelter and the Astroturf was drier and softer than the ground.

The closeness of the houses is important, I thought. This is a local lad trying his luck, not a sophisticated seducer. One scream would have brought people running. That's why I didn't believe that he started out to kill Naomi. If he had, he would more likely have taken her over the fields away from The Rec. Instead, he chose to stay close to the houses and would have to run past them when he finished.

There are various possibilities for what happens next. Perhaps he tries to kiss Naomi and starts touching her. Because of the sanitary towel, I think it less likely that Naomi wanted to have sex and would have needed some persuasion. She refuses and the knife comes out. She won't scream now, she's frightened and does as she's told.

I looked again at how her shoes had been found. One had been removed with the laces undone but, by contrast, the other shoe had a complex knot – not something that comes undone with the tweak of a bow. In the darkness he wouldn't have been able to see the knot so I think it's likely that Naomi undid the lace. Then he helps her pull her jeans and pants down, but they're only removed from one leg. There is no expectation here of a lengthy sexual interlude – it is going to be over very quickly.

Her buttocks are pushed into the ground and her sweater and bra are pulled up over her breasts. Naomi may go part of the way, but he can't stop. With the bite, everything changes. Now she just wants to get away, but his anger at her surges and transforms a speculative sexual opportunity into a full-scale attempted rape.

Naomi is on her back, with her jeans down and a man lying on top of her. She won't have lubricated and perhaps after the bite, she locks her thighs and he can't force penetration. Because he's sexually unsophisticated, he doesn't know his way around this problem. This person is already prone to explosive rages, especially when frustrated and now he becomes extremely angry. There are so many possible triggers – he might blame her for teasing him, or changing her mind, or menstruating. He takes the knife to her and her silent fear becomes terror as he slashes her across the throat. Then he grabs whatever is nearby, perhaps a bottle, and assaults her with considerable force.

Afterwards, when he realizes what he's done, there are mixed feelings. On the one level he thinks, 'Well, I sorted her out,' and on another level he's quite numb with shock. The absence of light on The Rec means that he won't have a strong visual memory of what happened. This is one of the things that normally causes a problem for such murderers. They can't forget the vivid pictures and it can prey on their memories. The darkness will lessen the impact of such an effect.

I hadn't discounted the possibility of there being more than one attacker. If this was the case, the scenario would have been different. There would be a diffusion of responsibility, where each of them sheds their sensation of blame or responsibility onto the other. They egg each other on and can't afford to lose face. Naomi becomes much less important as a person because at that moment, it is the relationship between her attackers that is more significant.

If more than one person was involved, it became more likely that Naomi was coerced at the children's slide and made to undress. Nothing I knew about her suggested that she would have readily agreed to group sex. They could easily overpower her and pin her down, covering her mouth when she became distressed.

On 21 September, a week after the murder, I returned to Bedworth Police Station to deliver my psychological profile. Early that morning detectives had arrested five men from houses in and around Ansley

Common. They seized knives, clothing and shoes that were to be tested.

I had no idea about the arrests until I arrived at the station. Apparently, the raids related to the activities of young people who frequented The Rec at night. The inquiry team had been puzzled why none of the dozens of young men and women who regularly gathered at The Rec had come forward. Bayliss suspected that some of them knew the murderer's identity and had deliberately withheld information, through fear of several ringleaders.

The five men were taken to different police stations for questioning.

Bayliss was particularly keen to see if any of the suspects matched with what I had to say about Naomi's killer.

'The offender is most likely to be in his teens to mid-twenties,' I said. 'He's not sexually sophisticated and doesn't have a track record of lots of girlfriends; or of being able to woo women. He's also not particularly experienced in the finer points of sexual behaviour.'

The bite to Naomi's breast was a sign of youthful immaturity rather than sadism, otherwise there would have been signs of a need to control and dominate. If he had wanted to inflict pain on Naomi, there were ways of doing this far more elaborately than a bite.

'The most important points are these,' I said, looking up from my notes. 'Firstly, Naomi knew her murderer passingly well and, secondly, he's very local. He'll live within four or five hundred yards of the scene. He knows The Rec even in the pitch-dark. He knows that he can take a fifteen-year-old schoolgirl a hundred yards from her home and not be disturbed.

'He's of no more than average intelligence, but nothing about the offence suggests that he's mentally retarded or slow.

'You are looking for someone who can become very angry and very disinhibited. He's got a short fuse and when he explodes is capable of using great force and violence. It's possible that alcohol and drug abuse could have fuelled this anger.

'His disinhibition may well have brought him into contact with the police previously for minor sexual offences, following and aggressively touching local girls.'

I looked up at Bayliss. 'With a lone offender, I think it's more likely that Naomi undressed herself to facilitate hurried, low-comfort sex, but I can't exclude there being more than one. If this was the case, she could more easily have been overpowered and undressed, without suffering defence injuries or leaving signs of a scuffle. It raises the possibility that she offered herself to the wrong man and the other one became angry. Either way, it would account for why no-one heard her cry out.'

I explained how the anger and exhilaration would have quickly been replaced by shock and fear. 'Because he's a local man, he's going to arrive home in a state that is considerably different from his normal behaviour. That's why folks around him are going to know or suspect.'

'So someone must be shielding him,' said Bayliss, having suspected as much. 'How confident are you that he lives so close?'

'Very confident.'

'Which means we must have talked to him already. We've knocked on every door.' He glanced at a map of Ansley Common on his office wall. 'We've got him in that area. Our job is to work on that.'

Because the offender was likely to be living with his family or in a communal setting I explained how this supporting cast was likely to become more deeply implicated as each day passed. If parents were involved, it became particularly difficult.

I don't think I've ever come across a mother who says, 'My son is a monster and I know he killed that young woman, I must go to the police.' This also applies to fathers but they are often more realistic. Mothers don't want to believe their child could do such a thing and even if they accept that something dreadful has happened, there must be a misunderstanding. Later this attitude can harden into a belief that their son must have been drawn into it, or the girl must have provoked him. Taking this one step further, the mother thinks, yes, that poor girl is dead but my boy isn't. Even though it happened, I know him, he's really a good boy. So what's the use in locking him up, it's not going to bring her back and I will watch him and make sure it won't happen again.

The scientists had come back with a positive DNA profile. This allowed Bayliss to take the decision to run a mass-screening operation, similar to 'The Bloodings'. He wanted to turn the pressure right up by asking men to give a mouth swab from which saliva would be used to create a DNA profile that could be matched against the one found at the murder scene.

The idea had become feasible because of the narrow search area established by the psychological profile. However, they wanted to build in insurance, so they extended the age and geographical ranges to every male aged between fourteen and forty living within a half-mile radius of the murder scene. This could mean testing 5,000 potential suspects at a cost of £200,000.

Bayliss had secured a budget of only £40,000, and at £40 a swabbing it meant that the money would only stretch to 1,000 tests. A rationale had to be found for choosing which men were tested and in precisely what order – something that would increase the likelihood of the killer being among those tested early and help to identify him quickly.

Bayliss decided to use the full psychological profile to narrow the search parameters. Using a newly developed computer system known as Watson, which bolted onto the HOLMES database, elements of the profile were used to tighten the list of potential suspects, bringing it down to 1,750 people and then down to 850.

The advantage of Watson is that it can be interrogated and used to follow an investigatory path through the mountain of information gathered during an inquiry. For example, a programmer might say, 'Show me all known male associates of Naomi Smith,' and this produces 395 names. Then he may say, 'Now show me which of these male associates are aged between eighteen and twenty-three? And then show me which of these men has a history of violence or indecency offences?'

In this way, the computer begins to rank individuals in terms of their closeness of fit to the psychological profile and produces batches of names based on the degree of closeness. The first saliva swabbing would be requested from the twenty men who most closely matched the profile. They would be followed by the next twenty, and the next twenty, until hopefully the killer emerged.

Unlike in Narborough, Enderby and Littlethorpe all those years before, the procedure had been refined and great care would be taken using photographs and witnesses to avoid someone taking the test for anyone else. Similarly, particular attention would be paid to anyone refusing the test or leaving the area.

Privately, Bayliss hoped that the news of the DNA operation might put pressure on the murderer's family or friends to come forward. He asked me to look at the press release and tinker with the wording, making it clear that this very powerful technology was being brought to bear on the case and it was only a matter of time before police caught the killer. If his family and friends realized the game was up, they might come forward rather than risk being accused of shielding him, or he might flee and make himself obvious.

On 23 September the news broke and led to national headlines such as 'DNA Dragnet' and 'Mass Testing in Naomi Hunt'.

The programme would begin the following day, said Bayliss, when a team of twenty officers would start calling at the homes of young men. 'It is now a question of "when" and not "if" we catch this offender. I am aware that there has been concern that the inquiry was losing its momentum. I can reassure you this is not the case.'

He added that the police had no power to force people to take part but if anyone refused without good reason, officers would probe more deeply into their backgrounds. Samples had already been taken from people at the scene on the night, including relatives, medical staff and police officers – to rule them out of the inquiry.

The five men arrested by police on the previous Thursday had all been released by Sunday, although inquiries had triggered new leads and detectives visited another thirty-three houses in Nuneaton and Bedworth. Morc than 1,800 people had been interviewed by the inquiry team and witness statements taken from another 441.

Even so, detectives faced criticism after the dramatic morning raids. Several of the men threatened legal action, particularly when their arrests were filmed by a TV crew given permission to cover the operation.

Over the next week I made several trips to the incident room, often dropping in on my way from a clinical appointment and collecting new statements. The inquiry had already generated a paper mountain and I could see men and women stretched to their limits trying to process it all. There comes a point when the requirements of a fast moving operation can outstrip the capacity of even twenty or thirty people to deal with the information being gathered. I'd seen this in the Abbie Humphries case where vital details had been in the system but buried amongst masses of other information. It had led to delays that could perhaps have been avoided.

Here again, I could see the need for a management system to deal with the diverse information coming in and to give it shape and order. This was hammered home to me at a large inquiry team briefing in a lounge area at Bedworth Police Station when Bayliss stood at the front and detectives filled every chair, table and empty space. The SIO gave an update and asked for reports on various aspects of the inquiry such as the house-to-house inquiries and the corroborating of various alibis. Detectives stood up, gave their information and then sat down again.

The meeting was powerfully good for motivating the troops but there were indications that one or two actions hung in the air, incomplete. Unfortunately, people often make assumptions or mistakenly believe that matters have been dealt with and that nothing of note has been found. Otherwise, it would have been signalled, they think. The absence of comment is taken to mean that there is nothing to comment upon.

Take for instance the woman living beside The Rec who hadn't been interviewed because various detectives all assumed that someone else had talked to her.

I had a long discussion about this with Tony Bayliss.

'How many actions [leads] has the inquiry raised?' I asked.

'I'm not absolutely certain,' he said.

'And how many of the actions have been completed and what's the outcome?'

'The incident room will know.'

'Fine, yes, but you're steering the train and have to know that the important details are pointed out to you immediately. Look at the question of whether Naomi had gone out looking for someone; for briefing after briefing that issue remained unresolved yet the answer was sitting in the system.'

Bayliss agreed that it should have been caught the first time through and we discussed how to improve the information management system so that he knew exactly what allocated actions had been followed up and each of the outcomes.

I suspect that the cause of this problem was because one of the most senior detectives in the inquiry had taken leave because of a death in his family. Because Bayliss and his team had worked well together, their separate roles had never been fully understood and the absence of one of them had negative effects that no-one predicted. It's like having a dent in the hull of a racing yacht. It still makes headway but not with the same speed and efficiency as before.

The inquiry continued across a broad front and on 27 September the coroner ordered a second post-mortem. This revealed the massive force used in the vaginal assault on Naomi and established the dimensions of the weapon at a minimum of ten inches long.

Increasingly it became clear that Naomi might not have been the quiet, average schoolgirl portrayed. One resident of Ansley Common had given a statement about seeing a ginger-haired girl matching Naomi's description on four occasions late at night or in the early hours of the morning.

The first time she'd been walking a black dog at about 11.00 p.m. A few weeks later at around two in the morning the householder had looked out his daughter's bedroom into a dark alleyway. He could see a figure approaching slowly from the direction of The Rec. When security lights lit up the garden and alleyway, he saw the ginger-haired girl who was wearing a short skirt and 'was dressed like an eighteen-year-old'.

She ran towards Ansley Common Road and out of sight and he thought, What's she doing out at this hour of the morning dressed like that? I certainly wouldn't allow my daughters out dressed like that.

He saw her again on another night in similar circumstances, wearing a short skirt. At that stage, he didn't know Naomi's name but he recognized her as a girl he'd seen in a papershop on Thursday afternoon, 14 September, when he went to pick up his daughter from school.

'On Friday morning when my daughter said to me, "Dad, a girl's been murdered on The Rec," my first words were, "I bet it's that ginger-haired girl." That came to my mind because of the odd times of the night I had seen her by herself.'

The police re-interviewed Emma Jones and she admitted that she and Naomi would sometimes sneak out late at night, usually to take the dogs for a walk. Naomi would leave the back door unlocked or take a key with her. They sneaked out when Emma stayed over, mainly because they were bored. Once outside, they walked around Ansley Common, keeping to where the street lights lit up the roads.

Emma said, 'We wouldn't see anyone, we'd just walk around until we got tired and then go back to Naomi's. The last time I sneaked out with Naomi would have been in May time this year.'

During various meetings with Tony Bayliss, we discussed the significance of Naomi's night-time excursions. The idea of her being out in the early hours of the morning wearing provocative clothes seemed to confirm the complexity of her life and that parts of her existence were hidden.

This created a problem for the SIO. Quite rightly, he had taken the position that in order to use the media most effectively and to encourage people to come forward, it was far better that Naomi be seen as a mono-dimensional, sweet, ordinary schoolgirl. If any speculation leaked out of promiscuity or drug use, it could dramatically stem the flow of information. At the same time, Naomi had been killed by someone she knew and therefore it was vital to trace every associate and track her every movement.

'The problem is, we don't really know Naomi,' said Bayliss. 'We have an area that is riddled with promiscuity and loose morals and living in the midst of this we have Snow White brutally murdered by a monster. On the one hand, she's a virgin waiting for Mr Right, but Snow White also has two condoms in her back pocket and an older boyfriend.'

I asked him, 'Remember when you were fifteen, Tony, did your folks know everything you were getting up to?'

He laughed. 'Hell no.'

'So you had secrets that you kept from your parents?'

'Sure.'

'If anyone knew your secrets, who were they?'

'Well, my mates I suppose.'

'Right. And who's Naomi's special friend?'

'Emma.'

Two days after the murder, Bayliss had called in a specialist to interview Emma. The woman officer was teaching cognitive interviewing to the Warwickshire Police – a sign of how far interviewing techniques had developed over the previous ten years.

However, Emma had been interviewed only hours after appearing at a tearful news conference with Naomi's mother and father. She had described her sadness at losing Naomi, her 'best and special friend'.

'Someone has taken her away from me. Her family and I will find it hard to live without her. She was the kindest person I have ever known. We just enjoyed being together and were happy together.'

Having so passionately and publicly shown her loyalty to Naomi and her parents, Emma would find it very difficult to reveal anything about her best friend that might harm her reputation or upset her family. She had set out her stall and would not easily tear it down. As a result, the interview with Emma did not expose the hidden elements of Naomi's life.

At Bayliss's request, I agreed to conduct another interview, however, first I wanted to speak to Brian Smith because there were aspects of his statement that still puzzled me. In particular, I wanted to see if I could unravel exactly how Naomi's body had been positioned when he found her.

Catherine Smith seemed very brittle as she met us at the door of the semi-detached house at Ansley Common; her grief was palpable. In the lounge Brian sat in an armchair watching an extremely large TV in the corner. A big man, with a full beard and receding hair, he wore silver tracksuit bottoms and a vest.

Sitting on a three-seater settee beside him, I tried to start the interview and eventually had to ask him to turn off the TV. We had a long, complicated and curious conversation and I was surprised by how much Mr Smith knew about Naomi's clothes and the make-up she used. He and Emma were also very close.

I took him through the entire day of the murder from 4.00 a.m. when he woke up and went to work at MGM Taxis, to that evening when Naomi popped out to post the letter for her mother.

Among the new details to emerge was the fact that Naomi's house-key had been left lying on the table in the corner of the room when she went out. She always did this if she wasn't going far or for long, he said. Again it indicated that she intended to come straight home from the post box.

Mr Smith said that it had been *he* who suggested searching The Rec and Emma had volunteered to come with him. This settled an anomaly in their earlier statements but didn't explain why Emma had gone ahead into the darkness.

Importantly, Mr Smith insisted that when the car's headlights shone onto the white shape of Naomi's body, she was lying beside the slide and not underneath it. He was adamant about this even though the bloodstaining showed it couldn't be true. He was sure that she was wearing both shoes and that her jeans and pants were pulled down but not removed from one leg. He couldn't be blamed for being mistaken; he was a shocked and traumatized father under pressure from within himself to know what had happened to his daughter. However, this did affect how much weight could be given to his account of how Naomi had been left.

Ultimately, the question would never be answered fully, although Mr Smith did reveal that Naomi's breasts had been exposed and he pulled down her jumper to somehow protect what dignity remained.

Five days later on Tuesday 10 October, I left the negotiator training course I run at Leicester and drove to the incident room for a meeting with Emma Jones. It wasn't going to be a straightforward cognitive interview which is normally only useful when someone has told police all they can remember. In this case I felt that Emma had more to tell but had been unable to do so.

In most of my clinical interviews when I first see a patient I tell them that I know they are going to feel that they have to conceal things from me and to tell me lies. I explained this to Emma.

'There are things in your life that you have never told anybody – you may even have hidden them from yourself. You certainly aren't going to tell a perfect stranger these things straight off. But as we go on, you'll feel more comfortable and you won't be embarrassed. At some point when I ask another question, you'll think to yourself, "Should I tell him that or not?" You have to know that I'm not going to call you a liar or think any less of you. I just need you to help me understand the truth.'

We were sitting in a room at Bedworth Police Station and Emma sat clutching a small stuffed toy that had belonged to Naomi. Mrs Smith had given it to her and she wouldn't let it go. A big girl, wearing a black leather jacket, she looked as though she had been through the mill. She hadn't been sleeping and feared the murderer would come looking for her now that she'd been named by the media.

I couldn't think of many more painful or difficult situations to endure. At age fifteen, she was on the boundary between being a child and an adult and had suddenly been plummeted into the middle of a dreadful murder inquiry. Not only had her best friend been killed but Emma had actually found her body.

'I'm sorry that I can't take the pictures away, Emma, I wish I could. But I promise you they will gradually become dimmer and, as things go on, they'll be moved out of the way by better things.'

I explained who I was and told Emma that in common with all ordinary fifteen-year-old girls, I knew that she had secrets that she only shared with her close friends. 'There are things you do and say that your mum and dad maybe wouldn't understand or approve of,' I said. 'Places you go and adventures that you have. Is that about right?'

She nodded.

'In order to know what happened and who hurt Naomi, it's really important to know as much as possible about her. Even though she lived with her mum and dad and loved them, there are things that mums and dads aren't ready for; things that you only talk about with your best friend. Most teenagers are the same.

'I need to know about Naomi and I need to know her in a way that only you can tell me. I know you promised not to tell anyone your secrets . . .' She nodded. 'But we're in a slightly different situation now. Someone has killed Naomi. If you think about it, if Naomi were here now, I think she'd say, "Emma you can tell."'

Emma blurted out, 'She does, she does talk to me.' She clutched the toy a little and explained that when she had her healing crystal with her, she dreamed of Naomi walking, talking and naming her killer. But without the crystal, she had terrible nightmares.

'Do you think Naomi would want you to help us catch the person?'

'Yes,' she whispered. I could see her relax a little.

Together we drew up a list on a piece of paper of the sort of secrets that teenagers might keep from their parents.

Sexual relationships
Stealing
Truanting
Drinking and smoking
Going out late at night
Staying out too long
Being with people she shouldn't be with
Drugs

As we began to go through the list, Emma admitted that Naomi wasn't a virgin and had slept with a number of her boyfriends. She preferred quite active partners but was only interested in boys in their twenties rather than anyone her own age. Apart from the condoms her dad had given her, Naomi had eighteen that she'd been given by someone else.

Naomi easily transferred her affections from boy to boy, but couldn't say goodbye to them so just went out with someone else. She liked to have sex indoors because it was more comfortable and wasn't so keen on sex outside because she thought it was 'indecent'.

As Emma realized that I wasn't going to criticize her, it became easier for her and almost a cathartic experience as everything came bubbling to the surface. She described how sometimes she and Naomi would go out at two or three o'clock in the morning dressed in miniskirts and 'tarty clothing'. Sometimes men approached them in cars, but the girls never accepted their offers.

'Naomi would brag about being looked at and having people say, "Hello, Sexy". Folks at school thought she was ugly but when she got dressed up guys thought she was sexy.'

Normally they just walked in the fields with Naomi's dogs, Sandy and Tammy, but the dogs had recently killed a cat so Naomi had given them away. Emma thought that if the dogs had been with Naomi, she wouldn't have been killed.

Describing the night, Emma said she initially thought Naomi might be up a particular alleyway with a boy that she fancied. 'I thought she'd gone to see him again – where I'd seen them before, up the alley.'

Back at the house, she volunteered to search The Rec with Brian Smith because she wanted to warn Naomi just in case she was up there with someone. 'I ran up to The Rec, waiting to shout in her face, "What are you doing?"'

Clearly, the picture that emerged of Naomi was of a girl far more worldly wise and able to use her female wiles than had come across previously. This didn't make her unusual, however. In fact it confirmed that she was a completely normal girl within the cultural value system in which she lived.

Naomi had been sexually aware and active, enjoying a broad-ranging series of friendships with young men, normally older than herself. Her dislike of sex out-of-doors made it unlikely that she easily agreed to a quick sexual coupling beneath the slide. At the same time, she tended to get into teasing relationships with men without fully understanding male sexuality and the inherent danger of lighting a fuse and then hanging around for the fireworks to go off.

In the first week of November, seven weeks after the murder, Tony Bayliss telephoned to say that the DNA testing had produced a match.

'We got him in the first sweep, damn near top of the list,' he said. 'Edwin Douglas Hopkins – his friends call him "Eddy" – he lives in Ansley Common, very close to The Rec.'

'Have you picked him up?'

'No. We're pulling together a history and a list of known associates. I want you to see the file.'

Bayliss knew that under the restrictions of the Police and Criminal Evidence Act (PACE), he needed to have the case against Hopkins nailed down tightly before making any arrest. Similarly, he had to establish if anyone had been shielding him since the attack.

The following morning, a lever arch file arrived at my office from the incident room. It contained dozens of statements and intelligence reports that related to Eddy Hopkins, a nineteen-year-old apprentice paint sprayer who lived at home with his mother and father and younger brother.

Hopkins had first come to notice on 18 September, four days after the murder, when he phoned Bedworth Police Station and told a policewoman, 'My mum suggested I call. I was in the area of Ansley Common that night. I am six foot tall with mousy blond spiky hair, I had a pushbike with me on that night.'

He made a statement on the same day, describing how he arrived home from work at 5.00 p.m. and after a bath and something to eat he went to his sister's house several doors away. Julie Hopkins, aged twenty-two, lived with her boyfriend, Steve, and her two young children. At about 9.30 p.m. Hopkins said he left the house borrowing Steve's mountain bike to ride along Ansley Common to the Triple A shop, a journey that took five to ten minutes. He didn't notice anything as he passed the Bretts Hall Estate.

He bought eight cans of Carling Black Label lager and about fourteen bags of 10p crisps from the Asian owner and then cycled back to his sister's house with a carrier bag in each hand. He arrived back at 10.00 p.m. and stayed there drinking until about one o'clock on Friday morning. That's when he heard the police helicopter circling over The Rec and he and his cousin John Simpson decided to walk their dogs down to the Bretts Hall Estate to see what was going on.

Officers making house-to-house inquiries on 3 October interviewed housewife Mrs Mary Oxford who said that her daughter Rachel Hamilton had told her in confidence that on the night of the murder Eddy Hopkins had called at her house in Ansley Common at 10.30 p.m., asking for some shampoo and aftershave because he wanted to take a shower.

Following this up, detectives interviewed Rachel, the girlfriend of John Simpson. She insisted that Hopkins had asked her for shampoo at 6.00 p.m. and not 10.30 p.m. According to her statement, he left her house at 6.00 p.m. with John Simpson and she didn't see them again until 11.45 p.m. when they both called into her house to take the dogs for a walk. They said that something had happened down at the Bretts Hall Estate and went off.

On 15 October, Hopkins had made another statement and revealed how he used to visit The Rec regularly when he went to Hartshill High School prior to 1992.

'I used to play football and meet with all my mates. It is considered a general meeting place. I have not visited The Rec for at least the last six months, in the main I go about with my cousin John Simpson . . .'

Hopkins retold his story of riding the push-bike to the shop in Birmingham Road to buy beer and crisps. He remembered seeing the shopkeeper's two sons restocking the shelves and getting ready to close up. It must have been 9.45 p.m. when he left the shop and he rode directly back to his sister's because it was spitting with rain.

He, his cousin and his sister's boyfriend had then played computer games until about midnight when they heard the loud noise of the helicopter. From the back of the house they could see the search-light sweeping over the Bretts Hall Estate, so Hopkins and Simpson went for a walk. They spoke to a police officer who had sealed off The Rec but couldn't learn what had happened. A few minutes later they spoke to a local girl who told them that Naomi Smith had been murdered.

'I knew Naomi to be a girl who lives in Bretts Hall Estate and is a friend of Emma Jones. I knew Emma because I used to go out with her sister Rebecca. I've seen Naomi and Emma around the village and occasionally spoken to them. We had just general conversations, usually they would have a dog with them. It may be a couple of months since I last spoke to either Naomi or Emma. I have no personal knowledge of any lads that they went out with or anyone else they may have been associated with.'

Intelligence files had already unearthed a rather disturbing incident involving Hopkins that dated back to March 1993. A local teenage girl had alleged that he had indecently assaulted her in the fields at the rear of The Rec. She claimed that Hopkins had followed her until they were out of sight and then tripped her. He allegedly dragged her leggings and pants down, sat astride her and pulled her clothing away exposing her breasts. Shortly afterwards he ran off.

Hopkins denied the offence and several witness statements gave conflicting versions of what had happened. Shortly afterwards the girl withdrew her complaint and the police had no choice but to caution Hopkins about his future behaviour and to drop the case.

As I read the details, I had no doubt that it had been properly investigated. Even so, if anyone had wanted an early blueprint of what had happened to Naomi Smith, here it was.

Edwin Hopkins had criss-crossed the investigation right from the very beginning and emerged as one of the first names from the computer when the DNA swabbing batches were compiled using the psychological profile. Even so, there was absolutely no suggestion that the police could or should have identified him any earlier. His apparent background and links with Naomi were no more spectacular or noteworthy than 100 other young men in the surrounding streets. If you wanted an Agatha Christie plot, set on a council estate instead of a grand country house, this was it. There were suspects everywhere.

For this reason, it had proved a perfect case in which to use psychological profiling to narrow down the field – not only acquiring a suspect who had otherwise deflected attention, but also saving considerable time and money.

At dawn on 16 November, detectives arrested Hopkins at his parents' terraced house in West View, Ansley Common. They raided twelve more houses in the area, making three arrests and taking the suspects to separate police stations in Bedworth, Nuneaton, Atherstone and Rugby.

The previous day, I had visited Warwickshire Police Headquarters at Leek Wootten and given my advice on how Hopkins should be interviewed. As with Gordon Wardell and Robert Napper, it was important that Hopkins confirm his earlier statements about not having been to The Rec for six months or having spoken to Naomi since the summer.

Similarly, the police had to give him the opportunity to restate his alibi story for that night. This would nail down any provable lies. Hopkins had already given police a story which he believed separated him from the crime, yet the police were holding DNA evidence that proved beyond doubt that he had to be on The Rec that night and had bitten Naomi during the assault.

As the interviews began, Hopkins said very little. Confronted with the DNA evidence he accepted that it linked him to the scene and to Naomi but maintained that he had not killed her. On 20 November, he appeared in Nuneaton Magistrates Court charged with the murder of Naomi Smith and entered no plea. Meanwhile, two other men aged twenty-three and twenty-one were bailed to appear at Bedworth Police Station in connection with allegations of intending to pervert the course of justice.

Fourteen months later, on 22 January 1997, Edwin Hopkins stood trial at Birmingham Crown Court. As the charges were read to him, the slightly overweight twenty-year-old looked directly at the jury of six men and six women and said, 'Not guilty.'

A lumbering youth, of average intelligence and popularity, he didn't strike anyone as looking particularly evil or menacing. In fact, Tony Bayliss later admitted to journalists, 'He [Hopkins] portrayed himself as a fairly inoffensive young man and there were no outward signs that he would obviously be considered a suspect in this case.'

Prosecutor Colman Treacy, QC, told the jury that Naomi had fallen victim to a 'warped sexual attack' and there could be no doubt about the person responsible. He revealed how the mouth swab taken from Hopkins during the DNA screening had suggested him as a strong suspect.

A further blood test, sent off for analysis, had resulted in a positive match with the DNA profile gleaned from saliva found on Naomi's body. As a result, there was only a one in forty-four million chance that someone other than Hopkins could have murdered her.

Further damaging evidence emerged from dental experts. Hopkins had fallen from a bicycle when he was seven years old and knocked out one of his front teeth. Other teeth had moved into the space and closed the gap so that his upper jaw was lopsided.

When Dr Andrew Walker, a forensic odontologist, compared a plaster impression taken of Hopkins' teeth he found that all the irregularities matched the bite mark found on Naomi's breast completely.

'It was probably better than if the killer had left his autograph,' Mr Treacy QC told the jury.

When Hopkins entered the witness box, he said he knew Naomi and would sometimes pause on his bicycle to chat with her and her schoolmates. For a while he dated Emma's sister Rebecca and, according to Emma, Naomi 'quite liked him' although they'd never been out together.

On the night in question, Hopkins maintained his story of drinking and playing Trivial Pursuit at his sister Julie's house in Ansley Common. He left at about 9.30 p.m. to buy lager and crisps from the off-licence – a round trip that had taken him about thirty minutes on a bicycle. Although he was in the same area where Naomi posted the letter, he couldn't recall seeing anyone on the way.

However, a tearful Julie Hopkins destroyed her younger brother's alibi when she told the jury that his trip to the Triple A shop had taken longer. 'I didn't want to see him get into any trouble,' she said, explaining why she had initially lied to the police.

Hopkins had been away so long that Julie feared that he'd been involved in an accident. When he returned forty-five minutes later, she noticed that he was wearing fresh clothes. He said that he'd been stopped for having no lights on the bike and she assumed he'd been caught in the rain.

Further evidence revealed that Hopkins had an unusual interest in machetes and Rambo-style knives which he hung from his bedroom walls and often carried around with him. His father had taught him to skin rabbits at an early age and the two would often go off hunting in the countryside around Nuneaton.

After hearing seven days of evidence, Hopkins displayed no emotion as the jury found him guilty.

Describing it as a savage murder with sadistic features, Mr Justice Tucker said, 'You are, in my opinion, a very dangerous young man. I bear in mind you are only twenty years old. I sentence you to custody for life.'

Tony Bayliss and Gino Varriale won't leave it there. Although the investigation was brought to a successful conclusion, they saw so much pain, confusion and holding back in that small community that they want to know precisely what happened, and, knowing now who it happened to, why it happened.

There is one person, Edwin Hopkins, who can finally answer these questions. Bayliss and Varriale won't rest until he does because then they'll be better equipped for the next time.

25

SINCE MY NAME FIRST BECAME PUBLICLY LINKED TO POLICE investigations, I have been conscious of the different ways in which people perceive what I do. The reality hasn't been helped by films such as *The Silence of the Lambs* and TV dramas like *Cracker*. Even family friends will make comments about how exciting my work must be. It took a long while before I could understand this reaction.

Some have a notion of the psychologist/detective treading lightly and gently over a murder scene which people tend to imagine is very clean and tidy as in Agatha Christie stories. In fact country house murders can be just as grubby as the death of a prostitute in a crack-ridden council estate, and be motivated by more abhorrent urges. A few regard the psychologist as fitting somewhere between a clairvoyant and a witchdoctor. They mistrust what they don't understand or alternatively embrace it without question.

One of the most chilling and disturbing things I can recall hearing is when another psychologist who had given advice on a murder described the experience as 'the most exciting, arousing and rewarding experience of my life. It was better than sex.'

I found this repugnant. I dread getting phone calls from the police and dislike every moment of reconstruction process.

So why do I do it? Well, that's easy.

Barely a week has gone by in the past fifteen years when I haven't seen the trauma and sadness caused by crime. I listen to the victims of rape and families who have been destroyed by losing someone they love. I also see and hear what predatory sex offenders and predatory murderers do and I know what drives them. Can there be a more powerful motivation than wanting to bring this to the end?

There is nothing exciting or heroic about this. Usually when I become involved somebody is already dead and I am constantly aware that if I make a mistake and misdirect the inquiry, then someone else might die. It's like standing on the front edge of oblivion and the only good time is when it's over.

When psychological profiling began in Britain in the early 1980s, it wasn't a question of how reliable, or how much weight police could give my findings. More to the point, they asked, 'What do we do with it?'

I might have been able to tell them why the offence had happened; that the offender was aged in their late forties or early fifties, with a particular sort of job, educational background, lifestyle, geographical base, and how they would respond to police actions, but unless the investigators decided to do something with this information, it had little operational value. Doing something meant committing themselves and devoting time, money and personnel. But how could they be surc I was right? What happened if I was wrong?

Most SIOs took my advice, a few ignored it, and some waited until one of my predictions proved correct and then went back and looked more closely at what I had said in total.

Over the years psychological crime analysis has developed and become more widely valued, the early doubters are now supporters. Using it to design the DNA screening for Naomi Smith's killer is a prime example of how far it has come to be relied upon in investigating serious crime since those early days.

I don't know how much longer I will continue dealing with murder and sexual violence. Years ago I came to the realization that instead of bringing my work home with me I left a small part of myself behind at each crime scene. I wondered what would happen when there was nothing left to leave behind.

I have been on a treadmill that has so far encompassed more than 100 serious crimes – more, it has to be said, than many senior officers will investigate in their whole careers. I could carry on, perhaps, but it now seems much more important to help the police *not* to need me, except in particularly challenging cases, and to develop master-classes and seminars which will allow investigators to recognize the basic psychological clues and the principles involved in different classes of crime.

More importantly, I will continue to become more involved in risk assessment and crime prevention. This means increasing my work in several different areas, including, vitally, how we can best train people to be more attuned and alert, lowering their chances of becoming a victim of crime.

I will also continue to advise companies and other institutions how to respond to threat and to organize their security arrangements to best effect. I've never forgotten the abduction of Abbie Humphries where the surveillance cameras at the Queens Medical Centre were so badly positioned that they provided a photograph that became one of the most destructive aspects of the entire investigation. It was so poor in quality that it served no useful purpose yet became the subject of heated debate over whether it should be shown or not shown to the public. Significantly, there were no pictures of the *nurse* from those vulnerable parts of the hospital where the risk was highest.

I also remember the Heinz baby food case where psychological advice proved to be critical in determining the investigatory response.

On a research level, we know what motivates people to murder so ways must be found to use this knowledge and to stop them in mid-flight. The urgency of this was underlined by the dreadful shootings at Dunblane Primary School. Even in the small amount of material I have read relating to Thomas Hamilton there were sufficient early signs to have said, 'Let's keep firearms away from this chap.'

I'm not suggesting that the killings could necessarily have been averted. Even without his guns, Mr Hamilton might well have found another way to kill the children of Dunblane, but as it was, he had the means to hand and by removing his guns it would at least have signalled a recognition that something was not quite right.

When I completed the International Review of Offender Profiling for the Home Office in June 1992, the recommendations were accepted and were aimed at making the UK the clear European centre of excellence for offender profiling within two to three years. Unfortunately, the speed of development has been much slower than this.

The problem is that too many personal agendas and personal investments are obscuring the objectives. There are petty jealousies in all fields of endeavour, but offender profiling, because of the publicity surrounding it, seems to have more than most. I was told a story about a BBC radio producer who wanted to do a programme on offender profiling and lamented, 'I have been in the business of making documentaries for a long time and in all my career I have never come across an area that is so bogged down in hostile politics and dreadful interpersonal difficulties as this.'

The time has come for other people to enter the area, people who haven't invested too much of themselves in being right in a particular case, or showing someone else to be wrong. The pure researchers must say, 'OK, let's look at psychological profiling; let's make it a field of work and study like memory, language and cognition; something which ceases to be associated with a half-dozen people and becomes an expertise that can be taught and improved upon and can lead to more effective investigating.'

This will bring in the detached experimental psychologists, whose interest is to prod it, shake it, challenge all aspects of it, weeding out the straw platforms and honing the body of knowledge that remains.

I have been fortunate in my career to work with some of the very finest police officers – intelligent, straightforward and pragmatic men and women, who have a wonderful grasp of complex detail and a wealth of experience. In general, they have taken the attitude that anything that can help them in their investigation should be utilized.

Sadly, the arrival of a psychologist at an incident room is often picked up by the media and highlighted. This can lead to noses being put out of joint – not necessarily within the inquiry teams but higher up among the policy-makers in the police service. They worry about being displaced or not receiving as much credit.

This will change. A few years ago it was forensic scientists who captured the headlines and the imagination of the public, inspiring crime novels, TV dramas and feature films. Now it is forensic psychology and 'offender profiling'. This will pass and soon profilers will be seen as simply another resource that the police can call upon.

In terms of its impact upon me, I see the world differently from when I started this work. I see things in terms of risk factors. I notice women who collect the mail in their dressing-gowns and leave their curtains open at night. This can be the only trigger that a voyeur needs. It's easy to think that if Samantha Bissett had lived on the second floor that she and Jazmine might still be alive. But it's just as easy to consider that if she'd kept her balcony door locked and blinds drawn at night, Robert Napper might never have targeted her.

Similarly, I see young women coming out of hotels, laughing as they walk along the street arm in arm. I look at them and I can rank them in terms of their likelihood of being at risk. We all contrive to manage the image we present through the clothes we wear, how we act and what we say. This allows an estimate of other aspects of our lives, which in turn influences the extent to which we are open to predation.

Nowadays, when I walk down the street I notice things that I didn't see fifteen years ago. I look at how people use their bodies, faces and voices; what they wear, how they drive their cars and relate to each other. It sounds terrible, but I think that one of the reasons that I tend to hold back from conversation is that now, without trying or wanting to, I learn things about people – not the detail of their lives but the shape of their personality and thinking. I find myself knowing more about them than I ever had any interest in knowing or wanted to know.

My son Ian, who is now my assistant, and Emma, my daughter, described it wonderfully one day when I picked up a slice of bread that had another slice stuck to it.

Ian said, 'I bet if you were a materials engineer, whether you wanted to or not, you couldn't help seeing the two slices of bread in terms of their tensile strength, friction coefficient and all the rest of it.'

Emma added, 'All you want is a slice of bread for a sandwich, but your training and experience would give you all this additional information.'

Looking back, I don't remember the victims' faces because usually the pictures I see are taken after death when the light has gone out of their eyes. What I do remember are their minds because so much of what I do involves learning the intimate details and rhythm of their lives. It's knowing them and knowing what happened to them that makes the pain and sadness of their deaths even greater. This is not enjoyable work.

The memories will never go away and they are the most potent reason why I can't say no when the police call. Each time I see the minds, hundreds of them, a sea of people who have been raped, murdered, abused and damaged; and somewhere there is a man who will continue to hurt. He's likely to be sitting and remembering what he did, savouring it and gaining sexual pleasure from recounting it. He's real and he's out there and eventually his urge will begin to build up again. I can't always predict when this will happen but I do know that unless he's stopped he is going to kill again and again and again.

How can I say no?

INDEX

Subheadings under Britton, Paul are divided into two parts: personal and professional life; involvement with crimes. Both are in chronological order of first page reference. All other subheadings are in alphabetical order.